ISLAND ENCLAVES

Island Enclaves

Offshoring Strategies, Creative Governance, and Subnational Island Jurisdictions

Godfrey Baldacchino

McGill-Queen's University Press
Montreal & Kingston · London · Ithaca

© McGill-Queen's University Press 2010

ISBN 978-0-7735-3716-3 (cloth)
ISBN 978-0-7735-3743-9 (paper)

Legal deposit third quarter 2010
Bibliothèque nationale du Québec

Printed in Canada on acid-free paper that is 100% ancient forest free (100% post-consumer recycled), processed chlorine free

This book has been published with the help of a Standard Research Grant from the Social Sciences and Humanities Research Council of Canada (SSHRC).

McGill-Queen's University Press acknowledges the support of the Canada Council for the Arts for our publishing program. We also acknowledge the financial support of the Government of Canada through the Book Fund for our publishing activities.

LIBRARY AND ARCHIVES CANADA CATALOGUING IN PUBLICATION

Baldacchino, Godfrey
    Island enclaves : offshoring strategies, creative governance, and subnational island jurisdictions / Godfrey Baldacchino.

Includes bibliographical references and index.
ISBN 978-0-7735-3716-3 (bound). – ISBN 978-0-7735-3743-9 (pbk.)

    1. Islands – Economic conditions. 2. Islands – Politics and government.
3. Jurisdiction, Territorial. 4. Economic development. I. Title.

HC59.7.B294 2010   338.900914'2   C2010-901635-1

This book was typeset by Em Dash Design in 10.25/13.5 Minion Pro

Contents

Abbreviations

ABC	American Broadcasting Corporation
ACP	African, Caribbean, Pacific States (within WTO)
AICIS	Åland Institute for Comparative Island Studies
AOSIS	Alliance of Small and Island States
APV	Asia Pacific Viewpoint
ÅSUB	Åland Islands Statistical Agency
BBC	British Broadcasting Corporation
BVI	British Virgin Islands
CA	Canada
CARICOM	Caribbean Community
CBC	Canadian Broadcasting Corporation
CFI	Canadian Fund for Innovation
CHOGM	Commonwealth Heads of Government Meeting
CIA	Central Intelligence Agency (U.S.)
CIGI	Centre for International Governance Innovation
CNMI	Commonwealth of the Northern Mariana Islands
COFA	Compact of Free Association
COMSEC	Commonwealth Secretariat
CPMR	Conference of Peripheral Maritime Regions
CRC	Canada Research Chair
CRRF	Canadian Rural Revitalization Foundation
CRSN	Canadian Review of Studies in Nationalism
DOM	*département d'outre mer* (France)
ECJ	European Court of Justice
ECLAC	Economic Commission for Latin America and the Caribbean
EEA	European Economic Area
EEC	European Economic Community
EEZ	Exclusive Economic Zone
ELAW	Environmental Law Alliance Worldwide
EMPS	Environmental Management Plan of the Seychelles
EPZ	Export Processing Zone
EU	European Union
FAO	Food and Agricultural Organization

FATF	Financial Action Task Force
FOC	Flag of Convenience
FP6	Sixth Financial Protocol (European Commission)
FPEIM	Federation of Prince Edward Island Municipalities
FSM	Federated States of Micronesia
G7	Group of the Seven Largest Industrialized Countries
GAO	Government Accountability Office (U.S.)
GATT	General Agreement on Tariffs and Trade
GCR	Global City Region
GDP	Gross Domestic Product
GIN	Global Islands Network
GLISPA	Global Islands Partnership
GNI	Gross National Income
GNP	Gross National Product
GR	Greece
HK	Hong Kong
HMG	Her Majesty's Government (Britain)
HTCI	Harmful Tax Competition Initiative
IANA	Internet Assigned Numbers Authority
ICAO	International Civil Aviation Organization
ICS	Institute of Commonwealth Studies, University of London (U.K.)
IGU	International Geographical Union
IIS	Institute of Island Studies, University of Prince Edward Island, Canada
INS	Immigration and Naturalization Service (U.S.)
IOC	International Olympic Committee
IPSA	International Political Studies Association
ISER	Institute of Social and Economic Research, NL
ISISA	International Small Islands Studies Association
ISO	International Organization for Standardization
ISSN	International Standard Serial Number
ITF	International Transport Workers' Federation
KIRC	Kish Island Reserve Commission
LDC	Least Developed Country
MAB	Man and the Biosphere Program (UNESCO)
MEPA	Malta Environment Planning Authority
MEUSAC	Malta – European Union Steering and Action Committee
MIRAB	Migration, Remittances, Aid, Bureaucracy

MIRAGE	Migration, Remittances, Aid, Government Employment
MIRTAB	Migration, Remittances, Tourism, Aid, Bureaucracy
MUN	Memorial University of Newfoundland, Canada
MURTAB	Migration, Urbanization, Remittances, Tourism, Aid, Bureaucracy
NA	Netherlands Antilles
NAF	North Atlantic Forum
NAIP	North Atlantic Islands Program
NASA	National Aeronautic and Space Administration (U.S.)
NATO	North Atlantic Treaty Organization
NBER	National Bureau for Economic Research
NFFB	New Football Federations Board
NL	Newfoundland and Labrador
NLFM	Newfoundland and Labrador Federation of Municipalities
NOAA	National Oceanic and Atmospheric Administration (U.S.)
Nord REFO	Nordic Institute of Regional Policy Research
Nord Regio	Nordic Centre for Spatial Development
NZ	New Zealand
OAS	Organization of American States
OCTA	Overseas Countries and Territories Association of the European Union
OECD	Organization for Economic Cooperation and Development
OECS	Organization of Eastern Caribbean States
OFC	Offshore Finance Centre
OSCE	Organization for Security and Cooperation in Europe
PAC	Pacific Access Category
PAC	Public Accounts Committee (House of Commons, U.K.)
PEI	Prince Edward Island
PGA	Professional Golfers Association
PMO	Prime Minister's Office, Canada
PNG	Papua New Guinea
PPP	Purchasing Power Parity
PRC	People's Republic of China
PROFIT	People, Resources, Overseas, Finance and Transportation
RFI	Radio France Internationale
RIHN	Research Institute for Humanity and Nature, Kyoto, Japan
ROC	Republic of China (Taiwan)
ROS	Republic of the Seychelles
RSC	Royal Society of Canada

SAR	Special Administrative Region (China)
SARTMA	South Atlantic Remote Territories Media Association
SBA	Sovereign Base Area (Cyprus)
SENSOR	Sustainability Impact Assessment: Tools for Environmental Social and Economic Effects of Multifunctional Land Use in European Regions
SIC	Shetland Island Council
SIDS	Small Island Developing States
SITE	Small Island Tourist Economy
SLRF	Sea Level Rise Foundation
SNIJ	Subnational Island Jurisdiction
SPIN	South Pacific Island Nation
SRG	Standard Research Grant, SSHRC
SSHRC	Social Sciences and Humanities Research Council, Canada
T&F	Taylor and Francis, Publishers
TCI	Turks and Caicos Islands
TOURAB	Tourism, Remittances, Aid, Bureaucracy
TR	Turkey
TRNC	Turkish Republic of Northern Cyprus
TRT	*The Round Table: Commonwealth Journal of International Affairs*
UK	United Kingdom
UKOT	United Kingdom Overseas Territory
UNCLOS	United Nations Conference on the Law of the Sea
UNCTAD	United Nations Conference on Trade and Development
UNDP	United Nations Development Program
UNESCO	United Nations Educational, Scientific and Cultural Organization
UNHCR	United Nations High Commission for Refugees
UOM	University of Malta, Malta
UPEI	University of Prince Edward Island, Canada
US	United States (of America)
USSR	Union of Soviet Socialist Republics
WCMC	World Conservation Monitoring Centre
WHO	World Health Organization
WHTI	Western Hemisphere Travel Initiative
WMO	World Meteorological Organization
WRSA	Western Regional Science Association
WTO	World Trade Organization

Acknowledgments

A wide circle of collaborators has been involved in supporting the research that made this book possible.

The Institute of Commonwealth Studies (ICS), School of Advanced Study, University of London – via its former director, Timothy Shaw – kindly hosted and co-organized a two-day project research workshop in April 2005 and facilitated the organization of another two-day workshop as part of the Commonwealth People's Forum accompanying the Commonwealth Heads of Government Meeting (CHOGM) held in Malta in November 2005. Through the ICS, and especially thanks to my good friend Peter H. Lyon, contacts were established with Andrew J. Williams (retiring editor), Terry Barringe, and other members of the editorial board of *The Round Table* (TRT), the prestigious and peer-reviewed Commonwealth journal of international affairs, which led to a special thematic and guest-edited issue of TRT (vol. 95, no. 386) dedicated to subnational island jurisdictions (SNIJs) in October 2006. The ICS and TRT, along with Taylor and Francis (Publishers) (T&F) hosted the launch of the TRT special issue in London in October 2006 which I attended, along with my long-time friend, academic sparring partner, and journal issue co-editor, University of Prince Island (UPEI) Professor Emertius David Milne. These good contacts in turn spawned an offer by Routledge, an imprint of T&F, to publish an expanded and updated version of that same collection, now published as *The Case for Non-Sovereignty: Lessons from Sub-National Island Jurisdictions* (London: Routledge 2008), with David Milne and me as co-editors. My thanks especially to Richard Delahunty and Vicky Claringbull at T&F for their support in this development.

The Nordic Centre for Spatial Development (NordRegio, formerly NordREFO), based in Stockholm, Sweden, has been a key supporter of the North Atlantic Islands Program (NAIP) initiative. NordRegio is supporting parallel, comparative research on a range of Scandinavian SNIJs: Åland, Bornholm, Faroes, Gotland, and Greenland (e.g., Karlsson, 2006). I have secured funding for this purpose from NordRegio and from ÅSUB, the Åland Islands Statistical Agency. (The Åland Islands, or course, are themselves a subnational island jurisdiction.) Bjarne Lindström, director of ÅSUB, has become a most respected friend. His energy and vision, plus that of the indefatigable Agneta Karlsson, led to the setting up of an Ålands Institute for Comparative Island Studies (AICIS), supported completely by private funds (www.aicis.ax).

In Canada, the Federation of Prince Edward Island Municipalities (FPEIM) and the Newfoundland and Labrador Federation of Municipalities (NLFM) have been valued non–academic partners and are especially interested in any practical lessons in governance that could apply to their respective island provinces. The Institute of Island Studies (IIS) at UPEI (with my colleague Irené Novaczek as director) and the Leslie Harris Centre of Regional Policy and Development at Memorial University of Newfoundland (MUN) (with another friend, Director Rob Greenwood, who was a doctoral student at the same time as me at the University of Warwick, U.K.) are regular and natural partners. Irené has, in particular, generously facilitated a couple of workshops that explored the implications of smallness and insularity on public policy. As the manager of Island Studies Press, she also supported my proposal to publish a book – now available as *Pulling Strings: Policy Insights for Prince Edward Island from Other Sub-National Island Jurisdictions* (Charlottetown: Island Studies Press 2008). This book, co-edited with Katherine Stuart, looks at lessons specific to Prince Edward Island from other subnational island territories.

Through its work under the European Union (EU) FP6 SENSOR project, the Malta Environment Planning Authority (MEPA) has undertaken a study on island regions in the EU and will use development indicators in order to describe key sustainability issues. MEPA has been collaborating with me in extending the island jurisdictional database in the environmental field. Hats off here to Marguerite Camilleri, Roberta Galea, Monique Hili, and Stefano Moncada at MEPA.

Various other individual collaborators from a range of disparate disciplines have connected with this project at various points. They include, in alphabetical order: Harvey Armstrong (University of Sheffield, U.K.); Joseph and Rose Marie Azzopardi (Gozo and University of Malta [UOM]); Barry Bartmann (UPEI); Geoff Bertram (Victoria University of Wellington, New Zealand); Peter Billing (Centre for Regional and Tourism Research, Bornholm, Denmark); Lino Briguglio (UOM); John Connell (University of Sydney, Australia); Eric Clark (Lund University, Sweden); Richard Crook (director, Institute of Commonwealth Studies, University of London); Michael Crossley (University of Bristol, U.K.); Richard Cullen (Monash University, Australia); Christian Depraetere (Laboratoire d'Étude des Transferts en Hydrologie et Environnement, Grenoble, France); Klaus Dodds (Royal Holloway, U.K.);

Yash P. Ghai (University of Hong Kong); Norman Girvan (University of the West Indies, Trinidad and Tobago); John R. Gillis (Rutgers University, New Jersey, U.S.); Jean-Didier Hache (Islands Commission, Conference of Peripheral Maritime Regions, France); Mark P. Hampton (University of Kent, U.K.); Pete Hay (University of Tasmania, Australia); Hiroshi Kakazu (University of the Ryukyus, Okinawa, Japan); Ilan Kelman (Centre for International Climate and Environmental Research, Oslo, Norway); Sandy Kerr (Heriott-Watt University, Scotland, U.K.); Lawrence Liao (UPEI and University of San Carlos, Philippines); David Lowenthal (University College London, U.K.); Grant McCall (University of New South Wales, Australia); Jerome L. McElroy (University of Notre Dame, Indiana, U.S.); private lawyer Dan McMeekin (Washington D.C., U.S.); Gert Oostindie (Leiden University, the Netherlands); Iain Orr (Biodiplomacy and Global Islands Network); Bernard Poirine (Université de la Polynésie Française); Bruce Potter (Island Resources Foundation); Robert Read (University of Lancaster, U.K.); Anthony Regan (Australian National University); Graeme Robertson (Global Islands Network); Stephen A. Royle (Queen's University Belfast, Northern Ireland); Henry F. Srebrnik (UPEI); Mark Shrimpton (Jacques Whitford and Memorial University of Newfoundland); Elaine Stratford (University of Tasmania, Australia); Paul K. Sutton (now at London Metropolitan University, U.K.); Edward Warrington (UOM); and Ronald L. Watts, Institute of Inter-Governmental Relations, Queen's University, Kingston, Canada. Many of these esteemed colleagues now sit on the International Editorial Board of *Island Studies Journal*, of which I am executive editor.

Clyde Sakamoto, director of the Maui Community College, accepted my proposal to run a specially organized SNIJ panel at the 9th "Islands of the World" Conference at Maui, Hawaii, in July 2006: seven papers were presented in a two-and-a-half-hour session. Targetted research and study visits between 2004 and 2009, usually accompanied by conference presentations and/or public lectures, consultations with key academics or informants, and media interviews, have involved such locations as Åland, Finland; Azores, Portugal; Barbados; Belfast, Northern Ireland; Bornholm, Denmark; Cebu, Philippines; Gotland, Sweden; Guernsey, British Isles; Reykjavik, Iceland; Jeju, South Korea; Kagoshima and Yakushima, Japan; Saaremaa, Estonia; Shetland, Scotland; St Lucia; Kinmen and Taipei, Taiwan; Hobart, Tasmania, Australia; Trinidad and Tobago; and Turks and Caicos Islands. I thank the various organizers and coordinators of these visits for their support and hospitality.

Then there are the students: Where would we academics be without them? The comparative and interdisciplinary nature of the research, its cutting-edge orientation, and its overall supervision and strategic leadership have made for a powerful formative and educational experience for various graduate students at UPEI. Students were encouraged "not to miss the proverbial forest for the trees": while focusing on specific islands or cases, they were urged to build up a more sophisticated understanding of what "offshoring" involves: its strengths, weaknesses, opportunities, and threats both to subnational island jurisdictions and to the metropolitan powers, and the world community at large, that may oversee them. The inner circle of such students was enlisted, over the course of three years (2004–07), to work on the compilation of the Sub-National Island Jurisdiction Database. This database has been put together with the help of the following graduate student research assistants: Faiz Syed Ahmed, Jean-Louis Arsenault, Ryan Boulter, Hans Connor, Douglas Deacon, Laura Fanning, Barbara Groome Wynne, Heather Gushue, Crystal McAndrew Fall, Margaret Mizzi, Ryan O'Connor, Janice Pettit, Ariana Salvo, and Kathleen Stuart, who acted as overall graduate student coordinator. Kathy, now a doctoral student, kindly acted as co-editor of the book *Pulling Strings* and continues to support assiduously the island studies program at UPEI.

Specific individuals, publishers, and institutions need to be thanked for conference organization, detailed feedback on drafts, and permission to reproduce material that has already been published.

I thank John R. Gillis, David Lowenthal, and Matt Matsuda, conveners of the "Islands on Our Minds" Conference held at Rutgers University, New Brunswick, N.J., in May 2004, which inspired the earliest draft of what became chapter 1 of this book, "Autonomy without Sovereignty: An 'Island Studies' Approach"; Christian Depraetere and Stefan Gössling for specific island-related information; and Eric Clark, Pete Hay, Jane Ledwell, and Stephen Royle for critical comments on an earlier draft of chapter 1. Parts of this chapter have appeared as "Islands as Novelty Sites," *Geographical Review*, 97, no. 2 (2007): 165–74. My renewed thanks to John R. Gillis and David Lowenthal who put this special issue together, and to Peter Lewis (permissions editor) and the American Geographical Society for permission to reprint.

Sections of chapter 2, "Borders within Borders and the New Offshoring," are based on my keynote address to the 7th "Islands of the World" Conference held by the International Small Islands Studies Association (ISISA) and hosted by the Institute of Island Studies, University of Prince Edward Island, in June 2002. My thanks to John Connell, Epenesa Esera, Mark Anthony Falzon, Pete Hay, Sandy Kerr, David Lowenthal, Grant McCall, David Milne,

Stephen A. Royle, Henry F. Srebrnik, and Unasa Felise Vaa for critical comments on an earlier draft. Parts of this chapter have appeared as "'The Coming of Age of Island Studies," *Tijdscrift voor Economishe en Sociale Geografie*, 95, no. 3 (2004): 272–83. Permission to reproduce this material has been obtained from the Royal Dutch Geographical Society through the good offices of Ronald Kranenburg.

Earlier versions of chapter 3, "Island Subnationalism and 'Upside Down' Decolonization," were presented at the international conference on the knowledge-based economy and regional economic development, Memorial University of Newfoundland, St John's, in October 2003; and at the Western Regional Science Association (WRSA) gathering in Maui, Hawaii, in February 2004. My gratitude also to Anthony Soares, Eammon Hughes, Satish Kumar, Maeve McCusker, Jonathan Skinner, and other organizers for inviting me to the Postcolonial Islands Conference at Queen's University, Belfast, Northern Ireland, in September 2007, for which event another draft of this chapter was presented. My thanks to Klaus Dodds, Rod Edmond, Carol Farbotko, Gert Oostindie, Stephen A. Royle, and Kathleen Stuart for their kind and helpful comments. An earlier version of the contents of this chapter appeared as: "Autonomous but Not Sovereign? A Review of Island Sub-Nationalism," *Canadian Review of Studies in Nationalism* (CRSN), 31, nos. 1–2 (2004): 77–89. That paper benefited from the mentorship of Thomas G. Spira, the long-serving editor of CRSN until his untimely death. My thanks to Klara Spira for permission to reprint.

I am grateful to the organizers of the "MIRAB + 20 Years" Conference, held at the Victoria Unversity of Wellington, New Zealand, in 2004, for the kind invitation to attend this international event and for soliciting the paper that became chapter 4, "A Review of Economic Performance: Tapping the Hinterland Beyond." (As it happened, a major snowstorm closed down Charlottetown airport and left me stranded on Prince Edward Island, but my paper was still presented at the conference by proxy.) My thanks to Harvey W. Armstrong, Jerome L. McElroy, Robert Read, Paul Streeten, and Geoffrey Wall and anonymous referees for critical comments, constructive criticism, and helpful research leads. Heartfelt special thanks go to Geoff Bertram for never failing, since 1991, to respond graciously to my all too frequent demands for collegial feedback. I am grateful also to Iain Orr for so much information on island goings on, including those on Svalbard (e-mail communication, 19 September 2003). An earlier version of the contents of this chapter appeared as "Managing the Hinterland Beyond: Two, Ideal-Type Strategies of Economic Development for Small Island Territories,"

Asia-Pacific Viewpoint (APV), 47, no. 1 (2006): 45–60. My thanks to Warwick Murray, editor of APV, for acceding to my request to reproduce the paper.

Special thanks to Doug Brown, Harvey Lazar, and Ronald L. Watts at the Institute of Inter-Governmental Relations, Queen's University, Kingston, Ontario, Canada, for the opportunity they afforded to Kathleen Stuart and me to discuss relevant issues and present a "work-in-progress" seminar at Queen's in October 2004. Thanks also to Timothy Shaw for co-organizing a workshop at the Institute of Commonwealth Studies, University of London, London, in April 2005, and again at the Commonwealth People's Forum held during the Commonwealth Heads of Government Meeting in Valletta, Malta, in November 2005, where the ideas contained in chapter 5, "Patterns of Creative Governance and Development," were fleshed out. I also thank Rob Greenwood and the organizers of the Canadian Rural Revitalization Foundation and the North Atlantic Forum conference held in Twillingate, Newfoundland, Canada, over 13–15 October 2005, who invited me to deliver a keynote address on which part of this chapter is based. Chris Dunn, Lawrence Felt, Mark Shrimpton, and Kathleen Stuart provided useful critical comments on an earlier draft. An earlier version of the contents of this chapter appeared as "Innovative Development Strategies from Non-Sovereign Island Jurisdictions: A Global Review of Economic Policy and Governance Practices," *World Development*, 34, no. 5 (2006): 852–67, reproduced herein with kind permission from Elsevier. Most of the "Canada-Newfoundland" portions of the same chapter appeared as "Governance in Small Places: The Unleashing of Asymmetric Federalism," in G. Baldacchino, R. Greenwood, and L. Felt, eds., *Remote Control: Governance Lessons for and from the Small, Insular and Remote* (St John's: ISER Press 2009), 114–34 . My thanks to Wayne Fife at ISER, as well as my co-editors Rob and Larry, for permission to reproduce this material.

Papers crafted from the content and arguments of chapter 6, "Offshoring Strategies: Lessons from Subnational Island Jurisdictions," have been presented at the 9th and 10th "Islands of the World" Conferences, organized by the International Small Islands Studies Association: the first at Maui Community College, Kahului, Maui, Hawaii, in August 2006, the second at the World Association for Island Studies and Jeju National University in Seogwipo, Jeju-do, South Korea, in August 2008. The section on Kish Island (Iran) is taken from the editorial introduction to *The Case for Non-Sovereignty: Lessons from Sub-National Island Jurisdictions*. My thanks to Richard Delahunty for permission to reproduce this material, on behalf of Routledge/Taylor and Francis.

For chapter 7, "Island Paradiplomacy and Smaller Island State Diplomacy Compared," I am indebted to my good friend and UPEI colleague Barry Bartmann for many ideas relating to para-diplomacy as it affects subnational jurisdictions, and to Justine Lloyd for our electronic conversation and sharing of research materials. Here, my gratitude also extends to the participants in the workshop on small-state diplomacy convened by Tim Shaw and Andrew F. Cooper at the Centre for International Governance Innovation (CIGI), Institute of International Relations, St Augustine Campus of the University of the West Indies, Trinidad and Tobago, over 20–23 February 2008. Special thanks, too, to Donna Lee, Vaughan A. Lewis, Debbie Mohammed, Keith Nurse, Naren Prasad, Baldur Thorallsson, and William Vlcek. Additional useful commentary on an earlier draft was also received from Philip Nel, Kathleen Stuart, and Jordan Blake Walker. An earlier version of parts of the contents of this chapter appeared as "Thucydides or Kissinger? A Critical Review of Smaller State Diplomacy," in Tim Shaw and Andrew F. Cooper, eds., *The Diplomacies of Small States: Between Vulnerability and Resilience* (Basingstoke, U.K.: Palgrave Macmillan 2009), 21–40. My thanks to Alexandra Webster at Palgrave for permission to reproduce this material.

A paper that included many of the ideas of chapter 8, "Environmental Policies and Politics: Economic versus Ecological Development Strategies," was presented as a keynote address at an international symposium on the theme "The Futurability of Islands: Beyond Endemism and Vulnerability," organized by the Research Institute for Humanity and Nature (RIHN) in Kyoto, Japan, 22–23 October 2008. My thanks to organizers Ken-Ichi Abe, Ryo Nakamura, Daniel Niles, Narifumi Tachimoto, Tokushiro Takazo, and Takakazu Yumoto, as well as participants John Cusick, Mark Gardener, Simon Haberle, Matthew Prebble, and Alma Ridep-Morris, for their collegiality.

Chapter 9, "An Enduring 'Rich Seam' of Jurisdictional Capacity," is essentially a synthesis of ideas already expounded upon in the text, as well as an attempt at looking forward in what is very much a field in flux.

The Appendix, containing the three maps and a selective listing of subnational island jurisdictions, has been painstakingly compiled and nurtured through various drafts by Kathleen Stuart and originally appeared in *Pulling Strings*, 178–85. My thanks to Kathy (again) and to Irené Novaczek of Island Studies Press for their permission to reproduce this work here. The artwork and layout of the original maps and listings are by our very capable Matthew MacKay, at Integrated Promotions, UPEI. Acknowledgement is particularly made to the CIA *World Factbook* (various editions); the web-based *Island Jurisdistions Index* moderated by attorney-at-law Dan

MacMeekin at http://www.macmeekin.com/Library/Jurisds/aaaindex.htm; and the Jurisdiction Project Database found at http://www.utopia.cs.upei.ca/jurisdiction/, which is supported by both the Canadian Foundation for Innovation (CFI) and the Social Sciences and Humanities Research Council (SSHRC), for much of the data that forms the basis for many of the arguments and examples contained in the Appendix.

Finally, I wish to single out for special mention and gratitude a few individuals with whom I have had some engaging conversations relevant to the book as a whole. The first is David Milne: we have been working together since 1996; having co-edited three publications with David, I count him as a friend and a respected senior colleague. The second is Mark P. Hampton, another long-standing friend, with whom I engaged in an extensive and frank discussion about the "morality" of offshore finance during a tour of the National Museum of Archaeology in Taipei, Taiwan, in November 2007, while we were both participating in the first conference of the newly inaugurated Islands Commisison of the International Geographical Union (IGU). A third is Bjarne Lindström, proud and visionary Ålander, with whom I have had warm yet vertiginous conversations while flying in his biplane over his Åland archipelago. Then there are Eric Snell and Tony Gallienne, both ambassadors extraordinary for the island jurisdiction of Guernsey. Eric, an artist, was gracious enough to invite me to deliver a keynote address at an international conference on *Art and Islands*, held at Castle Cornet, St Peter Port, Guernsey, in September 2008. Tony, whom I got to know much better while in Guernsey, had earlier sent me a copy of his autographical and critical book *Guernsey in the 21st Century*, which makes a truly wonderful and inspiring read. Subnational island jurisdictions can, and do, write back.

My deep gratitude also goes to those who have journeyed closely with me over the years, patiently nurturing me with their love and understanding: my wife, Anna, and our fine boys (now young men): James and Luke.

Island Enclaves is an anti-thesis of what a global village purports to be. It seeks to trace the potential power embedded in material place, as well as the place and potential of regulatory power in the modern world. I earnestly hope that the book will be, at the least, appreciated as a modest contribution to the study of islands. But, as with other studies that focus on islands, it purports to go much beyond that. Islands can be synecdoches: their understanding facilitates a "coming to terms" with a more complex whole. With its forays into politics, economics, international relations, and environmental studies, *Island Enclaves* is offered as a global and critical inquiry into how much islands can inform us about such dynamics as the evolution of decolonization, post-colonialism, globalization, paradiplomacy, ecological development – and perforated sovereignty generally. The book is more than a review of what islanders do, and can do; and what is done, or can be done, to them by others.

Of course, the usual disclaimers apply: full responsibilities for all sins of commission and omission remain my own. Handling so many islands, and grappling with so many cases, within the same book may be disconcerting to, and may be found wanting by, readers. At times, I may miss the proverbial forest for its individual trees, or get carried way by sweeping generalizations which fail to account for each and every case. Some readers may plead for more detail, just as others may ask for less. My sincere apologies if the book doesn't quite clinch it.

Godfrey Baldacchino
Charlottetown, Prince Edward Island, Canada
January 2010

Preface

THE CONTEXT

As I started to write this book, the 2008 Olympic Games were about to open in the People's Republic of China (PRC). All the games were to be held in Beijing, except for the equestrian events, which were staged in the territory of a different member of the International Olympic Committee: Hong Kong (HK). The paraolympic equestrian events, which followed the main Olympic spectacle, were also held there.

It is intriguing that Hong Kong was selected to host an Olympic event. Why is that so? It is not just because Hong Kong has world-class equine care facilities and medical services for horses in place. Hong Kong also has recognized quarantine protocol arrangements with many countries. Given the prevalence of equine diseases in Beijing and other mainland cities in China, Hong Kong's islandness – a condition that facilitates quarantine services – emerges as a key factor swaying the decision as to where to host the only Olympic events involving animals (*The Economist*, 2007b).

Hong Kong is a special administrative region (SAR) of the PRC. Its Basic Law serves as its constitutional document. It was adopted in April 1990 by the seventh National People's Congress of the PRC, and went into effect on 1 July 1997, replacing the Letters Patent and the Royal Instructions, when this former colony of the United Kingdom was handed over to the PRC. There is crucial debate as to whether this Basic Law is merely a consequence of exclusively domestic legislation, or whether it derives its authority directly from the Sino-British Joint Declaration of 1984. The HKSAR has a high degree of autonomy and enjoys executive, legislative, and independent judicial power, including that of final adjudication. "Hong Kong's Court of Final Appeal may invite foreign judges from common law countries to sit on its panels and may invoke precedents from common law countries in reaching its judgements" (Krasner, 2001a: 18). Its population of almost seven million is governed by its own unicameral legislative council (known as LegCo), which dates back to 1843. Hong Kong has its own flag, its own stamps, its own currency (the Hong Kong dollar), its own Internet domain name (.hk), and its own Court of Final Appeal. It has been (with Singapore) the "top Pacific Basin offshore financial centre" (Roberts, 1993: 102). As stated above, it is a distinct member of the International Olympic Committee. Hong Kong has the specific authority to forge international agreements and participate independently in international organizations and conferences as "Hong Kong, China." Indeed, it was admitted as a member of the World Trade Organization (WTO; then, in 1986, still the General Agreement on Tariffs and Trade, or GATT) before the PRC. But Hong Kong is neither a country nor a sovereign state. It is, according to Article 1 of the Basic Law, "an unalienable part" of the PRC. Hong Kong is governed under the principle of "one country, two systems," under which the PRC has agreed to give this region a high degree of autonomy and to preserve its economic (capitalist) and social systems at least until 2047 – fifty years from the date of the handover (e.g., Zeng, 2003).

Hong Kong is, most aptly, called "special"; its arrangements are "without direct parallel in international law" (Mushkat, 1997: ix). Yet, in a number of respects, Hong Kong is not special enough to be unique. The PRC itself has a number of other special regions; some are tolerated because of inherent qualities; others are crafted from above. All enjoy different degrees of autonomy, and most are the subject of heated debate: just think of "the autonomous region" of Tibet. The others are, like Hong Kong itself, either islands or mainly islands: Macao, the other SAR; Hainan and Xiamen, both special economic zones; and Taiwan, to whom the "one country, two systems" formula was orginally offered, in the late 1970s (McCall Smith, 2001: 107). Hong Kong is thus one excellent contemporary example of a subnational (mainly island) jurisdiction: a member of a class of polities that is hard to define and are more easily placed in that limbo that persists between full state sovereignty (as in independent countries) and administrative autonomy (as in municipalities).

This book argues that there is, first of all, a constellation of subnational island jurisdictions that, in spite of their many differences, merit collective scrutiny. They share various relevant features of innovative governance. They are not just relicts from a bygone age but are a response to the opportunities afforded by globalization (which include offshoring strategies). They represent quite fascinating examples of "the resourcefulness of jurisdiction," illustrating the flexibility and tenacity of global capital, of federal politics, of smaller autonomous territories, as well as of sovereignty and the geography of power generally – and not necessarily in that order.

THE BOOK'S STRUCTURE

Sustaining an argument that embraces such a diverse category of islands, or island-based jurisdictions, ranging from Taiwan and Puerto Rico to Rodrigues and Pitcairn, is daunting, to say the least. This book tries to do it by means of eight substantive chapters.

The terms of engagement, and its cast of essentially two sets of actors, are set out in chapter 1. The creation of offshore is explained, and its historical precedents identified; it is also argued that the practice of offshoring is an initiative by either island jurisdictions for themselves or by other (larger) players who have specific designs in mind for islands. The emphasis on islands is predicated on their relevance as sites of novelty, experimentation, and historical understanding: enclaves par excellence.

The vigorously (re-)assertion of the significance of place is the main thrust of chapter 2. Borders both *between* and *within* countries have assumed a messiness and vitality never seen before – conditions that also apply to our understanding of what *is* a country – even as we wax lyrical about a borderless world. Subnational island jurisdictions are presented as sites where such "inbordering" is clearly manifest.

How can one understand why the majority of the smallest, typically islanded, colonies and associated territories have refused to embrace, let alone struggle for, political independence? Political affiliation with(in) a larger, richer state can grant substantial economic, fiscal, and security advantages, as well as special status, to smaller, non-sovereign units, even as these flex their autonomy to craft their own laws and regulations. Chapter 3 reviews mainstream notions of colonialism, decolonization, and post-colonialism, and suggests that so many "mainland-island" relations can be better understood on the continuum of "shared rule versus self-rule" that is at the heart of federalist studies.

Chapter 4 presents the economic argument for subnational island jurisdictions. An island territory's lucrative engagement with the external hinterland, and the rents that this relationship provides, explains much of its economic performance – even if, ironically enough, tapping such externalities is in turn often dependent on domestically generated, political regulation. This chapter suggests a model of economic development based on the use of jurisdictional capacity as an economic resource, with a keen interest in leveraging such a capacity in terms of five select policy areas: finance, natural resources, air and sea transportation, free movement of persons, and tourism.

The policy intent of such "asymmetric federalism" is reviewed in chapter 5. The use of creative political capacities is described: flexing jurisdictional clout (including by stealth); expressing subnationalism and indigeneity; involvement in paradiplomacy. A case study of a recent colourful showdown between the (largely island) province of Newfoundland and Labrador with the federal government of Canada illustrates such capacity in action.

Chapter 6 offers a global survey of actual episodes of "mainland-island relations." The content is largely descriptive, with various, and non-exhaustive, illustrative examples of the role of offshoring and innovative governance practices *on* or *by* subnational island jurisdictions. Here is the political economy of island enclaves in action.

We move into the realm of diplomacy and international relations in chapter 7. This is no longer the preserve of sovereign states, as subnational units develop a selective presence in regional and international bodies and fora. Resorting once again to various examples, this chapter compares the paradiplomatic fortunes of subnational island jurisdictions with those of smaller island sovereign states. The balance sheet emerges in favour of the subnational units.

Various smaller island sovereign states have been involved in a flurry of environmental diplomacy, intended to alert the world to their plight as a consequence of sea-level rise. The next chapter takes the environmental debate to a higher level, seeking to look at development from a longer-term perspective. The debate here lies between economic and ecological criteria of development. Thus, chapter 8 invites a reconsideration of the impact of physical geography on development, and of the role of conservation and heritage management, in the context of a changing relationship between "nature" and "human culture." Of significance here is the crafting of national parks and internationally listed natural and/or cultural spaces, as well as wholesale privatization.

Finally, chapter 9 provides a brief synthesis of the overall discussion, outlining some of the main challenges and dilemmas in the reconceptualization of development as has been proposed in the earlier chapters. An Appendix with a series of maps and a listing of populated, subnational island jurisdictions completes the book.

THE GARDEN PROVINCE

Having such a book written by a scholar based at the University of Prince Edward Island in Canada should, one hopes, not come as a surprise.

That Prince Edward Island (PEI) is a jurisdiction *at all* is itself largely an outcome of a quirk of history. The Island, formerly the French colony of Île Saint-Jean, had been annexed to Nova Scotia by the British government in 1763. The ownership of almost the entire colony was allocated via a "land lottery" held in London, England, on a single day in 1767, to some one hundred absentee proprietors. The latter agitated for political control and successfully lobbied the British government to revert the Island to its former autonomous standing: thus was born the separate colony of St John's in 1769. The granting of such separate status led, in the same year, to the creation of an Executive Council of twelve persons appointed by the crown to advise and assist the governor in the exercise of his functions. An elected Legislative Assembly on the Island followed in 1773. The islandness of the place, with its geographically defined borders and relative remoteness from the colonial outpost of Halifax, and the logic of acceding to its demand for governance by endogenous (domestic) elites no doubt swayed the British government's decision to grant autonomy as an expeditious measure. (Britain also granted approval to change the colony's name from St John's Island to Prince Edward Island in 1798.)

Through the course of history, PEI and its Islanders have often referred to their small size as a source of pride. This is a province that can be covered in a day's drive: a place that, as Wade H. MacLauchlan, UPEI's president and vice-chancellor, is fond of saying, "we can get our arms around." The unique rural-urban balance that is a function of its size and scale is a major draw for the tourism industry of this "Garden Province," as well as for various immigrants and urban refugees. Its human- and community-centred way of life, combined with affordable housing, a "small town" feel, job availability, and a variety of natural resources, give Prince Edward Island a distinctive appeal (Baldacchino, 2007a: 7). The "positive virtues of landscape, family and community" (Bumsted, 1982: 32) – along with the not-so-positive traits of local gossip and a suspicion of outsiders – resonate in the twentieth-century works of what is perhaps the Island's most famous citizen, Lucy Maud Montgomery, author of *Anne of Green Gables*. Such values remain surprisingly relevant to this day and age on PEI.

At the same time, and almost paradoxically, the Island's small size in both physical and demographic terms – a land area of 568,439 hectares (5,660 km^2 or 2,184 square miles) and a current population of around 138,000 – is seen as a chronic and structural handicap towards its full development. The aspirations of the Island's people are often felt to be achievable only thanks to a sustained flow of revenue from external sources. Keen to emphasize its limited resources, the province has sought the benefit of federal programs and financial assistance, while fearful of external domination and warily resisting the homogenizing effects of national programs and standards. This stance has been, throughout the years, PEI's key defining role within the Canadian federation (Milne, 1992).

And yet, beyond Ottawa, there is another kind of resourcefulness, one that is PEI's to call upon. It speaks to the Island's own ability to generate and stamp its own signature on a globalizing world, via the resourcefulness of jurisdiction.

"Jurisdiction" is not a neutral, passive, or static term. It does not simply suggest a space, a place or territoriality. It signifies a legitimate and constitutionally engrained political autonomy that is thus recognized and respected by other players. It suggests a repository of powers which political actors are entitled to use, and which they may misuse, abuse, or not use at all. It proffers a series of levers, drivers, or tools that allow policy makers to tweak and craft the development trajectory of their land and its citizens in specific directions. In other words, *jurisdiction is a resource*. In recognizing PEI as a jurisdiction in this very active and strategic sense, the emphasis is not on being a *small* province, but on being a *province*.

The shift may be subtle, but it is neither semantic nor academic. Prince Edward Island is seen to be so small that many, particularly in central Canada, express frustration and question the Islanders' right to exist as one of the family of ten, a province with as much weight de jure as Alberta, Ontario, or Quebec (Baglole et al., 1997: 2). Small size has been touted as the cheap excuse for not treating PEI at all in scholarly discussions about certain provincial practices in Canada (e.g., Thompson et al., 2003: 10). Others mutter, in private more than in public, about the perceived advantages (mainly cost savings) of an eventual Maritime Union, whereby PEI would be joined to Nova Scotia and New Brunswick as a single province, with a total population still smaller than that of any other province in Canada except Newfoundland and Labrador. The construction and opening, in 1997, of the "fixed link" across the Northumberland Strait has added fuel to such arguments, now that PEI is, in a strictly geographical sense, no longer an island (Baldacchino and Spears, 2007: 63). Presumably, PEI would have most to lose from such a Maritime Union because it would certainly forfeit at least some of its current jurisdictional resourcefulness. No doubt, the prospects of such a loss would be aggressively contested by Prince Edward Islanders.

Since the mid-1980s, some awareness of the powers of jurisdiction – which include legislative, executive, and judicial prerogative – has been displayed by Prince Edward Island-based academics and policy makers. Although by all standards a small provincial university, UPEI spearheaded comparative research into the political and economic capacities of smaller island states and territories, mainly thorough its Institute of Island Studies, set up in 1985 with Harry Baglole as director. New possibilities were glimpsed during the *Islands Living* International Conference held at Brackley Point, PEI, in September 1992. This meeting of minds, organized by the IIS at UPEI, explored patterns of autonomy and dependence in the North Atlantic and provided a catalyst for making further connections which were to become more evident through the North Atlantic Islands Program – now the North Atlantic Forum (NAF) – a regional partnership that was spawned by the IIS and other partners after that pioneering 1992 conference. The focus was strictly regional, but an awareness of constitutional differences between island states, autonomies, and non-jurisdictions and their impact on economic capacity was a key outcome of the project (Baldacchino and Greenwood, 1998b; Baldacchino and Milne, 2000). The NAIP's emphasis on showcasing *successful* models of island economic development contrasted with the "doom and gloom" that still dominates the scholarly literature, with its emphasis on vulnerability (e.g., Harden, 1985; Briguglio, 1995) or consumption-maximizing and aid/rent-seeking strategies (Bertram and Watters, 1985; Kakazu, 1994; Poirine, 1999). Only lately has there been serious talk about *resilience* (Briguglio and Cordina, 2004; Briguglio et al., 2006) or "good governance" (Armstrong and Read, 2002).

A PERSONAL NOTE

I came to UPEI as the Canada Research Chair (CRC) in Island Studies, positioned as the appreciative beneficiary of a "gift" by the federal government of Canada to the people of Canada on the occasion of the 2000 millennium: 2,000 research chairs, federally funded for up to ten years each, were allocated to all tertiary education institutions in the country. Out of the slate that fell to UPEI, the university authorities, decided – bravely, to be fair – to allocate one such chair to "island studies," and I took up this post in 2003. This book very much distills my research ramblings in global island political economy during the six-year period that has since elapsed.

Soon after my installation, I applied for and was successfully awarded my first SSHRC standard research grant for an examination of "Patterns of Sub-National Autonomy amongst the World's Islands" (SRG Application No. 410–2004–0397). It was thanks to this generous funding that I could launch some timely pluri-disciplinary research into subnational island jurisdictions. "The Jurisdiction Project" has enabled a detailed, comprehensive, and global profiling exercise of the economic and political capacities of some 120 subnational islands and archipelagoes around the world. The dossiers were painstakingly built up over time and will require regular updating. The Sub-National Island Jurisdiction Database is now in the public domain (http://utopia.cs.upei.ca/jurisdiction/), part of an island studies website developed with assistance from the Canada Fund for Innovation and the support staff at UPEI's Robertson Library: let me single out Librarian Mark Leggott, and technical support staff Grant Johnson, Peter Lux, Paul Pound, and Kent Villard, for my heartfelt thanks. The analysis of the rich information that the database contains is proceeding apace in various scholarly publications and journal articles, and includes this book. A fresh SSHRC grant ("Offshoring Strategies from/for Sub-National Island Jurisdictions"; SRG Application No. 410–2007–0577) has since been obtained. Together, these two research grants have supported pioneering research activity along with various research visits combined with scholarly or public presentations in a variety of locations in Canada and beyond that speak to the subnational island jurisdiction perspective and its potential for scholarly work, especially where insights into the workings of globalization are concerned, as well as public policy. A number of publications have followed in hot pursuit; these so far include six authored or co-authored papers in peer-reviewed scholarly journals, a thematic co-edited journal issue, other papers by research associates, and three other edited and co-edited books. *Island Enclaves* is one of them.

Since I am mentioning publications, I must confess the peace of mind of having this book's proposal accepted by Philip Cercone at McGill-Queen's University Press. The text has benefitted from a very professional and supportive team, including Megan Elizabeth Hall, Joan McGilvray, Brenda Prince, Ryan Van Huijstee, and copy editor Curtis Fahey. Curtis told me that the manuscript "made me think of islands in a whole new way, and forced me to grapple with issues that had never occurred to me before." May such uplifting comments be forthcoming from the book's readers!

ISLAND STUDIES

Meanwhile, that I should even attempt such a book may warrant some jusitification. I do not consider myself a political scientist, nor an expert in federalism. Perhaps I could call myself a political geographer, although I have not had any formal and rigorous training in either political studies or geography. My undergraduate work was mainly in literature and social science, my graduate work in development studies and labour relations. In habitually presenting myself as an "islands scholar," I leave many confused: *island studies* is not exactly recognizable language in the world of academe.

And yet I may be cheapening myself unduly here: the study of islands on their own terms today enjoys a growing and wide-ranging recognition. "Island" initiatives have been undertaken by major international institutions, including: the United Nations (via its Small Island Developing States [SIDS] Program) and its specialized agencies, such as UNESCO's Small Island Voice and the United Nations Development Program (UNDP), as well as the forty-three-member-strong Alliance of Small and Island States (AOSIS) active in the General Assembly; the World Bank and its small states forum; the European Union (mainly via its Regional Policy Directorate-General, the Committee of the Regions, and the Islands Commission within the Conference of Peripheral Maritime Regions); and regional fora (such as the Pacific Islands Development Program, the South Pacific Forum, the Baltic Seven Islands Cooperation Network, the Indian Ocean Commission, and the Caribbean Community). A Global Islands Network (GIN) is active and maintains an impressive website and news-alert service (www.globalislands.net). The International Small Island Studies Association (ISISA), set up officially in 1992, continues its well-attended series of biennial conferences; its website is maintained by the University of Tasmania (www.geol.utas.edu.au/isisa/). The Japan Society of Island Studies (Nihon-Tosho-Gakkai) was set up in 1997. The Island Institute in Maine, United States, has celebrated its twenty-fifth anniversary and was recognized by a National Oceanic and Atmospheric Administration (NOAA) Excellence Award for Coastal and Ocean Resource Management in 2008, in recognition of significant contributions supporting coastal- or marine-resource programs. The Small Island Cultures Research Initiative (SICRI), set up in 2004 and now based at Southern Cross University, Australia, is a recent welcome addition, as is its scholarly journal *Shima* (www.http://sicri.org and www.http://shimajournal.org). A score of universities – including those of Hawaii, Kagoshima, Malta, and the West of Scotland – have an island-related centre, institute, or research program. The University of the South Pacific has a Faculty of Islands and Oceans. Queen's University Belfast, Northern Ireland, now has a professor of island geography. International Publishers Pinter (U.K.) launched an "Island Studies Series" in 1996, while Ashgate has a growing "Small States" series of publications. There is a commitment to small-state, mainly island, scholarship in the British Commonwealth, where thirty-two out of the fifty-three member states are small and mainly island jurisdictions with populations of less than 2 million.

And all this is in addition to the initiatives under way at the University of Prince Edward Island.

There is sufficient evidence that islands – small islands in particular – are distinct enough sites, or harbour extreme enough renditions of more general processes, to warrant their continued respect as subjects/objects of academic focus and inquiry. The core of "island studies" is the constitution of "island-ness" and its possible or plausible influence and impact on ecology, human/ species behaviour, and any of the areas handled by the traditional subject uni-disciplines (such as archaeology, economics, or literature), subject multi-disciplines (such as political economy or biogeography), or policy foci/issues (such as governance, social capital, waste disposal, language extinction, or sustainable tourism). And this is not to mention the aspect of small islands as somewhat closed (read: manageable) systems, amenable to study: most scholars – who are not necessarily islanders – enter into the study of small islands precisely in order to test and explore conceptual schemes and spe-cific hypotheses emerging from academic and policy debates at a mainland, regional, or global level. One could also argue that there is much academic and public-policy mileage yet to be made – especially by and for islanders who are active in academe or in the policy field – by looking critically and comparatively at island experiences and at "pan-island" approaches to similar challenges. This book is, I hope, further testimony to the power of an island-studies imagination.

THE MIRACLE OF MALTA

I moved to Canada in 2003 from Malta, my birth country: a smallish, arid, archipelagic island state with 400,000 citizens perched on just 316 km² of land. That such a sovereign state (independent since 1964) exists, and thrives as a moderately developed economy (since 1993, it is no longer recognized as a "small island developing state"), continues to fascinate me. Good gover-nance, some measure of good fortune, but also islandness and location, have played their part in this "miracle." As a student, and then as a member of the academic faculty, of the country's only local university – the University of Malta – I developed a better appreciation of how geographical positioning has shaped not just my country's history but also much of its economic and politi-cal fortunes. I prepared my doctoral thesis at the University of Warwick from 1990 to 1993; titled "Labouring in Lilliput," it explored labour-management relations among multinationals in the hospitality industry, within a context of the small and island states of Malta and Barbados. I developed courses that explored the sociology of small-scale societies, and taught these not just at the UOM but at tertiary-education institutions in Barbados, Canada, Fiji, Iceland, Mauritius, and the Seychelles. I continue to support the work of UOM's pioneering Islands and Small States Institute, as well as its Centre for Labour Studies, of which I was appointed director in 2002. The Council (Board of Governors) of the UOM uniquely granted me an open-ended leave of absence in 2003 in order to take up my CRC at UPEI: for this I am deeply grateful to my alma mater.

While in Malta, I was also one of six "technical experts" on a nationally representative Malta-European Union Steering and Action Committee (MEUSAC) that participated in the detailed negotiations, led by the minister of foreign affairs, on the adoption of the *acquis communautaire* between the Maltese government and the European Commission. This was in the run-up to a national referendum in March 2003 and Malta's eventual entry into the European Union in May 2004. Malta did not achieve all that it had hoped for – it did not manage to obtain an exemption from the use of plastic containers for beverages, for example. However, Malta *did* manage to secure the largest number of exemptions (seventy-two) from the *acquis* among all ten candidate countries at the time. These included a much bigger, and very demanding, state – Poland – which came away with the second largest number of exemptions (forty-three); Latvia came third with thirty-two. Malta even secured the only permanent derogation from the *acquis* among this group of accessing states: blocking non-permanent residents from buying second homes in Malta. I agree with a colleague at the University of Malta, Roderick Pace, who has argued that "Malta has used its small size to advantage in negotiating" (*The Economist*, 2004b). This was one of my own personal encounters with "the power of powerlessness" that can be wielded to good effect by policy makers in small jurisdictions and that is also featured and critiqued in this book.

ISLAND ENCLAVES

1

Autonomy without Sovereignty:
An "Island Studies" Approach

Islands are detached areas physically and readily detached politically.

Eileen Churchill Semple (1911: 436)

Dreaming of islands – whether with joy or in fear, it doesn't
matter – is dreaming of pulling away, of being already separate,
far from any continent, of being lost and alone – or is dreaming of
starting from scratch, recreating, beginning anew.

Gilles Deleuze (2004: 10)

INTRODUCTION

What goes around, comes around. Back in the winter of 1990–91, I was a
freshly minted doctoral student at the University of Warwick, reading fever-
ishly in order to come to better grips with what I wanted to concentrate on
as my thesis topic, without wanting to admit to others or to myself that I
was then hopelessly adrift. In any case, I found very welcome support from,
among others, sociology professor Robin Cohen, for whose work I had developed an appreciation in my earlier forays in development studies. Cohen
was kind enough to allow me free and unencumbered access to his campus
office on Fridays – when he would be typically working from home. During
that time, I would rummage gleefully through his many books and papers.
One particular collection I thoroughly enjoyed was his *African Islands and
Enclaves* (Cohen, 1983). There, I started coming across conceptualizations of
smaller[1] island states as "special cases" (e.g., Kaplinsky, 1983). Cohen had also
started collecting manuscripts for the book chapters of a sequel – provision-
ally titled *More African Islands and Enclaves* – which, however, was never
published but which I also pored over.

What did not strike me then but did so recently, more than seventeen
years later, is that Cohen does not appear to have realized that there was a
deep connection between the two targets of his volumes: islands and enclaves.

He juxtaposes them, perhaps assuming that they are mutually exclusive notions, never flirting with the idea that *an island could also be itself an enclave.*[2] In fact, the enclaves that feature in Cohen's 1990 book – Gambia and Cabinda (Angola) – are thus located on (and not off) the West Coast of Africa. Equatorial Guinea, also featured in the book, with both continental and island properties, carries elements of both concepts. Yet the concepts remain separate, mutually exclusive.[3] The terms "islands" and "enclaves" appear together in the same phrase just three times in the book: in the last three pages of its editorial introduction. Their possible interrelationship is never articulated. Cohen can be excused for missing out on a hidden relationship between the two terms in that particular text. Otherwise, *Island Enclaves* may never have been conceived.

PERSPECTIVE

This book investigates the carving out of islands, and even parts thereof, as jurisdictional enclaves – by and for themselves, or by and for other powers – in the context of idiosyncratic governance. Excising, zoning, detaching, niching, outbordering, dislocating, insulating, unbundling, quarantining, or offshoring are some of the performative active verbs that can be used to describe a clutch of different initiatives that share many basic characteristics. Deliberate or serendipitous, the method would involve the endowment of a specific place with particular and closely circumscribed privileges and powers, often ratified by law. The physical and geographic boundedness and distinctiveness of islands – fashioned, as they often are, by nature, but of late also engineered from scratch by human hand or mind – make these spaces especially attractive, and often default candidates of choice for such a thrust of political design that presupposes its own boundedness and distinctiveness. Simply and banally put, if one wishes to transform a place in order to endow it with the possibility of doing something different, perhaps shady, perhaps unconventional, perhaps dangerous, whether utopic or dystopic, or simply exceptional,[4] and in any case requiring both containment and distance, then that place should be on an island, or an island in toto.

Such a differentiation of geography comes about because governments are prepared to use that key capacity of sovereignty – the right and ability to make laws – with a view to better organize their relation to "things," in order to "optimize the health and wealth of the state and its people" (e.g., Braun, 2000: 12). Such a politically rational "reading" of territory is comparable to M. Foucault's concept of governmentality – defined as the right disposition of things, including the smart employment of territorial resources" (Foucault, 1991: 93; Kuehls, 1996: 67). Such a capacity is referred to in this book as "jurisdiction"; but the latter also includes extraterritorial outreach: the pursuit of pecuniary gain by drawing rent surpluses from *other* jurisdictions directly, or from the citizens thereof (Fabri and Baldacchino, 1999: 48; Palan, 1998: 630; 2002: 154; 2003: 59; emphasis mine). Governments "surrender some of their sovereignty-derived regulatory powers, or more precisely choose to use them in a particular way," in order to encourage non-local transnational actors to make use of their regulatory environment (Hudson, 2000: 270). The expansion of the offshore world is, in part, an expression of the spreading out of "sovereign bifurcation," whereby states deliberately and strategically bisect their domestic, intraterritorial sovereign space into "heavily and lightly regulated regimes" (read: *onshore* and *offshore* respectively) as a "competitive strategy" (Palan and Abbott, 1996; Palan, 2003: 8). These methods speak directly to the ways in which "imaginative geographies" (Said, 1979) "fold difference into distance, producing and performing an ever increasing separation between 'us' and 'them'" (Gregory, 2004: 320). As William Vlcek (2007: 333) argues: "The crucial point to recognize … is that the creation of an offshore space emerges from the use of sovereignty to carve out a regulatory and legislative space with the specific intention of creating a space of reduced regulation in comparison with [other] … states."

It is, however, not just sovereign states that exercise this function: even non-sovereign, subnational units with their own right and ability to make laws – which, granted, *may* have been devolved or bestowed formally or constitutionally by sovereign states – can perform, or be crafted to perform, this task. Many "dependencies" of sovereign states have resorted to their own "actorness" (e.g., Vlcek, 2008: 3) to develop offshore strategies, precisely because they *can* do so, given that they have the right to make their own laws within their territories: a crucial attribute of sovereignty that, however, can also be claimed by, or accorded to, such subnational units (Palan, 2003: 21). These candidates may have actually perfected the skill to a higher level, since their own fuzzy political status allows them to exploit more nimbly, selectively, and securely the spaces afforded by going after rents, or "jurisdictional shopping" for other purposes. Many of these places embody the broad personalities of federal or confederal cultures: a combination of "leave us alone" with "let us in" on major decisions affecting the national or collective whole (Duchacek, 1986: 296).

While forty-three of the world's sovereign states (22 per cent of the total) are exclusively island or archipelagic territories (CIA, 2009a), an additional

100-plus subnational island jurisdictions are known to enjoy a degree of autonomy without sovereignty (Watts, 2000; Baldacchino and Milne, 2006; Stuart, 2008). Examples of the exercise of "creative political economy" – by both sovereign and non-sovereign island jurisdictions – include the sale of stamps and commemorative coins, Internet domain sites (such as .nu for Niue, .to for Tonga, and .tv for Tuvalu), and telephone dialing codes (Aldrich and Connell, 1998: 76; Prasad, 2004); the hosting of movie productions (Malta, New Zealand, Rapa Nui) and religious pilgrimages (Amritsar, Iona, Skellig Michael); offering flags of convenience (FOCs) (Bermuda, Cyprus, Marshall Islands, Vanuatu); serving as *gulags* and detention centres (Guantánamo Bay, Christmas Island, Nauru, St Helena, Solovetsky); acting as offshore finance (Vlcek, 2008), electronic-gaming (Alderney, Antigua and Barbuda, Malta), and casino centres (Macao, Christmas Island); selling passports (Marshall Islands, Nauru, Samoa, Tonga, and Vanuatu); and attracting other, rent-based revenues (Baldacchino, 1993; Kakazu, 1994; Sidaway, 2007b: 354). Other islands have exploited, or have been exploited for, their "in-betweenity" (Baldacchino and Greenwood, 1998a: 10; Baldacchino, 2008b) or "betweenness" (Coutin 2005) in physical space (Ascension, Iceland, Kinmen) and/or in terms of time zones: the Cook Islands, for example, is the last centre to open for business in the international trading day (Aldrich and Connell, 1998: 85). For a more extreme form of time warp, note the island of Sark, until recently "the last European fiefdom" (Murphy, 2007). These places thrive by being between a rock and a hard place. Various island states and territories today may have not just deployed, but actually traded in, their sovereignty, or part thereof, in exchange for economic largesse, by exploiting this limbo granted by peripherality. R. Palan (2002: 172) argues that they have gone so far as to have prostituted their sovereign rights.

Even the realm of the literary and fictional is not immune from similar insights. On the mysterious and isolated islands of the mind, standard biological or political processes need not apply. Imagined geography, as A. Balasopoulos (2002: 59) reminds us, can legitimately conjure up the ideal (or fictitious) commonwealth of *Utopia* (More, 1516), as well as the microcosm of Lilliput and the mobile panopticon of the flying island of Laputa, both in *Gulliver's Travels* (Swift, 1726, Parts I and III respectively). Meanwhile, the "geographical precision" of an island (Weale, 1992: 81–2) exacerbates a sense of psychological distinctiveness and specific identity. Literature by writers from islands is replete with struggles to articulate particularity (Hay, 2003; Wood, 2008).

EIGHT HISTORICAL ANTECEDENTS

Palan (2003) does an excellent job in describing how the contours of the commercialization of state sovereignty developed surruptiously and in different locales; they were not methodical developments crafted by some conspiracy of politicians or business persons who foresaw what they were engineering. In his case, he focuses mainly on the offshore finance industry, and how various distinct components of what is now an integrated industry emerged sporadically, even chaotically, and then spread out and became consolidated thanks to that unfailing market mechanism: the demonstration effect.

This book considers the nature of "offshore" to go far beyond the geography of finance. And so this historical review will be broader, even if necessarily partial and sketchier. The point, however, is to illustrate how various special practices – legal niches in their own right – emerged historically and in largely uncoordinated fashion, although within a context of state formation and capitalist expansion. In their own turn, these practices then provided examples and precedents for similar strains of innovative governance. They are historico-spatial configurations that have given rise to particular, socially produced, modalities of "seeing" and "knowing" "enisled" spaces (Braun, 2000: 18).

Take, for example, the concept of *sanctuary*. The concept is a widely prevalent and variable one, appearing in the guise of such terms as safe haven, cocoon, or shelter (e.g., Gaudet, 2007). As a specially protective space, it harks back to the Judaic Law of Moses, which held that fugitives from human laws could take refuge at the altar of God, who, as the ultimate source of justice and mercy, would offer His protection if they were innocent. Later on, at a time when the separation between church and state was blurred and subject to tense negotiation, the Christian Church in Europe broadened the idea to include the blanket protection of the presumed guilty from the pursuit of human law. (The gypsy Esmeralda was granted sanctuary inside Paris's Notre Dame Cathedral in Victor Hugo's *The Hunchback of Notre Dame*.) As the political power of the church retreated, governments retrieved their jurisdictional reach and ensured that any fugitive would be liable to pursuit and capture, even in holy places. Various chapels and churches would then have made it clear – particulary to the desperate on the run – that sanctuary therein did not apply any longer, with appropriate visual notice. In my own birth country of Malta, the Latin phrase *Non Gode Immunita Ecclesias* (meaning: immunity does not apply) was thus stamped on ceramic tiles on the façade of religious sites, following an order by British Governor Frederick Cavendish Ponsonby, as late as 1828. More recently, symbolic offerings of sanctuary were offered to various draft dodgers during the Vietnam War, with various members of the clergy appearing to be "delighted with the opportunity to use their houses of worship in what they feel is an openly defiant way of supporting dissent" (*Time Magazine*, 1968). Perhaps the contentious application of Islamic Sharia Law in otherwise liberal-democratic polities today speaks to a similar "carving out" of jurisdictional practice.

It does not take much to shift from using special spaces to keep the people inside safe from bodily harm or legal retribution to using similar spaces still to keep people inside but with a view to restrain their freedom of movement and thus protecting others from their actions. The association of islands with *prisons* is an old one: pagans often located their demons offshore; Christianity locates them in Hell, which could also be imagined as an island (Turner, 1993); Dante located his *Inferno* on an island in the Southern hemisphere. A graduated spatialization of fear has led to islands being favoured sites for penal colonies, or even as wholesale prisons: Elba, and then St Helena, incarcerated Napoleon; Devil's Island (in French Guiana) held Alfred Dreyfus; Robben Island held Nelson Mandela; while Alcatraz – also known as Hellcatraz (Gardner, 1939) – held Al Capone. Apart from the penal colony on the Australian "mainland" proper in the nineteenth century, several offshore islands served as the equivalent of higher security prisons: Sarah, Melville, Stradbroke, Norfolk, Rottnest, and the quasi-island Tasman peninsula (Gillis, 2007; Pearn and Carter, 1995; Royle, 2001: 50–1).

Another enclaving of jurisdiction, also involving chapels, and one that persists and has become institutionalized in present-day international relations, is *extraterritoriality*. This crafting of a jurisdictional enclave owes part of its origins to the so-called embassy chapel problem. The needs for states to maintain open and ongoing diplomatic channels and relations often conflicted with the exigencies of national law: one effective response to that quandary, and in spite of the "abuse" that such immunity engendered (e.g., Trimble, 1946), was to devise an arrangement whereby "the house and equipages of the diplomatic agent are regarded as the territory of the power by whom he [*sic*] is accredited" (Online Encyclopedia, 2006). In what can be seen as an extension of the principle of sanctuary into the secular world, the agent of extraterritoriality – typically, a resident ambassador – is not subject to the receiving government and thus is exempt from local taxation and civil jurisdiction. For similar reasons, political or criminal offenders, and citizens who may feel that their civil rights are threatened, may and do seek asylum in a foreign embassy: a dramatic recent example of such behaviour would be then Zimbabwe presidential candidate Morgan Tsvangirai, who took refuge in the Dutch Embassy in Harare in June 2008 (CBC News, 2008). This mechanism was an imaginative resolution to an otherwise thorny impasse, concerning in particular the religious practices of ambassadors after the sixteenth century. It would have been simply intolerable for the most Catholic kings and queens of Spain to tolerate the English ambassador participating in a Mass according to the rites of the Church of England on Spanish soil; and just as impossible for the kings and queens of England, themselves head of the Anglican Church, to permit Spanish ambassadors to freely indulge in the "papist" rites of the Catholic Mass on English territory (e.g., Ruggie, 1993: 165).

A fourth relevant historical development, again taking us physically offshore, concerns the practices of *piracy and corsairing.* Piracy had been a "natural way of life" in the Mediterranean Sea at least since the tenth and eleventh centuries, with Pisa, Genoa, and Venice being the main maritime cities involved in the practice while also maintaining fleets to ward off foreign pirates in their own waters (e.g., Unger, 1980: 102). By the fourteenth century, however, a distinction in naval plundering emerged: corsairs emerged as entrepreneurs who would have some form of licence or permission from a parent state to commit aggressive acts. In principle, assaults were restricted to times of war and only against enemy vessels. But, human nature being what it is, these were not "reliable business partners." They frequently attacked friendly ships and were sometimes reluctant to share the profit with the shipowner. The Knights Hospitaller of St John, in particular, became well-known privateers in the sixteenth century and their targets were by no means confined to Muslim ships and states (Atauz, 2004, passim). Thus, a risky but potentially lucrative economic activity emerged whereby the same action could be deemed legitimate or otherwise, depending on whether it was somehow sanctioned.

Fifth, and with another Venetian connection, is the concept of *quarantine.* This term, associated with health practices, owes its origins at least to 1377, when the rector of the seaport of Ragusa, then belonging to the Venetian Republic, officially imposed a thirty-day isolation period for ships, which became forty days for land travellers (the number forty is *quaranta* in Italian and a group of approximately forty is *quarantaine* in French). In 1423 Venice set up one of the first known *lazaretto* (quarantine stations) on the island of Santa Maria di Nazareth near the city, and the Venetian system became a model for other countries to emulate (Gensini et al., 2004: 259; Sehdev, 2002). The zoning practice in this case was an act of containment, codified at law, to ensure that communicable diseases that might have been contracted elsewhere – by sailors, passengers, and animals – would not spread to local populations. The surrounding sea made the possibility of escape, and thus widespread contagion, that much less likely. The similar ease of containment, along with the difficulty of escape, explains why many islands have hosted prisons – see above – or hospitals that treated leprosy or contagious diseases (e.g., the "leper colonies" of Molokai and D'Arcy Island).

Sixth, moving into the twentieth century, and on the theme of economic activity, is the emergence of *export processing zones* (EPZs). With business organizations developing their own legal personality, culture, and behaviour patterns (e.g., Morgan, 1996), the export processing zone applies a similar logic to a whole cluster of firms that decide to share location. An EPZ is a designated area into which companies can import raw materials or semi-finished goods which they can then finish and export (e.g., Palan, 1998: 634). Their legal regimen usually includes relaxed labour and environmental laws, with preferential customs duties on selected import items, thus presenting an attractive proposition to foreign export-oriented capital. The EPZ becomes an enclave protected from the typically more stringent regulatory framework of the rest of the country: in some exceptional cases, and to prevent accusations of "two weights, two measures," a whole island jurisdiction can transform itself into an EPZ, as Mauritius has done, with a thriving garment industry (e.g., World Bank, 1992). To assert the role of airports as sites of innovative governance (about which more in chapter 2), one of the first onshore EPZs was the duty-free Shannon International Airport in Ireland in 1959. Many airports remain duty-free enclaves today.

The full-scale, free *trade* EPZ model was pioneered in the United States after the passage of the Celler Foreign Trade Zones Act in 1934. The first such free zone came into being in 1937 at Stapleton, Staten Island, New York, known as the New York Foreign Trade Zone No. 1 (Palan, 2003: 119). The model was then perfected with respect to Puerto Rico and Operation Bootstrap. This island's relationship with the United States is a truly "special case" and belongs to an "undefinable category" (Duchacek, 1970: 184–5). Without delving into the details of the arrangement, it can be said that the island's local administration enticed U.S.-owned companies to relocate and set up operations on Puerto Rico by providing labour at costs below those on the mainland, access to U.S. markets without import duties, and profits that could enter the country free from federal taxation. The investment of external capital, importing of raw material, and exporting of finished products to the U.S. market were all supported by the state. Owing to this clutch of measures, the island industrialized fast, overtaking for some time even the "Asian tigers" in its staggering rate of growth. Consultants associated with the Puerto Rico experience were directly involved in setting up Taiwan's first EPZ (suggestively, on an artificial island in Kaohsiung harbour) and in Indonesia (on Batam Island, just off Singapore) (Palan, 2003: 122). The policy then started to stagnate in the early 1970s; in Puerto Rico itself, a large public sector and a pervasive welfare state dampened the motivation for enterprise (Goldsmith, 1979; *The Economist*, 2006b). Since then, however, the model has enjoyed exponential growth: at least half the countries defined as "developing" by the United Nations had EPZs by the 1990s (Emadi-Coffin, 1996: 142). Palan (1998: 639) refers to "700 free trade zones of various descriptions."

Another twentieth-century development is the emergence of countries offering *flags of convenience*, defined as those that "offer their maritime flag registration to owners from another country." Much cheaper and more hassle-free ship-registration fees, low or no taxes, and freedom to employ cheap labour are the typically cited motivating factors behind a shipowner's decision to "flag out" (International Transport Workers' Federation [ITF], 2008). Thirty-two countries have been declared FOCs by the ITF's Fair Practices Committee; of these, nineteen are island states or territories. A jurisdiction like the Marshall Islands has been developed by the United States to provide such services (Van Fossen, 1992); its shipping registry is run out of Reston, Virginia, by International Registries (Palan, 2003: 53). As with export processing zones, flags of convenience are especially appealing to smaller jurisdictions who lack "internal profit making capacity" (Johns, 1983). Smaller jurisdictions lack hinterlands; they have no "space" in which to employ a "defence-in-depth" economic strategy, something that is inherent to the nature of a larger economy (Baldacchino, 2006e; Vlcek, 2008: 85–6). They can thus bring in more revenue by lowering transaction costs because, in doing so, they widen their revenue/tax base (Dommen and Hein, 1985: 166).

Eighth and lastly, a similar logic lies behind the emergence of *offshore finance centres* (OFCs): jurisdictions that have at least one significant institution geared towards accepting deposits and investment funds from foreigners (Van Fossen, 2003: 268n.1).[5] The key trigger for this development appears to have been the emergence of a so-called Eurodollar market in the late 1960s, centred in London, United Kingdom, where – given the glut of U.S. dollars in the post-Second World War reconstruction boom in Europe – U.S. banks in particular could make loans in US$ without having to comply with any reserve requirements (Roberts, 1994: 94; Vlcek, 2008: 19). Today, such locations are markets for currencies, loans, bonds, and a raft of other, increasingly sophisticated financial instruments which exist beyond the regulatory reach of other national economies (Roberts, 1994: 93). In a 1994 listing of offshore financial centres, twenty-eight out of forty-three identified locales are on islands (ibid., Figure 5.1). A 2002 list details seventy-one such markets, of which forty-six are whole islands or on islands (Palan, 2003: 37–9). Professional lawyers and accountants assign novel interpretations to the fluid concepts of territorial boundary, legal personality, business entity, residence, domicile, citizenship, and nationality in order to enable capital to escape domestic politics and shelter in favourable offshore jurisdictions (Picciotto, 1999). One-third of the wealth of the world's high net-worth individuals, or nearly US$6 trillion, may today be "held" offshore (Vlcek, 2008: 51). And yet "holding" is not the correct term. One novelty in this industry is that we are increasingly dealing with fungible, intangible (often furtive) movements of capital; they are financial transactions that – unlike the products that find their way to, from, and through export processing zones – are essentially electronic or accounting flows and do not necessarily occupy material space.

The above categories may appear relatively clear-cut, but they mask the myriad interesting interrelationships that crop up among the above eight historical developments. These include: islands as sanctuaries for pirates throughout history; the promotion of OFCs as "financial piracy" (Vlcek, 2008: 23) or "economic piracy" (Baldacchino and Milne, 2000: 6); or the attempt by The Pirate Bay (a private company) to use Sealand (an artificial island, previously used as the base for a pirate radio station) as a sanctuary (read: safe haven) from international copyright laws (e.g., Owen, 2007).[6]

ISLAND GEOGRAPHIES

Looking at these and at similar and historically more recent systems of economic thought, experiments in innovative governance, and border politics – like offshore casinos, electronic gam(b)ing, and refugee security zones – it is clear that islands are the premier geographies of choice for these forays into spatial-juridical enclaving. The notion of a sanctuary enisles a particular space; an overseas embassy effectively becomes an enclave, immune from most of the legal obligations of the surrounding host state. Their relative smallness and essential marginality camouflages the pivotal role of islands within global capitalism. Islandness increases the disposition for internal confidentiality and endogenous control of information, in a setting that resembles a "self-contained universe" (Brock and Smawfield, 1988: 232; Fabri and Baldacchino, 1999: 142). Islands are the quintessential "visible territorial enclaves" (Palan, 1998: 626). Explains Michael Taussig (2004: 294):

"An island allows one to hold the world in one's hands, play with it, observe it from different angles, and provide it with different fates."

Throughout history, islands have been locales where both nature (via evolutionary processes) and humankind (via creative political economy and civil engineering) have undergone many interesting "experiments," whether intentional or fortutious. In this respect, I do not wish to draw any hard and fast parallels between biogeographical and politico-economic or engineering developments. Suffice it to be said here that, according to the principles of evolutionary theory, islandness, compounded by size and distance from the nearest mainland (and the latter's own size), has had an impact on the number and types of biota that have developed on islands (MacArthur and Wilson, 1967). Oceanic islands in particular, born de novo out of volcanic or coralline activity, habitually develop endemic species over time. It was research on island archipelagos like the Galápagos in the eastern Pacific and the Aru Islands in eastern Indonesia that independently inspired both Charles Darwin and Alfred Wallace to stumble upon the theory of evolution by natural selection (Darwin, 1859; Wallace, 1880).

Similarly, perhaps, other islands have departed from the legal and regulatory orthodoxy of their time. In his study of the colonial history of St Helena, S.A. Royle (2007) describes a polity that was a contained and conveniently located site for administrative experimentation as a "company island," where the East India Company could very much "play God." In a detailed study of the world's first fully fledged astronomical observatory on the Danish island of Hven, we read that the island was entrusted in 1576 to astronomer Tycho Brahe as a "fief"; his plans involved considerable social upheaval, with the local peasants and fishers drafted as cheap construction labour for at least eight years (Christianson, 1999). Today, the islands of Samsø and Aerø, in Denmark, are models of communities run exclusively by renewable energy (Turner, 2007: 27–44, 65–70). Unlike mainlands, whole islands can also be bought or leased, a new pastime for the rich and famous (FT Expat, 2002; Private Islands On-Line, 2008; Vladi Private Islands, 2008). The engineered Palm Islands of Dubai, or "The World" archipelago close by, are contemporary examples of this pseudo-manufacture (Jackson and Della Dora, 2009; Junemo, 2004). Islands are hot private regions even within the virtual spatiality of Second Life (2009), offering "the most flexibility and privacy." In line with various creation myths, islands have definitively shifted "from the register of the 'found' to the register of the 'made'" (Sloterdijk, 2005: 279)[7]. In contrast, mainlands, with their sprawling hinterlands and unfathomable complexity, overwhelm and frighten.

Moreover, being on the edge, out of sight and so often out of mind, exposes the weakness of mainstream ideas: paradigms tend to be weakest at their peripheries; challenges to sovereignty are most apparent at the margin, where power is more clearly contested (e.g., Hudson, 2000: 277). Such a tense condition also foments and entertains alternatives to the status quo. Islands thus tend to stand out as sites of novelty; they are disposed to act as advance indicators or extreme reproductions of what may be present elsewhere, or future everywhere: a shape of things to come?

ISLANDS AS NOVELTY SITES

Thanks to a self-evident vulnerability, "the island," with fallacious simplicity, can be conceived as a convenient platform for any whim or fancy. An island is for all seasons and for all tastes. An island can be both paradise and prison, both heaven and hell. An island is a contradiction between openness and closure, between roots and routes, which islanders must continually negotiate (Clifford, 1997; Connell and King, 1999: 2; Jolly, 2001; Kirch, 1986; Péron, 1993: 16; Villamil, 1977). Islands are paradoxical spaces that are difficult to pin down: "Islands … absolute entities … territories, territorial; relational spaces – archipelagos, (inter)dependent, identifiable; relative spaces – bounded but porous; isolated, connected, colonized, postcolonial; redolent of the performative imaginary; vulnerable to linguistic, cultural, environmental change; robust and able to absorb and modify … utopian and dystopian, tourist meccas, ecological refugia" (Stratford, 2003: 495).

A significant component of the contemporary intoxicating lure or fascination of islands has to do with the fact that islands suggest themselves as tabulae rasae: potential laboratories for any conceivable human project, in thought or in action (Baum, 1996, Baum et al., 2000; King, 1993). There is something about the insular that beckons alluringly. It inspires a greater malleability to grand designs. It is a condition that erodes inhibition. It is a proneness to a more genuine, "gone there, done that" (even if psychological) finality. It provides an opportunity for a more thorough control of intervening variables which then are more likely to guarantee successful outcomes (e.g., Baum et al., 2000: 215). Yet the smaller, remote, and insular subject also suggests peripherality, being on the edge, being out of sight and so out of mind; such and similar situations expose the weakness of mainstream ideas, orthodoxies, and paradigms while fomenting alternatives to the status quo.

The combined outcome of these features is a presentation of islands as sites of creative conceptualization. More scope for tinkering is generated; there is a greater readiness for either making the strange familiar (breaking out of the mould) or making the familiar strange (finding your soul). Thus, Innisfree Island, in Ireland, is marketed as one such "refuge for the soul" (Royle, 2001: 12), with the Sligo Tourist Board seeking to capitalize on the text of "The Lake Isle of Innisfree" by the Irish poet William Butler Yeats (1893). Or else, take Ricardo Montalbán, who as Mr Roarke fulfilled the wildest dreams of his rich and eccentric clients every week on *Fantasy Island* (ABC, 1978). The more remote and smaller the island, the greater its propensity to innovation. Islands are the first, the harbingers, the pioneers, the miner's canary (Baldacchino and Milne, 2000: 241). In the words of former United Nations Secretary General Kofi Annan, islands are the frontline zones where many problems associated with the environment and development are unfolding (UN, Special Session of the General Assembly, 1999).

It should therefore come as no surprise to us that islands, both real and earthy as much as concocted, or even those occupying the fuzzy space in between, stand out as sites of novelty, of coy experimentation, of deliberate or coincidental path-breaking events. This is one of the many diverse roles that islands perform as objects of representation.

CELEBRATING ISLANDS AS EXPERIMENTAL, EXTREME, OR FRONT-LINE SITES

At first sight, Charles Darwin's study of finches on the Galápagos Islands (Darwin, 1859) and Alfred Russel Wallace's study of birds-of-paradise on the Aru Islands (Wallace, 1880) may have appeared to be inconsequential, island-based, island-specific fieldwork. And yet crucial, new insights, particularly in our understanding of evolutionary biology and zoogeography, emerged from these investigations. The forays of Borislav Malinowski among the Trobriand (or Kiriwina) islanders of Papua New Guinea (1922), of Margaret Mead to Samoa and the Admiralty Islands ([1928] 2001, [1934] 2002), and of Raymond Firth to Tikopia ([1936] 1983) led to the birth of ethnography and the consolidation of social anthropology as a discrete social-science discipline with its own methodological rigour (Deloughrey, 2001: 35; Baldacchino 2004b). More recently, researchers have been "islanding" with a view to exploiting the laboratory potential of smaller islands for deducing observations of an extraordinary and extra-insular relevance, as in the case of Daniel Simberloff and Edward Wilson's (1969) controlled experiments among the mangroves of the Florida Keys. As prototypical ethnoscapes, islands have also spearheaded the study of how locales are conceived and produced in the human imaginary (Appadurai, 1996: 180; Baldacchino, 2006d). Islands tend towards clairvoyancy. They act as advance indicators for what will occur in the future, or as extreme renditions of what exists elsewhere in less exceptional form (Baldacchino, 2007b).

Insights from the Natural Sciences

Consider first the evidence of islands as front-line zones, sites of novelty or exaggeration as emergent from the natural sciences. D. Quammen (1996) surveyed Aldabra, Aru, Angel de la Guarda, Galapagos, Guam, Hawaii, Komodo, Madagascar, Mauritius, Rakata, and Tasmania to support his assessment that we are witnessing widespread ecosystem decay. Insularity has been described as "the flywheel of evolution," with copious island-based examples of endemism, including giantism (such as the Solomon Island rat) and dwarfism (such as the Icelandic horse) (Carlquist, 1974). A. Cropper (1994) confirms that between 66 and 97 per cent of endemic plant species on the Lord Howe, St Helena, Rodrigues, Norfolk, Ascension, Juan Fernandez, Canaries, Seychelles, and Galápagos islands are rare, threatened, or extinct.

Islands occupy 1.86 per cent of the Earth's total surface area (and just 1.47 per cent without Greenland) (Depraetere and Dahl, 2007; Global Shoreline Database, 2005), but 18.7 per cent (166 out of 890) of UNESCO's World Heritage sites are on islands (139) or are islands in toto (27) (UNESCO, 2009 – see Tables 8.3 and 8.4). The latter category would include Chile's Easter Island, Ecuador's Galapagos, Gambia's James Island, Greece's Patmos, and Russia's Solovetsky, to name but a few. Papua New Guinea is the world's largest depository of language diversity (Crystal, 2000). The island of Mafia off Zanzibar is the World Health Organization test site for the elimination of advanced lymphatic filariasis or elephantiasis (*The Economist*, 2003a). The islanders of Tristan da Cunha may hold the key to asthma and lung-cancer genes (Scott, 2003). The Micronesian islands of Pingelap and Pohnpei have the highest known incidence of achromatopsia (colour blindness) (Sacks 1997; Gabilondo 2000). Iceland is a leader in genetic decoding, owing to its extensive and well-documented genealogical heritage (Vesilind, 2000).

In geophysical terms, every place is born. Islands, however, can be and are born quickly (e.g., Surtsey, off Iceland; or Kavachi, in the Solomon Islands (Nunn, 1994); and they can have their entire living biota wiped out (e.g., Anatahan Island, in the Northern Marianas) (NASA, 2003) or be totally annihilated as a consequence of natural activity (e.g., Krakatoa in Indonesia) (Whittaker 1999). They can also suffer terribly at the hands of humankind, as has Bikini Atoll in the Marshall Islands, where fifty years ago the world's largest nuclear-bomb test explosion took place. Sea-level rise may be to blame for the wholesale disappearance of at least two uninhabited islands in Kiribati – Tebua Tarawa and Abanuea (*Independent on Sunday*, 13 June 1999, cited in Royle 2001: 39) – and India's Lohachara Island, once home to 10,000 people (*The Independent* [U.K.], 2006). It may also be responsible for the imminent depopulation of the Carteret Islands, Papua New Guinea (Tweedie, 2009).

Insights from the Social Sciences

Consider next the social sciences. G. Bertram and R.F. Watters (1985) examined Tuvalu, Niue, Kiribati, Cook Islands, and Tokelau, identifying in the process the mutually reinforcing features of a rent-driven, "MIRAB" economy (explained in more detail below). This departs from the more orthodox conceptualization of economic development as driven by indigenous productive forces (Baldacchino, 1993), surviving instead on out-migration flows that provide remittances and on foreign aid that finances a local bureaucracy (more on this in chapter 4 below). J.A. Barnes (1954) and J. Boissevain (1974) developed the foundations of social-network theory from their respective fieldwork on the Norwegian island of Bremnes and in a village in Malta. G.V. Doxey (1976) set up his "irridex" (a tourism-irritation index) after fieldwork in Barbados. Both A. Crosby (1986) and R.H. Grove (1995: 9) remind us that Mauritius was the site of the modern world's first environmental debate, involving the extent to which, if at all, alien biota should be deliberately imported into other territories. D.S. Landes (1998: 69) documents the island groups of Azores and Madeira as the world's prototype plantation economies, a technique then perfected in the island Caribbean (Beckford, 1972; Best and Polanyi Levitt, 2009).

The separateness, distinctiveness, and more manageable, smaller size of islands render them obvious starting points for designing sustainable ecotourism programs through biosphere reserves, national parks, and other diversity-rich areas (Di Castri and Balaji, 2002). Chumbe Island, near Zanzibar, has been one of a few successful prototypes for ecotourism projects among warm-water islands (Gössling, 2003); various cold-water islands – like Greenland and Svalbard – appear to have more hopeful prospects for sustainable tourism (Baldacchino, 2006f). The fishers of Isla Tiburón, Mexico, practise sustainable fisheries management (Hirsch, 2009). The residents of Sanibel and Captiva Islands, Florida, voted to become a town in 1974 in order to adopt a sustainable housing master plan (Cameron, 1998: 213–15).

The impact of tourism is nowhere more sudden, pervasive, transparent, and perhaps even irrevocable or unsustainable than on smaller islands and their (more fragile) habitats and/or communities (Conlin and Baum, 1995; Briguglio et al., 1996; Lockhart and Drakakis-Smith, 1996; Apostoulopoulos and Gayle, 2002; Gössling, 2003; Baldacchino, 2004c). UNESCO recognized this island condition early on in reviewing case studies of tourism effects in five island territories: Bali (in Java), Bermuda, Cyprus, Malta, and the Seychelles (De Kadt, 1979).

Examples of very high population density and its effects as played out on a bounded territory can be glimpsed from life on the atoll of Malé, Maldives, with a population density of 5,200 persons per km^2. Population-density figures for Singapore, Bermuda, Majuro (Marshall Islands), Malta, and South Tarawa (Kiribati) are not much less (UN, Earthwatch Island Directory website). All these islands, however, lag far behind Ap Lei Chau, Hong Kong, with its 80,000 people in an area measuring just 1.3 km^2 (Island Superlatives website, 2007).

Insights from Literature and Fiction

Consider, too, that the realm of the literary and the fictional is not immune from similar insights, even if the discovery is of one's soul, one's mission, or one's self, rather than of buried material treasure. Islands, especially smaller islands, lack hinterlands (Baldacchino, 2006e), but that does not prevent islands from serving as material or spiritual hinterlands for others, as tourists would readily attest. Many fictional characters who travel to islands in the course of a story, whether alone or in company, usually return disturbed, broken, refreshed, redeemed, resolute, shaken, or somehow transformed by the experience (e.g., Lawrence, 1927). Islands shake their visitors out of the complacency of contemporary social mores, whether by releasing the atavistic anarchism as in Golding's *Lord of the Flies* (1954), by giving free rein to the noble intentions of social engineering as in Wells's *The Island of Dr. Moreau* (1894), or by catalysing a spiritual experience as in Glover's *Elle* (2003), where the heroine (for a change!) is marooned on the Île des Demons.

As William Shakespeare reminds us (via prototype islander Caliban) in *The Tempest* (1611), that early specimen of island-framed literature which melds reality with illusion, "be not afeard, the isle is full of noises" (3.2: 138). Noisy it is indeed. The theme of island redemption is central to Western historical inscriptions of island sites (Deloughrey 2001, 35). As J.R. Gillis (2004) points out, the cultural history of "the West" is primarily an island story. Such islands became "the loci of imagination, desire, hopes and fears, the goal of dreamers and mystics and misfits, multiplying, drifting, disappearing and reappearing moulds into which cosmographers and cartographers could pour both art and science, material spaces which the merchant venturer, pirate, colonist and governor could penetrate and exploit" (Cosgrove, 2005: 302).

Many former island colonies now desperately seek to market themselves as tourism destinations on a similar (though repackaged) mythical allure, laced with whiffs of fecundity and exoticism for the erogenously inspired and/or spiritual healing for those tickled by what is beyond the flesh (e.g., Gabilondo, 2000: 99). The magnetic attraction of such unsullied fantasies continues unabated. In 2001 the box-office hit *Castaway* (starring Tom Hanks) was filmed on Monuriki Island (Yasawa Group, Fiji) (Zemeckis, 2000), while separate rounds of the massively popular television serial *Survivor* were filmed on the islands of Aitutaki (Cook Islands), Efate (Vanuatu), Koror (Palau), Nuku Hiva (Marquesas Group, French Polynesia), Pulau Tiga (Malaysia), and Vanua Levu (Fiji Islands).

ISLAND JURISDICTIONAL ENCLAVES

Island creativity also extends to the distinct subfield of political economy. Hence the focus of this book. The intellectual effort to come to better grips with this phenomenon has been much slower than developments in the real world (Elazar, 1994: xii). So much so that, today, it is quite common for various islands to trade in their sovereignty, or part thereof, in exchange for economic largesse. The contemporary world has a staggering number of "jurisdictional enclaves" which occupy the fuzzy middle ground between full sovereignty and conventional municipality. The large majority of these are islands, or on islands: a relationship that is spawned by the natural logistical tendency of an island to be self-administered, especially if it is remote from its metropolitan power.

The vast majority of these jurisdictions are *not* seeking sovereign status, nor do they wish to lose their autonomous powers; and the metropolitan power responsible for them is often all too willing to accede to their political agenda. For the islands themselves, this behaviour emerges as an increasingly rational and strategically appropriate one, resulting in net material gains for the jurisdiction, particularly at a time when security concerns are real and when sovereignty has largely *not* delivered relatively high levels of economic prosperity. Being a subnational island jurisdiction typically bestows a solid safety net supported by a metropolitan power, while granting enough discretion to safeguard national identity, local culture, and the general exercise of local power. The metropolitan player can meanwhile exercise a "soft imperialism" (Hettne and Soderbaum, 2005), which does not typically raise eyebrows among the members of the United Nations Committee on Decolonization, and can target its smaller island beneficiaries with its munificence: a relatively small amount of money can go quite a long way on a limited land area and/or a smaller population. Why, and how, is this so? Is there a benign relationship between the jurisdictional condition (and its intersecting governance levels) and economic prosperity? Is there a pattern to the practices behind such a condition entered into by the various SNIJs around the world? If so, is it worthy of more systematic investigation and further scrutiny?

Exclaves were quite common in medieval Europe, but they disappeared rapidly with the ongoing territorial consolidation of states and the adoption of the principles of Westphalian sovereignty. Until recently, these exclaves were assumed to be anachronisms, relics of a past political system (Muir, 1975: 43). And yet exclaves have persevered and now survive with a newly found purpose, often in some symbiosis with a sovereign state to whom they may owe their current non-sovereign but (to some degree) autonomous juridictional status.

With the suspension (July 2006) and then collapse (July 2008) of the WTO's Doha Round of trade talks, there is suddenly more scope for bilateral, asymmetric deals between states. Countries are once again likely to turn their energies to striking "preferential deals" with individual countries or regional blocks (e.g., *The Economist*, 2006c). And that is what subnational island jurisdictions have been doing all along: they lead the way in manifesting creative expressions of governance within typically asymmetric relationships with a much larger state. The economic and political tools that they deploy are in part a function of a negotiated outcome of a bilateral relationship with a (usually benign) metropole; a colonial inheritance; the vibrancy of a local "subnationalist" culture; and the ability of local elites to govern, represent, and advance "subnational" interests.

This book may be the first to investigate and discuss the modalities and practices of subnational island jurisdictions globally, discerning how populated SNIJs provide lessons in multilevel and intersecting governance; how they have the capacity to act and interact in their (changing) environments; how equipped they are to navigate, and how well or badly they manage, multiple levels of political economy; how they expose the limitations and "fuzziness" of sovereignty; and how they provide evidence of alternative yet (in their own way) viable models of "development" that are not based on large pools of resources or economies of scale, such as are liable to be found in large cities, industrial clusters, or knowledge-capital concentrations.

NEW THINGS TO CONSIDER

Islands have historically served as refreshment and revictualling stops on long maritime journeys (Deloughrey, 2001: 28). They can still serve that purpose, but this time to provide refreshing ideas and practical examples on certain natural and human (including political) conditions: "The heretofore obscure histories of remote islands deserve a place alongside the self-contemplation of the European past – or the history of civilizations – for their own remarkable contributions to an historical understanding. We thus multiply our conceptions of history by the diversity of structures. Suddenly, there are all kinds of new things to consider" (Sahlins, 1987: 72).

This observation is in sharp contrast to the imperialist (often fatal) contact that transformed many such islands into cargo cults (Worsley, 1957) and welfare-dependent communities, wedded to the metropole. Islands are increasingly acknowledged as sites of agency, depositories of "new things." The fragmenting, continental narrative of the "many islands of the world" – which summarily leaves such bothersome dots out of maps (Hau'ofa, 1983) – can yet be profitably replaced by the pan-archipelagic script of "a sea of islands" (Hau'ofa, 1993). The treasures that islands deliver include powerful messages, bearing the fullness of new and vital noises.

2

Borders within Borders and the New Offshoring

We need to throw out Ptolemaic, nation-based models with which we interpret the world's events.

Kenichi Ohmae, 1990: 213

INTRODUCTION

There are only two countries in the world that share a border stretching over 8,890 km, are both members of the Organization for Economic Co-operation and Development (OECD), share the same international telephone prefix, trade extensively in goods and services, and whose majority of citizens speak the same language, watch similar TV programs, and get to play in each other's major sport leagues. Those countries, of course, are Canada and the United States.

One would imagine that such a relationship could only broaden in the context of a "borderless world." But the contrary has happened: in April 2005 the United States government announced the Western Hemisphere Travel Initiative (WHTI), whereby all travellers to and from the Americas, including Canadian citizens, must present a valid passport to enter the United States. Effective 23 January 2007, a passport has been required for air travel to the United States from Canada (as well as from Mexico, Central and South America, the Caribbean, and Bermuda). As of January 2008, the passport requirement was extended to all land border crossings and sea travel.

Such a development may have caught some observers by surprise – as it did various prospective travellers who inundated passport-issuing offices with their urgent requests, in some cases with holiday packages already booked and paid for – before and after the two January deadlines elapsed. The WHTI represents what appears to be a step backwards in the overall inexorable march towards making the world a smaller, more connected place.

Kenichi Ohmae is just one prominent interlocutor for this phenomenon: the globalization of consumer tastes, the rapid dispersion of information and communication technologies, the relentless flow of information – what Canadian Marshall McLuhan (1964) termed and presaged as resulting in "the global village." The compression and convergence of time and space – a consequence of things becoming easier and cheaper to communicate faster (Janelle, 1969: 359; Harvey, 1990) – can, it seems, be thought of only in terms of a force that erodes national borders and renders them redundant. Services are following products into the realm of portability and non-site specificity. The "end" or "death of geography" concept is beguilingly simple and has become a fashionable narrative in business and marketing circles: because of improvements in transportation, hyper-mobile capital, media technologies, and commercial organization, the actual physical site of money blurs, and even the location of physical customers becomes irrelevant to their ability to receive seamless service from their chosen suppliers – and especially so if the product at stake is weightless (e.g., Cairncross, 1997; Martin, 1996; O'Brien, 1992).

Yet, just as geography is being laid to rest in some conceptions of the "knowledge economy," the *significance of place* is being vigorously (re-) asserted elsewhere. The redefinition of the Immigration and Naturalization Service (INS) of the United States as the Department of Homeland Security suggests such a reconceptualization: between those to be protected inside borders and those they are allegedly being protected from. "Place branding" is all the rage in marketing: note campaigns meant to limit the use of the name "champagne" to a specific region in France, "sherry" in Spain, or "port" in Portugal (e.g., Dow Jones Newswires, 2007). The identification of the economic-development benefits of "physical proximity" by Paul Krugman, and of "clustering" by Michael Porter – both Nobel Laureates in economics – have reaffirmed the importance of place (and geography) in mainstream economic theory (e.g., Krugman, 1991; Porter, 1990). Ironically, even as computing – a borderless utility icon – is fast emerging as a "cloud" of disembodied services accessible from any place that has an Internet connection, the data, or hosting, centres that contain this cloud need a physical location, preferably with cheap power, fibre-optic cables, a chilly climate, and dry air (e.g., Lawson, 2000; *The Economist*, 2008e).

In his relevant and broadly representative critique, K. Morgan (2004) argues that the alleged death of distance is overstated because it undervalues "tacit knowledge" (including trust building), which is both person-embodied and context-dependent: thus, it has to be local, "nested-in-place," or spatially "sticky." Moreover, and more pertinent to this discussion, Morgan charts the growth of what he calls "territorial innovation systems": local or regional assemblages of firms and their subnational network of institutional supports. These seek to develop and exploit regional economic-development strategies. Thus, geography matters, since the invisible economic hand of the market will continue to be tweaked by policy and politics, which are, in turn, location-based and driven. (What else is politics essentially about?) A system in which nations, regions, and cities seek to influence the trajectory of economic development in their respective jurisdictions is essentially a *political* one; this speaks to the reality of uneven development, and to the disadvantages that small peripheral jurisdictions face when they simply follow market forces (e.g., Poot, 2004).

It is with the logic, tenacity, and recent manifestations of spatial differentiation that this book is concerned. The "death of geography" narrative does have its validity, especially with regard to the scope and tempo of globalization and the disposition towards sameness that follows. But there is merit in observing and documenting expressions of idiosyncratic and creative governance which are perhaps mainly intended to invent or preserve difference (e.g., Storper, 1987). Such practices have national, regional, and local nuances. They are policy-driven, though also with an eye to market niches. In each of these, place matters a lot. In the context of such a return to realism, R.D. Kaplan (2009) calls this approach "the revenge of geography."

And so the demonstrably global village in which we find ourselves living today is experiencing messy, contradictory dynamics. There is a "flexible, non-uniform adaptation to the penetrative flows of various interactions across the territorial divides" (Duchacek, 1986: 296), and yet a corresponding attempt to wield public policy as a tool to subvert, exploit, or even mastermind such penetrations. The threat of terrorism (itself, ironically, a function of globalization) has been the main inducement for the United States to render the U.S.-Canada border less "porous," to the chagrin of those who used to take the fluidity of the crossing for granted. One could say the same about the "security fence" built by Israel to separate itself from the Palestinian-run territory of the West Bank, although, in this case, strategic long-term geo-politics is probably an equally pertinent reason (Bard, 2007). The case of clandestine immigration is a different threat altogether: again, a function of globalization and its encouragement of the free movement of persons, it is the main explanation for the U.S.-Mexico border, which has dramatically become much less "borderless" and increasingly militarized with extensive fencing (e.g., Wolfson, 2006). And, while the current twenty-five European countries of the Schengen Area (all EU member states except Bulgaria, Cyprus, Ireland, Romania, and the U.K. – plus Iceland, Norway, and

Switzerland) have removed the obligation for internal border checkpoints and controls between each other (Schengen Visa, 2008), the EU maintains a much stronger vigilance on its borders with non-member states. This is nowhere more dramatic than in the two Spanish enclaves on North Africa: Ceuta and Melilla. The two city statelets were surrounded by "a ten-foot high fence, with double razor-wire, electronic sensors, and infra-red cameras on top" (Young, 2003: 67). A third wall, "using the most advanced technology aimed at keeping out undocumented immigrants," was built more recently, and the fence has been doubled in height (Drago, 2005).

Actual terrorism and illegal migration, and their respective potential threats, are thus key contemporary issues which have seen states taking national measures to protect their respective sovereign territories.[1] In our allegedly borderless world, individuals crossing borders need not only passports but often also visas (permitting entry) and work permits (permitting entry for purposes of paid employment). These technologies are themselves subject to increasing sophistication: from biometric passports and fingerprints to retina scans and dental records, available online at the "biometric border" (Amoore, 2006; Ng and Whalley, 2008). The conditions and fears that, some 2,000 years ago, led to the building of the "Great Wall of China" – at 6,350 km, the longest human-made structure to date – are still with us. Far from extinguishing the national state, the new "thickening" measures along borders reassert national concerns and national interests, are codified by means of national law, are accompanied by nationally prescribed powers, are executed by national personnel, and are accompanied by symbols and icons of national identity – like flags, logos, uniforms, and passports.

Yet borders, as dynamic, political, and discursive constructs, do not define and prescribe only the space *between* countries. For similar, mainly security-related reasons, even spaces *within* sovereign states have been carved out and designated to fall under specific regulations which, often deliberately, do not apply to the rest of the state. Obvious places to look for such practices, related to the "free ports" of pre-modern Europe, and being as they are at the front line of the threat of both terrorism and immigration, are the so-called "international ports." Even though international airports and seaports are quintessential "spaces of flows" (Castells, 1996), and though they may deal mainly with international (non-national) travellers and cargo (including those "in transit"), these ports are nevertheless *very national* institutions: they function to screen and exercise discretion about who (by Immigration, Homeland Security) and what (by Customs, Agriculture, Pest Control) is allowed to proceed beyond and into the national space. This feature becomes all the more assured when air/seaport terminals are subject to a specific status and regulatory regime. In practically all international airport and seaport terminals today, there are clearly designated zones where (apart from the ubiquitous security personnel) only bona fide passengers and certain types of "carry on items" and personal affects are permitted and where even passenger behaviour is tightly regulated: one must take off one's coat and shoes, remove metal objects from one's pockets, shepherd objects through X-ray machines while one passes through metal detectors, allow for body searches and swabs (to test for traces of explosives), and, all the while (as I am reminded every time I travel), respect staff and avoid using abusive language in their regard. *Only Passengers with Valid Boarding Passes beyond This Point* scream the notices. Meanwhile, a tactic that has long been in place at Ben Gurion International Airport, Tel Aviv, Israel, has been brought on stream in many other airports: covert, plainclothes security officials watch for "suspicious behaviour" and practise "active positive profiling" (BBC News, 2002b; Baum, 2006). We are told that there is such a thing as "pre-crime" and that one can actively pre-screen passengers and identify "people who have hostile intent" (*The Economist*, 2007a). *Project Hostile Intent*, under development in the United States, goes further: it will use video technology to scrutinize fleeting "micro-expressions," probing for those "certain behaviours" that previous research has shown to be "statistically indicative of deception" (Department of Homeland Security, 2008: 5). To travellers' chagrin, such positive profiling is bound to increase after the failed attempt to blow up Northwest Airlines Flight 253 on Christmas Day 2009.

These spaces represent exemplars of "fractal sovereignty" and "ambiguous zones" (Lloyd, 2002; 2004), and not only because of the self-contained regulatory regime under which they operate. Such spaces can also be conceived as "non-spaces," what George Agamben (2005) calls "camps": locations that are devoid of identity, organically arisen relationships and history (Augé, 1995: 101). Since an airport is a non-space where most people (practically all, other than its employees) are "in transit," and are only there to leave, the locational, interstitial, and transitional identity *of the air/seaport itself* lends itself to some imaginative prescription. The notion of an air/seaport as a duty-free zone, pioneered at Shannon International Airport, Ireland, has already been referred to in chapter 1. Many international air/seaports today are "free ports," though they tend to be called customs areas, customs zones, or international zones. A designated "waiting zone" in a port organizes the border as a space of exception which deliberately dislocates the territorial order (Chowra, 2006). Thus, Frankfurt-Main, Germany's main international airport, has been a legally declared detention and "extraterritorial zone" since 1993: the presumed intent of this provision is to deny any asylum seekers the opportunity to claim a right to asylum status simply by having landed at that airport. Naimah H., a forty-year-old Algerian woman, hung herself there, after having been held under arrest within the airport – and thus not on "German territory" – for seven months (Zimmermann, 2000). Eighteen-year-old Ghanaian footballer Ayi Nii Aryee spent seven months in legal limbo at Macapagal International Airport in the Philippines over 2006–07. With a voided working permit and an expired passport, he was unable to travel to his destination as well as back to his point of origin (*The Global Game*, 2006). In 1999 Esquimalt Naval Base in British Columbia, Canada, was likened to an international airport and designated "not-yet-Canada" so that six hundred Chinese migrants could not claim refugee status (ECLAC, 2002; Perera, 2002).

Extraterritoriality and the creation of non-space, however, do not work only in the interests of the national state. As is typical of human agency and strategic opportunism, individuals can and do at various times exploit a situation to serve a purpose for which it may not have been intended by those who originally crafted the regulations. Sanjay Shah lived in the duty-free section of Nairobi's International Airport for thirteen months before he was told that his application for full British citizenship was approved (Mynott, 2005). Merham Karimi Nasseri, an Iranian man who lost his papers while in transit, lived in a "waiting zone" (in French, *zone d'attente*) – in Terminal One of Charles De Gaulle International Airport in Paris – for no less than eleven years before his request for immigration was acceded to by the French authorities (Moseley, 1999). This episode served as the core inspiration of two films: *Tombés du Ciel*, starring Jean Rochefort (Lioret, 1993), and *The Terminal*, starring Tom Hanks (Spielberg, 2004).

We seem to be witnessing here a new definition of "perforated sovereignty" (Duchacek, 1990), "overlapping sovereignty" (Lindström, 1999: 86), or "multi-layered sovereignty" (Hocking: 1993a; 1993b). We can also explain these episodes as a political geographic (or spatial) rendition of what Aihwa Ong (1999: 217) calls "graduated zones of sovereignty," leading to situations of "variegated citizenship." We have an explicit engineering of *borders within borders*, where spaces are circumscribed and assigned specific powers and functions.

This is not a new phenomenon. Gentrification, ghettoization, and segregation are evidence of de facto "borders within borders" or enclaves within many urban settlements and are key patterns in their transformations across time. Such internal differentiations could serve as examples both of cultural diversity (Toronto, London, New York, Sydney) and of tension and violence (Derry/Londonderry or Belfast in Northern Ireland from the 1960s to the 1990s [e.g., Smyth, 1995; Whyte, 1990] or contemporary Baghdad in the throes of Sunni-Shia strife). Other examples of such *inbordering* would include the resort to export processing zones, free trade zones, and tax-free zones, about more of which below. Limbo, clearly, is not just the stuff of Christian teachings about the afterlife.

SUBNATIONAL JURISDICTIONS

What is perhaps new in this game is the manner and extent to which inbordering is taking place, and the purposes to which it is being applied. This book examines the existence and practices of enclaving within, by, and by means of wholesale jurisdictions that exist today at the level just below that of the fully sovereign state. Some of these may be little better than privileged local authorities, but – as in the case of the Shetland Islands – their considerable local clout, supported by revenue, cannot go unnoticed. There are a variety of units that exist within federal arrangements, and typically within territories that have a large land mass and/or large population. These include the "states" constituent of Australia, Brazil, India, Malaysia, Nigeria, and the United States; the German Lander; the 83 "subjects" of the Russian Federation; some regions of Spain; and the provinces and territories of Canada: these are equipped with powers that are explicitly articulated but typically subject as well to ongoing negotiation with the central government. There are "special regions" that benefit from distinct legal provisions (like international treaties, as apply in the case of both Svalbard [Norway] and Åland [Finland]), or that respect history, culture, and economic stability (as with the "special administrative regions" of Hong Kong and Macau within the People's Republic of China). And, at the extreme end of this range, there are candidates that may be construed as "states within states," with or without the blessing of the larger government: entities like Abkhazia and South Ossetia (Georgia), South Mindanao (Philippines), Kurdistan (Iraq), and, until recently, Tamil Eelam (Sri Lanka). These units possess broad capacities in relation to revenue, coercion, and institutionalized political representation. Some – including Abkhazia, Nagorno-Karabakh, Somaliland, South Ossetia, Trans(d)niestra, the Turkish Republic of Northern Cyprus, Western Sahara, and Taiwan – are de facto states, exercising all aspects of sovereignty inclusive of proto/paradiplomacy but not enjoying broad international recognition (Bahcheli et al., 2004).

The bulk of these "wholesale jurisdictions" would, however, have been called colonies until recently – fragments of former empires or trust territories that enjoy locally representative government yet maintain strong ongoing relationships with Amsterdam, Canberra, Copenhagen, London, Paris, Washington, and Wellington. Finally, examples like modern-day Nauru – an effectively self-bankrupted smaller island state, which has been rocked by a major money laundering scandal (e.g., Van Fossen, 2003) and which has performed asylum-processing services for payment on behalf of another state (Australia) – is (for want of a better term) less than its purported full sovereignty suggests. That critique could apply equally well to the "sovereign" states of Palau, Federated States of Micronesia (FSM), and the Marshall Islands: these have, since their "independence," assigned their defence and security (and thus perhaps in practice also their foreign policy) to the United States in the context of a Compact of Free Association (COFA) whose fiscal generosity basically underwrites their economic (and possibly even political) viability (e.g., Rosenblatt, 1998; Underwood, 2003): they might not have entertained independence without that financial lifeline. Even with those generous financial guarantees, the Northern Mariana Islands decided to break away from the FSM and struck a separate deal with the United States, with the latter's full encouragement. The islanders secured for themselves commonwealth status with the United States (1985) and U.S. citizenship (1986) (Anckar, 2003: 118; McPhetres, 1983: 169–70). As with Guam, Puerto Rico, American Samoa, and the Virgin Islands, the United States controls their foreign policy, in exchange for pledging to defend them from any "foreign aggression" (Fowler and Bunck, 1995: 117).

Most of these "autonomies" have been called "non-central governments" (Duchacek, 1986: 240; Hocking 1993; 1999: 17). They have also been called "non-sovereign jurisdictions" (e.g., Fabry, 2000). R. Kaiser (2002) calls them "subnational governments." H. Catt and M. Murphy (2002) use the term "sub-state nationalism." I.D. Duchacek (1984) has also referred to them as "subnational self-governments." My preference is to call this highly assorted collection of political entities *subnational jurisdictions*. This emphasizes that they are usually not simply "top down" creatures of strategic constitutional ingenuity by a typically larger state; they may also harbour, or develop through time, some characteristics of national identity which yet is subsumed to some extent within another, overarching (state) identity. Moreover, they are not necessarily interested in sovereignty. Indeed, most of them harbour an anti-sovereigntist practicality – as amply demonstrated by the case of the Northern Marianas – as will be discussed further below. And then it is also perhaps both advisable and preferable to define something by what it *is*, rather than by what it is *not*.

Of course, the selection, or exclusion, of members within this list can prove contentious. Mainland Chinese may protest at the inclusion of Taiwan, which they officially regard as their rogue island province. In my defence, I will simply state that I am driven by pragmatism and my inclusion of Taiwan is to be considered not as justifying its existence but simply as reporting a fact.[2] Many Sri Lankans may be appalled at the simple mention of Tamil Eelam, which is interpreted in many circles to have served as the cover for a terrorist organization; yet, for some time, it was a renegade Tamil homeland which operated much like a jurisdiction, with "its own banks and law courts" (*The Economist*, 2009b). In other situations, and in any case, my decision may prove arbitrary: should I have included the "Kingdom" of Redonda (Redondan Foundation, 2008)? Or the "newly independent nation" on one-hectare Forvik Island (Quinn, 2008)? Or the similarly sized Kingdom of North Dumpling Island in New York State (Cooper, 2007; Dunford, 2009)? The subject matter of this book deals with the soft underbelly of sovereignty, and so some disagreements as to candidature are to be expected.

WHAT IS A COUNTRY, ANYWAY?

In fact, the reference to *countries* in this book speaks to a similar kind of vagueness. Except for the obvious members of federations considered in this volume, all the other "units" – from associated states to autonomies, from collectivities to "special status" territories, from Bermuda to the Cook Islands, from Guernsey to Guam – could easily be called countries.

It is commonly understood that there are 194 sovereign states in the world today – defined as enjoying (a) a permanent population, (b) a defined territory, (c) government, and (d) a capacity to enter into relations with other states: these are the principles of "customary international recognition" as stipulated by the 1933 Montevideo Convention. The latest additions have been Timor Leste (2002), Montenegro (2006), and Kosovo (2008). Of these 194 states, all except Vatican City and Kosovo enjoy full membership of the United Nations. This number excludes nine states under customary international law, six de facto states, and forty-five other "countries": a motley collection of thirty-six inhabited "dependent territories," five areas of "special sovereignty," and the four constituent countries of the United Kingdom (England, Scotland, Wales, and Northern Ireland). Of this batch of forty-five, all but two – French Guyana and Gibraltar – are islands, while one deals with sovereign military enclaves on an island (Akrotiri and Dhekelia, on the island of Cyprus).

Such authoritative numbers suggest a false sense of definitional agreement. In reality, a clear-cut line between sovereignty and non-sovereignty can prove difficult. The jury is still out on both the quantity and the quality of countries.

Number-wise, the annual CIA *World Factbook* provides comprehensive entries for – in the latest, 2009 edition – 266 "nations, dependent areas and other entities." (The differences between these is, perhaps, deliberately vague.) The U.S. Department of State (2008) lists 194 "independent states" – with additionally Taiwan all by itself as "other" – along with 66 "dependencies and areas of special sovereignty" on its website. A rather dated United Nations publication, from its Statistics Division, lists 232 "area codes," along with various disclaimers (UN, 1999). The International Organization for Standardization (ISO) has 246 "country codes" under its 3166–1 list (Classification Unit = Countries). The Internet Assigned Numbers Authority (IANA) recognizes 243 top-level, Internet "country" domain names. The Internet-based Wikipedia (2008) lists 245 "entities [that are] considered to be countries." M. Schmidt (2008) lists 248 "countries or territories" which have: an ISO two-letter country code, a UN three-digit numerical code, and an extant IANA-assigned country code top-level domain. By the way, Taiwan has all three.

This ambiguity is also extended by the glib usage of the word *country* in the context of information and communication technologies. For example, Adobe Acrobat Designer has an importable "countries" box that can be easily incorporated into data-management sites on the World Wide Web. Thus, when asked to "pick your country," the drop-down list that materializes could include 202 "choices" plus "another country" as a residual option.[3] (It appears that the programmers prefer to err on the side of caution, seeking to be as inclusive and exhaustive as possible on their list. There is no point in leaving potential customers out.) And so Puerto Rico is listed as a "country" – the most populous one on the list – as are also (in alphabetical order) American Samoa, Anguilla, Aruba, Bermuda, Cayman, Gibraltar, French Polynesia, Montserrat, and New Caledonia.[4] The absence of Taiwan from some (but not all) of these lists no doubt spares some embarrassment to the People's Republic of China.

Quality-wise, a jurisdiction like the Cook Islands is a fully self-governing entity with its own international representation (including in the United Nations Food and Agriculture Organization [FAO], the International Civil Aviation Organization [ICAO], UNESCO, the WHO, and the World

Meteorological Organization [WMO]), even though it is not a member of the UN and is in free association with New Zealand. Montserrat is a full member of the Organization of Eastern Caribbean States (OECS). International representation is today a practice indulged by various cities and subnational units of larger states and can no longer be seen as a sovereign state prerogative or monopoly. The Sovereign Military Hospitaller Order of Saint John of Jerusalem of Rhodes and of Malta has formal diplomatic relations with over one hundred states and maintains permanent observer status at the United Nations (along with Palestine, the European Union, and the Vatican). What makes this entity unique is that, though sovereign, it has no territory, no economy, and just three citizens: its grand master, the deputy grand master, and the chancellor – possibly a harbinger of things yet to come, if global warming totally submerges such countries as the Maldives, Marshall Islands, Kiribati, or Tuvalu.

On the other hand, notionally fully sovereign states may not be able to practise certain allegedly "core" features of their sovereignty. The cases of Nauru and the three Pacific "Compact" states have already been highlighted above. S.A. Kerr (2005) astutely reminds us of Cyprus, a fully recognized sovereign state which, however, cannot unilaterally change its constitution.

WHY ISLANDS?

That many of these cases should be islands, or on islands, should not come as a surprise. Ninety per cent of subnational jurisdictions are islands, or on islands, anyway (Watts, 1999). Islands predominate in "large unit-small unit" federal relationships. Why? There are several reasons.

First, islands are conveniently delineated by geography: as pieces of land surrounded by water, they have a natural demarcation and therefore lend themselves as obvious enclaves – or exclaves – where a different governance regime may prevail. This inclination towards a specific unitary form of island governance is borne out by the evidence: the sheer number of sovereign island states, and the very small number of divided or shared island jurisdictions (more about this later).

Second, being islands, these territories are typically cut off from mainlands and may even be remotely located with respect to reference territories. This makes access (to would-be invaders, intruders, or just visitors) more difficult, and so traffic to/from the island is arguably more manageable. This is an advantage when a location is strategically prized, whether for military (naval base, air base, listening site), aeronautic (space monitoring, satellite tracking), or commercial purposes (time zone, exclusive economic zones, offshore tax havens).

Third, discrete pieces of land separated by stretches of water from mainlands are difficult to administer "by remote control." There is therefore a logistical tendency for an island to be self-administered, especially if distant from its metropolitan power (Peckham, 2003: 503).

Fourth, geography and identity reinforce each other: finite island geography nurtures a sense of identity contiguous with territory (Anckar, 2005; Baldacchino, 2004a; Srebrnik, 2004). This again explains why so many island jurisdictions exist today in the first place. Even if initially triggered by administrative convenience, the jurisdictional capacity thus nurtured would, of itself, fuel the growth of nationalist sentiment. Such fervour can even militate against archipelagic unity.[5]

Fifth, being typically small apart from isolated, there is some guarantee that, whatever idiosyncrasy may be foisted on the island, it would be containable on the same island and will not spread beyond its shores. Thus, a privileged status of some kind is more likely to be condoned by envious neighbours, or even by other subordinate units of the same overarching state. It would be, moreover, conveniently located beyond one's visual and psychological horizon: out of sight, out of mind?

Sixth, islands – especially smaller islands – are much less subject to competing territorial claims than mainlands (except in toto);[6] and, barring a few dramatic examples,[7] they are less liable to internal ethnic "pillarization" or factional differentiation. The story with mainlands is different: contiguous powers may haggle over the exact demarcation of a border;[8] whether a town or city should be assimilated within one jurisdiction or split between contending claimants;[9] and how to secure the rights and freedoms of national minorities.[10] Border skirmishes and incursions, and fractious relations more generally, are much more difficult to avoid, or camouflage, with land borders.[11] An operation by sea against an island needs more careful planning: S.A. Royle (2001: 135) argues that islands are less likely to be attacked than mainlands; once invaded, though, they are more likely to succumb to the invading force.

In at least these ways, carving jurisdictions (including "non-spaces") on islands is (generally speaking) less complicated, and more acceptable within international relations; and even more so if they are subnational entities. Somehow, it also seems the natural thing to do. There is a long history of considering islands as both *terra nullius* (empty land) and yet also as *locus amoenus* (a beautiful place), and therefore easy and ready objects for big-state (including imperialist) indulgence. Part of the difficulty of securing an acceptable resolution to the "Cyprus problem" (e.g., Stefanidis, 1999) stems from an obdurate belief, particularly strong in the Greek camp, that an island destiny requires a single whole, a unitary state: island partitions are somehow distasteful (e.g., Baldacchino, 2002b). Perhaps the same can be said about the island of Ireland and (for totally different reasons) Sri Lanka.

WHY ENCLAVES?

Of course, enclaves are already islands of sorts. But they are not necessarily surrounded by the sea. Non-island enclaves like Gibraltar, Tibet, Ceuta, and Melilla may be more enisled by geography and location than most "pure" islands. Indeed, one ongoing debate in island studies concerns the essentialization or otherwise of the concept of "island." Ought the term extend beyond its strict physical geographical meaning? But, once it does so, how do you stop from referring to everything as an island?

In Margaret Mead's pioneering anthropological research in the Pacific, she refers to locations of human isolates that go beyond "small Pacific islands" and include "dense African jungles or Asiatic wastes" (Mead, 1973: 11). Although she never studies these places professionally, Mead is one of many scholars who invite a flexible definition of "island." In this, she partakes of a long tradition that identifies the sea as just one of a series of media which act as frontiers or barriers, as obstacles to transfers. Jean Brunhes, Sherwin Carlquist, David Pitt, Russell King, and William Newmark have postulated a broader definition of islandness (Brunhes, 1920: 160–1; Carlquist, 1965; Pitt, 1980; King, 1993: 15–19; Newmark, 1987). To them, literal or material islands, those that are permanently surrounded by water, are only a subset of much broader insular conditions in our universe. Many geographical features are island-like: together, they behave just like archipelagos. Consider lakes – "anti-islands," according to C. Depraetere (2008: 27) – which are presumably as much islands for the fish and amphibians that inhabit them; or the effective insularization of a tree-dwelling species of animal that inhabits a small dot of taiga (a subarctic conifer forest) surrounded by wastes of tundra (a subarctic treeless plain) (MacArthur and Wilson, 1967: 3–4). The (aptly named?) rocky inselbergs emerge from the vast flatness of tropical plains (Barthlott and Porembski, 2000). Is our obsession with only one type of island – the literal, physical, and material one – fuelled by a jaundiced, mainland-driven impression of the sea as "the most effective barrier of all" (Carlquist, 1965: 4)? What if an expanse of ocean proved easier to cross than a mosquito-infested jungle, a desert, a mountain range, or a continental ice sheet? A more supple rendering of the subject matter of island studies could help avoid sterile debates – as to whether, say, an island connected by a bridge to a mainland is any longer an island (Baldacchino, 2007c).

The purists, however, will be sure to cock an eyebrow. The richness of literary and cultural islanding could be so obtrusive and pervasive that it could actually threaten and dismiss the physicality of islands as "real lived-in places." P. Hay (2006: 30) argues emphatically: "So powerful is the metaphorical idea of the island that it can be deployed in the absence of even the slightest reference to the reality of islands. Those who live real lives on islands are entitled to resent this." One could say that the epitome of the objectification of islands would be reached when the island metaphor thrives on its own, as a *simulacrum*, without any trace of its physical referent (Baudrillard, 1988: 170). That would once again render islands as victims, this time of hyper-reality, a form of post-modern "reality by proxy." The first set of essays in a volume edited by J. Skinner and M. Hills (2006), part of a section titled "Conceiving Islands," is "not about islands at all but about metaphors of islandness" (Lowenthal, 2006: 259). In a theoretical review of multilevel governance, L. Hooghe and G. Marks (2003: 234) refer to five distinct literatures, and their associated terms, as "islands of theorizing" because "the density of communication within each of them is much higher than that among them." B. Holm (2000: 59–82) tells us that his piano is an island. Readers may not necessarily have, as I do, an island in their kitchen, but they are bound to have hormone-producing islands of Langerhans in their pancreas.

How to reconcile, or at least come to terms with, these opposing traditions? In particular, one wonders how islanders themselves react, if at all, to the slippage in the analysis of their condition, where they continue to be ritually "aesthesicized, sanitized and anaesthetized" (Connell, 2003: 568). Like other contested, and contestable, border regions – the ocean depths, the high seas, outer space, and increasingly the Arctic – islands (and, of course, islanders) are treated as fair game for mainland subjugation and organization. They find themselves conscripted as actors in a play about "island life" that they rarely control. They find themselves targets of an incessant regimen of construction, which would have them behave this way and that, in ways that fulfil the desires and dreams of all, for all seasons and for all tastes. Resentment, as Hay put it, is only one of a variety of ways in which islanders can "react."

The notion of enclave, and its linkage with issues of governance and political economy, may help to contain and ground this particular discussion of material islands. However, this does not exempt those very physical islands from being the subject of dreams and inventiveness. Indeed, one may validly argue that, certainly today, one cannot plausibly separate the material-physical island from the metaphorical-mythical one. Islands are now, unwittingly, the objects of what may be the most lavish, global, and consistent branding exercise in human history. They find themselves presented as locales of desire, as platforms of paradise, as habitual sites of fascination, emotional offloading, or religious pilgrimage. The metaphoric deployment of "island," with the associated attributes of small physical size and warm water (again, not always borne out by material evidence – see Baldacchino, 2008a: 40), is possibly *the* central gripping metaphor within Western discourse (Hay, 2006: 26; emphasis in original). Yi Fu Tuan (1990: 247) claims that four natural environments have figured prominently in humanity's (including non-Western) enduring and endearing dreams of the ideal world. They are: the forest, the shore, the valley ... and the island. Why else would a widely distributed, recent full-page credit-card advertisement list "Visit an Uninhabited Island" as one of twenty-one "things to do while you're alive"?[12] Via a long historical and marketing project, islands have thus matured into enclaves.

NICHES TO EXPLOIT

Throw in a dash of public policy into the mix, and the configuration for the active engineering of island enclaves is set. Especially in recent history, and with possibly increasing momentum, states and elites have resorted to creative governance in order to exploit niches in the internationalization of production, trade, and finance, turning inherent small size and insularity into net advantages while challenging state-centred conceptions of property rights and capital accumulation (Dodds and Royle, 2003: 489). The development has taken place at the same time as rising rich-nation wages and decreasing trade, transaction, and communications costs mean that firms that had previously bundled together most or all stages of manufacturing in one country now find it profitable to unbundle, out-source, and/or "off-shore" some (especially labour-intensive) stages of their production, assembly, and/or distribution to other, lower-wage countries (e.g., Baldwin, 2006: 14). Locational competition by the latter has led to packages that are even more attractive to capital, which exploits its increasingly fine-tuned footloose nature to "divide and rule" the competition.

Island microstates, or larger states that have island components, have been quite innovative in excising suitable island enclaves (meaning whole islands as enclaves, or enclaves located on islands) by granting immunities or privileges, or else withholding the same – with a view to serve a variety of special, specific political and economic purposes. What these states have crafted include: 1) export processing zones, which include free trade zones, special economic zones, bonded warehouses, free ports, and customs zones (e.g., Atler, 1991; Glick and Roubaud, 2005; Singa Boyenge, 2003; Grundy-Warr, 1989); and 2) offshore finance centres: lower-tax, lightly regulated regimes which specialize in facilitating the formation of offshore companies (e.g., Abbott, 2000; Brittain-Catlin, 2005; Hampton, 1996; Le Rendu, 2004; Vashistha and Vashistha, 2006). In setting up EPZs and/or OFCs, these islands, or their parent states, have *either* excised parts of their territories from the regulatory regime extant in the rest of the country, *or* designated their whole territory for such purposes. Thus, for example, Hainan (PRC) and Kish (Iran) are whole-island EPZs, while Bermuda, Cayman, and Jersey are whole-island OFCs. None of these five exemplars is a sovereign state. SNIJs are the quintessential masters, or victims, of "offshoring," not only in the sense of going beyond the legal conventions of "onshore" export-processing, banking, and finance (probably the best-known usages of the term), but also in extending, and perhaps eroding, other central principles of sovereignty. They call for a re-evaluation of the role of the state, challenging conventional notions of agency and change in international affairs: for example, via "para-diplomacy" (Aldecoa and Keating, 1999; Bartmann, 2007; Hocking, 1993).

ISLANDS AS NON-SPACES; ISLANDS AS LOCI FOR CREATIVE JURISDICTION: THE *TAMPA* INCIDENT

It may appear brazen for a government to define part of its territorial space as non-space for specific purposes, but pragmatic considerations can fuel such inventiveness. Australia made history by deploying creative governance with respect to its subnational island jurisdictions – and being much criticized by human-rights activists for its efforts. On 26 August 2001 a Norwegian freighter, the *Tampa*, picked up 433 passengers and crew from the leaking Indonesian ferry *KM Palapa* and was later forced by asylum seekers (among those picked up) to head towards Christmas Island. Next day, the John Howard government in Australia (and backed by the Labour opposition) announced that the *Tampa* would not be given permission to land in Australia or any other Australian territory. When, on 29 August , the *Tampa* nevertheless entered Australian waters, special forces were sent to board the ship: its human cargo was eventually transferred to Nauru and New Zealand for "processing." On 11 September an Australian Federal Court judge pronounced that the asylum seekers should be brought to Australia, they having been held on the vessel "without lawful authority" and in breach of the common law principle of habeas corpus (Saunders, 2001). The full bench of the Federal Court, however, overturned this decision on 18 September (Federal Court of Australia, 2001; Betts, 2001).

Following this incident, the Australian legislature amended the Migration Act in order to limit the country's obligations with respect to migrants. It does so by designating portions of its sovereign territory as 'non-Australia' for the strict purposes of claiming asylum. These portions include Christmas Island, Ashmore Reef, Cartier Islands, and the Cocos (Keeling) Islands (Connell, 2006: 55). Moreover, the sovereign states of Nauru and Kiribati were officially designated by the same act of federal Parliament as "offshore processing centres" (read: immigration-detention facilities) for those claiming refugee status in Australia.

Moral and ethical issues apart, this so-called "Pacific Solution" case illustrates the manner in which a (typically large) country – in this case, Australia – can deliberately re-engineer the identity of some of its component units, especially if they happen to be "offshore," in the interests of national policy. But what is even more telling is that another *country* – in this case, the island states of Nauru and Kiribati, and eventually also Papua New Guinea – can take on a set of tasks for another state in exchange for payment that may suggest the status of a feudal fiefdom or a "tributary state," and not of a modern sovereign state.

The assumed absence of hierarchy in the post-Westphalia sovereign state architecture makes it impossible to conceptualize a suzerainty, or a tributary state: those could exist only under feudal law. There can be, by definition, only juridical independence and no hierarchical subservience between one sovereign state and another. While the model of a tributary state is argued to be suitable to address such thorny issues as the status of Taiwan or Tibet, and possibly Kosovo, the concept is deemed to be "absent" from the toolbox of contemporary international relations (e.g., Krasner, 2001b: 326). "In modernity, sovereignty is the dominant ordering principle of regulatory landscapes" (Hudson, 2000: 275). Further, "the central attribute of modernity in international politics has been a peculiar and historically unique configuration of territorial space" (Ruggie, 1993: 144). And yet the situation "on the ground" invites some healthy scepticism: the Nauru and Kiribati cases suggest that some sovereign states are – to borrow an Orwellian aphorism – "less equal than others," since they demonstrate that the practice of hierarchical subservience can exist within the realm of political possibility, fuelled by dire economic expediency (e.g., Carty, 2007). The example of the United States, with the three "Compact" states of Palau, Marshall Islands, and the Federated States of Micronesia, suggests a similar status. Likewise, the behaviour of the large industrialized nations (the G7) in relation to offshore finance centres and so-called tax havens (many of which are islands) – which effectively has applied pressure via "public shaming" on how the latter run their economies – is just as glaring an example of how we may, de facto, be living in a "multilayered system of sovereignties" (Palan, 2002: 173).

Indeed, "hierarchy" between states is more than a historical quirk and cannot simply be ignored in the study and practice of international relations. Sovereignty is often treated as indivisible, much like the binary numeral system: it is either 0 or 1: you either are sovereign or you aren't, with no room for dithering in between. Yet H.W. Armstrong et al. (1998: 639, 641) and Armstrong and R. Read (2005, passim) advise timely improvements in how "sovereignty" is measured and caution against the glib and reductionist use of binary (sovereign/non–sovereign) variables. The European Union has developed into a more flexible, yet more complex, "multi-speed" institution with various countries enjoying various levels of opt-out (e.g., Warleigh, 2002). Indeed, unusual authority relations are quite typical in the international domain; and the rationale for their existence and operation may be steadily increasing, as will be discussed later. Decades ago, W.W. Willoughby and C.G. Fenwick (1974) identified various candidates for "restricted sovereignty" or "colonial autonomy." In reviewing such cases as Taiwan, Bosnia, Tibet, Hong Kong, and Palestine, S.D. Krasner (2001a) speaks of "problematic sovereignty." D.A. Lake (2003: 310) goes so far as to suggest a gradation or "a continuum of increasing hierarchy in international relations." He suggests (ibid., 314) that "anomalies may be more commonplace than we often realize," and he is not alone in making such a pitch: E.C. Dommen (1985) has proposed a stratified continuum of jurisdictions, starting from a bottom stratum comprising uninhabited islands not recognized as belonging to any territory; followed by islands normally uninhabited but belonging to a territory; and moving on through dependent and "more or less independent" jurisdictions up to the top-most layer of "altogether independent" states. Kerr (2005: 504) undertakes a similar exercise, using actual cases to illustrate different points on his continuum (see Table 2.1).

Without sounding like a justification for neo-imperialism, perhaps one needs to look especially at islands to realize just how many, and of what form and variety, these anomalies are. This book is, I hope, a contribution to such an overdue acknowledgment and its unfolding analysis.

TABLE 2.1: A hierarchy of jurisdictions?

	LAYERS / STRATA OF GOVERNANCE	
New Zealand	Independent 1907	Member of UN
Samoa	Independent 1962. Reliant on aid, protected trade, and remittances	Member of UN
Cyprus	Independent 1960. Constitution difficult to amend. Overriding powers by GR, TR, UK	Member of UN
Isle of Man	Self-governing crown land – Pays UK for overseas representation and external defence	
Tokelau	NZ Colony. Largely self-governed by traditional village institutions	
Galápagos	Province of Ecuador 1973. Special Law. Local Control over Resources, Immigration, etc.	
Orkneys	Local authority (council area) of Scotland	
Lindisfarne	Populated island – part of mainland region	
Sable Island	No permanent population – part of Nova Scotia (CA)	
Rockall	No permanent population – subject to contested claims	

Source: Based on Kerr, 2005.

CONCLUSION: A NEW OFFSHORING

Ohmae is correct, but perhaps not precisely as he intended: it is fair to argue that the (nation-)state is less capable of providing a suitable reference or explanation to contemporary dynamics, but the explanation is not only to be found in the borderless world. Subnationalism, as exemplified by island autonomies around the world, certainly presents itself as a force to be reckoned with. To be sure, it harbours contradictory traits: it may be crafted, or condoned, by virtue of the capacities that accompany sovereignty, and yet its practices are premised on such exceptionalism and asymmetry that they can be seen to threaten the very stability and unity of the overarching state.

Some subnational island jurisdictions find themselves in a chronic dependency with a benign metropolitan power that effectively "kills their economy through kindness" (Hintjens, 1991: 51), but others have managed to deploy the "resourcefulness of jurisdiction" (Baldacchino and Milne, 2000), extracting asymmetrical concessions from the metropole and using the resulting political space to carve out a more sustainable economic development trajectory (Baldacchino, 2006a). *Offshoring* sums up the manner in which this deployment of jurisdiction occurs: this typically refers to outsourcing and the relocation of business processes to another country, based on comparative advantage (e.g., Carmel and Tjia, 2005; Robinson and Kalakota, 2004; Thondavadi and Albert, 2005). But these jurisdictions, or the powers who oversee them, now appear to have taken the concept of "offshore" to a higher level. The differential use of legislation, or of condoned de facto behaviour,[13] means that these small island territories behave *as if* they were another country, even though they are not sovereign and lie within the (itself fuzzy) purview of a larger, orthodox, sovereign state. They gamble with claims for specific, often innovative deals, even in – and especially in – this current age of liberalization and globalization, because they are small and so hope to get away with it (Palan, 1998: 625).

With their disposition towards administrative independence, as well as ethnic or cultural specificity, islands predominate as "autonomies" within bilateral, "small unit-large unit" relationships. The opportunities that "offshoring" provides, in a world of multilevel governance, positions islands as platforms of innovative realpolitik (Hudson, 1998).

3

Island Subnationalism and "Upside Down" Decolonization

Little places ... can throw up big principles, especially where the
evolution of post-colonial relations are concerned.

Helen Hintjens, 1995: 26

INTRODUCTION

Subnational island jurisdictions are spaces that illustrate some interesting
departures from the conventional realms of political possibility. The case
of the "tributary state" is one example, described in the preceding chapter.
This chapter will identify at least one other example of such an idiosyncrasy:
a decolonization experience that is stalled by virtue of the colonized party
stubbornly preferring the status quo and refusing independence. In so doing,
and with a sensitivity to both historical context and post-colonial theory, it
elaborates more thoroughly upon the characteristics of "island subnationalism" and presents models for its patterning and categorization, drawn from
studies of federalism.

A FAILED PROGNOSIS

In 1987 political scientist Paul Sutton confidently predicted that ten erstwhile non-sovereign territories – Aruba, French Polynesia, Greenland,
Montserrat, Namibia, New Caledonia/Kanaky, Western Sahara, and parts of
the Trust Territory of the Pacific (Palau, Marshall Islands, Federated States
of Micronesia) – would be seeking and achieving political independence over
the following five years (Sutton, 1987: 5).

The year 1992 has come and gone. With the advantage of hindsight, Sutton
(2008a) can now graciously accept that he had been "overly optimistic" and
that his prognosis has proved to be substantially incorrect.[1] From his list, only
Namibia has sought and obtained full independence, in 1990. The progress of
Western Sahara towards full independence has been stalled for years. Other

new sovereign states – like Eritrea or East Timor – were not on the Sutton list; nor were there any of the offspring from the break-up of the Soviet Union, Yugoslavia, and Czechoslovakia.

All the other candidates on the Sutton list, and various others besides, have not obtained full sovereignty, even today, more than two decades later: not so much because independence was denied to them, but rather, in most cases, because they have not requested or desired it in the first place:

- In 1983 the Dutch and Netherlands Antilles governments agreed that Aruba should receive separate status from 1986, aiming for independence by 1996; but, after achieving *status aparte*, Aruba backtracked and halted the movement towards full independence in 1990 (Hoefte, 1996). As of 2010, Curaçao and Sint Maarten, other components of the former Netherlands Antilles, should start enjoying a status similar to that of Aruba (Oostindie, 2006).
- French Polynesia, formerly an overseas territory of France (*territoire d'outre mer*), has been an overseas country (*pays d'outre mer*) since 2004, giving it more autonomy over local affairs. In spite of a considerable groundswell of support for independence, fuelled by France's controversial nuclear tests at Mururoa Atoll in the mid-1990s, a pro-independence leader was not elected until 2004 (*Sydney Morning Herald*, 2004) and the pro-independence cause appears to have abated since (Mercer, 2008).
- In New Caledonia/Kanaky, a self-determination referendum organized in September 1987 was boycotted by 94 per cent of Kanaks (the indigenous Melanesians). Agitation for independence over two decades, which included abduction and violence, ended in the 1998 Noumea Accord, which, over a period of fifteen to twenty years, has been transferring governing responsibility from France to New Caledonia. As part of this accord, locals will have another opportunity to vote in a referendum sometime after 2014. If held, this should determine whether the territory remains a part of the French Republic as an overseas collectivity or whether it will become an independent nation (Chappell, 1999). However, "despite greater autonomy, New Caledonia/Kanaky has moved little closer to independence after two decades of struggle" (Connell, 1987; 2003).
- Greenland/Kalaallit Nunaat achieved home rule from Denmark in 1979, followed by full self-government in 1981, and voted to leave the European Economic Community (EEC) in 1982 (the only territory so far to do so, and thus cutting the EEC's land area by 50 per cent in one fell swoop). In 1998 the Danish Parliament granted Greenland

the right to full, uncontested independence, should that be desirable. Greenland currently relies on Denmark for nearly 40 per cent of its Gross Domestic Product (GDP); but, as global temperatures rise, they are melting Greenland's icecap, freeing up farmland and unlocking revenue from the exploration for oil, minerals, and diamonds. Following a 2008 referendum, a "road map" has been agreed upon between Nuuk and Copenhagen, envisaging the phasing out of Danish subsidies and possibly launching the territory – at over 2 million km^2, the world's largest island – into independence. Yet "the road to independence will be a long one" (Boyes, 2008).

• What was thought to be the imminent independence of Montserrat was such a foregone conclusion that, when it joined the Organization of Eastern Caribbean States in 1981, the territory was accepted as a full member. But any such plans were derailed, perhaps permanently, with the eruption of the island's Soufriere volcano in 1995–96, leading for a time to the wholesale exile of its population to the United Kingdom (Skelton, 2000). Montserrat has been a United Kingdom Overseas Territory (UKOT) since 2002.

Meanwhile, during the last four decades, various referenda have polled electorates on their interest in achieving full independence. Such referenda have been held in Bermuda (1995), Bonaire (2004), the Cook Islands (1974), Curaçao (2005), Mayotte (1976), the Netherlands Antilles (1993 and 1994), Niue (1974 and 1999), Puerto Rico (1967, 1993, and 1998), Saba (2004), Sint Maarten (2000), St Eustatius (Statia) (2005), and the U.S. Virgin Islands (1993). Of course, the exact language and the specific economic and political circumstances were different in, and peculiar to, each case. And yet the result in all instances has been a rejection of independence, typically by huge margins (McElroy and de Albuquerque, 1996; BBC Caribbean, 2004; Bea, 2005; Cohn, 2003). The August 1998 vote held in Nevis (Premdas, 2001), and the 2006 and 2007 votes held in Tokelau (BBC News 2006b; *Scoop News*, 2006, 2007; Hillebrink, 2008: 42n.171), were exceptional in that they were approved by some 62, 60, and 64 per cent of the voters respectively, but they still fell short of the required two-thirds majority for the referenda to succeed: the last of these by just sixteen votes (see Table 3.1).

Moreover, in 2003, voters in both Martinique and Guadeloupe rejected proposals to streamline their administration. Note the choice of words: "The aim of the reform was to eliminate a tier of local government, but many

TABLE 3.1: Referenda that failed to endorse sovereignty on island jurisdictions (1967–2007)

DATE	JURISDICTION	% IN FAVOUR OF INDEPENDENCE
1967	Puerto Rico	0.6
1974	Niue	less than 34%
1976	Mayotte	0.6
1993	Puerto Rico	4.4
1993	U.S. Virgin Islands	invalid: only 31% of eligible voters participated
1995	Bermuda	15
1998	Puerto Rico	2.5
1998	Nevis	61.7
1999	Niue	less than 40%
2000	Sint Maarten	14.2
2004	Bonaire	0.5
2004	Saba	1.0
2005	Curaçao	4.8
2005	St Eustatius	0.6
2006	Tokelau	60.1
2007	Tokelau	64.4

Sources: Various, including Baldacchino (2004a).

voters appear to have *feared* it represented a step towards *autonomy* – in spite of assurances from Paris" (Caribbean Net News, 2003; my emphasis).

In most other subnational jurisdictions, there has only been a minimal interest in considering sovereignty, and so referenda on this matter have not even been proposed.[2] Indeed, since 1984, the dynamics of decolonization have "changed dramatically" (Kashou, 1997: 163). The only small territories to struggle and obtain *full* independence since that year – in other words, serving as classic examples of decolonization – were: East Timor, in May 2002, with its independence referendum in September 1999 endorsed by 78.5 per cent of voters (e.g., Chomsky, 1999); Montenegro, in June 2006, with an independence referendum narrowly endorsed by 55.4 per cent of voters (BBC News, 2006c); and Kosovo, with a contentious unilateral declaration of independence in February 2008 (CNN News, 2008). These three cases are actually exceptions which justify the rule, since they were all societies emerging or escaping from various levels of repression, violence, and insecurity.

Deliberately excluded from my list of recent independent states are the three former members of the Trust Territory of the Pacific: the Federated States of Micronesia, the Marshall Islands, and Palau. While legally sovereign small island states (and members of the United Nations), they are not fully independent (e.g., Jonsson, 1997: 4) but operate within a Compact of Free Association with the United States, which accords the political status of free association to these island territories and grants the United States defence rights and obligations while denying access to these island territories by other third-party states (Friberg and Holen, 2002). Compacts between the United States and the Federated States of Micronesia, as well as between the United States and the Republic of the Marshall Islands, were signed in 1982, endorsed via referenda in 1983, and ratified in 1986 (COFA, 1985). The COFA with the FSM was amended in May 2003. The Republic of Palau negotiated a separate compact, effective beginning in 1995, after no less than eight referenda. Indeed, these three "hybrid jurisdictions" (Levine and Roberts, 2005) represent attempts at exploiting the advantages of both sovereignty and an autonomy supported by a benign patron state. In some studies (e.g., Bertram, 2004; McElroy and Mahoney, 2000), all three are treated as effectively non-sovereign. Had the United Nations used the same criteria as the League of Nations did in refusing the application of Liechtenstein in 1919, the Pacific trio would, in all probability, have shared a similar rejection. The league's admissions committee had reasoned that, because Liechtenstein had "chosen to depute to others some of the attributes of its sovereignty … we are of the opinion that the Principality of Liechtenstein could not discharge all the international obligations which would be imposed on it by the Covenant" (League of Nations, 1920: 667, quoted in Bartmann, 2008b: 62). Times have changed.

DECOLONIZATION, UPSIDE DOWN

The active and dogged pursuit of extended colonial relationships requires a more adequate conceptual assimilation, especially within post-colonial theory. Such behaviour has been aptly described as "upside down decolonization" – a phrase apparently coined by Dutch scholars in the process of observing the unfolding situation in the Netherlands Antilles, where it was the metropolis, and not the former colonies, which was pressing the latter for independence (Hoefte and Oostindie, 1989; 1991: 93). This is described as "an unusual situation" (Allahar, 2005: 132) whereby the mother country seemed willing, even anxious, to free itself from the responsibilities of empire[3] but the colonies in question would demur and not let the mother country off the hook (Oostindie and Klinkers, 2003: 116, 145). The persisting seven colonial powers – Australia, Denmark, France, Netherlands, New Zealand, the United Kingdom, and the United States – find themselves in an "*enforced* colonial condition," while their wards "*opt* for dependency status" (Skinner, 2006: 185; my emphasis).

It would, however, be fairer to state that the above situation is neither unusual nor paradoxical. The politics of "upside-down decolonization" are the norm rather than the exception in today's non-independent territories. With some exceptions, sovereignty does not appear to be any longer the obvious trajectory of peoples who see themselves as dispossessed political entities or at the losing end of federalist developments (e.g., Trompf, 1993: xxv; Baldacchino and Milne, 2006). In the contemporary world, there may be solid definitive advantages in *not* being independent. Yet the value-laden discourse of mainstream political science, along with the scrutiny of the United Nations Special Committee on Decolonization, belie an enduring obsession with the mantra of sovereignty as an intrinsically laudable, and almost historically unavoidable, evolutionary route.

How can one explain these manifestations of "upside down decolonization" in a historical context? It appears, in retrospect, that small size and islandness may have something to do with this dynamic. The four decades of failed independence referenda described above have dealt exclusively with smaller and island jurisdictions.[4] They are the candidates that have remained unaffected by the grand wave of decolonization that has swept the world, creating over a hundred new sovereign states in its wake.[5] Colonialism has been the main explanatory variable underlying small-island autonomy and small-state sovereignty. As colonization retreated after 1945, it left in its wake small puddles of jurisdiction, with the largest territories obtaining sovereignty first, the smallest territories following last, and the really *very* smallest units stubbornly refusing to budge. Indeed, a close look at the sequence of decolonization these past seven decades suggests that territories with larger populations – and their elites – were much more eager to struggle for, and achieve, independence. In fact, there is a clear correlation between population size and year of independence, certainly up to the break-up of the Soviet Union, Yugoslavia, and Czechoslovakia in the early 1990s. Only the case of Bangladesh (which achieved independence from Pakistan rather "late," for its population size, in 1971) breaks the quinquennial pattern that prevailed until the early 1990s (see Table 3.2). The larger the population base of a territory, the earlier has been its achievement of independence (see Table 3.3 and Figure 3.1).

TABLE 3.2: The largest go first: The direct relationship between population size and achievement of independence (1941–87)

5–YEAR EPOCH	NO. OF COUNTRIES SECURING FULL INDEPENDENCE DURING THIS TIME	TOTAL (ROUNDED) POPULATION AT INDEPENDENCE	AVERAGE POPULATION PER NEWLY INDEPENDENT COUNTRY
1941–47	10	511,200,000	51,120,000
1948–52	8	112,800,000	14,100,000
1953–57	6	41,000,000	6,833,000
1958–62	28	143,600,000	5,128,500
1963–67	12	36,700,000	3,058,300
1968–72	10	77,700,000	7,770,000
1973–77	13	23,300,000	1,792,300
1978–82	9	8,300,000	922,000
1983–87	4	340,000	85,000

POPULATED, AUTONOMOUS BUT NON-SOVEREIGN TERRITORIES	SAME, BUT EXCLUDING PUERTO RICO, MACAO, HONG KONG, AND WEST BANK
42 (38 being islands)	38 (37 being islands, or mainly islands)
Total Approximate Current Population = 17,168,000	Total Approximate Current Population = 3,183,000
Mean Population per Territory = 408,700	Mean Population per Territory = 83,760

Sources: CIA *World FactBook*, https://www.cia.gov/library/publications/the-world-factbook/index.html. Population at year of independence obtained from NationMaster (2008), in its turn based on World Development Indicators. For raw data, consult Table 3.3.

TABLE 3.3: Countries by year of independence and population at independence (1941–2008)

COUNTRY	YEAR OF INDEPENDENCE	POPULATION AT INDEPENDENCE (MILLIONS)
Ethiopia	1941	15
Lebanon	1943	1*
Iceland	1944	0.2
Korea, North	1945	10*
Korea, South	1945	20
Vietnam	1945	29
Jordan	1946	2

TABLE 3.3 (cont.)

COUNTRY	YEAR OF INDEPENDENCE	POPULATION AT INDEPENDENCE (MILLIONS)
Syria	1946	4
Pakistan	1947	30
India	1947	400*
Israel	1948	0.8
Sri Lanka	1948	9
Burma	1948	20*
Bhutan	1949	1
Laos	1949	3
Taiwan	1949	7
Indonesia	1949	70
Libya	1951	2
Cambodia	1953	4
Tunisia	1956	3
Morocco	1956	10
Sudan	1956	10*
Ghana	1957	6
Malaysia	1957	8
Guinea	1958	3
Cyprus	1960	0.6
Gabon	1960	0.5
Mauritania	1960	1
Congo	1960	1
Central African Republic	1960	2
Togo	1960	2
Benin	1960	2
Somalia	1960	3
Chad	1960	3
Senegal	1960	4
Niger	1960	4
Mali	1960	5
Burkina Faso	1960	5

TABLE 3.3 (cont.)

COUNTRY	YEAR OF INDEPENDENCE	POPULATION AT INDEPENDENCE (MILLIONS)
Cameroon	1960	8
Cote d'Ivoire	1960	5
Madagascar	1960	6
Congo, Democratic Republic of	1960	16
Nigeria	1960	43
Kuwait	1961	0.5
Sierra Leone	1961	2
Samoa	1962	0.1
Trinidad and Tobago	1962	0.9
Jamaica	1962	2
Burundi	1962	3
Rwanda	1962	3
Uganda	1962	7
Algeria	1962	11
Kenya	1963	9
Malta	1964	0.3
Zambia	1964	4
Malawi	1964	4
Tanzania	1964	11
Maldives	1965	0.1
Gambia	1965	0.4
Singapore	1965	2
Barbados	1966	0.2
Guyana	1966	0.6
Botswana	1966	0.6
Lesotho	1966	0.9
Nauru	1968	0.01
Equatorial Guinea	1968	0.3
Swaziland	1968	0.4
Mauritius	1968	0.8
Tonga	1970	0.09

TABLE 3.3 (cont.)

COUNTRY	YEAR OF INDEPENDENCE	POPULATION AT INDEPENDENCE (MILLIONS)
Fiji	1970	0.5
Bahrain	1971	0.2
Qatar	1971	0.1
United Arab Emirates	1971	0.2
Bangladesh	1971	75
Bahamas	1973	0.2
Grenada	1974	0.09
Guinea-Bissau	1974	0.6
São Tomé e Príncipe	1975	0.08
Cape Verde	1975	0.3
Suriname	1975	0.4
Comoros	1975	0.3
Papua New Guinea	1975	3
Angola	1975	7
Mozambique	1975	11
Dominica	1976	0.07
Seychelles	1976	0.06
Djibouti	1977	0.2
Tuvalu	1978	0.01
Solomon Islands	1978	0.2
Kiribati	1979	0.06
St Vincent and the Grenadines	1979	0.1
Saint Lucia	1979	0.1
Vanuatu	1980	0.1
Zimbabwe	1980	7
Antigua and Barbuda	1981	0.06
Belize	1981	0.1
St Kitts and Nevis	1983	0.04
Brunei	1984	0.2
Marshall Islands	1986	0.03
Federated States of Micronesia	1986	0.07

TABLE 3.3 (cont.)

COUNTRY	YEAR OF INDEPENDENCE	POPULATION AT INDEPENDENCE (MILLIONS)
Namibia	1990	1.4
Yemen	1990	12
Estonia	1991	1.6
Slovenia	1991	1.9
Macedonia (Former Yugoslav Republic of)	1991	1.9
Latvia	1991	2.6
Armenia	1991	3.3
Lithuania	1991	3.7
Croatia	1991	4.6
Moldova	1991	4.4
Turkmenistan	1991	4
Kyrgyzstan	1991	4.5
Georgia	1991	5.2
Tajikistan	1991	5.6
Azerbaijan	1991	7.5
Belarus	1991	10.2
Kazakhstan	1991	16.3
Uzbekistan	1991	21.9
Ukraine	1991	52.2
Bosnia and Herzegovina	1992	3.7
Serbia and Montenegro	1992	10.5
Eritrea	1993	3.1
Slovakia	1993	5.3
Czech Republic	1993	10.3
Palau	1994	0.01
East Timor	2002	0.76
Montenegro	2006	0.7
Kosovo	2008	2

* Approximation.

Source: Interpolated from "World Population Prospects," held by the Population Division, Department of Economic and Social Affairs, United Nations Secretariat, http://esa.un.org/unpp.

FIGURE 3.1: Plotting year of independence by the log value of the population at independence (1941–2008)

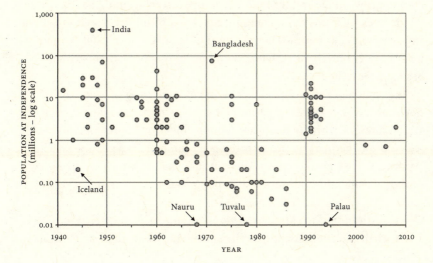

Thus, India – the largest remaining colony – was one of the first to achieve independence, and a traumatic partition, in the post-Second World War period. The smallest colonies took the longest to achieve independence (if at all), also because their colonial masters had serious doubts regarding their presumed viability and stability as independent states (Diggines, 1985; Pirotta et al., 2001; Plischke, 1977: 9–10). And so it has been said, for example, that "independence is an extravagant and improvident recipe for the remaining small territories" (Wainhouse, 1964: 133); and that "in the 1980s, Britain was left with a few colonies, mainly islands, too small by any standards to become independent nations" (Chamberlain, 1985: 51). Indeed, the presumed non-viability of small countries was so ingrained that initial attempts at their decolonization were geared towards federative solutions.[6] Meanwhile, what are typically the very smallest territories have not sought or achieved independence at all.[7] The bottom right quadrant of Figure 3.1 remains tellingly empty.

Insularity, isolation, and small size provide the geographical, if not also the administrative, logistic, cultural and historical, properties to render the existence of such jurisdictional pockets and enclaves, whether sovereign or merely autonomous, much more likely.

CONSTITUTIONAL CATEGORIES, AND THEIR RATIONALE

A dominant trend in world politics over recent decades has been for countries to grow smaller rather than larger, by fracturing along national and ethnic lines. Will this trend continue any longer? This drive seems to have stopped short of its assumed natural conclusion, that is, sovereignty, certainly for islands. However, the rush for other, smaller (but non-sovereign) entities has not been halted.

The contemporary political map is strewn with cases of island jurisdictions, and the non-sovereign examples far exceed the sovereign ones. R.L. Watts identifies "forms of political relations which combine autonomy [read: self-rule] and partnership [read: shared-rule] within federal political systems" (Watts, 2000: 23–9; 2008: 33–8). These include the following five categories,[8] each of which in turn includes contemporary subnational island exponents:

- *Constitutionally centralized unions.* Examples include New Zealand (North and South Island); St Vincent and the Grenadines; and Trinidad and Tobago.
- *Constitutionally decentralized unions.* Examples include Antigua and Barbuda; Fiji; Indonesia; Japan; Papua New Guinea; Solomon Islands; Vanuatu (bearing island constituents of archipelagic states); Corsica; French Polynesia; New Caledonia; Wallis and Futuna (island autonomies within a mainland state – France); Sicily and Sardinia (island autonomies within a mainland state – Italy); Zanzibar and Pemba (island autonomies within a mainland state – Tanzania); Anguilla; Bermuda; British Virgin Islands (BVI); Montserrat; Pitcairn; Turks and Caicos (island autonomies within a larger island state – United Kingdom); Tokelau (an island autonomy within a larger island state – New Zealand); American Samoa; Guam; U.S. Virgin Islands (island autonomies within a mainland state – United States).
- *Federations.* Exclusively island-based federations include: Comoros; Micronesia; and St Kitts and Nevis. Federations encompassing islands as fully fledged constituent units include: Argentina (Tierra del Fuego); Australia (Tasmania); Canada (Newfoundland and Labrador, Prince Edward Island); China (Hainan); Comoros (Njazidja, Mwali, and Nzwani); Malaysia (Penang, Sabah, and Sarawak); Micronesia (Kosrae, Pohnpei, Truk, and Yap); St Kitts and Nevis (St Kitts and Nevis); Spain (Balearics and Canaries); United States (Hawaii, *but not* Rhode Island, which is primarily mainland).

- *Federacies* (mainly ex-colonial associations). These are dissolvable by mutual consent. They include: Faroe Islands and Greenland (in relation to Denmark); Åland Islands (in relation to Finland); Azores and Madeira (in relation to Portugal); Isle of Man, Guernsey, Jersey, and their dependencies (in relation to Great Britain); and Northern Marianas and Puerto Rico (in relation to the United States).
- *Associated states*. These are dissolvable unilaterally. They include the Netherlands Antilles (in relation to the Netherlands, but now defunct); and Cook Islands (in relation to New Zealand).

J. Connell (1994) and J.L. McElroy and M. Mahoney (2000) explain candidly how political affiliation continues to grant substantial economic advantages to small, non-sovereign, island units. These benefits include: free trade with, and export preference from, the parent country; social-welfare assistance; ready access to external capital through special tax concessions; availability of external labour markets through migration; aid-financed infrastructure and communications; higher-quality health and educational systems; natural-disaster relief; and the subsidized provision of external defence and security. Autonomy without sovereignty also does not hinder the development of flourishing tourism economies, and may actually facilitate them because of easier terms of access and security. Most of these special conditions have emerged in the context of a history of a relatively benign colonial relationship, typically one that was dominated by strategic rather than economically exploitative interests. A recognition of the rights of indigenous peoples also acts to spawn such subnational decision-making capacities.

A second explanation for the lack of a drive for independence is the existence of an ample dose of existing jurisdictional prerogative or self-determination. Many small islands, because they are islands, enjoy some degree of administrative autonomy. This same feature supported the transition of some two dozen small islands or archipelagos to sovereign statehood, starting with Iceland, in the period 1944–84. Furthermore, because they are also small and somewhat isolated, and irrespective of independence, such island jurisdictions usually manage to extract some special advantages from their respective metropole. Those that have refrained from sovereignty typically enjoy – jurisdictionally (de facto) or constitutionally (de jure) – more discretionary powers than any similarly sized, or even larger, blocks of "mainland" (Poirine, 1998). S.A. Royle (1989: 108) identifies forty-one populated territories with overseas territories, associated status, compacts of free association, or some other special, separate arrangement with a larger state.[9] Four of these are fully fledged "overseas" departments of France, to which will be added a fifth – Mayotte – in 2011, following the outcome of a referendum in March 2009 (RFI, 2009). Fagerlund (1996) describes the Faroe Islands, Åland Islands, Isle of Man, and the Channel Islands as four autonomous European island regions enjoying a special relationship, this time with that provisional supranational state, the European Union. It appears that the independence candle for islands has been snuffed, at least for this historical era. The current status is regarded as "the best of both worlds" (Sutton, 2008b). These island statelets are provided with many of the benefits associated with political sovereignty, while they themselves delegate responsibilities to a larger, and typically richer, *patron*, thanks to whom they also reap vital security and material benefits.

Thirdly, and related to the above, one must address a twist in the contemporary articulation of nationalism. National identity is and remains one of the most powerful forces in modern history and lies at the root of much civil strife and violence. However, while the articulation of nationalism can become jurisdictional, it need not become sovereigntist. "Insular particularism" may be rife, but there remains "little or no sense of nationalism" in many subnational island jurisdictions (Killingray, 2005: 7).

Fourthly, there may have been a "demonstration effect" at work. The phase of decolonization has been long enough for non-independent territories to observe the outcomes of independence. The economic well-being of the citizens of subnational jurisdictions has remained significantly better than that of many of their counterparts in independent territories; the gap may have even widened. Moreover, in the Pacific, coups in Fiji and secession movements in Papua New Guinea and the Solomon Islands have not been very reassuring to those other territories in the region contemplating independence. This may explain why even pro-independence movements, as in New Caledonia, shifted their position, certainly as far as "immediate independence" was concerned (e.g., Mrgudovic, 2005: 74).

BENIGN COLONIAL RELATIONS

Yet how have these measures of autonomy been secured by some territories and not by others? Why have some territories struggled to obtain independence against the desires and plans of their colonial rulers, while others have undergone, or experienced, exactly the opposite?[10] And why has the latter turn of events been most strikingly visible among the world's smallest and enisled jurisdictions? The answers to these key but difficult questions possibly lie in the manner in which colonial relations were differently introduced, developed, and contested in many small and island locations. Four exploratory suggestions are proposed.

First, while small islands have taken longest to consider independence (Doumenge, 1989: 51), they have also been – especially those in the North Atlantic and Indian Oceans, as well as the Caribbean Sea – among the earliest territories to be colonized and so have retained colonial links for longest (Caldwell et al., 1980: 960). J. Feyrer and B. Sacerdote (2006) go so far as to suggest that, the longer an island spent as a colony, the higher its present-day living standards and the lower its infant mortality rate: each additional century of European colonization is associated with a 40 per cent boost in income today and a reduction in infant mortality to 2.6 deaths per 1,000 births (for a critique, see Bertram, 2007).

Second, the islands in question may not have had an indigenous population at all – or, if they had one, it had gone extinct – and were thus appropriately "discovered" or re-established de novo by Western explorers.[11] In other cases, the natives, having no hinterland to retreat to (Hintjens, 1991: 38), were utterly and quickly wiped out following contact with the West. This *terra nullius* scenario conveniently avoided the need to subjugate or somehow come to terms with indigenous populations, because they did not (or did no longer) exist. Instead, so many island societies and cultures have thus not been colonized but created *ex nihilo* by colonial penetration from the outside (Houbert, 1986: 146).

Third, the nature of the colonial impact and experience on small islands was not just longer; it was also more total and profoundly intimate. Again, the absence of a geographical but also psychological hinterland meant that a close and regular engagement with the colonial presence and its psyche was inevitable for most local island populations. In some cases, it was the only access to formal employment (as in public administration) and formal education.

Fourth, many small islands had hardly anything valuable worth exploiting in economic terms: unlike "plantation islands," rich in agricultural products or mineral resources, they were more prized for being strategic "fortress islands" (Warrington and Milne, 2007), defending sea routes or possessing sheltered and deep-water harbours. In such a situation, the colonial power just had to ensure the loyalty of the local population: in other words, the sympathy of the locals at large (and not just that of the narrow elite) had to be guaranteed at all costs in order to maintain the security of the military or naval base, and particularly at times of threat. Blatant economic exploitation had thus to be avoided, the preferred strategy instead being deliberate and assiduous assimilation, through such techniques as social advancement via civil-service jobs, workfare, opportunities to migrate to the metropole, and overall benign paternalism: breeding widespread civic loyalty to the imperial cause.

This interrelated battery of conditions has nurtured colonized nations (and not just elites) with Western tastes, Western ideals, Western languages, and Western religions, especially in the Caribbean: "manufactured societies ... creations of empire" (Naipaul, 1972: 254). These are clear manifestations of cultural incorporation, even if, at times, fleshed out in non-Western ethnicities and even if unrequited by the colonial motherland.[12] Even independent island micro-states have long been identified as "more Westernized" than neighbouring but mainland states (Newitt, 1992). Micro-insular domestic politics have been enthusiastically deployed at forestalling or postponing independence rather than clamouring for it. Greek Cypriots sought Ἕνωσις (*Enosis*, meaning unification) with Greece, while both Malta (in the mid-1950s) and the Seychelles (in 1971) went as far as lobbying for integration with Britain, a policy platform that can be described as the very antithesis of decolonization (Drower, 1992: 114; Hillebrink, 2008: 96). In mid-1987 officials from the Turks and Caicos Islands offered the Canadian government the opportunity to annex the islands. According to the Turks and Caicos representatives, polls then indicated that 90 per cent of islanders favoured some form of special relationship with Canada. The idea continues to surface (CBC News, 2004).

In some instances, the motivation for enduring colonial links has been triggered by a desire to escape being, or becoming, a dependency of a neighbouring jurisdiction. Anguilla successfully seceded from the independent state of St Kitts-Nevis-Anguilla, preferring to remain "in association" with Britain (and in spite of the latter's attempts to force the island into independence in coalition with its island neighbours). In July 1967, 1,813 residents of that island voted in favour of Anguilla's secession in a referendum, while only 5 voted against (Government of Anguilla, n.d.) In 1978 the Ellice Islanders chose independence (as Tuvalu) to thwart becoming a junior partner of an independent Kiribati. And both St Martin and St Barthélemy voted in 2003 to each become – as of February 2007 – fully fledged *collectivités d'outre mer* of France, rather than remain subdependencies of Guadeloupe. In so many other cases, small island dependencies cling proudly and tenaciously to their colonial status (Guillebaud, 1976; Miles, 1985; Winchester, 1985/2003).

The analysis of the above dynamics suggests that many island people are comfortable in displaying evidences of *subnationalism*, much like a regionally or geographically anchored ethnicity. Typically, there is a morbid interest in outright independence, a lukewarm (at worst) but deep-seated sympathy for maintaining links with former colonial patron states, and a sense of pride and identity with their island jurisdiction in the context of having a more powerful but arms-length protector. The intermittent willingness to interpret or test the "shared rule versus self-rule" divide constitutes the hard core of local politics. The key ideological schism is not in terms of left versus right, but in terms of autonomy/secessionism versus integration/irredentism (e.g., Mørkøre, 1996). The electorate will judge local political leaders mainly on their ability to work and negotiate the balance of power with the larger player in the political dyad, including the ability to extract funds or concessions from the latter. This dynamic is well captured by the Latin phrase *Parva Sub Ingenti* ("The Small under the Protection of the Great") found in a didactic poem on agriculture by the Roman poet Virgil (*Georgics*, Book II). This same phrase is also, not coincidentally, the motto of Canada's smallest (and only fully enisled) province, Prince Edward Island (Fraser, 1997).

EXPLANATIONS

Unless a territory has enjoyed separate status within a colonial relationship, such a territory appears most unlikely to have the basic political raw material which eventually could be nurtured into being a sovereign state, or even a quasi-sovereign one. This situation would have resulted because the administrative boundaries legitimizing a distinct political identity were developed both out of sheer convenience as well as within the comfort of an internationally and domestically recognized framework of colonial rule.

In the case of continental states that have island provinces or regions without a history of a separate colonial boundary, the metropole is usually careful not to create the circumstances for any eventual devolution, unless obliged to take such action under *force majeure*: witness recent overtures to Corsica (and, as described earlier, to New Caledonia) by the centralized French state, in the wake of violence and strong moves for separatism.[13] Such a strategy could be undertaken, for example, by deliberately avoiding the creation of exclusively island-based administrative or political units or by ensuring that geographic "island regions" are incorporated within larger subnational units,[14] or are themselves broken down into smaller, subnational units, as occurs in large archipelagic states such as the Philippines and Indonesia. Opportunism may create historical conjunctures which facilitate such a withdrawal of autonomy, and the availability of prized resources may provide the material pretext to do so.[15]

Meanwhile, failing the colonial card, island regions must rely on diplomatic acumen and leadership to extract discretionary powers from a central state. How is this done? At least three, interrelated approaches can be distilled from practice.

One is to use the existence of a supranational institution to somehow circumvent the local state. This is one intended outcome of the islands' lobby within the European Union, which has identified no less than 286 island regions as the targets of "specific measures" since the adoption of the Treaty of Amsterdam (Planistat Europe and Bradley Dunbar Associates, 2003). The sheer act of being defined and recognized as an "island region" could, in itself, be seen to represent an, albeit tokenistic, political victory of sorts (e.g., Hache, 2007).[16] Similarly, in 1982, once Australia had enlisted an international organization – UNESCO – to carve out the Tasmanian Wilderness and add it to its World Heritage List, the territory could be protected from commercial interests, even if the latter were supported or entertained by the Tasmanian state government (Hay, 2000).

A different, and more radical way is to embark unilaterally on a style of "rogue politics" which may set an island region on a confrontational path with a central government but where critical local public opinion may be swayed in favour of the lurch and thereby act to legitimize its stance democratically, if not legally or constitutionally. Whether such politics may indeed be deemed "maverick" is probably a matter of interpretation. Fully sovereign island regions may be more likely to adopt such a system and could therefore rely on the momentum or "extantism" that sovereignty provides, in their confrontation with other, larger powers (Bartmann, 2002).[17] Examples that come to mind include Iceland and the "cod wars" with Great Britain in the mid-twentieth century (*The Economist*, 1971), Malta's negotiations with the United Kingdom over the military facilities on the island in the 1970s (Wriggins, 1976), and the drive by Vanuatu and the Solomon Islands for a nuclear-free Pacific in the 1980s (Trompf, 1993: xv–xvi). Anguilla's tactics in preventing a quiet absorption into the proposed state of St Kitts Nevis-Anguilla, which led to a British "invasion" welcomed by the locals, is a classic example drawn from a subnational island jurisdiction that wanted to remain so (Westlake, 1972).

A third approach connects with the ascendancy of the governance rights of indigenous or aboriginal peoples. Native peoples have been quite successful of late in securing decision-making powers from the metropole, and all the more so when they are islanders.[18] This applies to the Aleutian Islanders (Alaska, United States), the Baffin-Ellesmere Islanders (Canada), the Maori (New Zealand), and the Torres Strait Islanders (Australia). The huge Canadian territory of Nunavut was established in 1999: it includes many islands, including Baffin, the world's fifth largest (and where Nunavut's capital and largest settlement, Iqaluit, is located). It is Canada's largest political unit by area and 82 per cent of its population of some 33,000 is indigenous Inuit (Légaré, 2002). The Akaka Bill, which was tabled in the U.S. Senate in 2005 but failed to become legislation, was designed to "provide a process for the recognition by the USA of the native Hawaiian governing entity" (Borreca, 2005). Meanwhile, native islanders of Sakhalin Island, in Russia, have protested against the expected negative impact of the world's largest oil and gas pipeline project, and sentiments for greater autonomy have been aroused (*Vladivostok News*, 2005). In this case, a small population base is also likely to facilitate the granting of more self-determination.

In the three routes identified above, smallness and cultural distinctiveness of population and/or land area, isolation, and islandness can act in concert to fuel a distinctive politics and to safeguard and differentiate the region from external "intervention."[19] Rather than consider such departures as exceptional, it would be wise to see them as examples of innovative governance, of carving out political niches where geography facilitates the action at the same time as it circumscribes the territorial scope of any achieved or granted powers and privileges.

Handsome benefits can result from the extraction and deployment of jurisdictional power (Baldacchino and Milne, 2000). These usually translate into a larger localization of control over economic and political decisions. Some enviable jurisdictional powers – which are far greater in relation to the small size of a land mass or resident population – have been achieved and assiduously cultivated, especially by some sovereign small states: fisheries policy by Iceland; the only successful exclusive enterprise zone in Africa by Mauritius; sustainable tourism policy by the Seychelles; and air-transportation policy by Iceland and Malta. But the political economy of success is perhaps even clearer among subnational island jurisdictions. More on this in forthcoming chapters.

REVISITING POST-COLONIALISM

This is not to dismiss the relevance or significance of local agitation for independence, and so presumably a more complex "ethnoscape" (Appadurai,

1990) of interpretations, identities, and memories of empire: at some point, even many of these island jurisdictions would have had at least one political party or civic movement advocating full independence – and that particular party (as in Bermuda, the Faroe Islands, and notably recently in Scotland and French Polynesia) may have also been elected to power and taken over the governance of the jurisdiction by itself or as a member of a ruling coalition. Nor do I intend to diminish the (often newly found) interest by the colonial/mainland state in extending its stewardship over island territories, whether for geo-strategic interests,[20] economic gain,[21] or simply what today could be described as politically correct imperialism: such as bestowing largesse or rewarding sympathetic governments with investment.[22]

And yet what does the above have to tell us about the epistemologies of post-colonialism? Of course, in spite of all the carnage, damage, and destruction it has caused, colonialism is not a non-problematically evil and negative process. In an age of uncertainty and globalization, there is an even worse fate for peoples and territories – that of being marginalized from world markets and cut off from tapping the wealth, largesse, and "rents" forthcoming from other, often larger, territories (e.g., Kakazu, 1994). Autarchy has never been a realistic option for islands,[23] in spite of a common but fundamentally erroneous opinion that islands – especially small islands – are, by geographical disposition, insular, closed, and complete spaces.

Rather, islanders have long been recognized as an internationally mobile citizenry (e.g., Wood, 1967: 95). The ingrained openness of small islands serves to orient their island inhabitants towards the metropole, for inspiration, vacation, adventure, shopping, education, and/or employment. Small-island literature is dominated by the migration theme (e.g., Markham, 1989; Brinklow et al., 2000). Often, emigration is the only medium that permits a viable "exit" option to the pervasive and stifling totality, monopoly, and intimacy of the local socio-cultural environment (Baldacchino, 1997). Islanders from developing nations are known to have a very high propensity to migrate to developed countries (Connell and King, 1999). The highest proportion of non-OECD graduates living in an OECD country in 2005 were from Guyana, Jamaica, Haiti, Trinidad and Tobago, Fiji, Angola, Cyprus, and Mauritius – all but two of which are small island states (*The Economist*, 2005a). High levels of urbanization at home act to dislodge residents from outlying villages or islands (in the case of archipelagos) and render them potentially more mobile regionally and internationally (Bertram and Watters, 1986: 55–7). For various island households, migration becomes a strategic resource, since offspring sent away can be expected to infuse remittances, in

cash or in kind, to the home economy, acting as a "transnational corporation of kin" (Marcus, 1981; James, 1991). In some instances (e.g., Cape Verde,
Philippines, Samoa, and Tonga), these are significant contributions to the
home island's gross national income (e.g., Ahlburg and Brown, 1998). At
any point, a significant percentage of an island population is likely to be
away at its respective metropole(s) (Baldacchino, 1997: 89; Lowenthal, 1987:
41–3). If one were to determine one key reason why island territories prefer to
maintain subnational status rather than "graduate" to full sovereignty today, it
would probably be the guarantee of the option to migrate to, and freely settle
in, metropolitan labour markets.

SLIPPING THE NET OF POST-COLONIAL THEORIZING

It is time to strike clear of the naive notion that the experience of colonialism constitutes, invariably and completely, a tragedy, a subjugation, a loss of
self-representation (e.g., Bhabha, 1994) and the resistance to colonialism is
an act of "conflictless brotherhood" devoid of internal contradictions (e.g.,
Mukherjee, 1993: 27). It is also time to debunk a reductionism that dismisses
"upside down decolonization" as merely an alienated strand of essentially
neo-colonial power relations (e.g., Hickling-Hudson et al., 2004). No doubt,
the full consequences of colonialism deserve attention, in all their embarrassing detail. Yet the relationship between colonial and post-colonial is
not necessarily a neatly dialectical one. In societies created and scripted by
colonialism, post-colonial need not imply anti-colonial, and even the *post* in
post-colonial may need to be critiqued (Baldacchino, 2010; Royle, 2007).[24]
Some places – and some smaller islands in particular – can perhaps be con-
ceptualized as permanent parts of empire (Drower, 1992). Helen Hintjens
(1990; 1995: 9) cogently asks whether the acquisition of a new citizenship
for former colonial citizens – American, Australian, British, French, Danish,
Dutch, or New Zealand – and the metropolitan integration it implies might
be regarded as a type of decolonization at the individual level. As a senator
from the French *department d'outre mer* (DOM) of Réunion argued: "For
the old colonies that have become departments, integration is a means of
decolonization, just as much as independence for those who have chosen
that" (Ramassamy, 1987: 8). These post-colonial island spaces embody a self-
definition which may not be determined by the experience of colonization
but which cannot imagine itself without it. R. Edmond and V. Smith (2003:
5, 6) correctly affirm that "island stories have tended to slip the net of post-
colonial theorizing … within theories of colonial discourse … islands are

regarded merely as metonyms of imperialism, rather than as specific locations generating their own potentially self-reflective colonial metaphors."

One could draw a similar observation and cautionary note with respect to other fashionable "posts." In presenting themselves as redeeming epistemologies, both post-structuralism and post-modernism can, in practice, act to appropriate and control their subject matter, obviating the relevance and damaging the credibility of alternative explanations (e.g., Tiffin, 1988: 170).

Especially for small island jurisdictions, there is quite a compelling case to be made today for autonomy without sovereignty. After all, "in an uncertain world, a substantial degree of autonomy, where culture and identity are respected and protected, reasonable access to employment and services exists, and security is guaranteed, has weakened the strength of the claim to independence" (Connell, 2003: 141). Some islands have been the sites of some of the most brutal colonial encounters; others have been construed as offloading sites for the metropolitan societies' worst citizens. And yet, in spite of this dystopic legacy, pushing any of the current island "colonies" towards independence could be even construed as a "repulsive colonial act" (Hoefte and Oostindie, 1989: 29; also Connell, 2008). While local politicians may continue to peddle the rhetoric of independence as a long-term goal, progress in that direction appears gripped by "an infinite pause" (Connell, 1994: 104) and "suspended under an imperial gaze" (Skinner, 2006: 201). More about this in chapter 9. An enduring, even if pragmatic, culture of colonial loyalty calls for deeper theorization into post-colonial research (e.g., Dodds, 2007). Meanwhile, current post-colonial research (e.g., Le Sueur, 2003) still finds it easier to pick on, and grapple with, Algeria rather than Mayotte, India rather than Bermuda, and Indonesia rather than Aruba.

A Review of Economic Performance: Tapping the Hinterland Beyond

INTRODUCTION

A small territory is especially obliged to use extraterritorial resources as its "hinterland" for economic success. Yet it is rare to come across a critical analysis which looks at islands as the strategic and candid promoters of a role as political and economic usufructuaries over external resources. Adopting a "jurisdiction as resource" perspective, this chapter notes how subnational island jurisdictions tend to perform economically better than sovereign island states, precisely by crafting themselves as efficient siphons for attracting rent surpluses from other jurisdictions, and especially (but not exclusively) from their patron metropolitan power and its citizens. The resources thus attracted extend over a whole range of goods and services. They can, according to the MIRAB (migration, remittances, aid, bureaucracy) model of small-island economic development, primarily consist of aid and remittances. However, these resources can alternately include access to investment, welfare, security, stable currency, international relations, specialized labour power, other fiscal transfers, and access to markets and specialized higher education. I thus propose a different model of small-island economic development, using the acronym PROFIT (people, resource management, overseas engagement and ultra-national recognition, finance, transportation), which favours a more active policy orientation and a disposition towards carving out procedural and jurisdictional powers. It is my contention that a small island territory's engagement with the external hinterland can be conceived as a position on a sliding scale, a strategic mix of options located between two distinct development trajectories, of which MIRAB is one and the PROFIT model the other. Overall, the strategy is a natural consequence of having an enclave status.

THE IMPACT OF NATURAL ENDOWMENTS

Economic historian William Green regards population density as a principal factor determining the nature of labour relations in post-emancipation Caribbean. High population density on a small and insular land area, he argues, led to the non-availability of plots of land for private use by emancipated slaves; the latter thus had little choice but to seek employment on plantations or emigrate. Moreover, the colonial presence was "sometimes intimate, and always weighty" (Green, 1984: 114). These conditions were not conducive to the development of an independent peasantry. Barbados presented the most extreme example: "[It] had almost no forest: it was fully cultivated, rifled with roads, and bestrewn with villages, stone churches, windmills and factories" (ibid.) As in such other island territories as St Kitts or Antigua, in Barbados "there was no sense whatever of the vast primeval forest that extended beyond the tiny squalid settlement at Belize and intruded deeply upon the social psyche of its inhabitants" (ibid.). Of course, population density, much like smallness or insularity, does not cause anything. It is a condition, not an attribute. There may be, however, something going on here that is worth reflecting on. Does the existence of a "vast primeval forest" have an impact on the social psyche of a population? Would the absence of any such forest have an impact as well? And, if so, how?

The comparative study of small islands confronts us with observations similar to Green's. Discarding the specific nuances of personalities, history, climate, time, and space, these observations suggest that the availability, or absence, of such a feature as a forest, or some other immense domestic natural endowment, can have a critical and determining effect on human behaviour generally, and on economic growth and development strategy specifically.

EFFECTS OF AN ABSENT LOCAL HINTERLAND

Various arguments drawn from a number of social-science disciplines suggest that the absence of a natural domestic endowment is an intervening variable in the economic development of a territory and the socio-psychological development of its people.

Helen Hintjens, Réunion-born political scientist, observes this much in relation to France's erstwhile colonies in the Indian Ocean. These islands became inhabited only at the time of the European "Age of Discovery." Thus, the settlers were the natives in the Mascaregnes: there were no tensions with aboriginal peoples, *because there were no aboriginal peoples.* With relatively small land areas and high population densities, the locals found no objection, and no alternative, to remaining culturally incorporated within the metropolitan regime. They had "virtually no physical or cultural hinterland to retreat to" (Hintjens, 1991: 38). Assimilation (Miles, 1985: 198–206) was well nigh total and complete. In spite of its limited administrative presence in the region, the cultural hegemony of France in the broad Indian Ocean has remained vibrant (e.g., Houbert, 1986; Mrgudovic, 2005).

Prior to Hintjens, Australia-based demographers J.C. Caldwell, G.E. Harrison, and P. Quiggin had already come to the conclusion that insular micro-states are more "Westernized" than post-colonial mainland states (Caldwell et al., 1980: 960). "They were part of the European maritime system at a time when the West did not have the economic strength to penetrate continental areas to the same extent" (ibid., 953). Proof of their "Westernization" was a higher propensity to migrate to developed countries; in the late 1970s, 85 per cent were predominantly Christian; 91 per cent had an official European language; 87 per cent had a majority of the population able to speak either a European or a Creole language (ibid., 954).

For U.S. economist Paul Streeten, the absence of a local, rural hinterland has pivotal significance to economic development. It exempts a territory from a dependence on "the slow-coach of agriculture" (Streeten, 1993: 199). In the case of small, densely populated island territories starved of land – such as the city states of Bermuda, Hong Kong, Malta, and Singapore – industrial or service-sector developments have been the inevitable and default growth poles, obliging a quick shift of mindset towards export promotion and the penetration of export markets. It also inhibits the formation of a land-owning peasantry or plantocracy which can become a formidable reactionary lobby in domestic and regional politics, seeking protection from cheaper imports and contributing to higher costs of food items to consumers.

A forest, a jungle, a desert, a swamp, or a mountain range is often seen as: 1) an outback, far from the centres of habitation and urbanization; 2) a place of refuge, escape, or "fallback," offering a defensive or regrouping position in time of war or pursuit; and 3) a reservoir, fount, or stock of diverse reinvigorating supplies and resources – physical ones such as agricultural produce, land, or lumber but also less tangible assets such as ancestral culture, spiritual refreshment, health, composure, inspiration, or crude energy.

This chapter will be referring to such places, real or imaginary, as *hinterlands*. I find the word apt since it synthesizes all three senses of being an outlier, a refuge, and a resource pool. It is the term already used by Hintjens and Streeten in their assessment of the development trajectories of small island territories. It is a term used readily in human geography to represent an outlying service centre feeding a metropolitan area, often acting as its "living space" (Cracknell, 1967); it is a relationship in which demand originates in one location but is satisfied in another (Greer and Wall, 1982: 227). The absence of an interior, a local hinterland, or a local territorial core area is a small-island characteristic recognized also by the United Nations (Griffith and Inniss, 1992). It would be very difficult to imagine Robinson Crusoe surviving on his island, with all his creature comforts, without the opportunity for him to make no less than thirteen trips to his wrecked vessel (Defoe, 1719; Hymer, 1971: 17).

The concept of a hinterland also connects easily with other, perhaps more current, terms. Take that of a "footprint," often applied to ecology (e.g., Gössling et al., 2002): it appears that, *ceteris paribus*, the smaller the territory and the higher the population density of its inhabitants, the more likely is it that its footprint extends beyond its shores. Extending the argument to the more familiar, although fuzzier, concept of "sustainability," one could contend that, as far as small islands are concerned, "speaking of sustainable development is a contradiction-in-terms" (Baldacchino, 2004c: 6; also Connell, 1988a; Bertram, 1993) since the small local-insular territory would not survive without drawing in resources and assets from, while flushing out excesses and undesirables to, a hinterland beyond. Drawing on the economic-vulnerability thesis postulated by L. Briguglio (1995), the model is faulty precisely for assuming autonomous systems and spaces of self-sufficiency. Adopting a territorially delineated, closed system or statist perspective leads one to conclude that many such states which depend on exogenous inputs survive only on the basis of "artificial props" (ibid., 1622). Parasitism remains a word with a heavy negative baggage (Baldacchino, 1993) and is looked upon with "scorn" (Poirine, 1998: 65). Development qualifies as non-sustainable because it is not underpinned by productive activity *within* the territorial boundaries of the island economy (Bertram, 1993: 248). Rather, islands, smaller islands in particular, must exhibit a generous degree of openness and integration with the outside world in order to survive (Baldacchino, 2000; Bertram and Watters, 1986: 52). So, by way of example, the handling of the aftermath of the volcanic eruptions in the 1990s on Montserrat – itself a subnational island jurisdiction – would have been a very different story were the small colony a closed system, not benefitting from external support, and particularly without the intervention of the United Kingdom.

It therefore does appear that a crucial distinction in the evolution of societies and economies has to do with the perceived availability or otherwise of a local hinterland. I have included the word *perceived* in the preceding sentence because, where human beings are concerned, there is no hard-and-fast, direct relationship between physical conditions and human behaviour. It was thus psychologically easier for Singapore to develop an export orientation since it had prospered with Malaysia as its hinterland until independence in 1965. Rapa Nui/Easter Island has become the classic example of a now extinct community which perhaps ended up consuming itself because, in the face of obvious constraints on finite material resources, it failed to recognize the option, or to develop the required technology, to expand beyond its shores (e.g., Diamond, 2004). Although extreme population densities (very low, as in Pitcairn; or very high, as in Singapore) can endanger people's lives and access to resources, it is also clear that many societies survive fairly well in what may be seen by others as simply unbearable, relatively extreme circumstances. Herewith a case in point: the inhabitants of Prince Edward Island often complain because theirs is the most densely populated province in Canada – but with just twenty-four persons per km^2!

POLITICAL-ECONOMIC BEHAVIOUR OF SMALLER TERRITORIES

These arguments, of course, are not new. They have been taken forward and elaborated upon to explain the political and economic behaviour of smaller territories.

Thus, Caldwell et al. (1980: 960) state that "on the whole, they [island micro-states] retained colonial links longer" (also Doumenge, 1989: 51). Few of these territories struggled *for* independence; most have waged intense diplomatic struggles to maintain or extend benign colonial links with their overseas hinterland, at times going so far – witness the cases of Malta and Mauritius – as to press for integration, the very antithesis of sovereignty (Baldacchino, 1997: 176–7; Guillebaud, 1976; Winchester, 1985). As discussed in chapter 3, an intriguing mathematical relationship presents itself in political geography, whereby, in the post-Second World War period, the larger, mainland colonies struggled and obtained independence first – with the largest extant (mainland) colony India being the first to do so, traumatically, in 1947. Meanwhile, the smaller, mainly island, colonies have either obtained political independence last or else stubbornly continue to refuse to shift gear from their current, non-sovereign status. There are at least forty-one examples of the latter, and the numbers are *not* falling (Royle, 1989: 108).

In the realm of economics, H. Kakazu (1994) has suggested that such small island territories be looked upon as harbouring rentier economies, offering their strategic location, investment potential, fishing rights, tax differentials, or tourism products to attract "rents" based on value added, that is, generated in hinterlands overseas. Such policies, where successful, have tended to see a shift from productive status to rentier status, and even stronger/deeper integration and convergence with metropolitan powers and their economic cycles (Bertram, 2004). When accompanied by the abandonment of what little commercial agriculture or fishing may have been possible, the shift becomes one "from subsistence to subsidy" (Connell, 1991: 271). In this case, domestic industrialization is not induced by the winding down of the primary sector, but rather summarily skipped (Baldacchino, 1998; Miles, 1986: 158). Small territories find themselves in the post-industrial era, without the scars and polluting effects of an industrial past, enjoying high levels of affluence and consumption predicated on an unorthodox, possibly shifting, combination of resources. Among these are: remittances from "transnational corporations of kin" (Marcus, 1981); bilateral and multilateral aid; public-sector employment and contracts; and philately, conch shells, international dial-up codes, and Internet domain names/sites (Prasad, 2004).

The common basis to the above arguments is that they suggest novel departures from more standard conceptualizations of development where the engagement with the hinterland falls under the rubric of less significant, marginal affairs. The stark truth of various small, mainly island, jurisdictions today is that they thrive mainly on such *external* relations. Whereas conventional economics treats *externalities* as often incidental by-products, often experienced by third parties, they are very much the essence of livelihood for many island citizens, their businesses, and their governments.

The MIRAB model (Bertram and Watters, 1985, 1986) is today arguably the most popular acronym for explaining this condition. The key hypothesis states that "there is today a class of economies and societies in which the combined effect of migration, remittances, aid and bureaucracy ... *determines* [rather than supports] the evolution of the system" (Bertram and Watters, 1985: 497; emphasis in original). The notion of "autonomous economic growth" in specific contexts is simply "false" (Watters, 1987: 33). In spite of a number of suggested alterations (MURAB by Munro, 1990; MIRAGE by Brookfield, 1986, quoted in Connell, 1988a: 81; TouRAB by Guthunz and Von Krosigk, 1996; MIRTAB by Ogden, 1993), the MIRAB concept remains steadfast and, perhaps, has even assumed of late the stature of a self-fulfilling prophecy, especially in the South Pacific. It is not only a welfare-maximizing strategy in line with the theory of competitive advantage (Poirine, 1998: 91); it now may, or may be seen to, legitimize, justify, and lock into place such an economic-development strategy in the long term (Treadgold, 1999). As long as sources of revenue remain secure, and as long as the shifting fortunes of any such "external" source are adequately compensated for by any other similar "external" source, existing or new, then that is, in practice, all that really matters – an unorthodox but effective sense of sustainability and entrepreneurship (Bertram and Watters, 1985: 512; Bertram, 1993: 257).

Is this a case of *plus ça change, plus c'est la meme chose*? The MIRAB cluster reveals itself as a standard "development" tactic for peripheral regions and territories the world over. In cases where there are metropolitan cores and stagnant peripheries – and where aren't there? – the MIRAB cluster of features constitutes the classic response to assuage the ailments of those on the edge, particularly if accompanied by a dominant ideology of professed redistribution and equalization – that is, unless the central power "is prepared to see living standards slide" (Bertram and Watters, 1985: 513). After all, the standard measures used by the core to support the periphery include an element of workfare (bureaucracy within MIRAB) and transfer payments (aid within MIRAB). Meanwhile, migration, internal this time, is also likely from the periphery to the centre, as people – particularly the young, the skilled, the educated, the ambitious – search for work and a still better education, occasionally visiting relatives back home or sending them gifts in cash/kind every so often (migration in MIRAB). The novelty of MIRAB, other than the fancy yet meaningless acronym, lies in identifying uncannily similar patterns operating *between* states as well as *within* them.

The MIRAB allure is quite remarkable. It seems that, once having named the beast of the apocalypse, there is no restraining its triumphant imperial project. When conceived in 1985, G. Bertram and R.F. Watters applied the syndrome primarily to just five Pacific island micro-territories, two of which were recently independent states (Kiribati, Tuvalu), with the other three being semi-autonomous, subnational jurisdictions (Cook Islands, Niue, Tokelau). Twelve years later (Bertram, 1999), Western Samoa (now Samoa), Tonga, French Polynesia, Federated States of Micronesia, other small U.S.-associated Pacific Territories, and Rapa Nui – as well as the outlying islands of so-called "non-MIRAB" island states, like Fiji, Papua New Guinea, and the Solomon Islands – were added to the pioneering five, or noted to have been added by other researchers. By 1998, the U.S. Virgin Islands, Guadeloupe, Martinique, Saint Helena, Saint-Pierre and Miquelon, and Mayotte had been added to the list from beyond the Pacific basin (Poirine, 1998). McElroy and Morris (2002) identify and confirm four African island states as MIRABs: Cape Verde, Comoros, Mayotte, and São Tomé e Príncipe. We have been told that "all SPINs [South Pacific Island Nations] match to a greater or lesser degree the model of rent-dependent MIRAB" (Fleming, 2002: 6). Connell (1991: 252, 270) had argued that the model is applicable, to a greater or lesser extent, to most small island countries, since most of these have moved "from subsistence to subsidy" (ibid.). It is not just the economic system described, but the model itself, which appears to be durable and persistent.

Yet is this really the case? Has MIRAB unwittingly become a convenient development paradigm that dismisses alternatives? If MIRAB has real explanatory value, this does not necessarily mean that it is the only measure of small-island development. There may be alternative small-island development syndromes, as equally distinct from conventional resource-based development models as MIRAB, at work among small-island territories today. There may be, in other words, non-MIRAB, pre-MIRAB, and/or post-MIRAB strategies for engaging with the hinterland beyond. Any such different combination of factors is, like MIRAB, as much at home in the realm of subnational as well as national or sovereign island jurisdictions. To appreciate this alternative, the reasons why many, mainly island, territories have not opted for political sovereignty merit being reviewed. The dynamics between the semi-autonomous territory and the larger, sovereign state (and often former colonial power) are uncannily similar to the purported advantages of a MIRAB strategy.

Earlier I reviewed how McElroy and Mahoney (2000) explain the manner in which political affiliation continues to grant substantial economic advantages to small, non-sovereign, island units. Meanwhile, a fair dose of jurisdictional clout inhibits any concerted drive for political independence. Many small islands, because they are islands, already enjoy some degree of administrative autonomy (Baldacchino, 2000), also as an unwitting benefit of colonialism. This same feature lies behind the credentials for, and eventual transition of smaller islands to, statehood. Furthermore, because they are also small, sparsely populated, and/or somewhat isolated or unique, such island jurisdictions usually manage to extract some special advantages from their respective metropole. Although they may have refrained from sovereignty, they nevertheless, jurisdictionally or constitutionally, typically enjoy more discretionary powers than any similarly sized or even larger chunks of "mainland" (Poirine, 1998). Thus, the idea of independence may appear to be set aside, at least for the moment, and in spite of any nationalist aspirations (e.g., Trompf, 1993: xxv). Links with the metropole are "an insurance against some of the vagaries of the world market, political upheaval, invasion and natural disasters" (Aldrich and Connell, 1992: 296).

More than that, these are also examples of alterations in geo-economic space. As economic power is transferred "upward, downward and outward from nation states" (Courchene, 1995: 3), jurisdiction is increasingly recognized as a very useful driver and primer for such purposes. It becomes the "catapult" which allows the entertaining of differentiation within the local state, as well as of developing an international (or better, an ultra-national) presence on the global or regional stage (e.g., McKercher, 2000). If the sovereign state continues to insulate itself in law, while the world market continues relentlessly to unravel beyond sovereign borders, the economic strategies pursued will increasingly seek to lure funds and value-added from other jurisdictions (Palan, 2002: 153). As Peter Drucker (1986) suggests, given what is more than just the "intriguing coincidence" of an integrating global economy and a splintering global and national polity, a coming to terms with this phenomenon would include using local rules to tap non-local resources.

The benefits resulting from the extraction and deployment of jurisdictional power call for increased recognition (Baldacchino and Milne, 2000). They usually translate into a larger localization of control over economic and political decisions. Of course, the apex of jurisdictional powers – powers far greater in relation to the small size of a land mass or resident population – has been achieved and assiduously cultivated especially by sovereign small, often island, states. But the political economy of success is even clearer among non-sovereign island territories. Discretion over taxation and offshore finance has been behind the success of such territories as Madeira, Bermuda, British Virgin Islands, Turks and Caicos, the Isle of Man, and the Channel Islands; discretion over language policy, shipping registration, and property owner-ship lies at the heart of the Åland Islands' autonomy from Finland; some jurisdictional autonomy of varying degrees is enjoyed by island provinces of larger states, in spite of usually small relative size of land and population (as in the cases of Barbuda, Gozo, Hong Kong, Kinmen, Nevis, Zanzibar, the *status apparte* of Aruba, French Polynesia, Labuan, New Caledonia, Svalbard, Hainan, Galápagos, Rapa Nui, Tasmania, the Balearics, the Canaries, and the Azores). What we have here is a combination of free-riding by the smaller, island party in the context of (at times deliberate) oversight by the larger, metropolitan party, crafting in the outcome some kind of regulatory legiti-macy. This persists while the island faction never completely relinquishes the potential resort to the metropole, if and when dire straits (such as budgetary shortfalls, economic recessions, environmental disasters, over-population, labour surpluses, or shortages) so determine or suggest. In this way, they avoid that chronic vulnerability which results from systemic closure and which is supposed to plague small, island territories most of all (Briguglio, 1995).

The key difference between these strategies and those falling within the MIRAB rubric is that the former are based on jurisdictional discretion, meaning the willingness and capacity to adapt local laws and regulations to suit the requirements of the micro-insular economy, even if these laws and regulations differ from those of the metropole in which the smaller territory finds itself politically incorporated. Neither (out)migration nor remittances, aid, or bureaucracy need depend on differential constitutionalism. Of course, a critical question to ask is whether any such departures from the norm are actually indicators of autonomy, acts of sheer desperation, or even mere manipulations driven and controlled by the central state to its own net advantage, often without any consultation or power-sharing arrangements with the island locals. Case in point: the decision to develop Batam Island as an exclusive economic zone within Indonesia, thus exploiting its proximity to Singapore, was a unilateral decision by Jakarta and intensified the powerlessness of the Batanese (Royle, 1997).

However, and following critical observation, utilizing jurisdiction as a resource is one way of compensating for the dearth of conventional economic assets (Baldacchino and Milne, 2000). It is another shrewd survival strategy based on a specific form of international relations: deploying a flexible and creative diplomacy, adopting free-riding (in such matters as international relations, defence, and security as well as currency issues), slipping free or through the nets of regulation, and/or cultivating special, ultra-national, economic linkages. All these measures constitute a skills repertoire that the small and powerless deploy and, being small, often get away with. They may, in the process, also be providing useful regulatory escape routes for their metropolitan patrons or elites, as perhaps best illustrated by offshore finance regimes. Such is the character of the dynamics of unequal dyads, or unequal federalist arrangements (Watts, 2000).

Subnational jurisdictions may be tempted in the near future to carve out policy discretion on a specific number of areas, and economic relationships with a specific clutch of attractive metropoles, in their favour. As the nation-state, already in itself a mythical construction of modernity, finds itself too big as well as well as too small to address key political problems (Bell, 1987), the pressures for internal devolution and internal federalism in the contemporary "fragmegrative" space (Rosenau, 2003) will increase, just as the incentive for supra and ultra-national agreements with other neighbouring states or components thereof will also increase. It is likely that, as in the cases of Malta and Mauritius forty years ago, political sovereignty as a fully fledged state will be seriously entertained or threatened only with some degree of bluff, if what is considered a better deal by the smaller player is absolutely unacceptable to the larger.[5] The same political contest is bound to occur at a supranational and regional level, as nations jockey to maintain policy autonomy while recognizing that "pooled sovereignty" is the only way forward to render such bodies as the European Union even more effective. The EU and the euro exist in the first place as the outcome of such a sober assessment. "Government" (meaning decision making by elected representatives) thus gives way irrevocably to "governance" (meaning decision making by a plurality of networked partnerships) (Roseneau, 2003).

A second observation concerns the financial dimensions of development. Conventional economic statistics rank countries according to Gross National Product (GNP), Gross Domestic Product, or Gross National Income (GNI). Wealth is often defined in such terms as GNP/GDP/GNI per capita, preferably using purchasing-power parity. Smaller, often island, territories are doing exceptionally well on these counts. In their powerful critique of the alleged structural vulnerability of many small (often island) territories, Armstrong and Read (2002) conclude that smaller jurisdictions actually perform economically *better* than larger states. This should not come as a surprise: as enclaves, most have institutionalized and "dug in" their relationship with one larger, richer mainland state, their key hinterland. Comparative research has shown that, on average, non-sovereign island territories tend to be richer per capita than sovereign ones (Poirine, 1998; Bertram, 2004). The citizens of French Polynesia, Aruba, Bermuda, and Iceland have been counted among the world's top ten richest people, even by conventional standards (*The Economist*, 2003b). That the first three of the above four territories are non-sovereign states is important, but, additionally, only the first can be considered a MIRAB-like economy. Stopping short of full independence, while negotiating access to spoils within a larger jurisdictional framework, appears to pay off. Yet is jurisdictional clout *only* there for the purpose of extracting more largesse from the core?

Alan Fox (1969), a British industrial-relations scholar, divides the spoils of the production relationship between manager and managed into two categories. He calls the first *substantive* rewards (meaning tangible results like wages, hours of work, or allowances) and the second *procedural* rewards (meaning details of process: such as who gets to decide on a promotion, or how workers are dismissed). It appears that MIRAB emphasizes the substantive gains – the *what* – to a small economy (at both macro and micro levels) but dismisses or downplays the procedural ones – the *how*. A second approach may treat the procedural goals as the priority, with the substantive results coming in eventually "downstream" as it were, as a consequence of the shrewd use of policy capacity.

CREATIVE POLITICAL ECONOMY: FIVE CAPACITIES

Armstrong and Read (1998: 13) have argued that many of the smallest states – most of which are island or archipelagic territories – have managed to compensate effectively for their small size by a high quality of "endogenous policy formulation and implementation." They also contend that "further investigation of the policy stance of successful micro-states, *particularly in the sphere of international political economy*, is likely to be fruitful" (ibid.; my emphasis). Earlier, Peter Katzenstein (1985) made similar remarks in relation to small European states. Such insightful observations can apply equally well to subnational considerations, and not just to international relations.

Island-based and island-biased literature suggests five policy areas as being most likely to fall within the remit of self-rule, looked upon by many subnational island authorities/spokespersons as policy concerns that they would most prefer to have under local control and as critical ingredients in shaping economic prosperity via offshoring strategies (e.g., Milne, 2000). Contestation over "who does what" in these policy areas has also been typically tense, especially in federal political systems, and may in itself lead to demands for more self-rule, its withdrawal, or its renegotiation between the parties concerned. These powers are, *like* the MIRAB, a constituent quartet, premised on effective governance; however, *unlike* the MIRAB quartet, they depend much more on the nurturing of specific, local, jurisdictional capacities or local powers. They comprise the management of external relations but, unlike MIRAB, this is done "by means of domestic policies and governing institutions" (Warrington, 1998: 101). Each of these selected five policy areas is briefly elaborated upon below.

Powers over Finance: Mainly Banking, Insurance, and Taxation but Also Gaming

It has been said that "the development of offshore banking illustrates how islands ... have been transformed into spaces apparently far removed from the 'normal' practices associated with state sovereignty and territorial jurisdiction ... [They also] challenge our state-centered conception of property rights and capital accumulation" (Dodds and Royle, 2003, 489; also Hudson, 1998).

Most offshore finance centres are located on small island territories. Out of 42 jurisdictions listed on a "low tax" website, 30 (71 per cent) are whole islands or on islands (Low Tax website, 2008a). This is because the latter habitually involve few significant domestic transactions, draw in "rent"-based surpluses from elsewhere, and are therefore not unduly troubled by low tax policies (Fabri and Baldacchino, 1999: 141; Kakazu, 1994). Hampton and Abbott (1999b: 7) argue that locating offshore finance centres on small islands helps to place the industry more closely within government oversight and thus increase investor confidence. Smallness and insularity may, however, precipitate a "capture of the local state" by international financial capital, such as international banks and large accountancy firms (Christensen and Hampton, 1999) as well as not-so respectable operations (Royle, 2001: 180). The G7 Task Force's published blacklist of fifteen territories where money laundering was allegedly taking place included ten island locations (G7, 2000). The Isle of Man and the other British crown dependencies have altered their fiscal policies under pressure from the European Union, in order to conform to the latter's code of conduct on business taxation (Bell, 2002). Successful finance centres in small economies also tend to "crowd out" pre-existing industries (such as agriculture or small-scale manufacturing), leading to increases in the price of property and skilled labour. This is the condition of such island territories as the Channel Islands (Hampton, 1994) and Madeira (Milne, 2000: 17–18).

The power to tax, and tax differently, can prove critical to economic prosperity in the global era. An exceedingly low-tax environment – via low corporate taxes and business rates, generous capital allowances, absence of capital gains tax, wealth tax, capital transfer tax, inheritance tax, and death or estate duties, along with low personal income tax rates (15–20 per cent) – goes a long way towards attracting both manufacturing and service industries (Baldacchino and Milne, 2000: 232), to the dismay of large continental countries that complain that such strategies do not constitute "fair competition." Such a clutch of fiscal powers lies largely at the basis of the success of Aruba, San Andres y Providencia, the Isle of Man (McKercher, 2000), Jersey (Le Rendu, 2004), Madeira, and Labuan (Abbott, 2000); all these have prospered with the backing of a much larger, reliable "patron" state – or, in the case of the Channel Islands and the Isle of Man, the city of London. Mauritius has been the largest and most successful EPZ in Africa (World Bank, 2001: 1), while Kish Island is one of three "industrial free trade zones" approved by Iran's Islamic Consultative Assembly in 1993 (Baldacchino and Milne, 2006).

The smaller special autonomous region of China, Macau, is now the world's biggest casino centre, taking over from Las Vegas. This city state, originally an island archipelago now largely turned peninsula, has 18,428 persons per km², making it the most densely populated jurisdiction in the world. It also received no less than twenty-two million visitors in 2006 (Barboza, 2007). (By the way, Macau is a subnational jurisdiction without any local hinterland par excellence: it has no arable land, pastures, forest, or woodland.) The gaming, tourism, and hospitality industry is estimated to contribute more than 50 per cent of Macau's GDP and 70 per cent of Macau government revenue. Macau is also an offshore finance centre, a tax haven, and a free port without foreign-exchange-control regimes. In seeking to emulate Macau's success – which includes attracting tourists from China – Taiwan's Parliament has voted to legalize gambling on the outlying islands of its Penghu archipelago (Sui, 2009).

A recent development that has once again seen islands at the forefront of innovative governance is the growth of the electronic-gaming industry. Attractive locations from which to operate online casinos and poker rooms now include Alderney (a sub-subnational island jurisdiction, since it is a dependency of Guernsey, itself an SNIJ), Curaçao, Gibraltar, and the Isle of Man, as well as the sovereign states of Antigua and Barbuda and Malta (On-Line Casino Locator, 2008). Gaming taxes are generally low: for example, in Malta, the gaming tax is 0.5 per cent of turnover; in Alderney, a maximum 20 per cent tax on company profits is being reduced to 0 per cent and there is no value-added tax on goods imported from European Union member states (States of Alderney E-Commerce, 2008). Companies that are granted a licence to operate are typically not permitted to take bets from the citizens of their respective island base (e.g., On-Line Casino City, 2008). Small jurisdictions are thus attractive to gaming companies, since only a fraction of their potential client base is legally excluded. (For the island jurisdictions themselves, any high social impact on gamblers from other countries is, presumably, not their concern.)

Locating international (offshore) finance centres, banks, gaming and insurance companies on (low/no-tax) islands allows for a reaping of the benefits of the industry, while containing any of the associated costs. If these islands are subnational units, or members of clubs like the European Union, they may additionally benefit from the purview and probity of a larger polity. Moreover, there is some evidence that financial institutions have a preference to invest in "dependencies" rather than newly independent states: the most vivid example was the flow of funds from the Bahamas to the Cayman Islands when the former was granted independence (Hampton, 1996: 99).

Powers over Environmental Policy, Particularly Natural Resources
The management of specific local resources desired by the central state – oil, gas, mineral deposits, fishing zones, strategic bases, tourism potential, or sheer political loyalty – can be, and has been, used as leverage for extracting some degree of policy autonomy.[6] The Canadian provinces of Alberta,

Newfoundland and Labrador, and British Columbia, as well as the Shetland Islands in the United Kingdom, have successfully negotiated some local powers from the central state over critical dimensions of their economy, largely in relation to jurisdiction over oil, gas, and other subsoil resources (Baldacchino and Milne, 2000: 234; Cullen, 1990; Blackadder, 1998). The same, however, cannot be said about the management of the Newfoundland fishing stocks (Baldacchino and Milne, 2000: 233). North Sea oil and gas has also led to some renegotiation of the power balance between Faroe Islands and Denmark (Olafsson, 2000). Svalbard (Spitzbergen) is a special case, with bilateral treaty provisions over mining access reached between Norway and USSR/Russia.[8] Sakhalin Island, with its priced oil resources, has its own governor, yet it is not a Russian federal district. Other islands have extended their economic zones over tracts of sea many times larger than their own land mass (Falklands). Still other islands – like Hainan (China), Batam (Indonesia), and Kish (Iran) – have benefitted economically by being designated special economic zones (see Chongyi and Goodman, 1997; Royle, 1997; and Ronston, 2005, respectively). What needs to be researched is whether such changes have been accompanied by a measure of power transfer from core to periphery.

Meanwhile, the contribution of islands to cultural, environmental, and biological diversity is proportionately much greater than the size of their territories or populations (e.g., Young, 1999: 253). As noted in chapter 1, islands – excluding the continents of Antarctica and Australia – account for a disproportionate share of UNESCO's World Heritage Sites (as of July 2008) (UNESCO, 2008). Island regions that in toto are also World Heritage Sites – like Rapa Nui or Galapagos – are run differently from "normal" mainland provinces, in this case, of Chile and Ecuador respectively. More about islands and the relationship between jurisdictional status, the environment, and development can be found in chapter 8.

Powers over Access, Particularly in Relation to Air and Sea Transportation

Transportation is often a triple problem of choice, time, and price for islanders. Generally speaking, islanders know that transportation options and frequencies decrease and verge towards monopoly provision, and that transit times increase and prices rise with increasing distance from mainland areas and with decreasing size of a specific island's population (CPMR, 2002: 25–6). Archipelagic islands compound these issues even further (Hamilton-Jones, 1992; Bayliss-Smith et al., 1988). Difficulties with transportation negatively affect tourism, have an adverse impact on the export of manufactured goods, and are compounded by diseconomies of scale. They also badly affect the provision of emergency off-island health care (Baldacchino and Milne, 2000: 234). Distance means high cost for the transport of goods, services, and people, and effectively reduces access to the metropole, even for those overseas areas where residents are citizens of a European mother country (Connell and Aldrich, 1992: 33). An analysis of the population history of the Irish islands suggests a clear relationship between levels of access and population decline (Royle and Scott, 1996; Royle, 2007). Island transportation is often in the hands of "governments" (Royle 2001: 113): but which, and at which level, in a federal arrangement? The Åland Islands' control over its shipping registry and the safeguarding of duty-free transactions on Åland ships flying the Åland flag have been crucial to the territory's economic livelihood (Lindström, 2000). The U.S. Virgin Islands, American Samoa, and the Commonwealth of the Northern Marianas are exempted from the protectionist Merchant Marine Act of 1920 (commonly known as the Jones Act), which elsewhere in the United States obliges all cargo transported by water between U.S. ports to be carried in U.S.-flagged ships that are constructed in the United States and are both owned and crewed wholly by U.S. citizens. In contrast, Niue's dependence on a weekly Air Nauru service led to a below-capacity operation for its fledgling tourism industry when that service was discontinued for over two years (S. Milne, 1992: 568).

Powers over Free Movement of Persons

Subnational island jurisdictions usually have small populations and a small land area. Given that smallness increases the disposition towards all-round volatility (e.g., Dommen, 1980; Easterly and Kraay, 2000), the threats of depopulation or overpopulation loom larger, as do the resulting impacts on labour supply and demand and housing-stock surplus or shortages. Archipelagic island territories must also contend with the additional dynamics of internal migration and urbanization. Acute emigration (and, more infrequently, immigration) are the safety valves readily available in response to all-to-frequent demographic, real estate, or employment imbalances. "Overall, it must simply be concluded that the problems of human resource planning are particularly acute in island micro-states" (Connell, 1988a: 23). Pitcairn Island is the extreme scenario of a territory risking depopulation (Connell, 1988b).

Many islanders from subnational jurisdictions look upon citizenship rights as a double privilege: it is a condition that grants the basis for property ownership and employment on their own island while providing them with a passport for potential emigration and freedom of access to the territory and labour markets of the metropolitan power. The citizens of the United Kingdom's overseas territories have enjoyed free access to that country since 1999 (a right until then extended only to the citizens of the Falkland Islands and Gibraltar); the citizens of Puerto Rico enjoy free access to the United States; and Lisbon granted citizenship rights in Portugal to almost all citizens of Macau before the transfer of that territory to China in 1999. Island autonomies with a special association with New Zealand – Cook Islands, Niue, and Tokelau – had half of their island-born population living in New Zealand by the mid-1980s (Bertram and Watters, 1986). Indeed, "unconstrained migration" to a mother country – typically the former colonial power – is perhaps the key benefit of negotiating self-determination without independence for small island territories (Connell, 1988a: 12). More is said about mobility, in the context of international relations and paradiplomacy, in chapter 7.

Migration policy extends to non-locals too. Concurrently, other island populations have swollen with the influx of foreigners. In the Spanish Balearics, 90 per cent of the population increase in recent years has been due to immigration for the purpose of retirement or employment (CPMR, 2002: 67). Territories like Åland, Bermuda, Jersey, and Malta have adopted immigration policies that favour a stream of limited but wealthy immigrants. Prevention of purchase of property by non-Ålanders in Åland was also a safeguard in Finland's Treaty of Accession to the EU in 1995.

Foreigners in Bermuda are more or less unable to buy land or property, other than houses with an annual *rental* value in excess of US$153,000. Currently, only 312 houses qualify. Some concessions were granted in 2002 to non-Bermudians with over twenty years of continuous residence and who have demonstrated good character and conduct, but only some additional four hundred persons are thus eligible (Low Tax Website, 2008b).

With half the population of Jersey not being born there, one hot political issue deals with housing rights. The Island's Housing Law renders the right to buy and rent property dependent on birth and is therefore intentionally "discriminatory" (Le Rendu, 2004: 60). Neither the European Union nor the United Kingdom have challenged these regulations, appreciating that they allow Jersey the option to maintain measures to limit population (ibid., 73n.33).

In 2002 Malta successfully negotiated a landmark permanent derogation with the European Commission, effectively preventing non-Maltese, non-resident EU citizens from buying property in Malta (*The Economist*, 2004b).

Both Sabah and Sarawak maintained separate control over immigration when they joined the Malaysian Federation in 1963. And had legislation on the management and ownership of customary land in Bougainville been in place, it may have staved off that island's civil war and the suspension of its provincial government from the mid-1990s (Ghai and Regan, 2000).

Meanwhile, there are downsides. Temporary residents (tourists) increase competition for local, scarce resources: many small islands annually receive numbers of visitors which are many times the size of the local population (McElroy, 1998). Temporary or permanent visitor influx acts to raise the price of housing, at times beyond the reach of local islanders, causing in turn commodification of finite space and gentrification, issues that can have serious social, economic, and political implications (Clark, 2005).

Powers over Tourism Policy

The association between small (especially tropical) islands and tourism is one of the best branding exercises in the history of marketing. The island mystique has been a tradition in the West for more than two thousand years, dating back to such ancient Greek epics as the *Odyssey*, repackaged in Western Europe's voyages of discovery, and perpetuated by painters like Paul Gauguin and pioneer anthropologists like Margaret Mead (Baldacchino, 1997: 59; Gillis, 2004). The image of islands as "Eden without apples" lingers on (Pitt, 1970: 1–3; Conlin and Baum, 1995), now exploited also by the media (in movies like *Cast Away* or TV serial blockbusters like *Survivor* and *Lost*), but not without its costs. Islands are among the world's most "penetrated" tourism locations (McElroy, 2003). The construction of large-scale hospitality facilities and infrastructure have filled in salt ponds, disfigured shorelines, and polluted near-shore waters with sewage (Pearce, 1989). Mass tourism may have contributed to the rise of an indigenous middle class and entrepreneurs, but it has also swamped local culture, contributed to domestic inflation, and damaged insular ecosystems, while not necessarily leaving much value-added to the local economy (Beller et al., 1990; Briguglio et al., 1996; Lanfant et al., 1995; World Tourism Organization, 2004, 2005).

McElroy (2003: 241) suggests that non-sovereign island territories may enjoy specific tourism advantages conferred by their political status. These could include geographical proximity to, and ease of travel (no passports, same currency) from, major mother-country origin markets; ready access to investment capital and aid-financed transport and communications infrastructure; and special tax and duty-free concessions. Apart from such advantages conferred via an association with a larger player, small islands – as well as their larger patrons – recognize the advantage of the specific, autonomous branding of their tourism "product." (There is, for example, a St Kitts and Nevis Tourism Board but also a Nevis Tourism Authority.) Moreover, strategic tourism management is often seen to be a pragmatic solution in the face of daunting logistics, while tourism remains a "safe" policy domain that does not threaten the authority of the centre.

Tourism is claimed to be a critical economic activity for most islands, whether measured in terms of income generation, employment creation, or foreign-exchange earnings (e.g., Armstrong et al., 1998: 654; Conlin and Baum, 1995; Royle, 2001: 188–209). Still, judging from the amount of imports that the industry requires (including food, fuel, and furniture), the massive leakages from the domestic island economy (when airlines, car rentals, tour operators, and hotels are not locally owned), and the disposition of tourism to create many low-skill, underpaid jobs which may also be taken up by expatriates, such a claim merits context-specific substantiation. One should not be surprised to find that "tourism" has been grafted onto the MIRAB syndrome as a form of economic dependency for islands which *erodes* (rather than *enhances*) local jurisdiction (e.g., Guthunz and von Krosigk, 1996; Ogden, 1993). A way ahead may lie in small-scale, low-density, comprehensively planned tourism where, ironically, an island's challenging location and relative inaccessibility may prove to be key regulatory assets (e.g., Weaver, 1998; Manning and Dougherty, 1999). Cold-water islands with extreme weather conditions – like the Scandinavian locations of Faroes, Greenland, and Svalbard – may be better models for generating greater local value from the industry. Shared jurisdictional powers to make this happen, while avoiding the slide into mass tourism, would be critical capacities (Baldacchino, 2006f).

DISCUSSION

These five capacities can be seen to form a unified whole, being, like the MIRAB model, the distinct strands of a broad strategy for securing unorthodox economic development: people considerations affecting citizenship, residence, and employment rights (P); resource management (R); overseas engagement and ultra-national recognition (O); finance (FI); and transportation (T).

PROFIT economies therefore differ from their MIRAB neighbours by being more interested in a shrewd immigration and cyclical migration policy; engaging in tough external negotiations concerning the use of local mineral, natural, political, and other imaginative resources; securing and controlling viable means of transportation; and luring foreign direct investment via very

TABLE 4.1: Comparing and contrasting MIRAB and PROFIT economies

MAIN SCOPE	MIRAB ECONOMIES SOURCING SUBSIDIES	PROFIT ECONOMIES ENHANCING DOMESTIC POLITICAL CAPACITY
Migration Flow	Out	In/Out
Remittances	High	Medium/Low/Nil
Aid	High	Low/Nil
Bureaucracy	High	Medium/High
Resource Management	Low/Nil	Medium/High
(Para)Diplomacy	Aid Seeking	High
Financial Management	Low	Medium/High
Transportation Management	Low	Medium/High
Agriculture	High (Cash Crops)	Low/Nil/Niche or Gourmet Products
Manufacturing	Low/Nil	Medium/Niche

low/no tax regimes. They flex their jurisdictional powers to affect international flows of financial and human capital, cargo, and tourism.

Rather than assume that the MIRAB model is the fundamental destiny of small economies, and that any departures from it constitute exceptions or periods of dormancy, we should think of a dynamic continuum with two extreme positions, MIRAB representing one of these extremes, as in Figure 4.1.

To what extent are the MIRAB and PROFIT syndromes similar and different? Can, and if so, how, does one graduate away from one syndrome towards the other? Is tourism one of the devices to escape the MIRAB mould?

In this respect, several points need to be made. First, both the MIRAB and PROFIT models constitute approaches towards managing the hinterland beyond via primarily non-agricultural, non-manufacturing, non-industrialization, non-commodity-production strategies. Both MIRAB and PROFIT economies are as likely to exhibit "bureaucratic dominance" (Watters, 1987: 50), given structural diseconomies of scale. Both are likely to depend substantially on "rent income" which accrues by virtue of identity and location (Bertram and Watters, 1985: 510). But one approach can ride piggyback on the other: in effect, a successful production strategy for small island economies lies in the "marketing of identity" (Fairbairn, 1988: 75; Baldacchino, 1999, 2002a; Baldacchino and Fairbairn, 2006) for what are typically more expensive, craft-based, lower-technology manufactures.

FIGURE 4.1: Relationship between MIRAB and PROFIT economies (schematic view)

MIRAB ⟵————————————————————⟶ PROFIT

Second, the contrast between some features of the two models can be construed as differences of degree rather than kind. When it comes to remittances, migration, or bureaucracy, clearly all contemporary societies are going to have elements of all three at any time; and so the dependence on any of these three sectors for economic purposes becomes a relativistic one.

Third, one key difference between MIRAB and PROFIT lies in the priority given to substantive as against procedural interests. The first – when successful – is an end in itself, the second is a means to a further end. The first relegates the MIRAB territory to a regime of subsidy, of aid with dignity, of consumer-led growth without development, of seeking the responsibility for economic benefits in exogenous, extraterritorial policy fora. The second – when successful – is a jurisdictional or constitutional tool, an endogenous instrument for public policy which local "governing wits" (Warrington, 1998: 105) can usually transform into economic prosperity. Attitude matters.

Fourth, it is possible for features of the MIRAB and PROFIT economies to co-exist. Indeed, at any point in time, most economies are likely to exhibit elements of both dispositions, especially if they both prove to be responses to windows of opportunity. Where choices are and can be made between one strategy and another, then, just like other economic decisions, the disposition to seek one road to largesse rather than another would depend largely on opportunity costs, track records of success, lower perceived effort, lower perceived risk, or higher perceived gain, just like any standard utility-curve transaction.

Fifth, it is practical to assume that, at a number of points, an economy may undergo a lurch from a MIRAB towards a PROFIT orientation, or vice versa. The collapse of civil law and governance structures in the Solomon Islands, the exhaustion of the phosphate mines and the mismanagement of their previous accumulated revenue in Nauru, the landfall of a hurricane or any other major environmental disaster – such occasions are likely to nudge small economies, steadily or suddenly, along the MIRAB path, for better or for worse, for a temporary period or an interminably long one. The opposite lurch is also likely. Watters (1987: 33) is self-critical enough to identify what he calls "exceptions" to the MIRAB pattern among the five prototype island economies which were documented in the pioneering 1985 article: the temporary citrus boom and the stimulus of a state-promoted cannery in the Cook Islands; and the high-level export of phosphates until their exhaustion in 1979 in Kiribati. Meanwhile, at a time when pearl farming in French Polynesia appeared to be reducing dependence on "geo-strategic rents" and shifting its economy towards a PROFIT direction (Poirine, 1998: 97), aid per capita fell by more than 50 per cent in real terms between 1992 and 1997 (ibid.). In spite of powerful vested interests from ingrained politico-economic elites, one *can* contemplate a "post-MIRAB economy" (Treadgold, 1999: 236), as also suggested for Guam and Hawaii (Poirine, 1998).

Sixth, one needs to appraise the impact of tourism on both MIRAB and PROFIT economies. Tourism comes with "genuine comparative advantages" for island territories (Connell, 1991: 265). M.L. Treadgold (1999) has argued that tourism has helped to break Norfolk Island, an SNIJ and previously classic MIRAB case, out of this structural mould. Tourism has now "erased" Norfolk Island's MIRAB characteristics or rendered them insignificant, it is claimed. However, tourism is in itself a rent-accruing activity bearing its own "geo-strategic" (that is sun, sea, salt, sand – and sex?) services, which hardly vest jurisdictional muscle in the provider; the industry remains fickle and vulnerable, mainly to economic uncertainty and both local and regional political instability; it is also a largely private-sector activity lying outside "managed" external-relationships syndromes. Or is it? Perhaps tourism can be seen as part of a "hinterland management" system if it is driven by special concessions from metropolitan powers or else benefits handsomely from tourists from the same metropolitan sites.[1] Small-island tourism economies (SITEs) were originally proposed as a new and distinct, small-island development syndrome altogether (McElroy, 2006), and more recently as a subspecies of the PROFIT syndrome (Oberst and McElroy, 2007; Parry and McElroy, 2009).

Seventh and lastly, it would be useful to find quantitative indicators that correspond to the PROFIT syndrome, much like the visually evocative analysis of the "jaws effect" (imports outpacing exports; expenditure outpacing revenue) (Bertram and Watters, 1985: 510) for the MIRAB model. Perhaps, as with the pioneering research of Bertram and Watters in the 1980s, one needs to identify a clutch of economies – some sovereign states, some subnational jurisdictions – and soberly analyse their economic statistics, migratory patterns, and public-sector financial health, with the goal of distilling some comparative patterns. Likely candidates for this exercise would include

Åland, Aruba, Bermuda, Barbados, Cyprus, Iceland (in spite of recent economic mishaps[2]), Malta, Mauritius, and the Seychelles.

CONCLUSION: MERODIA

The archipelago of Merodia, population 200,000, is a region of the republic of Lagado, a member state of the enlarged European Union (CPMR, 2002)

It would only be an act of historical continuity to resort to imaginary islands for didactic purposes. Jonathan Swift created Lilliput to satirize British high society; Daniel Defoe invented Robinson Crusoe and his island to present an account of the development of capitalism (Hymer, 1971); Jules Verne's *Mysterious Island* demonstrates humankind's superiority over nature in the epoch of industrialism (Loxley, 1990); the island in Shakespeare's *The Tempest* is the setting for a critique of ethnicity and colonialism (Brinklow et al., 2001).

The smaller the territory and the smaller the resident population, the more likely is it for that territory and that population to rely on external inputs for sheer survival. The fictitious Merodia is one attempt, by the Conference of Peripheral Maritime Regions (CPMR), at mulling and moralizing over the role of external support for island development. It seeks to demonstrate how a "European islands policy combining understanding, flexibility and solidarity with regard to these [island] regions leads to their full integration within the [European] Union" (CPMR, 2002: 129). Furthermore, the implications of such a policy would "affect Europe as a whole" (ibid.). Merodia becomes the contemporary experiment – and whether the outcome is a utopia or dystopia is seen to depend ever so much on "managing the hinterland." The "permanent and pervasive realities" of islands call for differential treatment, argues the CPMR (2002). The MIRAB syndrome, as much a series of economic transactions as an "in-its-own-way" sustainable cultural lifestyle, is certainly one response towards the recognition of this special handling.

And so there are other responses beyond MIRAB. Size of land area, population levels, regional location, or political status do not appear to pre-empt the consideration of non-MIRAB options, and allow for even messier "mix and match" approaches. That is why the MIRAB model, the PROFIT model, or any other model for that matter is best seen as an abstract, ideal type: seductively elegant in its conceptual simplicity but not present in its pure form anywhere in the real world (Weber, 1949: 89–95).

Economists A. Alesina and E. Spolaore (2003) have convincingly argued that smaller jurisdictions are likely to prosper when trade is liberalized and markets are open. Free trade is likely to reduce the costs of secession and independence. True; but smaller countries are likely to prosper *even more* when the rules of the game are skewed in their favour. The key point to make here is that the strength of many small, often island economies often do not correlate with geographic distance to markets: they are not necessarily better off by being physically closer to the metropole. A better indicator of economic strength is the extent of that island economy's current *political* integration with a typically larger, more affluent, state (even if the latter is far removed geographically) (Bertram, 2006; Bertram and Karagedikli, 2006). In the case of sovereign island states, this is likely to be the former colonial power; in the case of non-sovereign jurisdictions, this *patron* is a federal government or a current colonial power (though this latter term is now no longer politically correct). T. Sorensen (2006: 2352) concludes that "paradoxically, there is a positive relationship between the strength of colonial embrace and economic well-being." Should he follow the arguments presented in this chapter, and appreciate the crucial role of the hinterland in securing and tapping revenue and opportunity for island jurisdictions, then he may just realize that there is nothing paradoxical about this rapport.

The volume edited by H.M. Hintjens and M.D. Newitt (1992) and the more recent chapter contribution by G. Bertram and B. Poirine (2007) sum it up nicely: there can be no such thing as island economics, especially for the smaller islands; there is only an island political economy.

5

Patterns of Creative Governance for Development

Linked to self-determination, [autonomy] achieves that without the disruption or break up of sovereignty. It defuses political conflict by providing alternative sites of power and patronage. It helps to accommodate sub-national identities, within a national identity, providing a basis for protection of regional cultures and languages. It can lay the foundations for a more pluralistic and democratic order, the development of regional political parties, and a new set of checks and balances. It provides a framework for inter-ethnic bargaining and so converts conflicts into disputes that are susceptible to formal processes. In some ways, it gives political weight to a community which it would not otherwise enjoy... Autonomy is both a way to recognize diversity and to involve all groups in the central state mechanism ... it is an extremely flexible instrument, capable of responding to different configurations of ethnic relations.

Y.P. Ghai, 2002: 44–5

Sovereignty rules can be violated in inventive ways.

S.D. Krasner, 2001c: 20

INTRODUCTION

The "development" agenda of smaller island states continues to be gripped by a paradigm of vulnerability, though a recognition of resilience now seems to be sneaking in (e.g., Briguglio and Cordina, 2004; Briguglio and Kisanga, 2004). Such disarming discourse vindicates the concerns of many observers and scholars about the presumed non-viability of smaller island polities and economies, expressed both before and after the wave of smaller state sovereignty took off in the 1960s (Cyprus –1960; Samoa – 1962; Malta –1964; Maldives – 1965), also propelled by the collapse of the West Indies Federation (starting with the independence of Jamaica in 1962). Independence for the smaller island territory was deemed extravagant or dangerous (Wainhouse, 1966; Guillebaud, 1976; Plischke, 1977; Commonwealth Consultative Group, 1985; Diggines, 1985; Harden, 1985) and, more recently, even a recipe for a "failed state" (Kabutaulaka, 2004) or a "security threat" (OAS, 2002). An "aid with dignity" scenario (Connell, 1988a) has gained ascendancy in the literature, perhaps best represented by the MIRAB acronym – standing for a reactive, sluggish economy totally dependent on four sources of in/direct income: migration, which fuels remittances; and aid, which maintains a relatively large bureaucracy (Bertram and Watters, 1985; Bertram, 2006). This condition has been reviewed in chapter 4.

Meanwhile, key players in (usually large) federal states debate nervously why and to what extent obvious differences (or asymmetry) in the size, geography, economic wealth, cultural fabric, or population of their constituent units (regions, states, provinces) should or should not be translated into asymmetric power, in practice or at law (for the smallest federal jurisdictions, see Anckar, 2003; for Canada, see below). Treating the constituent members of the same state differently is often heralded as a recipe for disaster: an incentive for spiralling devolution, fuelling secession, catalyzing the eventual implosion of the state. Is this not the main explanation behind the heavy-handed measures of states which see themselves thus threatened, like Indonesia, Russia, or Spain today (and explaining their refusal to recognize Kosovo as a sovereign state?) or the United States in the early 1860s (e.g., Anderson, 2004: 101–4)? In any case, resorts to "autonomy," often by smaller communities, were looked upon as "anomalous, annoying or even amusing exceptions" to the sovereignty rule (Stevens, 1977: 178).

There is, however, a different story to tell, although it has not been as well publicized as the previous two. However wealth is defined, a number of smaller island territories score exceptionally well (Armstrong et al., 1998: 644; Easterly and Kraay, 2000: 2015; Armstrong and Read, 2002). Moreover, most such territories partake of some form of stable *asymmetrical federalism* (Stevens, 1977) with(in) a typically larger state. Is the (unexpectedly above average) economic performance of such territories related to their jurisdictional status?

PROPOSITION

This chapter suggests that "autonomies" need to be recognized as viable politico-economic units in their own right, rather than insignificant relics from a bygone age or messy examples of territories whose transition to sovereignty is taking longer than most. An autonomy should not, in most cases, be seen naively as a case "in transit" towards full sovereignty.

Autonomy (that is, the *concept*) can be used to refer to independence of action on the internal or domestic level; in legal-political language, it denotes self-government (e.g., Dinstein, 1981: 291; Heintze, 1998: 8). However, this "independence" is always beholden to some political link. And so an autonomy (in this case, the *jurisdiction*) would, for example, have its own local police force for the supervision of internal security and public order (Hannum and Lillich, 1980: 860); but there would tend to be decisions on international status and political unity that are excluded from an autonomy's remit, often foreign relations, defence, and currency matters. Still, the power to conclude international agreements concerning cultural or economic matters may reside with the autonomous entity. Interestingly, the right to self-determination (or self-government) of peoples, while enshrined in the United Nations Charter of 1945, does *not* imply the right of secession (UN, 1945: 296).

A comparative "island studies" approach would identify close to 110 subnational – and autonomous – island jurisdictions in the world today which have a permanent civilian population, most (if not all de facto) existing in conditions of asymmetric federalism and varying in population size from Taiwan (22 million) and Puerto Rico (3.7 million) to miniscule Pitcairn, which, in spite of its 47 citizens, has protested against external interference in widely reported child-sex abuse trials (e.g., Middleton, 2005). Such an experience of asymmetry can go back many years, to 1204 in the case of Jersey (Everard and Holt, 2004). These autonomies may benefit by sharing knowledge, lessons, and insights concerning strategies for both international economic competitiveness and dyadic political stability, emerging from what appears to be an idiosyncratic political economy. Perhaps more important for a wider audience, extant "mainland-island relations" can serve as lessons and provide insights into larger and other smaller players, beyond the strictures of both vulnerability and sovereignty. The complex political and economic dynamics of "subnationalism" make increasing sense in a world where levels of governance are expanding both above (e.g., supranational) and below (e.g., municipal) the level of the sovereign state. It may be timely for autonomies to be recognized, or to recognize themselves, as possibly significant models in an international system struggling with integrating economies and splitting polities (Drucker, 1986).

Meanwhile, as D.L. Horowitz (1985: 619) notes: "Federalism, or at least some devolution, has conflict-reducing possibilities for many more countries than have so far contemplated it." Indeed, frustration over restricted powers can stimulate the desire for independence (Thorndike, 1989). By sanctioning the action by a shared government for certain common purposes, together with the autonomous action by its constituent units for purposes that relate to maintaining their distinctiveness, federalism is often touted as a formula for stability in large sprawling countries with diverse populations and/or ethnic or national diversity (e.g., Watts, 1999). Studies of federalist arrangements among smaller island states and territories are few and far between (Anckar, 2003). Having said that, however, federalism is generally seen as an improved form of territorial group protection, irrespective of size or scale, since the components are units that have their own local legislature, government, and judiciary. Y. Dinstein (1993: 235) suggests that, in a federal arrangement, "the constituent states [or provinces] are equal or at least balanced in their influence." But one can have arrangements whereby some of the constituent units within a federal system have more extensive powers than others relative to the central government (Brown, 2005; Stevens, 1977). A. Stepan (1999: 31; emphasis in original) observes that, with the possible exception of Switzerland, *all* federations that are constitutionally symmetrical – Argentina, Australia, Austria, Brazil, Germany, and the United States – are "mono-national": that is, each full member (canton, state, autonomous region, province, or Lander) of the federation has exactly the same constitutionally embedded obligations and rights. In contrast, Belgium, Canada, India, and Spain are "multi-national" and all their federations are asymmetrical. More than forty years ago, C.D. Tarlton noted that cultural, economic, social, and political factors in combination in all federations have produced asymmetrical variations in power and influence of different elemental units (Tarlton, 1965; Watts, 2005).

ASYMMETRIC FEDERALISM: A CANADIAN TALE

> I guess it is referred to as asymmetrical federalism, where you try to evolve a system, where you give a bit more power to Québec to satisfy its needs, but you do not give all those same powers to the other provinces because then you dilute, in a very significant way, the central government authority.
>
> Manitoba Legislative Task Force on Canadian Unity, 1997

> Prime Minister Paul Martin struggled yesterday to dampen internal party dissent as more senior Liberals accused him of opening a "constitutional Pandora's box" with his new policy of asymmetrical federalism.
>
> R. Fife, 2004

Asymmetrical federalism is often seen and discussed in Canada as a device for meeting the specificity and aspirations of the singular province of Quebec for control over its cultural and social life without removing it from the Canadian federation, where it coexists with nine, largely (so far) English-speaking, provinces which have more in common culturally and socially. The Canadian constitution does not formally recognize such a system, yet arrangements over the past several decades have introduced asymmetrical federalism piecemeal. Quebec today has extensive authority over immigration, health care, pension plans, and use of employment-insurance funds for parental-leave provision within its borders, matters that are largely or totally handled by the federal government in/for all the other provinces.

Most Canadians saw a series of events that took place following Christmas 2004 as nothing short of extraordinary. They witnessed what they interpreted as a unique unfolding of asymmetrical federalism for the most anglophone Canadian province of all, Newfoundland and Labrador (NL), which the 2006 census reports as the province with the largest proportion of residents who claim the English language as their mother tongue: 98 per cent (Statistics Canada, 2006, slide 17). A showdown between then Canadian Prime Minister Paul Martin and NL Premier Danny Williams signalled a readiness to consider tactics and manoeuvres that had been thought to be confined to Quebec. Moreover, the outcome has shown that, on the one hand, in exploiting political-historical circumstances present at the time, such tactics can be successful in achieving subnational goals, with debatable consequences for the Canadian polity. On the other hand, unless legalized or somehow codified, a new government in Ottawa can rescind on the commitment of its predecessor.

High Drama, on and off the Flag Pole

> The fundamental basis for federalism in Canada ... was and
> remains the need to reconcile, balance, and accommodate diversity.
>
> R. Simeon, 2002

On 14 February 2005 the government of Canada guaranteed that NL would keep 100 per cent of its offshore oil and gas revenue, and this without endangering its equalization payments. The event followed in the wake of a walkout by Premier Williams from negotiations over the distribution of offshore oil and gas revenue, and a dramatic Christmas and New Year, during which the feisty premier ordered the Canadian flag pulled down from all government buildings in the province. During those eighteen tense days, the province appeared to be seriously contemplating secession from the Canadian federation (Dunn, 2005).

The "flag flap" exposed many sore points in Canadian federal-provincial relations. Many Canadians were not amused by the grandstanding and much less with the outcome of the deal: they were quick to decry the agreement as foul and unfair. Having the cake and eating it too was just not right. In contrast, for Newfoundlanders and Labradoreans, the showdown reignited their sense of pride and dignity as a people who had a right to manage effectively their offshore resources (do a better job with them than the federal government) and cash in on the benefits. For their premier, Danny Williams, it meant a strong and welcome surge in popular local support. Anger and disgust over a newspaper column by Margaret Wente in the *Globe and Mail*, which downplayed the Newfoundland case with deliberate condescension and paternalism (Wente, 2005), was widespread in the province. Premier Williams's brazen leadership style, tested in this showdown, won him a landslide victory in the provincial elections of October 2007.

One could go to extreme lengths in order to portray the deal as a unique achievement; however, it is also one of various examples of an underlying reality in Canadian politics. A large country with enormous imbalances – in such areas as geography, resource wealth, population, employment opportunities, religious affiliation, and national sentiment – has been carved into a federal mould to respect this diversity, while maintaining a modicum of stability and cohesion.

For this reason, it is pertinent to place the "Martin-Williams" showdown of early 2005 in a wider critical context. In Canada, provinces, territories, and municipalities – as well as First Nations, cities, and universities – are all engaged in decision making, often within interlocking and overlapping policy regimes. Moreover, all over the world, subnational, often island, or mainly island, jurisdictions – like Newfoundland and Labrador – are key actors in this contemporary game of intersecting governance, recognizing their jurisdiction as an economic resource. They often seek to exploit the economic opportunities offered by their jurisdictional capacity in such sectors as tourism, financial services, or industrial promotion, while maintaining an umbilical cord to a much larger, and richer, state and/or regional power which (at times begrudgingly) comes in to cover the costs of social services, inject heavy capital investments, or stave off economic downturns. Their small size, strong political organization, and shrewd "glocal" positioning typically serves them well; nor is this necessarily a "zero sum game" (Ordeschook, 1986; Ordeschook and Shvetsova, 1997: 29; von Neumann and Morgenstern, 1953).

Within a federal political system, some extent of self-rule is granted to subnational levels. This allocation of jurisdiction can defuse political conflict by providing alternative sites of power and patronage. It can help to accommodate subnational identities *within* an overarching identity as a country. It can provide a basis for protecting regional cultures and languages. It can give political weight to a community which it would not otherwise enjoy (Ghai, 2002: 44–5). Federal politics is largely framed by carefully worded constitutions that declare what powers are held by whom, but it is then consumed by negotiations between the national core and the subnational periphery as to how to interpret the fine print – and how to balance, usurp, or renege on the rest.

However, with multiple peripheries negotiating with the centre, as is the case in Canada, one would assume that the logical route to take is that of equal treatment. Whether one is dealing with fiscal transfers, executive powers, tax measures, citizenship rights, or level of public services, arguably, the safest and fairest approach is an even and impartial division. But how can one treat Prince Edward Island equally to Ontario? How can one treat a province like a territory? How can one reconcile the unique demands of the *nation Québecois,* and those of various aboriginal peoples, for more self-governance and/or resource control?

For the sake of the maintenance of the central Canadian state (how else to protect effectively against the unilateralism of the United States?), it appears that any idiosyncratic powers held by the provinces, Quebec, and First Nations must be curtailed. Otherwise, in order to assuage demands for subnational and provincial autonomy, then it is the federal cast which holds the country together that would be dangerously weakened. The situation has the hallmarks of a "catch 22." Yet only by foregoing the basic principle of equal treatment can the Canadian polity accommodate different forms of partnership simultaneously. An "imperial temptation" (Laforest, 1998) by the central government, a priority for advancing, country-wide, basic human rights and freedoms (as during the Trudeau era), the myth of a uni-national Canada (Kymlicka, 1998) – such and similar initiatives may have stymied this centripetal development. The situation now appears to have changed, and it continues to unfold following the election of the minority Conservative governments of Stephen Harper. Opportunities for a resort to de facto, asymmetric federalism in policy making continue to present themselves in the guise of pragmatic provincial governments willing to risk "cutting their own deals" with Ottawa, fiscal flexibility, and a need to expand into north-south relations that reflect commercial transactions (RSC, 2005).

Meanwhile, Quebec – now recognized by Parliament as "a nation within a united Canada" (Thompson, 2006) – has been granted formal representative rights in UNESCO, an international organization: a measure of diplomacy and international relations typically reserved, even in federal countries, to their central government (PMO, 2006; also Gwyn, 2005).

Canadians may be angry, worried, and confused; one doubts whether there are (as yet) any clear ideas of what is being spawned in the medium to long term. The extent to which asymmetry is politically acceptable and legally and administratively legitimate is also driven by political values, and yet no broad consensus on such values appears to exist in Canada (RSC, 2005). Moreover, the Martin-Williams deal, like a similar one brokered at the same time with Nova Scotia, was not reached as part of a broader national program, and its ad hoc nature smacks of political opportunism; the Conservative governments in Ottawa since 2006 have appeared inclined to reopen "the deal" and, according to NL Premier Danny Williams, have "reneged shamelessly on their commitment" (Government of Newfoundland and Labrador, 2007). In any case, the outcome may hold new challenges for devolution and innovative governance, both in/by provinces (Alberta?) and in/by smaller and remote rural regions.

A Case for Difference

First of all, to some extent, the provinces *have* been, and expected to be, treated differently all along. Asymmetry has been the name of the game with respect to a raft of "jurisdictional powers and duties, the shape of central institutions, or the application of national laws or programs" (Milne, 2005). Specific provinces (mainly, but not only, Quebec) have secured, or been given, specific arrangements – whether enshrined in the 1867 Canadian constitution – as in the cases of: 1) denominational education, the qualification of judges, and language (for Quebec) as well as the unequal representation of the provinces in the Senate; 2) provincial acts of union, as in the commitment to a steamship and telegraph service to Prince Edward Island; 3) recognition of provincial control over natural resources in Alberta, Saskatchewan, and Manitoba since 1930; regional development (such as the Atlantic Canada Opportunities Agency, only for Atlantic Canada) as well as foreign policy (the provinces of New Brunswick and Quebec being represented in La Francophonie); and 4) de facto program implementation, as in immigration, child care, tax collection, student-loan plans, health care, and many other policies pursued by the province of Quebec (Milne, 2005; Hogg, 1977). Yet de facto provisions, not codified in constitution or legislation, can be rescinded: it had been common practice to appoint at least one minister from Prince Edward Island in each federal cabinet. This was no longer so under the Harper government of 2006–08: perhaps the Island was made to suffer the consequences of having been the only province not to send a single Conservative MP to Ottawa in the 2006 federal election.

Second, a totally different driver of asymmetrical autonomy arrangements relates to the defence of minority rights and the promotion of minority identity. This driver has found its most obvious expression in Canada with regard to the rights of indigenous peoples. Land rights, revenue-sharing arrangements from land-based resources, and other forms of autonomy with First Nations have been negotiated in recent years, others are in the offing, and others still are being contested. Indigenous governance practices, including the resort to consensus, non-party politics, communal decision making, and a totally different relationship with air, sea, and land, are instructive procedures.

Third, note the particular struggles of the (in retrospect, short-lived) Martin Liberal minority government to secure its own political survival and eventual re-election on a stronger footing, as it hung on by the smallest of margins in a budget confidence vote while sitting on the largest and continuous series of budget surpluses in Canadian history and with "peak oil" heralding deep federal pockets for years to come. This fortuitous combination of circumstances created an unparalleled historic opportunity for the provinces to demand their share of the additional national wealth: each in ways that satisfy particular interests, with no attempt at interprovincial harmonization and with a strong likelihood that each would actually get most of what it asked for ... if only it acted fast enough. Newfoundland and Labrador's Atlantic Accord of February 2005 is one such result. Nova Scotia secured its own, similar deal concurrently. Ontario was pledged a refund of $5.75 billion over five years in May 2005. Prince Edward Island and New Brunswick sought to follow suit with their own $100-million deals apiece (Thibodeau, 2005), but these deals were not secured prior to the demise of the Martin government in January 2006.

There is yet a fourth, and more compelling, move that does not respond to the constitutionally established centres of executive power. Recent years have seen a major interest in *cities* as new jurisdictions. We have at hand an "urban asymmetry," one that creates cleavages through the historical fabric of the Canadian federation. This term means that the federal government has actively flirted with pursuing direct relationships with the larger urban centres and agglomerations of the country, and also with other players like universities and other special-purpose bodies (e.g., the Canada Research Chairs program: www.chairs.gc.ca). It is premised on two key rationales.

The first basis for this new relationship is *needs*. Canada, the world's second-largest country by land area, is the world's most urbanized state. While the population density averaged out over the whole country was a meagre 3.3 persons per km^2 in census year 2001, 79.4 per cent of its population lived in communities of more than 1,000 persons *and* with a population density of more than 400 persons per km^2 at the same time (Beckstead and Brown, 2005). A further 19.4 per cent lived within commuting distance of an urban area with a population of at least 10,000 residents: the so-called *urban shadow* (Polèse and Shearmur, 2002). Moreover, the pattern is set to continue: 74 per cent of the country's recent immigrants – who number around 250,000 annually and now represent the major form of population increase nationwide – settle in Toronto (46 per cent), Vancouver (15 per cent), or Montreal (13 per cent) (*The Guardian*, 2003).

The second rationale is *economic potential*. The transformation of the world into a series of "prosperous city regions" (Ohmae, 2000: 33), with the remainder doomed to poverty and political marginality, is gripping policy makers. Cities are thus the only viable route to economic prosperity. They are the dynamic export and innovation platforms of the new knowledge economy. They may lack formal constitutions, but only they have the critical mass of people, educational institutions, markets, talent, and finance to undertake research, compete, and create value. "As go our GCRs" [global city regions], argues Tom Courchene, "so goes Canada" (Courchene, 2005: 31; Dunn, 2004).

Cities had successfully convinced the Martin Liberal government that they cannot simply remain creatures of provinces: they can and will manage their affairs better and more economically if they are recognized as legitimate actors in the constellation of federal governance, and legitimate recipients of federal funds, bypassing the provinces (e.g., Plunkett, 2004). Theirs is a strong case for implementing subsidiarity. While provincial concerns persevere in support of rural settlements, and their challenges of employment, service provision, and population growth, many federal pundits have been extolling the virtues of urbanization. They are advising that, unless cities are granted more fiscal autonomy and stability, the basis of Canada's prosperity (read: "urban" prosperity) will be eroded (e.g., Slack and Bird, 2007). And so Canadians are now witnessing "a new inter-governmental relations nested in an increasingly complex set of sub-provincial [and *ultra*-provincial] partnerships" (Dunn, 2004: 42).

Currently, asymmetrical federalism is even more *de rigueur*, even if its introduction is piecemeal and driven by pragmatist considerations. This is a very different climate from what obtained nationally some twenty years ago, when the Charter of Rights and Freedoms enshrined a language of common and equal rights (Constitution Act, 1982).

AUTONOMY WITHOUT SOVEREIGNTY

To add more grist to the mill, there are various successful examples of asymmetrical federalism beyond Canada, where subnational units enjoy some level of autonomy as well as privileges or powers that other subnational units within the same state do not necessarily share. The very large majority of these units are islands, on islands, or mainly islands.[1]

These island autonomies, in spite of their obvious diversity and geographical spread, are largely characterized by one, or more, various "special" endowments: 1) they are non-sovereign states with, however, strong levels of internal autonomy, whether de jure, de facto, or both; 2) they are *sub*national, meaning that they continue to be associated with a usually much larger, sovereign state – in some cases, this would be their former colonial master; 3) they are sub*national*, meaning that they have a distinct society and culture, and are often recognized as constituent "nations" within the larger state; 4) they are islands, physically cut off from mainlands and often geographically remote from their metropolitan powers, which therefore presents pragmatic cases for administrative autonomy; 5) the bulk of their citizenry supports local politicians who are neither integrationist nor sovereigntist but who delicately and carefully exploit "the best of all possible worlds" (Everard and Holt, 2004: 188), using their jurisdiction as a key economic and political resource; and 6) they either escape regulation or customize it in order to suit *their* interests – or else have it thus crafted so as to suit the interests of the metropole – whether it is tax policy, language policy, citizenship rights, or transportation costs.

The usage of the word *autonomy* continues to challenge the current, post-Westphalia (1648), dominant configuration of politics as being strictly state-centred. The modern nation-state – as an assemblage of public bodies asserting exclusive authority over a territorially defined space and its citizens – gradually proliferated over three and a half centuries as the legitimate manifestation of collective human organization (e.g., Picciotto, 1997: 13), a political structure that has also been exported globally through imperialism. Divergent factions and regional power blocks *within* states were discouraged, but not necessarily obliterated or accommodated, as politics became central-ized. However, and especially in the wake of decolonization, the territoriality over which governance has been assigned and since exercised has not always corresponded neatly to "the nation": meaning the people who see them-selves as rightfully and naturally co-governed citizens. As a result of the disequilibrium between statehood and nation, there are "nations in waiting," "proto-nations," or "nations without states" (Bahcheli et al., 2004; Eriksen, 1993: 14; Gottlieb, 1994), which, according to P.P. Streeten, have included "Kurds, Basques, Armenians, Palestinians, Québécois, Cree Indians, Scots, Welsh, Cornish, Croats, and many others, but ... not Gozitans" (Streeten, 1994: 201).

These "nations" have been given increasing recognition, mainly via federalist arrangements (Watts, 1999: 6–7), with governments endors-ing devolutionary or "power-sharing" strategies, as in Papua New Guinea with respect to Bougainville (2002) or in Indonesia with respect to Aceh (2005), and/or via strengthened regional policy (as in the European Union or the Nordic Council). Some candidates on the Streeten list above have since secured full political independence (Armenia, Croatia), been granted forms of substate self-determination with democratically elected assemblies (Scotland, Wales), or, as I write, appear heading long-term in that direc-tion (Kurdistan) (*The Economist*, 2005b). In the other cases, including Gozo (Bezzina, 2005), as with many other cases (see especially chapter 6), the search for a more appropriate form of self-determination via negotiation goes on. Autonomy need not, however, be sought or granted simply to assuage nationalist sentiments. In fact, more often – in the case of smaller islands distant from their metropolitan heartlands – it could simply have been a his-torically pragmatic response to often formidable logistic and administrative challenges (Baldacchino, 2004a: 80).

Various scholars insist that an empirical justification for the effects of "islandness" is either absent, insignificant, ambivalent, or otherwise difficult to test for, especially given severe data constraints (e.g., Armstrong et al., 1998: 654; Armstrong and Read, 2002: 451; Easterly and Kraay, 2000: 2025n.5; Liou and Ding, 2002). However, the focus on *island* subnational jurisdictions in this chapter is deliberate. Islands represent quintessential platforms for nation-states, since "as a 'limited' sphere, a discrete bounded space that is at once knowable and, because of its consolidated form, readily defensible, the island functioned ... as an ideal embodiment of the state's relationship to the nation" (Peckham, 2003: 503).

The finite island geography smoothens the nurturing of a sense of identity that is contiguous with territory (Anckar, 2005; Baldacchino, 2005; Srebrnik, 2004).

JUST FOURTEEN DIVIDED ISLANDS

As if to prove this empirically, of the world's thousands of populated island territories, *only fourteen* are shared (de facto or de jure) by more than one national jurisdiction, and in some of these cases the sharing has not happened without resistance by those who would see them eventually under unitary control. Two are Borneo (shared between Malaysia, Indonesia, and Brunei Darussalam) and Cyprus (the messiest example by far, shared between the Republic of Cyprus, the de facto Turkish Republic of Northern Cyprus [TRNC], and the United Kingdom via its Sovereign Base Areas [SBAs] of Akrotiri and Dhekelia; note also that the Greek Cypriot villages of Xylotymbou and Ormidhia, also in the Republic of Cyprus, are enclaves surrounded by the Dhekelia SBA. One may wish to add the buffer zone administered by the United Nations to complicate matters further). These two are currently the only islands in the world whose jurisdiction is carved up between (at least?) *three* countries.

Then there are the twelve jurisdictions divided between two countries. These are (Royle, 2001: 150–1; *The Economist*, 2008d): Hispaniola (Haiti-Dominican Republic); Ireland (Republic of Ireland-Northern Ireland); New Guinea (West Papua Province of Indonesia–Papua New Guinea); Sebatik (Indonesia-Malaysia); Saint Martin-Sint Maarten (France-Netherlands); Tierra del Fuego (Argentina-Chile), Timor (Indonesia-East Timor); Usedom-Uznam (Germany-Poland); Svalbard (belonging to Norway but with an autonomous Russian settlement); Bolshoi Ussuriysky on the Sino-Russian border, as of 2008; Cuba (given the effective control by the United States of Guantánamo Bay); and Mindanao, where the Autonomous Region in Muslim Mindanao has existed since 1989 (e.g., Bacani, 2005).

Various other, previously divided, islands have also since been unified: examples include Corsica, Newfoundland, Sakhalin; Sri Lanka (following the demise of Tamil Eelam; and, of course, Britain (until the Act of Union of England and Scotland in 1707, though that may change in the near future should Scotland become independent). Moreover, islandness reduces the likelihood of enclaves or exclaves that interfere with territorial demarcation in contested non-island scenarios: Abkhazia, Brussels, East Jerusalem, Euskadi,

Gagauzia, Kaliningrad, Kashmir, Kirkuk, South Ossetia, and Trans(d)niestria come to mind (Bahcheli et al., 2004).

A focus on subnational island autonomies seems especially appropriate since they are spread across all oceanic basins; are diverse is size, climate, topography, and environmental values; and showcase a wide repertoire of economic structure and jurisdictional discretion. The overwhelming majority of contemporary subnational jurisdictions are archipelagos, single islands, or parts of islands anyway. An extension of this "island" analysis to include non-island, subnational jurisdictions would, in any case, be a promising research pursuit.

CREATIVE ECONOMIC CAPACITIES

The a priori claim that islandness is, in principle, negatively correlated to economic development, "since islands suffer additional disadvantages associated with remoteness/isolation in addition to that of small size" (Armstrong and Read, 2002: 447), has been contested of late. Current scholarship appears now more inclined towards treating aspects of topography beyond islandness (such as being mountainous and/or landlocked) as more serious obstacles to development (e.g., Armstrong and Read, 2005). Moreover, most of the current empirical economic literature agrees that subnational dependencies tend to enjoy higher living standards than independent states (Betermier, 2004: 63–4; Armstrong and Read, 2000: 303). Using 1998 GNP data for 108 territories (of which 75 are archipelagos, islands, or on islands), Armstrong and Read (2003) infer the *negative* impact of sovereignty on per capita income. Using a Pacific data set and ordinary least squares regression, G. Bertram and O. Karagedikli (2004) report subnational jurisdictions enjoying per capita incomes – at purchasing power parity (PPP) – *ten times greater* than those of newly independent small states, and without evidence of any regional convergence. Bertram (2004: 353) also concludes that, in the Pacific, "independence did not pay as well as continued political dependence." Similar conclusions are presented from a Pacific and Caribbean data set (McElroy and Sanborn, 2005). The above is consistent with B. Poirine (1999) and his analysis of how metropolitan powers maintain aid flows in exchange for "strategic services," a relationship that is harder to break in non-sovereign territories.

CREATIVE POLITICAL CAPACITIES

Chapter 4 looked critically at five key economic policy areas for subnational island jurisdictions: finance, environment, transportation, migration, and tourism. While acknowledging the very real difficulty of a plausible, even if conceptual, separation, this chapter looks in turn at the four critical political capacities deployed by, and for, island enclaves. To be sure, the set of political capacities associated with such a condition of subsovereign jurisdiction is, just like its economic corollary, often particular to each case: fair treatment would require a critical understanding of specific political, historical, cultural, and constitutional issues. However, a roughly common pattern suggests itself from the literature, based on four distinct though interrelated conditions.

Jurisdictional Clout

One explanation for the lack of a drive for independence is the existence of an ample dose of existing jurisdictional prerogative. Many small islands, *because* they are islands, naturally enjoy some degree of administrative autonomy. (This same feature supported the transition of some two dozen small islands or archipelagos to sovereign statehood, starting with Iceland, in the period 1944–84.) There is a manifest logistical tendency of an island to be self-administered, especially if distant from its metropolitan power (Peckham, 2003: 503). Furthermore, because they are also small and somewhat isolated, and irrespective of independence, such island jurisdictions usually manage to extract some special advantages, or power niches, from their respective metropole. Those that have refrained from sovereignty typically, whether de facto or de jure, enjoy more discretionary powers than any similarly sized or even larger blocs of the "mainland" (Poirine, 1998). Their current status has been described as "the best of all possible worlds" (e.g., Everard and Holt, 2004: 188). These island jurisdictions deploy many of the benefits associated with political sovereignty while they are delegating responsibilities to, enjoying the security provided by, and reaping the material benefits of remaining in association with, a larger, and typically richer, *patron*.

One example of island territories clinching "jurisdiction by stealth" is evident in the world of sport. This may be seen as a relatively harmless and innocuous initiative, yet it can convey significant international visibility and take on the attributes and functions of paradiplomacy (see below). This book opened with an appreciation that Hong Kong, while not a country, enjoys distinct membership within the International Olympic Committee (IOC). So does Taiwan (under the euphemism of *Chinese Taipei*) and (as of August 2008) twelve other territories that do not have membership in the United

Nations. (While the 2004 charter of the IOC states that only a country that is "an independent state recognized by the international community" is eligible to field a team, numerous exceptions have been made for smaller (and typically island) entities. Meanwhile, for the next Olympic Games, slated for London in 2012, there will, most likely, still not be a national "Great Britain" team competing in the football competitions. This is because the world's four oldest football associations (England, Scotland, Wales, and Northern Ireland) have each maintained separate affiliations within the world's football federations. The Scottish National Party, running a coalition government in Scotland since 2007, would wish to see Scotland fielding its own Olympic team (and not just in football) in the 2012 event (Gordon, 2007). And, sticking to football, the New Football Federations Board (NFB), set up in 2003, is mainly made up of teams that represent "countries" which remain unrecognized as sovereign states. Members include Chagos Islands, Easter Island/Rapa Nui, Gozo, Greenland, Sealand, Yap, and Zanzibar, as well as the sovereign state of Kiribati.

Expressions of (Sub)national Identity

A second explanation is related to the articulation of national identity. The assumption of a common people enjoying exclusive jurisdictional rights over a distinct territory – the classic nation-state arrangement – as an ultimate objective looks increasingly passé, redundant, unable to handle issues requiring either more powerful or more local organization. Instead, one often finds the expression of an island-based *sub*nationalism: much like a regional or geographically anchored ethnicity, which is, however, not keen on outright independence, manifesting rather a sympathy for maintaining links with a (typically ex-colonial) patron state and a sense of pride and identity with their island jurisdiction in the context of having a more powerful but arm's-length protector (Baldacchino, 2004a). In rarer situations, one comes across "infra-nationalism" (Weiler, 1991: 96), which is a political and institutional structure beyond the constitution, a de facto island state apparatus existing in a taunting defiance of the main state, with which relations are *not* harmonious: examples include Taiwan, Southern Mindanao, and, until 2009, Tamil Eelam (as well as, perhaps, the Mafia in Sicily?).

Promoting the Rights and Identity/ies of Minority/ies and Indigenous People

A third driver towards non-sovereign autonomy arrangements relates to the defence of minority rights and the promotion of minority identity/ies. "Appropriate local or autonomous administrations" are recognized by Article

35 of the Copenhagen Declaration on the Human Dimension, a document issued by the Conference of Security and Cooperation in Europe (precursor to the Organization for Security Co-operation in Europe [OSCE]), as one of the possible means for promoting the ethnic, cultural, linguistic, and religious identity of certain minorities (Ghai, 2002: 33). This driver has found its most obvious expression with regards to the rights of indigenous peoples.

One may validly raise a question here: Why should the subject of indigenous peoples be brought up within a study of subnational jurisdictions? H. Catt and M. Murphy (2002: 7) argue why such a challenge would be misguided: despite obvious differences, these two groups share several characteristics, including "self-identification as separate societies with distinctive languages, cultures and traditional forms of economic activity and governance [as well as articulating] a similar claim to collective self-determination."

Over 130 native American (Indian) tribes existed as de facto federacies within the United States by the mid-1970s (Elazar, 1994: 289); by 1997, 60 "self-government compacts" had been negotiated covering 202 different tribes (Catt and Murphy, 2002: 80–1). The number has since increased. The new arrangements apply to such diverse groups as the Aleutian Islanders (Alaska, United States), the Baffin/Ellesmere Islanders and those of Haida Gwaii/ Queen Charlotte Islands (Canada), and the Torres Strait Islanders (Australia). Since North American Indian reservations have limited sovereignty, and can therefore exist outside direct state regulation, they have developed, for better or for worse, into niches for operating gambling businesses. The U.S. Indian Gaming Regulatory Act (1988) set out the parameters for how native American tribal entities are permitted to operate casinos and bingo parlours. Some tribes have attempted to "offshore" their casino, locating it out of their indigenous homeland, usually near a large urban centre (*San Francisco Chronicle*, 2006). Online casinos can theoretically operate from any location that has a server connected to the Internet. While some countries have made it illegal to operate within their jurisdiction, other jurisdictions, especially islands and other enclaves, have actively encouraged casinos to operate on their soil and will license them for such activity (for more, refer to chapter 4). The Mohawk Council of Kahnawake (in Quebec, Canada) established its Gaming Commission in 1996 (Kahnawake Gaming Commission, 2008).

Para-Diplomacy

Fourthly, the devolution of representative power to institutions above or below the nation-state has taken on some momentum in recent years. Notable here is the increasing demand for political power by cities and large urban metropoles in a burgeoning knowledge economy. In Europe, the Committee of the Regions within the EU is one such legitimate advisory body (Christiansen, 1996; Keating, 2004). Such paradiplomacy has involved subnational governments setting up offices in Brussels or in other countries, within and outside the EU. The (ambiguously named) twenty-one-member Overseas Countries and Territories Association (OCTA) is one such active lobby, set up by the Treaty of Rome in 1957 (European Commission, 2005). A component of such devolution finds expression in the flurry of international activity by subnational "authorities." The Catalan government has been a striking example: part of a wider process of the ongoing transformation of the EU into a structure of multilevel and multi-speed governance. These cases defy those who, within a sovereigntist mould, had been able to imagine Europe's future only as a collection of nation-states or as a new country called Europe.

There are other cases too. The Canadian province of Quebec is an active (though non-sovereign state) member of La Francophonie. The Riau Islands are the target of a Singaporean-Indonesian collaborative effort to kick-start development projects by creating jurisdictional enclaves, bolder than the exclusive economic zones of earlier development strategies (Grundy-Warr et al., 1999). De facto states in the international system – like the Turkish Republic of Northern Cyprus – press for recognition on the international stage, seeking to bypass other regimes (Bahcheli et al., 2004). Most of the Netherlands Antilles has now broken up, its island constituents preferring direct links with Amsterdam than through Curaçao. Åland has been a member of the Nordic Council since 1954. Anguilla, Montserrat, and the British Virgin Islands are associate members of the Organization of Eastern Caribbean States (OECS, 2005; see also Ramos and Rivera, 2001). The Isle of Man, Guernsey, and Jersey have been active in signing conventions with other states and international organizations, especially in the fields of finance, the environment, and trade (e.g., OECD, 2004). Other (but non-island) proponents of paradiplomacy include Tatarstan in Russia (Sharafutdinova, 2003), the German Lander, and the Belgian region of Flanders (Aldecoa and Keating, 1999). In the world of intersecting jurisdictions, such paradiplomacy is not one of the net advantages of autonomy without sovereignty.[2]

CONCLUSION

Various, typically large, states are finding it convenient to develop a creative use for usually small, far-flung, and remote island jurisdictions within their orbit, facilitating activities that could be anathema on home ground. The rationale is not uni-directional, however: there are also various plausible reasons for small island territories to aspire to an arm's-length, customized relationship with a larger, benevolent, "mainland" patron. Thus, various subnational island jurisdictions partake of some form of asymmetrical federalism with(in) a larger state. A recognition of the rights of distinct and indigenous peoples to a level of self-determination also acts to spawn such subnational, decision-making capacities.

This chapter has only scanned the surface of the comparative analysis of the creative competitiveness strategies and governance practices of subnational island jurisdictions. Its goal has been primarily to demonstrate the benefits of such a comparison, and to invite others to take the project forward. On the basis of a global, largely inductive, and discriminatory analysis, four political capacities have been suggested as being characteristic of the innovative development strategies practised today by various island "autonomies." Extant "mainland-island relations" can provide insights into other smaller, non-island as well as larger players, beyond the strictures of both economic vulnerability and sovereignty.

The chapter's rather optimistic and sanguine tone also calls for some qualification. Autonomy can, and does, have its limits. Managing a steady stream of resources from overseas is not always within the grasp of small island polities. The transnational dynamics and demands of effective tourism, finance, or natural-resource management can foster a new, often neo-colonial dependency (Hampton, 2004; De Kadt, 1979). Jurisdictional power can be, and has been, abused, particularly given the towering part that not just big international capital but also key individuals play in small polities where role multiplicity (and hence role conflict) is normal, gossip is rife, accusations of nepotism are difficult to avoid, and "everyone knows everyone else" (e.g., Baker, 1992; Crocombe, 1979; Richards, 1982; Singham, 1968). S. Betermier (2004: 64) has suggested that metropolitan powers actively "choose to retain" territories in line with strategic self-interest. The Ilois/Chagossians, island citizens of the British Indian Ocean Territory, were summarily removed from their homeland when their presence clashed with superpower strategic interests, a situation unchanged in spite of various decisions by the high courts (Harwood, 2002; Winchester, 2003; Pilger, 2006). St Helena was meant to get an international airport by 2010 (SARTMA, 2005), but this initiative has now fallen victim to the 2008 global credit squeeze, much to the disappointment of the island's residents (Bowcott, 2008).

To sum up, while it is tempting to see islands as "too small, too weak, too defenceless to manage in the modern world" (Royle, 2001: 158) and merely "places without power" (ibid., 57), such a view is fundamentally incorrect. After all, the evidence is mixed. Power (Foucault reminds us) is never unilateral, and a case can certainly be made for the creative solutions to difficult economic challenges that *some* (and not necessarily *all*) non-sovereign island territories have developed, often as a direct outcome of utilizing the resourcefulness that their jurisdictional status and capacities permit.

To echo B. Lindström (1999), one can today safely speak of a post-sovereign political landscape, where sovereignty is split or divisible. Is it not increasingly relevant to address and acknowledge territories where there is a shared exercise of power (Lindström, 1997: 249) and where "subnationalism" is not a contradiction in terms but a recipe for political stability, a dignified compromise between separate statehood/secession and a unitary state (Ghai, 2002: 31; Baldacchino, 2004a)?

The practice of asymmetric federalism merits further analysis and recognition by economists and political scientists (Congleton et al., 1999: 2). Islands, with their disposition towards administrative independence, and with their proneness towards unique recognition through the geographical coupling of location and small relative size, predominate as "autonomies" within bilateral, "small unit–large unit" relationships.

In a future world order, as the explosion of governance outwards, downwards, and sideways gains momentum, island autonomies may prove no longer to be the quirks and the exceptions of the system, but the rule. They will no longer be seen as anomalies, paradoxes of history (e.g., Anderson, 2004) or "inherently problematic" (Aldrich and Connell, 1998: 1), but rather as entities normalized within an architecture of comfortably overlapping lines of power and authority, parts of a nexus of multiple regional centres of executive capacities (Joenniemi, 1997). Moreover, while the analysis of the category of small island developing states still remains driven by vulnerability considerations, an analysis of the category of subnational island jurisdictions suggests a markedly different set of endowments: when J.L. McElroy and K. Sanborn (2005) compared sixteen dependent (i.e., SNIJs) and nineteen independent (i.e., SIDS) from the Caribbean and the Pacific, the difference in the results is statistically significant (to 0.025 or 0.001 levels) on no less than seventeen out of twenty-five distinct socio-economic and demographic variables. (More details in chapter 7.) This warrants the authors to claim, daringly, that "the dependents ... have come to represent a new, successful, insular development case" (ibid., 11).[3]

Similarly, the key objective of this chapter has been to suggest that there is potential in investigating the intricacies of "decolonizing without disengaging" (Houbert: 1986). F. Constant's observation (1992: 51) remains valid: "This strange phenomenon remains little known and is still under-researched ... and it has not yet been adequately theorized." Analysing the creative (and, in their own way, often sustainable) development strategies deployed by, and on, subnational island jurisdictions may prove timely.

6

Offshoring Strategies: Lessons from Subnational Island Jurisdictions

A kind of paradigm shift is occurring: we are perhaps now acceding to a new, invigorated sense of looking at the struggle over geography in interesting and imaginative ways.

Edward Said (1994: 21)

INTRODUCTION

Saint-Pierre and Miquelon is the smallest jurisdiction in North America, off the southern coast of Newfoundland, a *collectivité d'outre mer* of France, with a population of around 6,500. It used to thrive on the cod fishery, before the Canadian government – which controls fish quotas – imposed its cod moratorium on the Grand Banks in 1992. The islands have since fallen into a sullen dependency on transfers from France. Their Exclusive Economic Zone is already quite unique and is completely engulfed by the Canadian one. It is 200 nautical miles deep, but just 10 miles wide – and is known, because of its shape, as the *baguette*. This EEZ is, in effect, a French maritime enclave, surrounded entirely by the sovereign maritime territory of Canada (De la Fayette, 1993; Charney and Alexander, 1998). Sitting just beyond Canada's Exclusive Economic Zone, and under the same continental shelf of which Saint-Pierre and Miquelon are part, may be lucrative and exploitable mineral deposits. The islanders feel that France should lay claim to these waters on behalf of its tiny and remote jurisdiction (Plantegenest et al., 2003). A web-based petition initiated by the islanders and addressed to the French authorities has insisted that they defend the islanders' claims to resources that lie on the segment of the continental shelf (Saint-Pierre and Miquelon, 2008). The French government has indeed officially announced in 2009 that it "wants to negotiate an agreement to share offshore energy wealth with Canada that would give the tiny islands of St-Pierre-Miquelon a share of any new energy discoveries off the Atlantic coast" (O'Neil, 2009). There is, however, one hitch: getting to these waters would require "leapfrogging" from the end of the *baguette* over/through Canadian-controlled waters (Law, 2006). This has never been done before. The concept "raises questions concerning the projection of sovereign rights that would, in effect, leapfrog over zones where other states exercised exclusive jurisdiction" as well as provide a mechanism for similar "shelf-locked states" to create a "discontinuous juridical continental shelf" (Boswell, 2005). As was to be expected, Canada has objected to the French claim, stating that it would "take all necessary measures to defend and protect its rights with respect to its continental shelf" (*The Economist*, 2009a; Reuters UK, 2009).

Islands, like Saint-Pierre and Miquelon, are tempting prizes to countries with imperial aspirations, and all the more so if their control endows a continental power not just with a strategic location but also with very large portions of ocean as a component of that power's Exclusive Economic Zone. In international maritime law, an EEZ is a sea zone in which a state has special rights to the exploration and use of marine resources. In what is another triumph of sovereignty in international law, owing to the deliberations of the United Nations Conference on the Law of the Sea (UNCLOS), a state's EEZ extends 200 nautical miles out from its coast, except where resulting points would be closer to another country's EEZ claims. Thus, France has the world's second-largest EEZ in the world (after the United States), thanks primarily to its far-flung subnational jurisdictions, all of which, except one (French Guiana), are islands.

The particular situation that Saint-Pierre and Miquelon finds itself in may be quite unique, and yet such a uniqueness is somehow patterned: it is typical of the power predicament of many of the world's subnational island jurisdictions. Some are chronically dependent on a benign metropolitan power that effectively kills their economy through kindness; but others have managed to deploy their jurisdictional power as a resource, extracting asymmetrical concessions from the metropole and using the resulting political space to "offshore": carve out a more sustainable and lucrative economic-development trajectory – based on niche manufacturing, tourism, shrewd use of environmental and heritage resources, banking, and finance. The differential use of legislation means that these small island territories behave *as if* they were another country, even though they are not sovereign and thus lie within the purview of a larger, sovereign state. They gamble with claims for specific deals – some, as in the case of Saint-Pierre and Miquelon, quite innovative in governance terms – in this current age of rampant liberalization and globalization, because they are small and hope to succeed. And sometimes they do.

Meanwhile, we must be careful not to assume that these jurisdictions behave merely and naively in their collective nationalist interest. Mainland-island relations are usually triggered by the interests of elites, and the ensuing tensions are as a much a manifestation of power play as of innovation.[1] And so, as in the case of Saint-Pierre and Miquelon, one also – and always – needs to raise the question: In whose interest would the innovation work?

OVERVIEW

Now that the Doha Round of "freer and fairer" trade talks, within the World Trade Organization, has been scuppered, there is much more scope in scrutinizing bilateral, preferential deals between jurisdictions (Baldwin, 2006; *The Economist*, 2006c). SNIJs are pioneers in creative governance expressed within typically asymmetric relations with much larger states, a form of "managed dependency" (Fabri and Baldacchino, 1998). The economic and political tools that they deploy are in part a function of a negotiated, at times tense, bilateral association with a (usually benign) metropole; a colonial inheritance; a federal arrangement; the vibrancy of a local "subnationalist" culture; and the ability of local elites to represent and advance "subnational" interests.

Small island territories have been "decolonizing without disengaging" (Houbert, 1986) over the last sixty years, starting with the departmentalization of four French overseas island territories in 1946 (Connell and Aldrich, 1992; Mrgudovic, 2005; Woolf, 1989), then the setting up of the Netherlands Antilles in 1954 (Oostindie and Klinkers, 2004), and dramatized by the secession of Anguilla from St Kitts-Nevis in 1967 (Westlake, 1972). Historical practice and/or international provisions have secured the autonomy of such locations as Åland, Channel Islands, Isle of Man, and Svalbard. Military interventions and/or sectarian strife have led to de facto semi-autonomous jurisdictions in Northern Cyprus, South Mindanao (Philippines), and Tamil Eelam (Sri Lanka). Constitutionally or legally engrained provisions frame and secure the autonomy of island provinces like Corsica, Hawaii, Kosrae, Njazidja, Prince Edward Island, Sicily, and Tasmania. Indigenous "first nations" increasingly enjoy self-determination in locations such as Nunavut, Haida Gwaii, and the Torres Strait. There are the various former colonies that are not interested in independence (as confirmed in various plebiscites) and engaged in evolving binary relations with Amsterdam, Copenhagen, London, Paris, Sydney, Washington, or Wellington. Specific legal subnational arrangements treat the Galápagos, Hong Kong, Jeju, Kish, Labuan, Madeira,

Nevis, Rapa Nui, Rodrigues, Sakhalin, Scotland, or Zanzibar differently from the rest of the respective state. There are strategic military enclaves like Ascension, Diego Garcia (British Indian Ocean Territory), and Akrotiri and Dhekelia (Cyprus). Taiwan can be seen as a government in-exile, sovereign state, or rogue province of China (Watts, 2000).

Sovereign states have reimagined islands; they resort to creative governance in order to circumvent international obligations, tolerate activities that would not be appropriate among large populations, and/or generally exploit niches in the internationalization of production, trade, and finance, turning inherent small size and insularity into net advantages (Dodds and Royle, 2003: 489). In setting up special regions or zones, these islands, or their parent states, have either excised parts of their territories from the regulatory regime extant in the rest of the country *or* designated their whole island territory for such purposes. Thus, SNIJs are the quintessential masters, or victims, of *offshoring*: not only in the sense of going beyond the legal conventions of "onshore" export-processing, banking, and finance (probably the best-known usages of the term), but also in extending, and perhaps eroding, other central principles of sovereignty. They call for a re-evaluation of the role of the state and challenge conventional notions of agency and change in international affairs (e.g., via "paradiplomacy": see Aldecoa and Keating, 1999).

Meanwhile, if the predicament of offshore finance centres can provide useful insights, then one must note that much international pressure has been brought to bear in recent years on these "tax havens" and their "unfair competitive practices" (Bell, 2002; Financial Action Task Force, 2005a, 2005b; G7, 2000; Hampton and Christensen, 2002; Vlcek, 2007). The international community *can* develop concerted action (coercive or moral) when departures from what are diagnosed as acceptable norms of legal and economic practice start to bite significantly. Likewise, in the United States, the Bush administration had faced relentless international pressure over the function of the "non-jurisdiction" of Guantánamo (U.S. Supreme Court, 2004; Greenhouse, 2006).

EXCEPTIONAL SOVEREIGNTY

The Treaty of Westphalia (1648) is crucial in the history of international political relations since it forms the basis for the modern international system of independent nation-states. It ushered in an international community of law between sovereign states of equal legal standing, guaranteeing each other their independence and the right of their peoples to political self-determination. The two most innovative principles proclaimed were sovereignty and equality among nations.

Sovereignty implies legitimate authority over a specific territory and the exercise of such authority over the residents of that territory. This means that the continental world can literally be "carved up" between contiguous "states," while the United Nations Law of the Sea allows an extension of such principles over large portions of ocean, measured outwards from land. As long as sovereign states respect each other's sovereignty, the stage is set for long-term political stability.

And yet there appear to be serious challenges to post-Westphalian governance practices today, although they often end up affirming and bolstering the powers of sovereignty. These challenges are mainly due to two complementary dynamics. The first is "from the outside in": the pressure and challenges of globalization and global competition oblige and encourage states to determine new, often ingenious, ways of exploiting niches of opportunity or of protecting themselves from economic liberalization. The second is "from the inside out": the bolder assertion of new "sovereign" claims by "nations," which need to be accommodated preferably without threatening the solidity and territorial integrity of the current state.

The outcome of these "pincer-effect" dynamics is often found in expressions of creative governance. After all, as Carl Schmitt (1922: 5) reminds us, "the sovereign is he [sic] who decides on the exception," such as declaring a tax exemption, or a state of emergency. The determination of a differential application of a law creates the legal edifice for imperial rule, which explains why colonial outposts gravitate naturally towards offshore status.[2]

One area where such dynamics are fleshed out in practice consists of the unique arrangements struck between a big player and a much smaller player (or players) within the recognized administrative competence of the same sovereign power. These arrangements lead typically to negotiated details of some form of federative or federacy arrangements, including a plethora of "non-state" jurisdictional expressions, that allow for a modicum of both shared rule and self-rule. Many of these "governance anomalies" – anomalous certainly from the point of view of the territorially compact, nation-state model – are being applied *by*, or *on*, islands which are usually much smaller than their metropolitan counterparts. Such "exception making," or offshoring, is nevertheless the quintessential exercise of sovereignty.

Small islands suggest themselves as tabulae rasae for such and similar purposes: potential laboratories for any conceivable human project. Relative small size, geographical boundedness, and the cultural specificity of the island

and its people promote a distinctive identity which calls for recognition, while at the same time ensuring that the "experiment" is clearly circumscribed and will not get out of hand.

Such experimentation is a moving target. It presents an opportunity to explore the tension between endogenous and exogenous pressures for political change. The evolution of offshore finance centres is one case in point: "The development of offshore banking illustrates how islands ... have been transformed into spaces apparently far removed from the 'normal' practices associated with state sovereignty and territorial jurisdiction" (Dodds and Royle, 2003: 489; also Hudson, 1998). It is the transformation of these spaces (and the context of dyadic or multiparty negotiation in which such a transformation can take place) that is the focus of this chapter. This is one attempt at critiquing the manner in which island space challenges our understanding of "boundary" and "identity," themselves terms that are synonymous with islandness and fraught with difficulty and misrepresentation (e.g., Baldacchino, 2006c).

ISLAND, BOUNDARY, IDENTITY

The discrete essence of islands is often deemed to be their key distinguishing feature. However, "boundedness is [often] confused with closure ... a facile but unwarranted assumption" (Kirch, 1986: 2). If there truly were insular islands, then we wouldn't even know of their existence. Barring human intent (as in the case of prison islands), very few island settlements – like Easter Island/Rapa Nui and Greenland/Kalaallit Nunaat – have been cut off for long stretches of time in their history; and this self-enclosure has jeopardized the very existence of such island societies (Diamond, 2005). Indeed, external "interventions" are often pivotal and central to islands, whereas, on a mainland, exports, emigration, remittances, and environmental or military interventions are considered "externalities" – things apart. It is fair to ask: *Are islands insular?* (Gosden and Pavlides, 1994); because they are usually anything but.

Thus, identifying islands as sites for "boundary studies" (e.g., Pitt, 1980) can be quite problematic. All island boundaries are, by definition, permeable and are better conceived as representing interfaces with the world beyond. Rather than a boundary, a better trope to represent islandness would be a beach, that ever shifting liminality where local and global meet (e.g., Dening, 2004).

The same difficulty arises in considering island identity. The ingrained openness of small islands serves to orient their island inhabitants towards the metropole, for inspiration, vacation, shopping, education, and/or employment. Their literature is dominated by the migration theme (e.g., Markham, 1989; King and Connell, 1999). Often, as noted earlier, emigration offers an escape from a suffocating local environment (Baldacchino, 1997). Small island citizens (and not just their elites) are more likely to emulate, and be assimilated into, Western culture (Harrigan, 1978; Caldwell et al., 1980; Miles, 1985). They are known to have a higher propensity to migrate to developed countries (Connell and King, 1999). International migration has in fact long been recognized as heaviest from the world's smallest territories (e.g., Wood, 1967: 95). For various small island households, migration becomes a strategic resource, since offspring sent away can be expected to infuse remittances, in cash or in kind, to the home economy: in some instances (e.g., Niue, Tokelau, Cook Islands, U.S. Virgin Islands), these are significant contributions to the GNP (Ahlburg and Brown, 1998). At any point, a significant percentage of an island population may be away at its respective metropole(s) (Baldacchino, 1997: 89; Lowenthal, 1987: 41–3). All this shuttling from island to mainland, often in the context of multiple visits and trips spread out over a lifetime, suggests that "brain rotation" or "brain circulation" are more appropriate descriptors than "brain gain" and "brain drain" (Baldacchino, 2006b). The end result is a difficult and painful coming to terms with identity if this implies a steady "rootedness in place." Many islanders would be "transnationals," deploying a specific pattern of de-territorialized and cross-boundary migration that challenges the concept of the temporality and spatiality of "homeness" (e.g., Duval, 2004; Hatziprokopiou, 2004; Vertovec, 2001). They are at the forefront of seeking to nurture and exploit the advantages of a *glo-cal* citizenship (Robertson, 1995; Courchene, 1995): just like "tidalectics," the backward and forward movement of water, observes Barbadian poet Edward Kamau Brathwaite (1984).

If the world is dominated, as M. Castells (1999) puts it, by "the space of flows," then islands and islanders are as much characterized by the *roots* of place as with the *routes* of mobility (Clifford, 1997; Jolly, 2001); or is it, perhaps, just a "rooted mobility" (Fog Olwig, 1993)? A. Appadurai (1996: chapter 2) argues that there are various "scapes," characterized by fluidity rather than fixity, that characterize the contemporary world. One may agree with Connell (1995: 276) that "dichotomies are no longer useful, as the world is revealed to be far more complex, involving movements in specific colonial, neo-colonial and post-colonial circuits, different diasporas, borderlands, exiles, detours and returns." Ex-islanders are not necessarily exiles (e.g., Bongie, 1998: 18–24).

The rigid and idealized nation-state struggles to maintain itself in this shifting and turbulent field. It does not simply find itself fighting a rearguard action against those who would seek to turn the precepts of sovereignty on their head. It also finds itself exploring departures from the "norm" to position itself more effectively in the face of perceived threats or potentially lucrative opportunities. Small islands appear willing players, or easy prey, in this game.

This is where a review of examples of the application of governance anomalies – both *by* islands and *on* islands – becomes pertinent.

INNOVATIVE GOVERNANCE *BY* ISLANDS

Islanders often want to have their cake and eat it too (Palan, 1998). And they can often get away with a "double standards" policy – in spite (or because?) of the global pressures for "a level playing field" that seeks to eliminate preferential, bilateral deals and agreements. They are pesky actors who, in the eyes of metropolitan officers who may have to deal with them and their antics, "punch above their weight": "these specks on the horizon … had a propensity to suddenly loom and smack the government straight in the face when it least expected it" (quoted in Drower, 1992: 82). Islands that are subnational units have managed to extract concessions, either *within* the jurisdiction of a sovereign state and/or (in alliance with their patron state) within the ambit of a confederate super-state, like the European Union. Key areas where such unequal arrangements have been secured to date regard: 1) citizenship rights (with associated rights of residency, property purchase, and work permit); 2) indigenous self-government; 3) paradiplomacy; and 4) economic sovereignty. All four areas question the strict definition of sovereignty and its imputed exclusive powers and obligations: regarding single citizenship; equal rights for all citizens; the rights of international representation; and local government transactions respectively.

Citizenship Status and Rights

The border – where the law is always suspended, and where one is neither citizen nor foreigner in the face of the border agent (Salter, 2006: 169) – is, in the words of Giorgio Agamben (2005), a permanent "state of exception," and especially so since 11 September 2001. Many subnational island jurisdictions forcefully lobby for and, once secured, defend their right to maintain metropolitan passports and citizenship that allows them to access the mainland at will and without encumbrance. Such rights are especially important in the face of very tight labour markets, as well as potential economic crises or total environmental disasters. The volcanic eruptions on Tristan da Cunha (1971) and Montserrat (1995) required total (albeit temporary) evacuations to the United Kingdom.

Yet the same territories have no qualms in exercising very strict restrictions on who can work, settle, or purchase property on their island; there is not even a quid pro quo. The defence-of-access rights in such locations is a fundamental one; it calls to mind Bertrand Russell's strong language on property rights (1938: 95): "Apart from the economic power of labour, all other economic power, in its ultimate analysis, consists in being able to decide, by the use of armed force if necessary, who shall be allowed to stand upon a given piece of land and to put things into it and take things from it."

Cook Islands, Niue, Tokelau

The 1,800 residents of Niue enjoy dual citizenship, as an independent nation in free association with New Zealand. Tokelauans are citizens of New Zealand, which gives them free right of access to that country. Under the agreement that establishes the Cook Islands as self-governing in free-association with New Zealand, the Cook Islanders are also New Zealand citizens and may move to New Zealand to live and work. (In the latter two cases, Tokelauans and Cook Islanders do not have a dual citizenship.)

Galápagos

Strict immigration measures have been put in place in the Galápagos Islands since 1998, even though they are part of the state of Ecuador. The inhabitants of the Galápagos Islands remain citizens of Ecuador and enjoy all the same civic rights as those on the mainland (Kerr, 2005).

Sabah and Sarawak

When Sarawak and Sabah joined the Federation of Malaysia, they negotiated arrangements that make them seem like semi-independent countries. These include the requirement of a passport or a specific official document to enter Sarawak or Sabah from any other part of Malaysia (Malaysia Immigration Department, 2006).

Northern Marianas

Under the Constitution of the Commonwealth of the Northern Mariana Islands (CNMI), only persons of Northern Marianas descent may own land in the CNMI. Leases of up to fifty-five years are available. Meanwhile,

U.S. citizenship was conferred in 1986 upon those people of the Northern Marianas who meet the necessary qualifications.

United Kingdom Overseas Territories

The British Overseas Territories Act (2002) has reaffirmed full British citizenship for the citizens of Britain's remaining fifteen overseas territories (of which fourteen are real islands and the fifteenth, the enclave of Gibraltar, a virtual one). This act also grants automatic transmission of citizenship to offspring; the right of abode, including the right to live and work in the United Kingdom and the European Union; the right not to exercise or formally to renounce British citizenship; and the right to use the fast-track European Union/European Economic Area (EEA) channel at the airport, free of U.K. immigration controls.

Within the U.K.'s overseas territories, perhaps the tightest and most one-sided arrangements for citizenship, residency, and work permits are to be found in Bermuda. Property ownership is highly restricted: expatriates may purchase only one of some 312 homes listed as available for sale to non-Bermudians; each of these cost an average of US$976,000 (June 2003 figures). In general, single-family dwellings in Bermuda with price tags of less than US$5.5 million cannot be sold to foreign nationals (Bermuda Online, 2010).

Moreover, the Bermuda constitution protects Bermudians only: although human rights exist, they do not apply to non-Bermudian residents in the same ways as they do to Bermudians. The employment of non-Bermudians is severely restricted and they cannot change employment without official permission and work permits that stipulate a specific employer.

The situation is much the same in the British Virgin Islands. Applicants for "belonger" status and residence must have lived continuously in the territory for the previous twenty years. As for those who applied for residency status after 1 January 2003 or will apply in the future, only twenty-five people each year will be granted residence and belonger certificates. The BVI government is adamant that individuals who are away from the British Virgin Islands for more than ninety days in a calendar year will be denied residency status. Controlling immigration in the territory is a "very serious challenge" and a "careful balance" must be struck between welcoming foreigners and protecting the rights and privileges of citizens (Connect-Project.net, 2008).

The situation somewhat repeats itself in Guernsey, one of the Channel Islands. There, housing is split into the local market (reserved for inhabitants and those with housing licences) and a smaller number of just 1,700 open-market (and much more expensive) properties for anyone else (Sherwood, 2008).

Faroes and Greenland/Kalallit Nunaat

The Faroese have their own separate passport because the Faroe Islands are not a member of the European Union, unlike Denmark. However, Faroese citizens are also Danish citizens. Likewise, Greenlanders have their own citizenship and passport separate from that of Denmark owing to Greenland not being a member of the EU. (Actually, in what is probably another act of innovative governance, Greenland is the only territory to have *left* the EU, in 1985.) Following a referendum in 2008, Greenland now has control of its police force, coast guard, and courts of law. The rules under which oil revenues are split between Greenland and Denmark have been revised in Greenland's favour. In addition, Greenlandic is now the sole official language (Lyall, 2009; McSmith, 2008).

Within the European Union

Within the EU, both the Åland Protocol attached to the accession of Finland in 1995 and the accession document relating to Malta in 2003 provide strong safeguards and limitations – amounting, among other things, to (in Brussels-speak) "permanent derogations" on the rights of settlement, which abrogate the otherwise hallowed principle of "the single market" in favour of the islanders because of the circumstances induced by very small population size (in Åland) and very small land area (in Malta). The status of Jersey, Guernsey, and the Isle of Man vis à vis the EU is governed by Article 299 (6) (c) of the treaty establishing the European Community and Protocol 3 of the United Kingdom's Act of Accession to the Community in 1973. The three SNIJs are not members of the EU but are part of the EU customs territory, so common customs tariffs, levies, and other agricultural import measures apply to trade between these islands and non-EU member countries. There is free movement of industrial and agricultural products between the three SNIJs and the EU, but no free movement of services, capital, or persons. Such a customized, à la carte relationship is quite unique within the EU.

Sovereign Rights by Indigenous Peoples

A second expression of governance "from below" relates to a concerted global movement for the recognition of aboriginal rights and their associated principles of self-government and self-determination *within* the parameters of a sovereign state. A United Nations Declaration on the Rights of Indigenous

Peoples was adopted by the General Assembly in 2006. This provides for the protection of the collective human rights of indigenous peoples, including their rights to self-determination, culture, spirituality, language, lands, territories, and natural resources. It applies to over 5,000 distinct indigenous peoples, numbering over 300 million worldwide, many of whom live on islands (UN, 2006).

Torres Strait Islanders

The right to ownership of land by Torres Strait Islanders according to their traditional customs was recognized in a landmark Australia High Court decision, *Mabo vs State of Queensland*, in 1992. This decision recognized for the first time native title rights and interests in common law. Torres Strait Islander people now hold and deal in substantial areas of land, and usually these lands are held through some form of communal title. However, the recognition by common law of native title rights has highlighted the difficulties of these arrangements. Indigenous communities own land under customary law as self-regulating communities with distinct rights but cannot, under current Australian statutes, organize their political structures in relation to this land. There are also substantial difficulties even in identifying the "community" which might organize such structures.

Andaman and Nicobar Islands

In an attempt to salvage their now depleted resources following the December 2004 tsunami, tribal councils on India's Andaman and Nicobar Islands are asserting their rightful ownership over tribal lands and preventing mainland settlers from returning to the islands. The islands are also protected under the Aboriginal Tribes Regulations (1956), whereby tribal land is not allowed to be transferred by way of sale, exchange, mortgage lease, or otherwise to any person other than a member of an aboriginal tribe. No person other than a member of an aboriginal tribe may acquire interest in any land situated in a reserved area or in any product of, or crop raised on, such land (Reuters Foundation, 2005).

Haida Gwaii/Queen Charlotte Islands

In Canada, the provincial government of British Columbia and the Haida Nation have agreed to co-manage a land-use planning process for the Haida Gwaii/Queen Charlotte Islands. The council of the Haida Nation was formed in 1980 with a mandate to protect and assert aboriginal title and the collective rights of the people. The Haida First Nation claims that it is the rightful owner of the Queen Charlottes, including the resource-rich seabed surrounding the islands which contains vast reserves of untapped oil and natural gas. In the 1997 *Delgamuukw* decision, the Supreme Court of Canada recognized the importance of aboriginal title and prodded provincial governments to get on with negotiating treaties with First Nations in order to unburden the court system with legal proceedings on the matter (Thom, 1999a; 1999b).

Hawaii

The Akaka Bill, tabled in the U.S. Senate in 2005, was designed to "provide a process for the recognition by the USA of the native Hawaiian governing entity" (Borreca, 2005). The intent in drafting this bill was to provide native Hawaiians with the opportunity to reorganize their governing entity for the purposes of a federally recognized "government-to-government" relationship with the United States (*The Economist*, 2005c). As it turned out, this measure was not passed, falling victim to land-title issues. If it had been, it would have constituted the first step towards the re-establishment of a native Hawaiian government since the overthrow of the Hawaiian monarchy in 1893 (McGregor, 2002: 348). Apart from correcting historical injustices, it would have created a sense of parity in the way the federal U.S. government deals with the indigenous peoples who inhabited the Hawaiian lands which have today become the United States.

Paradiplomacy

The affirmation of subnational territorial identity and jurisdictional competence can only induce the elaboration of paradiplomatic relationships and thus reinforce the blurring of distinctions of status and privilege that were once at the core of international diplomatic practice. Paradiplomacy is the outreach of non-sovereign jurisdictions to actors beyond their own borders (Bartmann, 2006).

Turkish Republic of Northern Cyprus

Such a practice is especially critical for "de facto states." The Turkish Republic of Northern Cyprus, recognized as a sovereign state only by Turkey, has representatives in London, Brussels, Washington, D.C., and the United Nations, as well as a Trade and Tourism Office in Baku, Islamabad, and Abu Dhabi. In Geneva, the mission exists physically and functionally as part of Turkey's permanent mission.

Many subnational jurisdictions, by virtue of *not* presuming to be sovereign states, have, however, managed to penetrate somewhat the sphere of international relations as legitimate players, raising pertinent questions once again about the presumed distinction between sovereignty and non-sovereignty. The matter will be discussed in greater detail, and with examples to match, in chapter 7.

Economic Sovereignty

In some instances, the largesse associated with economic opportunity has been shrewdly translated into political mileage.

Shetland

The Shetlanders were initially quite ambivalent about the late-1960s discovery of North Sea Oil and the subsequent plans to turn Sullom Voe into a major oil terminal facility, now owned by a consortium including British Petroleum and Shell. Luckily, some shrewd policy making secured exceptional jurisdictional capacity for the local government. The Zetland County Council Act approved in 1974 enabled the Shetland Island Council (SIC) to acquire land, become a port authority, set up companies, and establish a reserve fund (Blackadder, 1998: 109–10). These led to the SIC receiving in time substantial payments from the oil industry, and profits that were saved up in trust funds have been used to promote local enterprise and development (Shetland Island Council, 2007). Although these trusts are theoretically independent charitable organizations, they actually permit the SIC to fund initiatives by proxy, circumventing United Kingdom and EU regulations that pertain to local government transactions. Almost 10 per cent of the Shetland labour force works directly for the SIC (Grydehøj, 2008). It would be fair to claim that, today, the SIC is not only the richest but also the most autonomous local council in the United Kingdom.

INNOVATIVE GOVERNANCE (IMPOSED) ON ISLANDS: THE EMPIRE STRIKES BACK

While the island citizens of subnational jurisdictions may be flexing their muscles and taking on characteristics that would have been deemed exclusive to sovereign states until recently, some mainland jurisdictions have set their sights on their own pet island projects. Consider, for example, the "sham federacies" in place today. These entities are similar to more traditional colonies except that they are cloaked in the guise of a partially sovereign arrangement. Though this sovereignty is not in fact acknowledged, their supposed autonomy allows these entities to fly under the radar of still rampant anti-colonialism (e.g., Rezvani, 2007).

Contending with Residents on Geo-Strategic Islands

Betermier (2004: 64) has suggested that metropolitan powers sometimes "choose to retain" territories in line with strategic self-interest and military expediency. The situation is made easier when these metropolitan powers deal with islands as tabulae rasae and do not, in particular, have to contend with civilian residents and civil law obligations. A measure that improves the ability to use an island for military or other geo-strategic purposes is either to depopulate it completely and/or engineer its exclusive habitation by military personnel. There are thus islands, and island enclaves, in the world today that are populated by only "non-residents" who operate under military discipline.

Ascension

Private ownership of land has not been permitted on Ascension Island, a U.K. overseas territory; all residents are housed in employers' quarters. Ascension has been operated like a classic company town throughout its economic history. Because of this, it has never had a permanently settled population; labour on the island has been subject to short-term contracts. This trend is expected to change over time, however, as some devolution processes continue. The U.K. government has asserted that no inhabitant of Ascension Island has a "right to abode": this is a point now in dispute by local council members, long-time employees, and their family members, as noted in the local newspaper *The Islander*. With the 2003 Wideawake Agreement between the United Kingdom and the United States, Wideawake Airfield on Ascension Island was opened to some civilian charter traffic. Previously, only military traffic had been permitted. The introduction of tax, the setting up of an electoral roll, and the introduction of the right to vote led to "certain expectations," which were, however, quickly dashed. The frustrated island council resigned en bloc in 2006, its members claiming that they "have been used as pawns by HMG [Her Majesty's Government] to legitimize a regime that is questionable, discriminatory, dishonest and unfavourable to the tax-payers of this island" (SARTMA, 2007).

Helgoland/Heligoland

Today, Helgoland is a small German island of less than two km². It is part of the European Union but excluded from the EU value-added-tax area and customs union; and much of the economy thrives on sales of cigarettes, alcoholic beverages, and perfumes to the visiting tourists. Formerly a British colony, the island was the subject of an embarrassing swap (involving another island,

Zanzibar), negotiated without the islanders' knowledge, between Britain and Germany in the 1890s. Later, it became the target of a controlled explosion in 1947 and a heavy-practice live-bombing range in 1950; it was initially also earmarked as a test site for a British atomic bomb. (The latter was eventually redirected to another island, Monte Bello, in Australia, and undertaken in October 1952.) A statement from the House of Commons debate expounds the stark facts about the island's suitability as a bombing facility, without even once hinting that there were islanders, transferred to the mainland after Second World War hostilities had completely devastated their island, who were desperate to get back home: "Heligoland has the advantage of being geographically in a position which can give practice to all sorts of other units concerned with air defence. We have got to have an island which is of a certain size. It must stick out a certain distance from the sea in order to be a good radar target to be bombed from a height" (House of Commons, U.K., 1950, quoted in Drower, 2002: 261).

Akrotiri and Dhekelia Sovereign Base Areas

The Sovereign Base Areas of Akrotiri and Dhekelia were crafted in the context of the Cyprus Independence Constitution of 1960. Their "residents" include 7,700 Cypriots, various support personnel, plus some 4,000 dependants. There are also nearly 2,700 locally employed civilians. Located close to the Middle East, the two sites continue to remain of immense strategic value. The SBAs have no elected government and no flag. Under the British Overseas Territories Act 2002, SBA residents did *not* automatically become British citizens with the right of abode in the United Kingdom. Their existence and operations have led to a number of clashes with Cypriots, as in the case of the military antenna installations in 2001 (Stefanou, 2005).

Okinawa

At the Futenma Marine Corps Air Station, on the outlying, densely populated SNIJ of Okinawa, the United States maintains its only large military base on Japanese soil. The rape of an Okinawan schoolgirl by three U.S. servicemen in 1995 caused a massive outcry: tens of thousands of Okinawans turned out to demonstrate against the American military presence on their island. That demonstration, combined with the determination of Okinawa's governor to see all American bases closed by 2015, suggested that the U.S. bases on Okinawa faced overwhelming local opposition. After ten long years of high-level negotiations, an agreement had been reached in 2005 whereby parts of the air station, including landing strips, would be relocated to northeastern

Okinawa, near Nago, in exchange for the withdrawal of 8,000 U.S. marines and their dependents to Guam. But Yukio Hatoyama, the new prime minister of Japan, personally promised Okinawans during the election campaign of 2009 that the Futenma base would be closed down, and not just relocated elsewhere in Okinawa. Will the Hatoyama administration dare break its promise to the islanders, or risk unravelling the Japan-U.S. alliance (Buckley, 2005; Kakazu, 2000; *The Economist*, 2010; Voice of America, 2009)?

British Indian Ocean Territory (Chagos Archipelago)

Britain summarily deported the entire 1,800 Ilois population of the Chagos Archipelago in the British Indian Ocean Territory and then leased the islands to the United States, which in turn built an ultra-sophisticated military base at Diego Garcia, the largest of the sixty-five islands in the archipelago. Over 1,600 km from the nearest land, this is the largest U.S. base outside the continental United States. Britain had first "detached" these islands from the territory of Mauritius as a condition for the latter's eventual independence in 1968. A decision by a London high court in 2000 invalidated the 1971 local immigration order that had evicted the Ilois from the archipelago, but upheld the special military status of Diego Garcia. An order-in-council or "Queen's order" in 2004 – a back-door method of legislation for overseas territories – overrode the 2000 decision; a High Court decision in May 2005 condemned this move as "irrational" and overturned it; and the U.K. government won its appeal in 2008 (CIA, 2009b; Harwood, 2002; Morris, 2008; Pilger, 2004, 2006; UK Chagos Support Association, 2006). The courtroom sagas drag on, have involved courts in the United States, and may now attract a new participant, the European Court of Human Rights. The U.S. lease on Diego Garcia expires in 2016, but it can be renewed for a further twenty years. To add to the political complexity, a Marine Protected Area is now being proposed for the territory.

Diego Garcia is also a space command-and-control centre, a spy station, and a suspected "black site" for secret detention and interrogation. It would be an obvious staging post for any future attack on Iran.

Meanwhile, the practice whereby British officials would, also via orders-in-council, gather up islanders, deport them by boat into exile, and then use the forcibly vacated island for economic or military activities has happened elsewhere: in 1847, to the Banabans in the west Pacific; and, in 1958, to the coconut gatherers on Christmas Island (Drower, 2002: 289–90). In another instance, Mururoa and Fangataufa were "ceded" to France in 1964 and so "legally belong to the *métropole*, rather than to French Polynesia" (Aldrich and Connell, 1992: 298).

Marshall Islands

The Americans, not to be outdone, summarily evicted the Bikini and Eniwetok Islanders (Marshall Islands) in the mid-1940s, transforming that space into a nuclear-testing facility. Those atolls were selected as test sites primarily for their proximity to a major U.S. military airbase on Kwajalein atoll (again, Marshall Islands) and for their remoteness from shipping lanes, airways, and fishing grounds (Hinz and Bendix, 1995: 36). That they were populated was immaterial. In 2008, a full fifty years after the United States ended its nuclear testing in the Marshalls (sixty-seven tests in all), a new Marshallese government began pressing for additional compensation for the ill-health, birth defects, and deaths suffered, and for a clean-up the radioactive mess left over. The United States insists that it has made full and final settlement under the first round of the Compact of Free Association (1986–2001) (*The Economist*, 2008a).

In 1995 the Marshall Islands government had appeared eager to accept the use of an uninhabited atoll as a nuclear-waste dump in return for payment, but local and international pressure stopped the plan before dumping began (Crocombe, 1997: 168–9).

Non-Populated Islands

Where non-populated islands exist, the intent of the larger powers is more clearly manifest. Given its extensive network of overseas bases, the United States is naturally concerned with the stability of the host nation of any potential base. Seeking out an unpopulated territory for military purposes avoids the UN's decolonization requirements and the resulting political issues of sovereignty or anti-Western sentiment (e.g., Morris, 2008: 6). An island like the uninhabited Palmyra Atoll, twelve km^2 in land area, in the northern Pacific, was used by the United States Navy during the Second World War to "dump enough munitions and 55-gallon diesel drums ... that it was later dubbed Black Lagoon for its resident pool of dioxins" (Weisman, 2007: 332). Being uninhabited except for a small group of scientists and volunteers, Palmyra Atoll remains currently the only *unorganized* incorporated U.S. territory. It was purchased by the Nature Conservancy in 2000 for coral-reef research.

In the United Kingdom, the small and uninhabited islets of Fuday and Sunray, near Barra in the Western Isles of Scotland, have been shortlisted as potential nuclear-waste dumps since the late 1980s (Edwards, 2005).

Excised Offshore Places and Other "Legal Limbos"

Strategic interests go beyond military and "hot" waste-disposal concerns and can spill over into broader security issues. In relation to such threats as global terrorism and illegal migration, large states have looked at islands with creative governance practices in mind, using them to hold detainees that they would rather not have on their own territory. The relative distance from mainlands means that island detainees are more difficult to reach; better hidden from the media, human-rights watchdogs, and the general public; and hindered in accessing judicial processes (Mountz, 2009: 11). But there is more to be extracted from the island condition.

Guantànamo Bay, Cuba

The United States has detained suspected terrorists and enemy combatants in "legal limbo" on its sprawling 115 km^2 island base at Guantànamo Bay in Cuba (U.S. Supreme Court, 2004).[3] On 29 June 2006 the U.S. Supreme Court repudiated the Bush administration's plan to put Guantànamo detainees on trial before military commissions, ruling broadly that the commissions were unauthorized by federal statute and violated international law (Greenhouse, 2006). Justice Anthony Kennedy emphasized, in his concurring opinion in *Rasul vs Bush*: "Guantànamo Bay is, in every practical respect, a United States territory" (U.S. Supreme Court, 2004: 487).

In choosing a place that is physically outside the nation itself, the U.S. administration has kept various arrested persons "abroad in a cynical attempt to delocalize liability on the use of torture" (Bigo, 2007: 19). Guantànamo Bay has effectively been crafted as a "juridical limbo," a "black hole," a "zone of indetermination," a "carefully constructed legal absence," and a field of experimentation because it is a threshold where the border between inside and outside is uncertain (Bigo, 2007: 17–18; Butler, 2002; Fletcher, 2004; Reid-Henry, 2007: 630). Guantànamo has become "an ambiguous space both inside and outside different legal systems" (Kaplan, 2005: 833). This situation recalls that of refugees (mainly from Haiti, but also from Cuba itself) held at Guantànamo Bay in the 1980s and early 1990s, who were denied any rights to appeal for asylum on the grounds that they were in a "lawless enclave" outside U.S. jurisdiction (Kaplan, 2005: 839; McBride, 1999). The resort to such "new technologies of rule with respect to those defined as 'non-citizens'"

(Reid-Henry, 2007: 638) transformed Guantànamo into something beyond a mere military base; a groundswell of international protest may have then obliged a (transient) policy change, just as it may have done again of late (Simon, 1998; Perera, 2002; Council of Europe, 2007; Neuman, 2007). As a veritable "state of exception" (Agamben, 2005; Reid-Henry, 2007: 631), the argument that the U.S. government lacks sovereignty over the territory of Guantànamo has long facilitated – rather than limited – the actual implementation of U.S. sovereign power in the region (Kaplan, 2005: 837). Thus, with Guantànamo being both inside and outside the law at the same time, the U.S. government could selectively expand its capacities to act as sovereign beyond its own borders (Marguiles, 2004).

As the Obama administration in the United States proceeds to fulfil its promise to close Guantànamo, it has started to offload its detainees onto other countries, including "island statelets": Palau has accepted thirteen detainees; Bermuda another four (*Globe and Mail*, 2009). Is "detainee dumping" (ibid.) ushering in a new, post-enforcement archipelago (Mountz, 2009)?

Lampedusa

The southernmost point of Italy, the island of Lampedusa (land area of 20 km^2), is situated 205 km from the island region of Sicily (of which it forms part administratively) but lies just 113 km from Tunisia, off the coast of North Africa. It is now best known as a key entry point to Europe for impoverished illegal immigrants from Africa. Thousands have been attempting the dangerous crossing across the Mediterranean sea; survivors located by the Italian coast guard have been held temporarily in a detention centre on Lampedusa prior to being transferred elsewhere in Italy for processing and especially for examining their case for asylum status. In 2008 Italy ranked as the fourth-highest asylum host country in the industrialized world, trailing only the United States, Canada, and France. In August of that same year, however, Italian Prime Minister Silvio Berlusconi stepped away from this processing procedure by externalizing Italy's borders to Libya "in the same way that Australia is externalizing our border to Indonesia" (Curr, 2009; see below). Following a US$5-billion deal with the Libyan government, the international waters between the two countries are more vigorously policed by joint naval patrols; many immigrants rescued at sea are often returned back to Libya, contrary to international refugee rights. The United Nations High Commission for Refugees (UNHCR) has expressed "mounting concern" about this practice, as with the state of the detention facilities on the island (e.g., France 24, 2009). The number of migrants attempting the Mediterranean voyage has fallen dramatically since this Italy-Libya pact has come into force (Human Rights Watch, 2009).

"Lampedusa stands as a blight on Europe: an outpost of the European Union where normal rules do not apply. Increasingly, governments around the world appear to be adopting an 'out of sight, out of mind' approach to these kinds of outposts: whether in the Australian desert, a military base on Cuba or small islands across the Mediterranean Sea" (Messineo, 2005).

Non-Australia

As we have seen in chapter 2, Australia declared parts of its territories and territorial waters to be "non-Australia" for specific purposes. Following the *Tampa* incident of late August 2001, the Australian legislature passed the Migration (Excision from Migration Zone) Act 2001 to amend the Migration Act in order to limit the country's obligations with respect to migrants. It does so by excluding portions of its sovereign territory for the purposes of claiming asylum. It designates Christmas Island, Ashmore Reef, Cartier Islands, the Cocos (Keeling) Islands, and Australian sea and resources installations as "excised offshore place[s]" deemed outside the country's "migration zone." Under the law, persons who enter these offshore places are defined as "offshore entry persons" and are unable to make visa applications, including requests for asylum, unless the minister exercises discretion on their behalf (Connell, 2006: 55). These spaces were thus effectively "de-territorialized" for the purposes of asylum seekers (Perera, 2007: 203). They are spaces which are both inside and outside the law, designed to isolate, contain, and punish asylum seekers (Kumar Rajaram, 2007). Such a technology of excision produces "spaces of exception" – spaces that manifest legalized lawlessness –via the very same exercise of sovereignty (Agamben, 2005).

Interestingly, Australia's border does not only "contract," as it excises outlying territories by design; it also "expands," as it effectively annexes the sovereign spaces of other states for its own specific intents (Perera, 2007: 206). The sovereign state of Nauru, as well as that of Kiribati, were both officially designated by Australia as "offshore processing centres" for those claiming refugee status. The government of Papua New Guinea – "an impoverished former Australian colony" – also agreed to incarcerate a number of asylum seekers in a hastily built detention centre on Manus Island, in return for an initial payment of AUS$1 million. Fiji and Palau were reported to be "considering" similar requests (e.g., BBC News, 2001). The Nauru detention camp, which held as many as 1,000 refugees, has since been closed, plunging the Nauru economy "into crisis" (Carty, 2007).

Manageable Havens at Arm's Length for Trading and
Interacting with the World

Kish

"From the palm-lined road nearby, the mountains of Iran's southern coast
are visible. But any shadow cast by Iran's repressive regime barely seems to
reach Kish's gentle sand. On this small island, 18 km off the southern coast
of the Islamic Republic of Iran, it is far easier to find a five-star hotel than a
mosque. That's because Iran's dictatorial government is trying to showcase
Kish not as a strict Islamic haven, but as an earthly paradise designed to win
over the international community" (Roston, 2005, 21).

Kish Island is one of three "industrial free trade zones" approved by the
Majlis (Iran's Islamic Consultative Assembly) in August 1993. Kish may be
small: just five km wide and seventeen km long. Still, it is administered semi-
autonomously by "an Authority organized as a company with autonomous
legal status, whose capital shall belong to the government" (Iran Trade Point
Network, 2008). Its very smallness and islandness lets Kish get away with
such a departure from fundamentalist theocratic rule.

Many readers can be excused for thinking that the above example is a
purely fictional one. For how could the most puritanical, hard-line, and anti-
Western of contemporary states – the Iran of the mullahs and the ayatollahs,
member of "the axis of evil" widely believed to be developing a nuclear
arsenal – tolerate shopping malls, "hypermarkets," theme parks, women in
high heels, and pool tables on part of its territory, an island that runs its own
(semi-private) airline and has plans for an eighteen-hole PGA golf course and
a Formula One racetrack (Roston, 2005; Watson, 2004)?

Yet Kish Island is very real and its modus vivendi is not that hard to
understand. Iran, like other states, is keen to attract international capital:
hence, the conversion of Kish into a visa-free trade zone and booming business hub. Kish's insignificant, remote, and peripheral island status provides
a tolerable and convenient diversion from the required austere life of the
mainland. Here, Iran can profitably experiment with a site that is small and
bounded, with no danger of destabilizing spillovers. Kish serves as an informal market for an international trade in avionics where Iran's air force fleet of
ageing U.S.-made F-15s, F-5s, and F-4s (bought during the reign of the Shah),
now under a U.S. embargo, can access desperately needed maintenance parts
and expertise (Baldacchino and Milne, 2008: 1–2). The island of Kish survives
as an "unofficial oasis of fun, where the religion police turn a blind eye to
things outlawed elsewhere" in the country (MacKinnon, 2008).

Reasserting the Rule of Law

Pitcairn

Pitcairn's very entrance into modern history had to do with an (albeit rebellious) act of innovative governance: it was the secret hideaway of Fletcher Christian and his band of British sailors who mutinied aboard His Majesty's Armed Vessel *Bounty* in 1789. Now the last remaining British overseas territory in the Pacific, Pitcairn is the only inhabited island of a group of four entities, collectively named the Pitcairn Islands, with a total land area of 35.5 km^2; Pitcairn itself is just 4.35 km^2. The entire population lives in the only settlement, Adamstown: in January 2007 there were forty-seven islanders and fifteen non-islanders.

Until recently, Pitcairn mainly sustained itself as a discreet "postage stamp republic" (Steinberg and McDowell, 2003: 60). Then, the islands were rudely thrust into the public gaze following a rather bizarre sequence of events. In 1996 the "first ever external administration official of any kind" (Aldrich and Connell, 1998: 34) was sent to Pitcairn. After a number of allegations of sexual assault, Britain posted a police officer on the island for six to eight weeks a year. In 1999 the officer reported two complaints of sexual assault. Following an investigation, various counts of rape and indecent assault were brought against seven men – almost the complete able-bodied adult male population of the island – under British law: sections 1 and 14 of the Sexual Offences Act, 1956. Their trials commenced on 29 September 2004 before the Supreme Court. On 11 October, the Judicial Committee of the Privy Council granted the islanders leave to appeal the pre-trial judgments but declined to grant a stay of proceedings. Instead, it directed the court to continue hearing evidence and, if the men were convicted, to indicate appropriate sentences. In findings announced on 24 October, the court acquitted one of the accused but entered convictions against the six remaining men.

At the start of the investigation, there had been no clear legislative, judicial, or correctional infrastructure in place to enable the trials or enforce any sentences. As a result, the British and New Zealand governments cooperated to replace a "relatively simple pre-1999 criminal justice system with an extensive array of new laws and institutions" (Angelo and Townsend, 2003: 231). Some forty new ordinances were introduced between 1999 and 2003.

The Pitcairners did argue successfully for their right to be tried at home. In 2002 and 2003, the British and New Zealand governments entered into an agreement to enable the Pitcairn courts to sit in New Zealand and allow for any sentences to be served in New Zealand. The agreement took legislative effect in the Pitcairn Trials Act 2002 (NZ) and the Judicature Amendment

Ordinance 2003. However, following submissions by the Pitcairners, a panel of judges sitting in the Supreme Court of Pitcairn Islands in Auckland directed the island's British administrators to conduct the trials on the island and rejected their claims that the logistics and expense of taking the court to the Pacific were "insuperable" (Foreign and Commonwealth Office, 2003).

What is much more interesting to this discussion, however, is that the criminal charges triggered a set of complex legal challenges to Britain's administration of Pitcairn before the Supreme Court and the Court of Appeal (Angelo and Wright, 2004; Power, 2007; Ryan, 2006; Trenwith, 2003; Wright, 2005). The defence sought to have the charges dismissed through a number of pre-trial applications, "the most fundamental of which is to challenge the jurisdiction of the United Kingdom over the Pitcairn Islands" (Pitcairn Islands Supreme Court, 2004: para. 4). Among the arguments brought forward by the defence were: that the Islands were never a British possession; that the islanders never acknowledged allegiance to the crown; that the Sexual Offences Act 1956 had not been published on the island; and that the English administration of justice over Pitcairn was operating in an occasional and ad hoc manner. In October 2006 the Privy Council refused the appeal against the islanders' convictions unanimously. As it did so, however, it admitted that the proceedings "involved an immense amount of research and study" and that the circumstances for the appeals were "most unusual" (Judicial Committee of the Privy Council, 2006). The men began serving their sentences on the island in November 2006, two years after they were sentenced. In January 2007, two more Pitcairners were convicted of rape and related offences in a special sitting of the Pitcairn Supreme Court in Auckland (Fletcher, 2008: 68). The arm of the law is long indeed. The outcome, in a way, represented a long overdue levelling of the score with the descendants of the former mutineers.

It appears that the intense particularistic relationships that mark the smallest, often island societies (e.g., Benedict, 1966), and the implications that these carry for social, and sexual, intimacy and abuse, are not restricted to Pitcairn. And, just like Pitcairn, when such events on an "island paradise" break news, they are avidly devoured by the media (e.g., Fletcher, 2008; The Economist, 2008b; Times Online, 2008). Moreover, such scandals could serve as excuses for the mainland state to intervene: a murder on Norfolk Island in 2002 – the first known murder in the island's history – may have provided a motive for Australia to seek to clamp down on the island's self-governing powers (The Economist, 2004a). More on this below.

CONTESTED SPACES

Since power is inherently contestable, one should not be surprised to find that there are various cases where "self-rule" confronts "shared rule"; where "mainland" and "island" interests are pitted in a dynamic clash to sway an island jurisdiction in a specific direction, either with a view to exploit "off-shoreness" and introduce asymmetrical powers with specific ends, as amply described above, or else with a plan to remove these asymmetries in order to regularize or neutralize the position of the island jurisdiction within a broader constitutional frame.

There are various indigenous island groups that are pressing for international recognition and for rights of self-determination. The Raizal, native islanders of San Andrés y Providencia, are considered Colombian citizens; however, they have been calling for self-determination in response to allegedly discriminatory government policies which have marginalized their community both socially and economically, displaced them from their lands, and overpopulated the islands with mainland immigrants. The people of Banaba (Ocean Island), within Kiribati, seek recognition as a nation: just over 200 still live on an island that has been ravaged by excessive phosphate mining, while others have been relocated to live on Rabi Island, in the Fiji archipelago (Abara Banaba website). The self-styled Tamil Tigers in Sri Lanka have been involved in a bloody civil war in pursuit of their claim for the independent jurisdiction of Tamil Eelam (Tamil Eelam News website).

There are many other cases, too numerous to mention here, ones that oftentimes refer to the attempts by a single individual to craft jurisdiction out of an island by invoking ancient laws or reinterpreting historical events. Meanwhile, a few more detailed case illustrations below highlight the specifics of some of these "mainland-island" power games, while also including subtexts of the conflicting or converging interests of elites in the respective territories.

Norfolk Island versus Australia

A case in point is Norfolk Island, an SNIJ of Australia, which became the first Pacific Island offshore business centre in 1966. It was then regarded by Australia as "a separate country" (Aldrich and Connell, 1998: 87) with respect to income earned outside Australia. By 1975, thousands of companies had registered on the island and thus avoided the high taxation rates of the Australian mainland. This concerned the federal government, and in 1976 the High Court of Australia unanimously ruled that the federal government had full sovereign powers over Norfolk Island, including areas of taxation. This effectively killed company registration on the island.

Moreover, in 1990–91, there was a renewed effort by a group of federal politicians to bring Norfolk Island into the Australian federal system. This sparked a referendum on the island, held in December 1991, in which 81 per cent of voters (801 of 986 ballots cast) opposed being integrated into the Canberra federal system. The Australian government proposed that only Norfolk Islanders with Australian citizenship should be allowed to run for, or vote for, the Norfolk Island Legislative Assembly. This was foiled, and the lone concession was that Australian citizens who wished to vote in federal elections were granted the right to do so. The residents' opposition to joining the federal electoral system is that they viewed it as a pretext to the imposition of federal income tax. In 1998–99 the Australian government once again created legislation to restrict on-island voting to Australian citizens. The bill was defeated in March 2000 in the Australian Senate. On 26 August 1998 another referendum was held, with 78 per cent of voters opposed to Australia making any changes to the Norfolk Island electoral process. A revamped proposal was defeated by 72 per cent of voters in another referendum held in May 1999. Under the auspices of the Joint Standing Committee on the National Capital and External Territories, in 2002 the issue of restricting voting in Norfolk Island elections and referendums to Australian citizens was once again raised. The commonwealth minister publicly announced that the federal government would follow this recommendation and introduce amendments to the Norfolk Island Act 1979 in order to bring the island's electoral policy in line with Australia's. The Norfolk Island government's view remains that, if any changes are made to its governance, such change should be implemented by the Norfolk Island legislation.

As if these controversies were not enough, in 1999 the Australian Human Rights and Equal Opportunity Commission found that Norfolk Island's immigration legislation violates Australia's protection of liberty of movement and freedom of choice of residence. It stated that Norfolk Island's immigration laws must be replaced by Australia's Migration Act 1958 and that the island government's power to pass legislation on immigration be revoked. Furthermore, it was stated that Norfolk was not justified in establishing its own immigration legislation because it was not necessary to protect the island's environment or Pitcairn heritage (Treadgold, 1999; van Fossen, 2002).

A former administrator of Norfolk has also recently submitted to an Australian Senate Select Committee that the island "is in urgent need of governance reform, federal financial support, and the associated necessary regularization of State (Territory) and Commonwealth financial arrangements." The island would thus "be more closely aligned with Australia within the construct of fiscal federalism" (Parliament of Australia, Senate, 2008). Chief Minister Andre Nobbs, reporting on discussions with the federal government, claims that there has been "significant progress in agreeing on a process for discussion and consultation and on the main areas where positive changes might be made in a cooperative manner" (Nobbs, 2008). The saga continues.

Vieques, Puerto Rico, versus U.S. Navy

In the Caribbean, the U.S. military purchased 60 per cent of the land area of Vieques, an island off eastern Puerto Rico, in the 1940s. The military used Vieques as a testing ground for bombs, missiles, and other weapons. Claims have linked Vieques's relatively high cancer rate to these tests, especially after the U.S. Navy admitted to the use of depleted uranium at least on one occasion in 1999. In March 1999 a Vieques native was killed by a bomb dropped by a military jet during bombing exercises. Native Viequense – who now number around 9,000 – and non-native pacifists seized upon this event as the flashpoint for ending military exercises there. Many travelled to Vieques to protest against the bombings and testings by illegally camping on the bombing grounds. The Puerto Rico legislature amended environmental legislation in 2001 so that U.S. Navy gunnery practice would not be permissible under new noise levels (Becker, 2001). The Puerto Rico governor began talks with the U.S. government seeking a solution to the problem; in 2001 an agreement guaranteed the military's vacating of the island in May 2003. Facilities and equipment were then turned over to the island's government by the U.S. Navy.

Kaho'olawe, Hawaii, versus U.S. Navy

A somewhat similar episode occurred in the Hawaiian archipelago. The island of Kaho'olawe, with a land area of 117 km^2, was nicknamed "The Target Isle": from the 1920s, it was used by the U.S. Navy as a ship-to-shore bombing target and (especially after 1941) as an artillery range. In 1976 native Hawaiian activists occupied the island in protest, causing a media splash. In 1990 then-U.S. President George Bush, Sr ordered a halt to the exercises after years of protests and lawsuits by native groups. The U.S. Congress authorized the clean-up of ordnance and other debris in 1993, which began in 1998 and is ongoing. In 1994 Kaho'olawe was conveyed back to the State of Hawaii as a cultural preserve until a (U.S. federal/Hawaiian state) government-recognized sovereign Hawaiian entity is established to manage it. The island, the physical incarnation of the sea god Kanaloa, is home to some of the most sacred historical sites in Hawaiian culture. Kaho'olawe persists as a cultural enclave run by a Reserve Commission (KIRC) which manages efforts to restore native vegetation, control non-native species, clean up trash, control erosion, and rehabilitate cultural structures. The island remains uninhabited and no one is allowed ashore without permission.

Meanwhile, the U.S. military has turned its attention to other islands. The Army is now conducting bombing and live artillery exercises at Pohakuloa on Hawaii (Big Island) and in the Makua valley on O'ahu. As much as one-fifth of the total Hawaiian land area is occupied by the U.S. military (Corbin, 2008; DMZ, 2008; Smith, 2002).

Sealand versus the United Kingdom, and the World?

The self-proclaimed principality of Sealand – which features its own flag, coat of arms, currency, stamps, and passports – was featured in numerous media reports as the "world's smallest country" and was made available for sale in January 2007. The history of Sealand involves a U.K. offshore defence structure, a Second World War relic, located some seven nautical miles off Suffolk, U.K., claimed under the law of salvage on the high seas by self-proclaimed "Prince Roy" of Sealand in 1967 (actually Paddy Roy Bates, a retired British army major). At that time, the United Kingdom's territorial jurisdiction extended to only a three-mile limit from the coast. Sealand was, therefore, outside U.K. control. A U.K. High Court ruling in 1968 reinforced this position. Subsequently, with the extension of U.K. territorial waters under the Territorial Sea Act in 1987, Sealand fell within the extended territorial limit. The precedent of the earlier ruling has meant that Sealand claims to have been able to maintain its claim to sovereignty; it continues not to recognize U.K. authority over its "territory." Hence, its "owners" allege that they have a right either to host a variety of businesses or to sell this right to other interested parties. Thus, Sealand is operating as a de facto independent territory, despite failing to meet the majority of the criteria required for statehood (Administrative Court of Cologne, 1978). Interest has been shown by some investors in relocating their operations to this offshore platform. The most notable of these are: 1) HavenCo, which has attempted to use Sealand as a base for a secure data haven since June 2000 (Markoff, 2000); and 2) The Pirate Bay, a popular torrent-tracking site that – for some time – has eyed Sealand as ideally suited to its requirements. The U.K. government has not formally challenged the legality of this situation since the 1967 High Court ruling. Will Sealand's use for digital money laundering, copyright infringement, gambling, or tax evasion, however, force the government into action? And, if so, what "action"? (see Principality of Sealand website, 2008).

DISCUSSION

The jurisdictional powers that island federacies enjoy are principally a result of bilateral negotiations between island political elites and a (usually benign, but possibly neglectful) metropole. This bargain is struck against the backdrop of a particular colonial inheritance, a local subnationalist culture, and/or the varying ambitions of local elites to win jurisdictional powers to advance subnational territorial interests. At other times, however, island autonomies arise as crafted, deliberately engineered devolutions of/by central governments, eager to exploit islands as distinctly (and preferably discreetly) "managed" zones for economic, commercial, military, or security-related activities in a globalized economy.

It may appear that "island studies" hold one answer to the burning question posed by Lloyd (2004: 2): "What is a border when it is not a point of contact between nations?" Contrary to much conventional wisdom, islands come with porous, permeable borders: they are spaces with osmotic properties, important tools in a contemporary game of economic prosperity, military strategy, or national security. Subnational jurisdictional status can provide a space *within* what might appear to be a de jure, unified, and indivisible sovereign unit.

This is clearly one of the many paradoxes and contradictions of globalization: on the one hand, rampant economic liberalization with its space (and time) compression (Harvey, 1990) that erodes transnational borders; yet, concurrently, the utilization of jurisdiction as a resource to engineer an inner space. This can accommodate peoples who are recognized as nations operating under some arrangement for self-determination and yet within the confines of other territorial entities. Moreover, jurisdiction can also be deployed (usually with the blessing of the law) with a view to developing an interstitial, insular "non-space" and therefore holding "non-citizens" – such as non-resident employees, prisoners, illegal migrants, or military personnel – subject to "non-rights."

CONCLUSION

Subnational island jurisdictions provide mounting evidence today of how fashionable narratives about the death of geography or distance (e.g., Ohmae, 1990; Cairncross, 1997) are somewhat exaggerated (Martin, 2004; Morgan, 2004). Building on Alfred Marshall's "localization economics" (1890, book 4, chapter 10) and Michael Porter's "spatial clusters" (1990), subnational island jurisdictions are clear candidates for locale-specific innovation in governance via "offshoring strategies."

Such subnational island jurisdictions are manifestations of a wider game: some states are now so engaged with extraterritorial activities that they have become distanced from the aspects of physical sovereign resources that led to their emergence as major powers in the first place. R. Rosecrance (1986; 1999) argues how the main drivers of developed states' success are no longer tied to the physical territory they have sovereign control over. Economic development is no longer reliant on extending sovereign control into other states' territories. From a "sovereignty-modern" standpoint (Jackson, 2003), such expansion can be seen as actively counter-productive to a state's interests. There is little to be gained from extending sovereign control if this brings responsibilities and costs associated with protecting this additional territory and providing for the needs (food, water, shelter, security, employment) of its own citizens: just note the situation in Iraq and Afghanistan. A far better option is simply to import required resources; the engineering and operation of subnational island jurisdictions is one manifestation of such a strategy. In this international political economy, looking at sovereignty itself as a possible commodity is a logical development. Sealand represents the lengths to which such a strategy may be taken.

If the predicament of offshore finance centres, among the latest arrivals to this offshoring game, can provide useful insights, then we have to take note that much international pressure has been brought to bear on these "tax havens" and their allegedly "unfair competitive practices," by the OECD, the European Union, and the G7's Financial Action Task Force (G7, 2000). The Isle of Man and various United Kingdom overseas territories have had to alter their fiscal policies under pressure from the European Union, in order to conform to the latter's code of conduct on business taxation (Bell, 2002).[4] The international community *can* develop concerted action – coercive or moral – when departures from what are felt to be acceptable norms of governance and civil and economic practice start to bite significantly. The U.S. government has been subjected to mounting international pressure over the operation of Guantánamo Bay as an extraterritorial detention centre;

and the Australian government has been under different pressure over its territorial "excision" by human-rights activists.

Not only that: big players can leverage their disproportionate strength and clout to counteract any gains that smaller economies might make at their expense. Herewith a case in point: although not a subnational jurisdiction, the sovereign state of Antigua and Barbuda successfully challenged the United States at the World Trade Organization on measures which prevented Antigua and Barbuda from supplying gambling and betting services to U.S. based players, an infringement, it said, of the international obligations of the United States. Admittedly, the use of the WTO dispute mechanism in this "David versus Goliath" showdown highlights the potential afforded to a smaller state by membership in an international organization (Vlcek, 2008: 160). And yet David did not win this slinging match; the outcome was "a big win" for the United States (Rose, 2005: 437). P. Clegg (2008: 232) notes: "After a four year struggle, and several favourable verdicts from WTO panels, [Antigua and Barbuda] has been unable to force the US to either alter its unfair trade rules or to win adequate compensation for the losses it has accrued because of them."

Yet, by and large, smaller jurisdictions hold their ground. C. Ingebritsen (2006: 289) credits smaller jurisdictions, inclusive of small states, with "greater freedom of manoeuvre than classic international relations theorizing suggests." Decades ago, R. Keohane (1971: 162) argued that such players "can pursue active, forceful and even obstreperous policies of their own." In spite of the forces that have been, and continue to be, brought to bear upon it, the practice of "offshoring" remains very much alive, and is likely to expand even further. The opportunities that it provides, to both mainlands and islands, to global international capital and to local nationalist movements and business-development strategists, continue to be explored, exploited, and negotiated.

Another case in point is Jeju Island, South Korea's most popular tourist destination and named the country's first special self-governing province. Its local government, as of 1 July 2006, has control over all internal matters not related to national security and foreign affairs, and is actively considering setting itself up as an offshore finance centre, even if Seoul is not exactly supportive (e.g., Ha and Prasad, 2008). Or take the Åland Islands, 27,000 strong, causing "headaches" for the Finnish government by demanding four special concessions in return for ratifying the European Union's Lisbon Treaty (e.g., Kirk, 2008). And then there is the case of the Raizales – "the indigenous native people of San Andres, Providencia, and Santa Catalina" – who are taking initiatives to reclaim "native self-determination" over their archipelago within the state of Colombia, in accordance with the terms of the Treaty of Annexation of 1822 (e.g., Colombia IndyMedia, 2007). Or examine the dramatic debates leading up to the 2002 presidential election in France, when Socialist Prime Minister (and presidential candidate) Lionel Jospin pushed ahead with his plan to grant the people of Corsica a recognition of their national identity, along with a delegation of limited legislative powers – a plan strongly opposed by the French right, which saw it as undermining the unity of the French state and a capitulation to a "violent minority" (e.g., Hossay, 2004: 425). The right won the election. A 2003 referendum that asked Corsican voters to accept a new territorial assembly and executive body that would manage more of the island's affairs was narrowly rejected: voters may have been "confused by its legalistic phrasing and suspicious of its true intent" (Bikales, 2004).

We could go on. Palan (1998: 641) predicts a scenario where "there will be a constant cat-and-mouse game of states and businesses innovating, with new offshore types of facilities counteracted by multilateral and bilateral responses effectively closing the loopholes."

This chapter has enlisted short but illustrative descriptions of "island-mainland" relations to flesh out the power play at the heart of the book's analysis. It has looked at examples from the global category of subnational island jurisdictions, critically assessing and analysing 1) how such SNIJs seek to take initiatives whose intent is to craft, exploit, or expand their "offshore" status; 2) how metropolitan states take countervailing initiatives with respect to islands, tasks that are usually more easily undertaken (or imposed) where such SNIJs are either depopulated or run by military personnel; and 3) how mainlands and islands negotiate the tension that arises when "offshoring" is enhanced, or reduced, by one party to the dismay or consternation of the other.

In a world of multilevel governance, islands continue to serve as epitomes of offshoring; they embody how economies can strategically reconfigure intimate relationships between identity, function, and location.

Island Paradiplomacy and Smaller Island State Diplomacy Compared

INTRODUCTION

The international community may be coming to terms with small, mainly island, subnational jurisdictions where the majority of resident populations is generally content to maintain and strengthen legally and economically dependent relationships with other countries, and which are still typically allowed considerable autonomy and latitude, even in relations with the outside world beyond their metropolitan centre. Indeed, the capacity of non-state units to engage the outside world through varying patterns of communication and representation, a phenomenon now widely termed *paradiplomacy*, is one development that invites a sober reassessment of these small islands' once conventional constitutional path towards full sovereignty.

The circumstances faced by these smaller island territories and the current options open to them are themselves striking evidence of a rapidly changing international system. Subnational island jurisdictions are among the least recognized players in conventional international relations studies, and yet many of them are now keenly engaged in unexpected external relations, acquiring means to enhance their regional and even global presence – whether in sports, cultural exchange, trade agreements, tourism promotion, disaster preparedness, and representation (via full or associate membership) in regional and international organizatons (Corbin, 2001: 136–59). As conventional distinctions of status and prerogatives seem to become increasingly blurred, particularly between internationally active subnational jurisdictions and sovereign states, the phenomenon and practice of paradiplomacy appears as both a cause and an effect of such developments. M. Keating (1999: 1) notes that globalization and the rise of transnational regimes have together "eroded the distinction between domestic and foreign affairs and by the same token have transformed the division of responsibilities between state and subnational governments." To be sure, these dynamics have led to "the reinvention of territory" as a distinguishing feature of the contemporary international system (Keating, 1996: 47–8; Bartmann, 1998: 239–50), as states look at ways and means to use geographical specificity – including sovereignty itself – to leverage concessions, privileges, or exceptions. Indeed, it is ironic that, just as subnational jurisdictions operate in an expanding international network, this very same network is effectively sanctioned by their metropolitan centres and consequently by the international system, itself still a system based on sovereign states (Bartmann, 2008b: 60).

The term "paradiplomacy" is used here to refer to all forms of "outreach" – those activities undertaken by non-sovereign jurisdictions with respect to external actors (including other subnational jurisdictions but especially sovereign states) – that simulate the formal, legal, and recognized diplomatic practices of fully sovereign states. Such activities are often functional (addressing a felt and immediate need); political (speaking to an enhancement or curtailment of the exercise of power, which is less case- or need-specific); or identity affirming (and thus mainly a source of symbolism, prestige, and collective pride) (Duchacek, 1986; Lubin, 2003/04: 22). They may not be intended as stepping stones to secession: B. Bartmann (2008b: 58) equates paradiplomacy to being an actor in the antechamber, "to the formal, legal and recognized diplomacy of the grand hall itself," although any such assurance would need to be examined in the context of such changeable variables as the fortunes and strategic calculations of political parties or coalitions in power. The threat of secession is also a noteworthy political ploy in itself, though metropolitan countries may be keen to call any bluff. In any case, the threat of secession is always more realistic when there are independence-leaning political parties in the running for power in the subnational jurisdiction.

EXAMPLES OF PARADIPLOMATIC ARCHITECTURE

To start off, the following is a broad sweep of paradiplomatic arrangements practised by various subnational island jurisdictions. Since the symbolism of diplomacy is inherently important, the mere fact of having and wielding international representation may be easily construed as an end in itself. In this respect, many of the island territories we are dealing with enjoy as much, if not more, legitimate representation and presence on the regional and international stage as like-sized sovereign states.

Montserrat

In the Caribbean, as noted in chapter 2, the United Kingdom Overseas Territory of Montserrat was accepted as a full member of the Organization of Eastern Caribbean States when that body was launched in 1981, on the understanding that it would soon be granted independence. However, any prospects for sovereignty were dashed in 1995–96 with the violent eruptions of the Soufriere volcano, which destroyed the capital, Plymouth, and forced the emigration of 8,000 islanders, almost the whole population. Around 5,000 have now returned and have recreated some semblance of normality. But the island's habitable space is confined to a small section of the northwest; Soufriere continues to erupt regularly and the island has been hit by various hurricanes.

Other Caribbean Autonomies

Meanwhile, two other Caribbean UKOTs – Anguilla and British Virgin Islands – are also full members of the OECS. The OECS maintains its own diplomatic missions in Ottawa and Brussels, and this allows these non-sovereign jurisdictions a direct diplomatic channel to the outside world. Anguilla, Bermuda, British Virgin Islands, Cayman Islands, and Turks and Caicos Islands – all UKOTs – are all associate members of the Caribbean Community (CARICOM), which maintains a permanent observer mission at the United Nations in New York: an especially useful channel of international outreach for its non-sovereign members. There are thirty-two consulates in Puerto Rico; fourteen in Bermuda; eight in the U.S. Virgin Islands; and four in the Cayman Islands (Embassy Pages, 2010). France has a consulate both in Anguilla and in the British Virgin Islands. Aruba, the (former) Netherlands Antilles, the British Virgin Islands, Tokelau, Cayman Islands, and Macao are subnational associate members in UNESCO (Corbin, 2001: 143).

Cook Islands and Niue

Turning to the Pacific, the Cook Islands and Niue, both self-governing states in free association with New Zealand, are full members of the sixteen-member Pacific Islands Forum. The government of the Cook Islands enjoys full executive powers; it has established separate diplomatic relations with over twenty states at the embassy or high commission level; there are no less than twenty-three states (including Australia, New Zealand, the United States, as well as the European Union) with full diplomatic relations accredited to the Cook Islands at the embassy or high commission level. And, while the Cook Islands remain an (albeit separate) part of New Zealand, Cook Islanders do not have their own but retain only New Zealand citizenship. Herewith a state that does not confer citizenship. Yet these particular islanders "are able to enjoy *all* the prerogatives of sovereignty with the most permissive and generous arrangements for international relations available to any dependent territory in the world" (Bartmann, 2008b: 72; emphasis in original). Only UN membership remains absent for the Cook Islands.

Niue's claim to paradiplomacy is much more modest. New Zealand has a high commission resident in Alofi, Niue, while Niue maintains a high commission in Wellington and shares an ambassador and embassy with the Cook Islands in Brussels, though the two states are accredited separately. Meanwhile, both the Cook Islands and Niue – which are "in free association" with New Zealand – enjoy *full* membership in UNESCO, raising intriguing questions concerning their international status.

Faroes

Consider next the three full members of the Nordic Council of Ministers which are not sovereign states. The first, the Faroes, which have been a "self-governing community within the Danish Realm" since 1948, have laid out a detailed "road map" for eventual full independence. Meanwhile, they currently maintain three representative offices: in London and Brussels with diplomatic status, and in Copenhagen without diplomatic status. The offices in London and Brussels "are located within the Danish embassies and the Faroese diplomats are formally accredited to the respective host nations as Danish diplomats working with Faroese affairs" (Isfeld, 2006). Moreover, since July 2005, the Faroese government has been able – on its own – to enter into negotiations and conclude treaties with other states and international organizations without previous consent from Denmark regarding all areas that are under the Faroese authorities (ibid.). There are now plans to open three more embassies. There are nine consulates in Torshavn, the Faroese capital: Finland, France, Germany, Iceland, Italy, Netherlands, Norway, Sweden, and the United Kingdom.

Greenland/Kalallit Nunaat

Second is Greenland, the world's large island (with a land area of over 2 million km^2) but with less than 60,000 citizens. It is the other Danish Home Rule island territory, achieving home rule in 1979. It maintains representative offices in Copenhagen and Brussels (Motzfeldt, 1997: 193–4). There are also nine consulates in Nuuk, the administrative capital of Greenland: Belgium, Canada, Finland, France, Germany, Iceland, Netherlands, Norway, and Sweden. As a result of a non-binding referendum in November 2008, home rule is being expanded in thirty areas, including the police, courts, and the coast guard; Greenland will be given a say in foreign policy and a more definite split of future oil revenue; Greenlandic will become the sole official language; and Greenland's financial subsidies from Copenhagen will be phased out. Greenlanders will also be treated as a separate people under international law, with the right to self-determination (Fletcher, 2008). Finally, as noted in chapter 6, Greenland is the only territory to have seceded from the European Union, having done so in 1985 (proving unwilling to lose domestic control over its fish stocks). The European Union lost half its land mass overnight.

Åland

Third is the autonomous and demilitarized Åland Islands and their 25,000 Swedish-speaking citizens within the state of Finland: this has been the subject of a unique international decision by the League of Nations in 1920 subsequently ratified by the Autonomy Act passed by the Finnish Parliament, which includes guarantees for Åland's language and culture. The story of these islands is also one of some creeping autonomy: they got their flag in 1954, started issuing their own stamps in 1984, and obtained their own Internet top-level domain – .ax – in 2006, which has since replaced .aland.fi. Notably, the islands secured duty-free status in the talks leading to the accession of Finland to the European Union in 1995. The economy of the islands now depends heavily on income from sales of duty-free and tax-free goods. These are sold on board ferries, many Åland-owned, which make a point of stopping at Mariehamn for this very reason. Although they are explicitly excluded from undertaking international representation by the Autonomy Act, the Åland Islands maintain representation in Stockholm, Helsinki, and Brussels, and there is an Åland representative presence in the Finnish delegation in Brussels.

Svalbard

In the same Scandinavian region, there is another island archipelago that has had its status determined via an international treaty, also agreed to in 1920. This is Svalbard (also known as Spitzbergen). The only place in Western Europe where migrants from developing countries do not need a visa or permit to be able to work (Kilner, 2006), Svalbard is completely controlled by, and is part of, the Kingdom of Norway. Yet the power that Norway exercises over Svalbard is limited to taxation, environmental conservation, non-discrimination, and certain military activity. Under the terms of the 1920 treaty, citizens of the signatory states have rights to exploit mineral deposits and other natural resources "on a footing of absolute equality" on Svalbard. As a result, there is a permanent Russian settlement, more or less autonomous, on the archipelago's main island. Thanks to its climate and geology, Svalbard is also the location of the Global Seed Vault since 2008: an underground facility, set up via an international agreement, to preserve safely a wide variety of plant seeds from locations around the world (Norwegian Ministry of Agriculture and Food, 2010).

Taiwan

The most pressing and problematic example of paradiplomacy remains Taiwan. This is at once a normal sovereign state, a government-in-exile, a rogue province of another much larger state, a prime candidate for the status of "special administrative region," and a de facto state "engaging in both official and internationally recognized channels of diplomacy in some cases and in cloaked para-diplomatic exchanges in others" (Bartmann, 2008b: 65). The rights of the indigenous people of Taiwan also need to be factored into this assessment.

The current status of Taiwan is not just that of a former government desperately grasping at steadily eroding vestiges of sovereignty. The Taipei government continues to maintain, after nearly sixty years, that it is the legitimate government of the whole of China. (In practice, the island government maintains authority only over Taiwan island itself and a handful of offshore islands and archipelagos). Still, in spite of the PRC's "peace offensive," now under way for almost four decades, twenty-three countries in the world (out of the UN's total of 192 country members as of March 2010) recognize Taiwan (as the Republic of China) and allow it to have an embassy on their soil (along with Panama, which maintains a Taiwan consulate general). Fourteen countries (Belize, Burkina Faso, Chad, Costa Rica, El Salvador, Gambia, Honduras, Marshall Islands, Nicaragua, Palau, Panama, Paraguay, São Tomé e Príncipe, Solomon Islands) have a resident diplomatic embassy in Taiwan. For sixty-six other countries, however, many with extensive and hugely important economic links to Taiwan, relations are of a purely paradiplomatic nature and – given the PRC's feelings on the matter – are marked by a highly sensitive nomenclature to describe "non–official" missions, though they may very well operate and behave in practice as "unofficial embassies" (Madsen, 2001: 175). (Indeed, the most common nomenclature for the Taiwan office in foreign countries is Taipei Economic and Cultural Office.) For fifty-seven of these countries, there are paradiplomatic resident missions in Taipei, with such names as the Argentina Trade and Cultural Office, the Malaysia Friendship and Trading Centre, and American Institute in Taiwan. The appropriate and at times tortuous nomenclature that allows Taiwan to participate in such international bodies as the Olympics has been referred in the opening pages of this book. Other than membership in the Asian Development Bank (under the name of "Taipei, China" since 1986), Taiwan's major activity in an international institution has been its membership in the World Trade Organization where it maintains a regular permanent mission, although it comes under the awkward title of "Special Customs Territories of Taiwan, Penghu, Kinmen and Matsu." And, on 18 May 2009, for the first time in thirty-eight years, Taiwan's health minister took a seat as an observer in the World Health Assembly of the UN-affiliated World Health Organization (WHO) in Geneva (*China Post*, 2009).

The situation remains in dramatic flux. There is considerable chequebook diplomacy going on, especially among small nations that see an opportunity to play one China off against another, with considerable financial assistance as the ultimate prize (Bartmann, 2008a; Harris, 2006; Madsen, 2001: 164; McElroy and Bai, 2008). Although there has been a lull in recent months, the diplomatic recognition by smaller states of either the PRC or Taiwan has replaced the polarity that characterized the Cold War and affords them a continuing opportunity to seek critical foreign aid "to the highest bidder". For example, the recently appointed president of Paraguay, Fernando Lugo, has been widely expected to switch diplomatic recognition from Taiwan to the PRC, unless perhaps Taiwan comes up with considerable funding (*China Post*, 2008). In fact, "governments have fallen and elections have been fought on the issue of who to support" (Nadkami, 2007). The situation in the South Pacific, where Taiwan maintains half a dozen "allies," has been nothing short of dramatic. A case is point is Vanuatu: from 3 November to 11 December 2004, this country recognized both the PRC and Taiwan: the only state ever to do so. It caused a vote of confidence in the prime minister, which he lost, and which in turn led to an election and a change of government (Crocombe, 2007: 260).

THE INSTRUMENT OF PARADIPLOMACY AND THE GLOBAL POLITICS OF DEVELOPMENT

And yet paradiplomacy is also, like diplomacy, a means to a further, functional end. International representation is primarily intended to influence decisions that will ultimately have an impact on the well-being of a territory's citizens. These decisions will mainly involve matters of trade, but security and environmental challenges are increasingly topical of late. When such an instrumental perspective to paradiplomacy is adopted, how do subnational island jurisdictions compare with their sovereign counterparts? The question is important since it serves as a litmus test of the viability of sovereignty or non-sovereignty in the contemporary world. It also may help to clear up some of the controversy about the presumed vulnerability of smaller, often island, jurisdictions.

In *The Peloponnesian War*, Thucydides (1972: 402) highlighted the effects of the general, overall weakness of smaller states vis-à-vis larger, more powerful ones in a key passage, where the Athenians remind the Melians that "you know as well as we do that, as the world goes, right is only in question between equals in power. Meanwhile, the strong do what they can and the weak suffer what they must."

Concerns about the vulnerability of small, weak, isolated states have echoed throughout history: from Thucydides through the review by Machiavelli (1515) of the risks of inviting great powers to intervene in domestic affairs and twentieth-century U.S.- and Commonwealth-led political science (Commonwealth Consultative Group, 1985; Handel, 1990; Vital, 1971). In the context of twentieth-century "Balkanization," the small state could also prove unstable, even hostile and uncooperative, a situation tempting enough to invite the intrusion of more powerful neighbours: a combination, according to Z. Brzezinski (1997: 123–4), of a power vacuum and a corollary power suction.[1] In the outcome, if the small state is "absorbed," it would be its fault, and its destiny, in the grand scheme of things. It has been recently claimed that, since they cannot defend or represent themselves adequately, small states "lack real independence, which makes them suboptimal participants in the international system" (Hagalin, 2005: 1).

Indeed, the appellative "small," alongside "vulnerable," has become a useful rallying cry for those that are strategically defining themselves as "small states." This composite condition, quantified into an index, has been used to lobby international support for special economic privileges to be granted to small economies. The international community has been politely supportive, acknowledging and taking note of the heightened vulnerability concerns of small developing states, including major references in both the Barbados 1994 and Mauritius 2005 declarations; yet the concept remains elusive and subject to some scepticism (e.g., Hein, 2004). The World Bank would only go as far as to agree that small states – and small island developing states in particular – have "special characteristics which should be noted by global institutions" (ComSec/World Bank, 2000; Payne, 2004: 626). Moreover, openness – one of the alleged components of economic vulnerability – is itself a key basis for the competitive export-orientation of small economies and may have prevented their lapse into protectionism and autarchy (Baldacchino, 2000). More recently, and reminiscent of P.J. Katzenstein (1985), a fresh flurry of research into the international relations of small states has emerged in the context of European integration (e.g., Thorhallsson, 2000): as if to add further confirmation of the absence of any rigorous definition of a small state, all the members of the European Union except the "big six" (France, Germany, Italy, Poland, Spain, and the United Kingdom), and all EU applicant and candidate countries except Turkey, are considered small (reviewed in Neumann and Gstöhl, 2004).

There is, however, a contrary, less notable but more extraordinary strand of argumentation that considers "the power of powerlessness" and the ability of small states to exploit their smaller size in a variety of ways in order to achieve their intended, even if unlikely, policy outcomes. The pursuance of smaller state goals becomes paradoxically acceptable and achievable precisely because such smaller states do not have the power to leverage disputants or pursue their own agenda. A case in point concerns the smallest state of all, the Vatican, whose powers are both unique and ambiguous but certainly not insignificant (*The Economist*, 2007c). Smaller states, as explained earlier, have punched above their weight (e.g., Edis, 1991), and, intermittently, political scientists confront their "amazing intractability" (e.g., Suhrke, 1973: 508). Henry Kissinger (1982: 172) referred to this stance, with obvious contempt, as "the tyranny of the weak."[2]

Imagine the consternation, surprise, and high drama among the international community when small island states seek to influence international relations according to their own interests … and succeed. Imagine the governments of two smaller island states, with no standing armies, with populations of less than a third of a million each, heading into a confrontation with the United Kingdom. The respective smaller state governments have either flimsy majorities or shaky coalitions. And yet, in both cases, the wishes of the smaller state prevailed over those of the ex-imperial power, and indeed with the support and additional pressure of the United States. In the context of the Cold War and the Soviet Threat of the early 1970s, both Iceland in the North Atlantic and Malta in the central Mediterranean played their cards, and won. In an obvious reference to the fictitious "teeny-tiny" European Duchy of Grand Fenwick, they were mice, and yet they roared (Sellers, 1959). The community of "great powers," including the United Kingdom, was not amused, however. *The Economist*, reviewing – and reviling – both Malta and Iceland in the same article, thought fit to title this feature "Damned Dots" (*The Economist*, 1971).

Malta and Iceland: The Mice That Roared

Much has been written about the stand-off between Malta Prime Minister Dom Mintoff and British Prime Minister James Callaghan in 1971–72 (e.g., Wriggins, 1975; Smith, 2007). In spite of a parliamentary majority of just one, Mintoff threatened to evict British military forces from Malta (then with a population of 325,000) and to turn over air and naval facilities – deemed to have "negative strategic value" to NATO and Britain – to the Soviet Union. In the outcome, deploying "maverick diplomacy," and playing the role of a "power broker" that has been described as "wholly unsuited for an economically weak, tiny island nation" (Micallef, 1979: 250), Mintoff succeeded, against all odds, in obtaining a 300 per cent increase in British development assistance to Malta (Baldacchino, 2002c: 202). Whether extracting more money from the British Exchequer was Mintoff's real long-term goal, we will probably never know.

At around the same time, in the North Atlantic, an Icelandic government composed of an unwieldy three-party coalition unilaterally expanded sovereignty over "its" fishing grounds by extending its territorial waters from 19.2 km (12 miles) to 80 km (50 miles), even in the face of an international agreement that had been earlier secured with the United Kingdom, and refused to recognize the jurisdiction of the International Court of Justice over the matter. Britain (population approximately 60 million) rushed to defend its economic interests by sending military vessels to the contested zone, while Iceland (population approximately 290,000) sent its coast guard vessels armed with trawl wire cutters. Iceland, comments M. Kurlansky (1997: 166), acted "shockingly tough." Britain's "using the Royal Navy to bully an unarmed small state" (Ingimundarson, 2003: 96), and Iceland's couching of the episode in heavy colonial discourse, generated much international sympathy for the Icelandic predicament, both from developing countries and from public opinion in the West; meanwhile, a nationalist discourse secured support at home. All along, the underdog argument was resorted to: "a small state was fighting for its economic survival against big powers, whose sole aim was to get their greedy hands on Iceland's economic resources" (ibid., 105). Moreover, this was not just *any* economic resource: Iceland was (and still remains) heavily dependent on its fishing industry.

When the tension subsided, and the two smaller states emerged better off from the confrontation, it might have been easy to conclude that, were it not for their respective strategic value, the United States would not have pressured Britain to accommodate these pesky microstates. And yet these two European economies were already squarely within the commercial and ideological circuit of the West; any isolationist policies would have spelled economic ruin, as U.S. President Richard Nixon hinted to Icelandic Prime Minister Ólafur Jóhannesson in June 1971 (ibid., 115). One may add with the benefit of hindsight that these strategies even led to political ruin, as both Malta's and Iceland's foreign policies eventually backfired. Indeed, may one suggest that the smaller states won their battle but not the war?[3]

It would be more appropriate to conclude that larger states do not want to be seen to bully smaller states, unless the smaller state can be convincingly depicted as harbouring communists, terrorists, or other reprehensible persons. Public opinion, at home and abroad, can be swayed and galvanized into protest action by such notions as imperialism or neo-colonialism. Moreover, the manner in which smaller states undertake international diplomacy is also typically both much more focused and more driven by "heroic" individuals (such as prime ministers) than would happen in larger, democratic countries, used to pluralism, internal consultation, and protracted deliberation by committee (e.g., Singham, 1968). This can disarm larger states, which find that victory in a showdown with an intractable negotiator is not necessarily a foregone conclusion (e.g., Pirotta, 1985). The stakes are also laid out differentially: a concession by a larger player to a smaller one may not be so onerous, and can always be dismissed as an act of generosity or gratuity; in contrast, the failure by a smaller state to secure its interests via international diplomacy with a larger state may be simply catastrophic, with possible negative implications for the larger state itself.[4]

ENVIRONMENTAL DIPLOMACY

Of course, these episodes may very well prove to be the exceptions that justify the rule. Indeed, if we fast-forward to the present, there are hardly any victories yet to be declared by smaller states when it comes to a different, perhaps more serious, topic of international statecraft: environmental vulnerability. In spite of a unity of purpose, the creation of the Alliance of Small and Island States, and a widespread recognition of the dual phenomena of global warming and sea-level rise, there is as yet no tangible evidence that smaller states are winning the argument. Why? Or, better, why not? Why have the lessons of the past not yet informed the present? Where are the contemporary Maltas and Icelands in the diplomatic war against environmental catastrophe? Let us consider three examples: the sovereign island states of Tuvalu, the Seychelles, and the Maldives.

Tuvalu

The 12,000-resident population of Tuvalu lives on nine coral atolls covering an area of just 16 km². The country, securing independence in 1979, became a member of the United Nations in 2000 and maintains a mission at the UN in New York. Tuvalu's only other diplomatic office is its high commission in Suva, Fiji. The promotion of concern about global warming and sea-level rise is Tuvalu's "major international priority" (U.S. State Department, 2007). Tuvaluan government representatives have been vocal advocates of the Kyoto Protocol, as well as champions of a global mitigation of climate change through reduced emissions. They have also expressed public disappointment with those governments that fail to manifest similar support (Sopoanga, 2003). As acting prime minister Maatia Toafa observed: "We in Tuvalu live in constant fear of the adverse impacts of climate change and sea level rise. With a height of a mere 3m above sea level, livelihoods and food security are already affected badly, with increasing salinity in ground water, land erosion, coral bleaching and total anxiety. The threat is real and serious, and is no different from a slow and insidious form of terrorism against Tuvalu" (Toafa, 2004: 4). The attempt to portray Tuvaluans as victims of terrorism does not seem to have triggered the expected response, however. In 2002 Tuvaluan Prime Minister Koloa Talake even raised the prospects of pursuing legal redress for climate-change damage in international tribunals and the domestic courts of the United States (the main terrorist threat?); so far, no litigation proceedings have been commenced (Farbotko, 2005).

More ingeniously, Tuvalu has appealed to Australia, a South Pacific hegemon, to arrange for the acceptance of its grand total of 12,000 citizens as "climate refugees." But Australia – during a period when there was much public debate about the country's policy towards asylum seekers – has refused even to discuss the matter, claiming that there is as yet no international recognition of such a refugee category. When Tuvalu turned to New Zealand for help, that country agreed to accept the whole of Tuvalu's population but only when that country becomes uninhabitable. Meanwhile, current applicants for entry to New Zealand remain subject to the conditions of the Pacific Access Category (PAC) that covers Tuvalu, Fiji, Kiribati, and Tonga. The PAC allows only seventy-five people to emigrate from Tuvalu to New Zealand per year and imposes a series of stringent requirements (Kenny, 2007).

Seychelles

The latest, smaller island state to attempt a major diplomatic exercise is the Seychelles. President James Michel took the lead in the setting up of the

Sea Level Rise Foundation in 2005 – a "global initiative to establish a platform of excellence on sea level rise" – and the Global Islands Partnership, which is trying to mount a common "global strategy" against the causes of this environmenntal crisis (SLRF, 2008; GLISPA, 2008).

Maldives

The Republic of the Maldives, a sprawling archipelago with a population of less than 300,000, has been very much on the front lines of environmental diplomacy, and for much longer. Flooding in 1987 threatened the country. More flooding, this time associated with the 2004 tsunami, submerged the whole archipelago, even if – mercifully – for just a few minutes. The Maldives government had raised the issue before the 1989 Small States Conference on Sea Level Rise, which it hosted and at which the Alliance of Small and Island States was initiated with this concern foremost on its agenda. The country was also the first to sign the Kyoto Protocol. Former President Maumoon Abdul Gayoon has campaigned vigorously on the international stage for the acknowledgment of the predicament of his country and that of similar SIDS, as well as for remedial action. His impassionate address to the United Nations at the June 1992 Earth Summit was poignant: "I stand before you as a representative of an endangered people. We are told that as a result of global warming and sea-level rise, my country, the Maldives, may sometime during the next century, disappear from the face of the Earth … Let this not be a time in the history of mankind when those who can really help decline to do so, while the very survival of the peoples of low-lying, small island nations is at stake. As I speak here today, there are 225,000 people in my country, and many tens of thousands more in other small island states, expecting strong and immediate international action to save our countries" (Gayoon, 1992). Democratically elected president Mohamed Nasheed, Gayoon's successor, landed a global media coup by chairing the world's first ever underwater cabinet meeting (MSNBC, 2009).

But, beyond perhaps expanding awareness, which "hasn't done much yet to slow down sea-level rise" (Hamilton, 2008), such political efforts have made little headway. And so the Maldives has turned to technological remedies: a massive sea wall, made up of concrete tertapods, that surrounds the entire capital of Male (2 km long and 800 m wide); and now Hulhumale, a brand new, flood-resistant island (CDNN News, 2004; DEME, 2008). Japan paid for the Male sea wall; international donors, one hopes, will pay for the man-made island.

Such expensive engineering strategies could mitigate or postpone the effects of sea-level rise, but they do not attack its causes or even represent a long-term solution. They are similar to the technology-driven measures being contemplated by developed countries threatened by sea-level rise, such as the Netherlands. The danger is that, as more states, small and not so small, consider adopting piecemeal engineering solutions to their own national problems, the urgency and thrust of a common collective position will be dampened. The resort to a global, largely diplomatic solution may no longer be seen as essential. And thus the pressure to reduce the causes behind sea-level rise may wane. Rampant technological optimism, and the belief in "science as miracle cure", may thwart any decisive steps that would otherwise attack the root causes of environmental vulnerability. So much for Gayoon's expected "strong and immediate international action to save our countries." Indeed, the Maldivian story may be an example of the "tragedy of the commons" (Hardin, 1968) and the frustration inherent in seeking a concerted global solution to a global problem; as has also been witnessed in the largely disappointing Copenhagen summit of December 2009 (e.g. Kanter, 2009). This is also an example of the resort to the more familiar "chequebook diplomacy" game with which smaller states are familiar (and which is perhaps one key reason why they assiduously call themselves *small states*). Larger, typically donor, countries are also comfortable with this stance since it allows them to display and offer munificence and development assistance.

Could it be that the attempt to seek international visibility via the issue of sea-level rise is construed as a ploy to arm-twist donors into a new line of credit? Environmental vulnerability may be replacing economic vulnerability as the new justifying mechanism for maintaining MIRAB economies (Bertram, 2006). Or is it also possible that the official leadership of SIDS may have fully internalized patterns of thought that represent them as weak victims of global trends?

THE FOREIGN POLICY OF SMALLER ISLAND STATES

The pattern that appears to emerge is that smaller states are especially good in diplomatic adventures where: 1) the relations are essentially bilateral (one-on-one); 2) the smaller state is able somehow to touch the heart of, and elicit some sympathy from, the citizens of the other party; 3) the smaller state commands the moral high ground such that it whips up both domestic support as well as manages to get an international media campaign to work in its favour, drumming up sympathy even from non-state actors; and 4) the issue at stake is essentially financial or economic. Locating the issue within the geo-strategic considerations of superpower conflict raises the stakes. Perhaps the most promising theatres for this to unfold in contemporary times are the PRC-Taiwan struggle for international recognition and the International Whaling Commission, where the commercial whaling interests of Japan can be seen to match the funding requirements of various smaller states (e.g., BBC News, 2006a; Bertram and Poirine, 2007: 365; Greenpeace, 2007). In spite of the considerable number of smaller states on the world stage, and their ability to make their presence – and their plight – felt in international fora, especially at the United Nations through AOSIS and, more recently, through SLRF and GLISPA, their lobbying has not generated much tangible benefit beyond rhetoric, sympathy, and applause.

Concern about such foreign-policy failure was already evident in the Mauritius International Review Meeting of 2005; and, while a study concluded that it would be unfair to say that AOSIS has failed, "the underlying goals of the coalition ... were not achieved" (Chasek, 2005: 135). Cooperative, smaller state, multilateral diplomacy has proved largely futile, *not* so much because smaller states have limited policy capacity, but mainly because no larger country has been sufficiently embarrassed by its failure to respond to smaller-state concerns, and no larger country has deemed its own economic or strategic interests unduly threatened by the slow sinking of the "languid sensual world" of tiny Tuvalu (Pollock, 2005), or even of a slightly less tiny Maldives. The Tuvaluans are meanwhile voting with their feet; already, there are more Tuvaluans living overseas than on their doomed archipelagic homeland. In spite of the islanders' attempts, the dangers posed to their smaller low-lying jurisdictions by climate change may not have turned them (yet?) into "the ecological conscience" of climate politics (Oberthür and Ott, 1999: 26; Payne, 2004: 633).

In his excellent review of smaller states in the context of the global politics of development, A. Payne (2004: 635) is quite dour in his conclusion; nevertheless, he is probably correct. On the international platform of environmental politics, as well as in the areas of international trade and finance, small states have played a marginal role at best. Payne asserts wryly that "vulnerabilities rather than opportunities are the most striking consequence of smallness."

Admittedly, various strategies pursued by small states are based on claims to special status and the resulting bending or quashing of global trade rules, and some of the big players and regional groupings have been keen to acquiesce; even so, such exceptions are usually temporary measures.

The seventy-one ACP (African, Caribbean, Pacific) states – many of them small – have enjoyed a one-way privileged market access to the European Union. While they violate WTO rules, the WTO members have granted waivers to the ACP accord (known as the Cotonou Accord) but only until December 2007 (WTO, 2001). The U.S. Caribbean Basin Initiative, the Caribbean-Canada (CaribCan) agreement, and the Africa Growth Opportunity Act have all introduced some favourable discrimination to small, often island, developing states.

PARADIPLOMATIC ADVENTURES

So, where small (often island) states are concerned, it is the Thucydides dictum that largely prevails. How does this compare with the paradiplomatic adventures of subnational island jurisdictions? Does the story have a similar script? Hardly.

The past is here instructive. Take environmental disasters; here, there have been at least two high-profile cases involving subnational island jurisdictions in recent decades. They relate to the evacuations of islanders from Tristan da Cunha in 1961 and from Montserrat in 1995, both due to volcanic eruptions and both undertaken with the (even if perhaps reluctant) connivance of the United Kingdom. Again, somewhat begrudgingly, the United Kingdom also took on the cost of infrastructure replacement and reconstruction (e.g., Killingray and Taylor, 2005).[5] Both these island jurisdictions were then, and still are, colonies/overseas territories of the United Kingdom, and so the United Kingdom had a measure of responsibility to ensure the well-being of their citizens. Both evacuations were temporary. Moreover, a volcanic eruption is a much more sudden and visually dramatic event than creeping sea-level rise: perhaps the former more easily captures the imagination of sympathetic onlookers than the latter. The ravages of the December 2004 Boxing Day tsunami, whose horrors were captured on amateur video and circulated worldwide via the Internet, similarly galvanized considerable international attention, from which affected islands were significant beneficiaries.

Unlike overseas territories like Tristan da Cunha or Montserrat, smaller island states are straddled with a sovereignty status which seems to have allowed other, larger, states to escape responsibility for the consequences of sea-level rise. No wonder these smaller but sovereign island states appear to have resorted to a combination of technology and feverish bilateral and multilateral diplomacy to seek some satisfactory resolution to their problem.

Maldives President Nasheed has declared that he will set up a "sovereign wealth fund" from tourism revenue as an insurance policy, which could eventually be used to buy land in/from India, Sri Lanka, or Australia to relocate all of some 300,000 citizens; whether sovereignty can thus be physically "transferred," however, is a matter of debate (e.g., Ramesh, 2008). But the option of "take up" by a benign state – the preferred solution sought by that other sovereign island state, Tuvalu – is not available, certainly not in the short to medium term. In contrast, the three-atoll subnational jurisdiction of Tokelau, New Zealand's last remaining dependent territory, with its highest point only 3.5 metres above sea level and therefore very vulnerable to climate change and sea-level rise, has no such pressing concerns. One terse statement sums it up: Tokelauans are New Zealand citizens. And, to prove it, already some 5,000 Tokelauans live in New Zealand and another 3,000 elsewhere. The population on the islands, which have a land area of just 10 km², is around 1,530. At some point, if the situation calls for drastic action, the last boatload of Tokelauans may calmly decide to relocate to their hinterland: Auckland, or perhaps Wellington. No fretful paradiplomacy is necessary.

Other subnational island jurisdictions have done equally well, in relation to a raft of different challenges. In the European Union, the so-called "ultraperipheral regions" – the island jurisdictions of France, Spain, and Portugal, plus the mainland enclave of French Guiana – have probably secured the best deal of all: a formal acknowledgment, in the Amsterdam Treaty of the European Union (1997), that their economic problems are a result of a permanent, chronic, and structural condition associated with their remoteness, insularity, and peripherality. As a result, they are the unchallenged beneficiaries of EU Structural Funds (Treaty of Amsterdam, 1999: Article 158, Article 299.2, and Declaration 30).

Portugal versus Malta[6]

The reference to Portugal allows an interesting comparison of how this country masterminded the emergence of an offshore finance centre, on the SNIJ of Madeira, in its run-up to EU membership in 1986. This case makes for a rather pointed contrast to that of another sovereign state – Malta – which did the exact opposite, deciding in 1994 to dismantle its intricate offshore finance legislation in preparing its credentials for EU membership, eventually secured in 2004.

The Malta International Business Activities Act came into force during 1989. Offshore business was restricted to non-residents; brass-plate and shell or "paper" companies were discouraged; the issuing of bearer shares (with their secrecy guarantees) was prohibited; and every offshore company had to have a resident nominee company which acted as its authorized and principal intermediary. By 1993, offshore business "was deservedly swiftly gaining recognition as an important sector of the Maltese economy in its own right" (Fabri and Baldacchino, 1999: 151). And yet, in 1994, the Maltese government decided on a "radical change of course" (ibid., 149). Offshore business was to be phased out, current registrations had to terminate offshore status by 2004, and new registrations were possible only up to December 1996. The "reforms" were explained as necessary in order for the laws "to be compatible with Malta's exisiting and forseeable international commitments" (Camilleri, 1995; quoted in Fabri and Baldacchino, 1999: 150). This was a veiled reference to the European Union, to whose membership the Maltese government had been clearly aspiring, certainly since 1987. The economic arguments in favour of maintaining an offshore finance sector, plus the sector's possible leverage as a bargaining chip in any eventual negotiations with the EU, were trounced in favour of the diplomatic argument: the Maltese government may have wished to send unambiguous signals about Malta's foreign policy and European vocation, dismantling an industry deemed incompatible with what Brussels might expect (Fabri and Baldacchino, 1999: 153–4). In so doing, given that the EU continues to tolerate offshore finance centres within its own territory (Luxembourg, Dublin, City of London), Malta, in retrospect, may be said to have been "holier than the pope."

The Portuguese story is spectacularly different. Indeed, the EU has been underwriting Madeira's International Business Centre, the latter recognized as a "special EU incentive to help the island bridge the development gap separating it from the rest of Western Europe" (quoted in Fabri and Baldacchino, 1999: 153). Madeira now has, in order of establishment, since 1980: a Free Trade Zone, an International Services Centre, an Offshore Financial Centre, and a Shipping Register. That Portugal has been able to transform Madeira in this way can be explained only by the European Commission's "explicit, albeit conditional, approval" (Levin, 2002: 45). State aid in any form, including taxation, is normally prohibited in the EU. There are, however, certain exceptions; and these have theoretically created the possibility for the so-called outermost regions to set up an offshore finance centre for development purposes. The only region to have done so is Madeira (ibid.: 27, 47). Of course, being part of Portugal, and the EU, imposes obligations: bank secrecy has been abolished, the EU directive against money laundering has been transposed, and regulation and supervision match onshore standards. And yet, "given that the EU has approved every stage of the process, Madeira's tax

advantages have faced little threat from the 'harmful tax practices' initiative
... In addition, Madeira is covered by the full array of EU legislation against
money-laundering, and is not known to be a target of criminal activity." It
is fair to conclude that "Portugal has been careful and clever in developing
Madeira's offshore economy" (LowTax.Net, 2010).

Did Malta – with a level of economic development similar to Portugal's
but (unlike Madeira) not an ultra-peripheral region of the EU – miss the
opportunity to become a second Madeira? Of course, we will never know.
Perhaps Malta – a sovereign state consisting of three populated islands, Malta,
Gozo, and Comino – should have more seriously considered an intraterritorial regulatory bifurcation: Gozo may have been (and may yet become?) to
Malta as Madeira has been to Portugal.[7]

Bermuda

Bermudans are entitled to be both Bermudan and British citizens with
the right to live and work in the European Union. Now the largest United
Kingdom overseas territory by population, its 65,000 residents enjoy a considerable degree of political autonomy, one of the highest per-capita incomes
in the world, low unemployment levels, and steady rates of economic growth,
even though it has virtually no natural resources and no industry. Britain is
responsible for the island's defence and external relations and plays a role
in its internal security arrangements. In a 1995 independence referendum,
73 per cent of voters opposed independence. Sir John Swan, a former premier
of Bermuda, has been quoted as saying in 1982: "With the Americans to
feed us and the British to defend us, who needs independence?" (quoted
in Aldrich and Connell, 1998: 129). Even so, perhaps because some political
mileage may be gained by an independence agenda among the black majority (Sanders, 2005), no other UKOT has experienced such an extensive and
detailed consideration of independence over the last four decades.

Falklands

Not surprisingly, the Falkland Islands can report "a strong and satisfactory
relationship with the United Kingdom, based on partnership, increasing self-
government and self-determination," one where "there is no movement ... for
independence" (Summers, 2007). The Islands have been enjoying a "fishing
fuelled prosperity," based especially on two types of squid (*The Economist*,
2002). Tourism is also picking up fast, especially where cruiseship visitations
are concerned (Royle, 2006; MercoPress, 2009).

Aruba and the Former Netherlands Antilles

Politicians in Aruba and the (former) Netherlands Antilles were "up in arms" against proposals by the Dutch government to introduce legislation that would make it possible to force criminal and deprived Antillean and Aruban youths who have lived in the Netherlands for less than two years – and who are considered Dutch citizens – to return to their Caribbean homes. The Caribbean policy makers have voiced legal objections to such "apartheid-like" laws that would effectively condone expulsion and that would be modelled on similar ones in force in the United States. More than that, the whole point of being integrated within the Kingdom of the Netherlands (and the European Union) is to ensure such mobility (*Daily Herald*, 2006; 2008). And how can one be expelled into another part of one's own country? The proposal is even more difficult to entertain now that Bonaire, St Eustatius (Statia), and Saba will become (the smallest) municipalities of the Netherlands. Their new status will be like that of a normal Dutch municipality, but – even then – the special circumstances of the Caribbean region will be taken into account. "This special status needs thorough negotiation for the islands to guarantee a desired standard of living to their citizens" (Saba Tourist Bureau, 2008).

The Bonaire-Statia-Saba development is actually similar to the "decolonization through integration" recipe that France long ago crafted for some of its many subnational jurisdictions (Houbert, 1986: 145). While many of these remain *collectivités d'outre mer*, Guadeloupe, Martinique, and Réunion (along with French Guiana) are *départements d'outre mer* (overseas departments), whose status is identical to that of metropolitan departments. These four (since 1946) are an integral part of France and (since 1957) part of the European Union. They are represented in the French Senate and National Assembly, as well as in the EU's Economic and Social Council; they elect a member of the European Parliament and use the euro as their currency.

DISCUSSION

Admittedly, brandishing paradiplomacy comes at a cost to the public purse. Indulging in frequent international travel (always so much more expensive to/from smaller islands) and manning missions and representative offices in expensive metropolitan cities (London, New York, Brussels) are taxing financially as well as in terms of scarce skilled human resources. SNIJs have done exceptionaly well in managing to offload even such costs on their metropolitan patrons, where possible.

N. Girvan (2004) has commented on how the processes of national market integration associated with the modern state have included measures which mitigate its "downsides": such measures include free labour mobility, a welfare system, income redistribution through taxation, environmental protection, and redress through national courts. The literature suggests that any drawbacks associated with the economic openness of smaller states are balanced by a strong and redistributive state (Cameron, 1978; Garrett, 1998). However, *no* similar measures are available when market integration turns international, a dynamic that is arguably even more problematic for smaller open economies. If anything, many countries are increasingly nervous and protectionist about opening their borders; and those that have done so may also entertain initiatives that reduce mobility – as the Dutch case above attests to. Subnational jurisdictional status emerges as one viable response to this facet of globalization. The same redistributive measures that have mitigated the negative effects of national market integration are made available to the subnational jurisdiction, such that the latter effectively operates within the same national labour market as its metropolitan custodian. This is the priceless and tangible "wild card," for which the absence of full sovereignty may not be such a high price to pay.

MEASURING THE DIFFERENCE

The difference between the functional effects of diplomacy and paradiplomacy can be measured, albeit indirectly. Seeking to better understand the lingering "insular propensity for dependence," McElroy and Sanborn (2005) collected data on sixteen SNIJs and nineteen SIDS drawn from the Caribbean and the Pacific regions.[8] Twenty-five variables were selected to test for distinct socio-economic and demographic differences. The results are tabulated, using mainly 2004 data, as Table 7.1.

There are various statistically significant differences between the two samples. They suggest that SNIJs have progressed further than SIDS in restructuring their colonial economies away from traditional low value-added staples (like banana, sugar, and copra) towards more income-elastic tourism and offshore finance. The SNIJs are considerably more tourism-penetrated. Such results also confirm Bertram's (2004) thesis on the significance of metropolitan linkages since it is demand in the main tourist-origin markets in North America, Europe, and Japan that fuels tourism growth in the Caribbean and Pacific peripheries. Significantly higher-life expectancy, lower infant mortality, and higher-than-average adult literacy rates (though the

TABLE 7.1: Paradiplomacy versus diplomacy? SNIJs and SIDS compared

VARIABLES	DEPENDENT ISLANDS (SNIJs)	INDEPENDENT ISLANDS (SIDS)	T-VALUES
Area	1871	7582	-1.76[*]
Population	139	375	-1.57
0–14	25.13	31.05	-3.17[***]
15–64	67.56	63.58	2.67[***]
65+	7.37	5.21	2.45[***]
Median Age	31.04	25.26	3.74[****]
Pop'n Growth	1.356	0.872	1.48
Pop'n Density	261	173	1.12
Crude Birth Rate	16.66	21.12	-2.65[***]
Crude Death Rate	5.36	6.68	-2.57[***]
Net Migration Rate	2.25	-5.66	2.97[***]
Infant Mortality Rate	10.14	22.60	-4.03[****]
Total Fertility Rate	2.1	2.689	-2.61[***]
Life Expectancy	77.02	69.93	6.89[****]
Literacy Rate	96.50	90.60	1.94[*]
Income (US$)	16381	6145	3.94[****]
% Agriculture	4.69	15.70	-3.42[***]
% Industrial	15.38	19.50	-1.37
% Services	79.88	64.80	4.43[****]
Labour Force Participation Rate	45.44	43.06	0.78
Unemployment	10.89	13.47	-0.98
Visitor Spending/Pop'n(US$)	6740	1174	3.68[***]
Tourism/ Pop'n	4.77	1.17	3.63[****]

T-Values are the result of a standard, two-sample means test.

* = Significant to .10 level;

** = Significant to .05 level;

*** = Significant to .025 level;

**** = Significant to .001 level.

Source: Table can be downloaded from: http://www.saintmarys.edu/~jmcelroy/Table%202%20
Dependent%20versus%20Independent%20Island%20Profiles.htm.

latter at a lower level of significance) manifest how the closer metropolitan ties of the SNIJs may foster access to superior health care, sanitation, and education. Finally, SNIJs are net immigrant jurisdictions, while SIDS are net exporters of people: this demographic difference is a telling indicator that distinguishes SIDS from their more affluent and dynamic dependent neighbours. People vote with their feet: the citizens of SNIJs have a per-capita income almost three times higher than those in SIDS (McElroy and Sanborn, 2005, passim).

CONCLUSION

We should therefore not be surprised to find that many of what are today small sovereign island states did not struggle for independence. For example, "the West Indies were the first colonies and they are determined to be the last" (Mills, 1972: 4). In Grenada, opposition to independence in 1973–74 erupted in violence and looting. Antigua and Barbuda's independence was delayed by the 1976 election of the Antigua Labour Party on a "no to independence" ticket (Thorndike, 1987: 102). Independence Day in Mauritius was not an occasion of universal rejoicing (Houbert, 1981: 87). "The Solomon Islands, Vanuatu and Mauritius [again] went to independence with as much trepidation as jubilation" (Aldrich and Connell, 1998: 246). Malta opted for independence only after its attempts to seek integration with Britain were dashed, mainly by the not-so-keen British themselves and by a nervous local Catholic Church (Baldacchino, 1993; 2002c). Although there are exceptions (Kiribati-Tuvalu, St-Kitts-Nevis, Indonesia-East Timor), many island-based secessionist movements are not instigated by yearnings for separate independence, but rather by estimates of their own territories' chances of associating with some larger, usually extra-regional state, thereby increasing the flow of development aid (Emmanuel, 1976: 5) and much more besides, rather than sticking to a possibly equally small, and equally poor, hinterland-starved partner. Witness such movements, some successful, in Anguilla, Aruba, Barbuda, Carriacou, Cayman, Mayotte, and the Northern Marianas.

The United Nations Special Committee on Decolonization remains hard at work. We have reached the end of the Second International Decade for the Eradication of Colonialism, and the "Special Committee of 24" has decided that "there are 16 non-self-governing territories remaining on the agenda of the United Nations." Until their status is "satisfactorily resolved," it continues to look for "innovative and practical ways to advance the decolonization process" (United Nations, 2008). Presumably, one of the options, if not the ultimate option, is full independence.

The Cayman Islands are one of the sixteen jurisdictions on the UN's list. In 1993 the special committee sought to visit the territory. The islanders made their intentions in favour of the status quo clear: "The People of the Cayman Islands do not want a mad rush forward into other forms of constitutional change," a government leader retorted. "In the case of the Caymans, we are fully committed to remaining a crown colony," another elected representative explained. "*Even the discussion of independence* is out of the question" (quoted from *The New Caymanian* in Aldrich and Connell, 1998: 142; my emphasis).

Representatives from the Falkland Islands attend the meetings of the UN's Decolonization Committee every year "to counter Argentine propaganda, and to set out our case to no longer be regarded as a colonial relic, but an internally self-governing territory that chooses to make its allegiance with the UK" (Summers, 2007). But such choices appear too bitter for the UN to swallow.

When Suriname was making preparations to achieve full independence in 1975, the Surinamese premier, Henck Arron, contacted his counterpart in the Dutch Antilles, Juancho Evertsz, and asked him whether he would lead his islanders to join Suriname into full sovereignty. The answer: "If you allow yourself to be hung, it does not mean that I will do the same" (quoted in Hoefte and Oostindie, 1991: 75).

Environmental Policies and Politics: Economic versus Ecological Development Strategies

INTRODUCTION

Much of the literature on the development prospects of smaller, often island, jurisdictions is steeped in pessimism, driven by a serious concern as to the ability of such players to exploit the opportunities of an increasingly globalized world and its emergent liberalized trade rules. It is common to argue that small size, islandness, low-governance capacity, and "vulnerability" – that is, a "proneness of susceptibility to damage or injury" (Wisner et al., 2004: 11) – conspire to exacerbate the existing marginalization of smaller economies and therefore create a condition that justifies ongoing, special treatment. These arguments, however, "are by no means uncontentious, and are part of an ongoing debate" (Horscroft, 2005: 41; 54n.1). L. Briguglio (1995: 1615–20), P. Encontre (1999: 265), WTO (1999), and UNCTAD (2004) are examples of sympathetic reviews of the special concerns of smaller economies, while T.N. Srinivasan (1986) and S. Page and P. Kleen (2004: 82, 89–90) represent even gloomier evaluations. Perhaps because I was born and bred in a small jurisdiction myself, I partake of a more pragmatic and optimistic view of the prospects for these territories and their citizens, who keep alive a portfolio of skills and revenue streams which enables them to migrate both intersectorally and transnationally, thus continuing to exploit opportunities and maximize economic gains in a turbulent and dynamic external environment (e.g., Baldacchino and Bertram, 2009a).

While there are real environmental threats associated with being a smaller and open economy – hurricanes, droughts, sea-level rise, water shortages, waste mountains – some such jurisdictions have done well and continue to do so. They are "developed," or have "graduated," not so much for having avoided major hazards but for having risen up to their challenge and prospered because – and not in spite – of their openness, perhaps becoming more resilient and nimble in the outcome.

In a globalized and interdependent world, all countries today face threats and dependencies. The United States, often referred to as the current "hyperpower," has had its fair share of recent, psyche-changing disasters, including 9/11 in 2001, Hurricane Katrina in 2005, and the Wall Street crash of 2008. All oil and gas importing countries have rediscovered their dependency on fossil fuels with the recent price hikes in these resources. Autarchy is hardly a policy option, and so some measure of trade dependence is a characteristic of contemporary jurisdictions. It is the responsiveness to threats, and not the existence of threats per se, that deserves kudos and analysis. The capacity to get up and move on in the face of various disasters deserves being celebrated and researched. Nor should such successes be simply dismissed as "special cases" (e.g., the Seychelles in Kaplinsky, 1983) or "paradoxes" (e.g., "the Singapore Contradiction" in Briguglio, 2002) that fly in the face of all-too-obvious vulnerabilities. They deserve critical recognition and serious scrutiny on their own terms.

This chapter proposes to move away from the "vulnerability-resilience" continuum that grips much of the debate on the economic viability of smaller states and territories today, replacing it with an alternative conversation: one between economic (high-density) and ecological (low-density) criteria of development. In so doing, one invites a reconsideration of the impact of physical geography on development, as well as the changing relationship between "nature" and "human culture." Such an approach also extends our discussion to a more longer-term analysis. Some might prefer to call this a "sustainable development" approach. I, however, prefer not to use this widely abused term, which, in any case, I consider to be an oxymoron (Baldacchino, 2004c).

Islands that are political units are also geographical enclaves that tend to have higher population densities than mainlands, since offloading people across the sea remains more problematic than offloading them onto a contiguous land mass. Moreover, around half of humankind dwells on or near coastal regions, because continental interiors are disadvantaged locations for settlement. These preferences are evinced from the much higher mean population density for islands than for continents. Excluding the large but practically empty mass of Greenland, island units have a mean population density of 144 persons per km^2 – *three times* the mean value of 48 persons per km^2 that obtains for Eurasia, America, Africa, and Australia combined[1] (see Table 8.1). Of course, if one is looking for extreme cases of population density, examples of *both ends* of the continuum are to be found on islands. In other words, island states and territories do not just provide scenarios of very high

TABLE 8.1: Population density on islands and continents compared (2009)

LAND MASS	POPULATION (A)	LAND AREA (KM²) (B)	POPULATION DENSITY (A/B)
1. Four Continents	6,550,435,000	136,071,330	48
2. As (1) above, less Australia	6,530,000,000	128,453,330	51
3. All Island States and Territories	588,807,050	6,263,612	94
4. As (3) above, less Greenland	588,752,050	4,088,000	144

population density – with places like Bermuda, Malta, and Singapore topping the list; they also provide examples of land areas with very low population density, as well as the *only* examples of completely de/unpopulated, geographically discrete areas on the globe. "'Uninhabited' is a word attached only to islands" (Birkett, 1997: 14). These locales are attractive, and in sometimes very contrasting ways. One could be the exploitation of their often unique natural qualities and apparent "underdevelopment" for the purpose of more sustainable living, exclusive retirement locales, or upscale, gated communities and/or niche tourism. Another could be the use of such islands, especially depopulated ones, as locales for offshoring undesirable "waste" (human or material) and dangerous experiments.

TWO DISTINCT PARADIGMS

Most of what are seen as successful island jurisdictions today have managed to avoid extensive resorts to industrialization. That means that they have also avoided the environmental fallout and rust-belt sites that such a development trajectory unwittingly implies. Other than the sovereign states of Fiji, Malta, and Mauritius, and the subnational Commonwealth of the Northern Marianas,[2] no smaller island jurisdiction has embarked on any significant industrial programs. Most have thus often managed to "leapfrog" nimbly from primary to tertiary sector production in the space of a few decades (e.g., Baldacchino, 1998). That being said, many of these successful smaller island jurisdictions today find themselves operating within one of two distinct and quite diametrically opposed development paradigms.

The first batch is typified by dynamic, aggressive, and competitive export producers who can depend on strong knowledge and capital pools. Such locations typically have high population densities, limited land areas, large pools of immigrant labour, considerable foreign direct investment, significant manufacturing sectors, and extensive overseas investments, but poor and degraded local natural environments (if any exist) and higher per-capita carbon footprints. "City states" such as Hong Kong, Malta, Monaco, and Singapore – as well as larger countries such as Japan – are leading examples (e.g., Debattista, 2007). These jurisdictions would not have any appreciable rural elite (Streeten, 1993: 199); this, in turn, is perhaps an outcome of poor soils, difficult terrain unsuitable for commercial farming, or the absence of a rural hinterland altogether. This cluster of features can be labelled as the *economic-development* approach.

In contrast, the second batch of examples is typified by island locales that flaunt their clean, serene, and pristine natural environments, often accompanied by distinctive cultural practices associated with indigenous communities. The absence of crowding – low populations and low population densities perhaps supported by remittances and transfers from elsewhere – help to maintain this more sustainable lifestyle, which in turn promotes a potentially more nature-friendly, more exclusive, tourism industry (Thomas et al., 2005; for a critical view, see Gössling, 2003). Dominica, Greenland, Iceland, Molokai, New Zealand, Samoa, Seychelles, Tobago, and the Faroes are apt examples (*National Geographic*, 2006). Many of these locales are associated with states that have dedicated significant portions of their land and/or sea to nature parks or have maintained their natural forest, tundra, taiga, or permafrost cover. Dominica's "mountainous terrain makes it inhospitable to massive hotel projects" (Osborne, 2008). For another example, note how five Micronesian governments (Palau, followed by the Federated States of Micronesia, the Republic of the Marshall Islands, the U.S. Territory of Guam, and the U.S. Commonwealth of the Northern Mariana Islands) have pledged to conserve 30 per cent of their near-shore marine resources and 20 per cent of their terrestrial resources by 2020 (Nature Conservancy, 2008). This second cluster of features can be labelled the *ecological-development* approach.

The main features of, and differences between, these two approaches are schematically described in Table 8.2. Different parts of the same country can exhibit these two sets of features. In sprawling archipelagic Japan, for example, metropolitan-high-density Honshu is contrasted to Yakushima Island (most of it being a UNESCO World Heritage Site) and the sacred island of Miyajima. The same can be said for the Bahamas, where two-thirds of the population lives on the island of New Providence, which has just 3 per cent of the country's total land area; or the Maldives, with almost the whole population living on one atoll. In Indonesia, the Moluccas (or Spice Islands) have a population density of 20 persons per km^2; contrast this to the population density of 2,070 for Java.

TABLE 8.2: Contrasting paradigms: Economic development versus ecological development

	ECONOMIC DEVELOPMENT	ECOLOGICAL DEVELOPMENT
Population Density	High	Low
Location	Nodal	Peripheral
Typology (*after* Warrington and Milne, 2007)	Entrepôt Island	Fortress Island
State of Natural Resources	Limited, fragmented, and strained	Significant, unadulterated, and pristine
Export Orientation	Aggressive (mass-market oriented)	Choosy (niche-market oriented)
Tourism Appeal	Mass	Exclusive
Carbon Footprint	High	Low*
Urbanization	High	Low

*One needs to exercise caution here. While domestic carbon footprints may be low, they may be excessively high in relation to, for example, the tourism industry. Thus, the Seychelles had a very high mean air-travel emissions level per tourist of 1,873 kg of carbon dioxide in 2005 (Gössling et al., 2008: Table 2).

The contrast between these two sets of island features can also be discerned from the same geographical region. In the island-rich Mediterranean, for example, population density ranges from a high of over 1,200 per km^2 for the Maltese Islands to 68 for Sardinia and just 32 for Corsica. In the latter two cases, a rugged topography makes settlement more challenging, and this difficulty of access conserves a rather unspoilt interior.

So it appears that geography and history conspire to render islands differently suited for development strategies. According to a typology suggested by E. Warrington and D. Milne (2007), island entrepôts have acted as magnets for significant incoming and circulating population movements and diversity; they are also well placed to exploit their "in betweenity" in another manner: to accumulate fiscal, human, and material capital for development. They are challenged to come up with solutions to the pressing problems resulting from an acute lack of space and associated high costs of land (e.g., *The Economist*, 2006a). They are thus well honed to take upon themselves an economic approach to their development. Meanwhile, island *fortresses* appear better suited at keeping newcomers away, making access to their shores more difficult, tortuous, time-consuming, challenging, or otherwise risky. These conditions suggest that an ecological approach to development may be a more natural option. J. Connell and R. King (1999: 3), echoing Churchill Semple (1911), observe that islands that find themselves at important crossroads – in a "nodal location" – tend to attract immigrants and may thus be challenged by overpopulation, whereas those that find themselves isolated, on the periphery, may be more adept at sending people away and may therefore suffer stagnant or declining populations in the outcome, risking depopulation.

That there should be at least two contrasting development paradigms in the first place may reveal a basic misunderstanding about the very nature and expression of development. The leading examples of *economic* development, with their significantly negative environmental impacts, may not be successful over the longer term. Their "success" may often depend on the ability to lure value-added from elsewhere, while exporting negative externalities offshore. The examples of *ecological* development (if any such term can be used), in contrast, maintain very low environmental footprints. A.L. Dahl (1996: 49) reminds us that "[in spite of] the 'eco' as a unifying concept ... the chasm between economics and ecology is a symptom of the malfunctioning of modern society which threatens our very future." Given the strong sense of place that they engender, islands are ideal spaces to experience the pernicious and dysfunctional chasm between these two separate "ecos" (Depraetere, 2008: 20; also Ritchie, 1977).

If we are to posit these two sets of island candidates as success stories, then we need to be better able to identify, critically but cogently, what led them to assume such a status. Are there (other) discernible patterns behind either of these two, apparently diametrically opposed, trajectories of success? Which political episodes (including crisis?) and dynamics (including non-democratic processes?) have galvanized these island societies and economies towards competitive economic or ecological prosperity? What particular set of goods and services have permitted these jurisdictions to occupy and secure export markets? What human-resource development policies have they pursued? What beneficial links with their respective diasporas have they fashioned? How have they exploited bilateral and multilateral agreements via shrewd paradiplomacy and international relations? Have higher education, tourism, financial services, and niche manufacturing been important contributors to economic growth? Is there an active concern with sustainability and visions of a future that will lower fossil-fuel dependency? These are some of the questions that beckon further, island studies research.

A second set of questions is also pertinent. These questions would connect with considerations or opportunities to shift gear from one developmental approach to another. What does one do if a particular island territory wants to be successful on *both* these development fronts? Can one be both economically *and* ecologically successful, and be known globally for both? How have island states such as Ireland and Iceland (e.g., *The Economist*, 2006d) managed to avoid this seeming contradiction by portraying themselves as "smart" (technologically savvy), without sacrificing their representation as places where nature is bountiful, where, for example, good whisky can coexist with cloning research (as in Scotland) and where quality milk chocolate can coexist with precision watches (as in Switzerland)? Can an island be both green and clever at the same time?[3] Or is this "best of both worlds" scenario only a myth, possible only via a deliberate foray into marketing spin and camouflage? Could especially archipelagic island states – such as the Bahamas, Fiji, Kiribati, Maldives, Seychelles, St Vincent and the Grenadines, and Tonga – but also mainland states with outlying island units – such as the United States with Hawaii, or Portugal with the Azores and Madeira, or Tanzania with Zanzibar – zone their territory in such a way so as to pursue differential development strategies via geographically delineated (that is, enclaved) policies?

ECONOMIC SUCCESS

The *economic* road to success is the easier to chart, because it follows well-worn, conventional principles and definitions. Standardized economic statistics rank countries according to GNP/GDP or purchasing-power-parity standards. Wealth is often defined in such terms as GNI/GNP/GDP per capita, with purchasing-power parity. Smaller, often island, territories do exceptionally well on these counts, while on average, non-sovereign island territories tend to be richer per capita than sovereign ones (Poirine, 1998; Bertram, 2004). The citizens of French Polynesia, Aruba, Bermuda, and Iceland (the latter before the recent collapse of its currency!) have been counted among the world's top ten richest people, in terms of these conventional standards (*The Economist*, 2003b).

Island-specific literature suggests five policy areas as being critical ingredients in shaping economic prosperity (e.g., Milne, 2000). Contestation over "who does what" in these economic-policy areas is typically tense, especially in federal political systems, and may in itself lead to demands for more self-rule, its withdrawal, or its renegotiation between the parties concerned. These powers are premised on effective governance. However, unlike other models that seek to explain the principles behind revenue flows to island economies,[4] these policy areas – especially finance, mainly banking, insurance, and taxation; environmental policy, particularly natural resources; access, particularly in relation to air and sea transportation; free movement of persons; and tourism[5] – depend much more on the nurturing of specific, local, jurisdictional capacities or local powers (Baldacchino, 2006a). They comprise the management of external relations "by means of domestic policies and governing institutions" (Warrington, 1998: 101). Looking at these policy areas more holistically, Bertram and Poirine (2007: 362) conclude that "the combination of offshore finance and high-quality tourism stands out as the strategy of the most successful island economies." These policy capacities have been reviewed in chapter 5.

ECOLOGICAL SUCCESS

The defining characteristics of *ecological* success are much more elusive. They typically include small populations enjoying longevity and healthy low-stress lifestyles, large proportions of undisturbed and pristine land, rich air quality, abundant local fauna and flora, and low carbon footprints, but these same features may be (mis)construed as those of a fledgling, late-coming economy. What, for example, is Greenland/Kalallit Nunaat? It is the world's largest island, with the world's largest national park (Northeast Greenland National Park – 972,000 km^2); a population of just 56,344 (in 2007), of whom 88 per cent are indigenous Inuit or mixed Danish and Inuit; and – thanks to challenging climate conditions, subnational jurisdictional status, and distance from markets – the beneficiary of relatively low but high-paying tourism (around 30,000 visitors annually). The tourism figures (via both air and cruise ship) are on a steady increase, and the official policy appears to be satisfied with expansion (e.g., Kaae, 2006). And so Greenland may be simply a very late starter for the conventional route to mass tourism. We could say the same about Madagascar, and other smaller islands. The march to conventional development grips such islands too: their populations –like their tourism numbers – may continue to grow unchecked, with a progressively more severe impact on finite and fragile natural assets.[6]

The trajectory from ecologic towards economic development is often a victim of the sheer momentum of democratic politics. Once local residents start buying into the tourism industry, they develop an interest in increasing tourism numbers, hoping to tap into the accruing wealth by landing an additional job or contract or else offering that one additional bed, meal, tour, or souvenir: a dynamic well explained in the "development phase" by R.W. Butler (1980) in his Tourism Area Life Cycle model, or by the "Tragedy of the Commons" as outlined by G. Hardin (1968). But more tourists do not necessarily translate into higher local value added, especially when a locale's exclusive charm is eroded and the local environment becomes irreparably degraded with the impact of tourist invasions – diminishing returns are a real threat, especially on the smallest islands. Politicians in democracies may be loathe, or find it difficult, to adopt unpopular measures that may, or are seen to, thwart the "trickle down" benefits – such as rents and employment – that may accrue from this industry.

Still, in spite of these real political challenges, there are some examples that suggest a fairly successful brake on the normal expansion of tourism and its creeping penetration on a smaller island's infrastructure, economy, and society. To illustrate, three "warm water" island cases are presented here. They manifest, to different degrees, how these islands have been able to buck the trend to a mass-tourism market, with its associated setbacks.

The Seychelles

This country has been one of the most stable, fastest growing economies in Africa over the medium term, having made a successful transition to democracy in recent decades. The arrival of 130,000 tourists generated US$112 million in 2000, corresponding to 20 per cent of GDP and 60 per cent of foreign-exchange earnings (Shah, 2002). The same number of visitors was reported for 2005. McElroy (2006) assigns the Seychelles a penetration index of 0.107. Tourism is thus a key pillar of the economy for this 112-island archipelago with a population of around 90,000. The Seychelles has adopted a strong-arm approach to the industry. It has limited the size of hotels (beyond tourism "villages") to a maximum of 200 rooms; it maintains a selective marketing approach where pricing acts as a filter for the type of tourism that the country desires. It has exploited its archipelagic nature, with the result that its tourist destinations most distant from the capital and the country's sole international airport – like Bird Island and Cousin Island – have higher occupancy rates even though they are costlier and both more difficult and expensive to get to. Prices per bed night per person reach €40, even in the simplest guesthouses (e.g., Rosalie, 2002). There are currently plans to attract a maximum of 250,000 tourists a year.[7]

Environmental legislation in the Seychelles was implemented in a top-down process under the one-party rule of President France Albert René in the mid-1970s. This policy continued even after the turn to democracy in the early 1990s. The institutional framework for environmental conservation was established with the creation of the Department of the Environment in 1989. As early as 1990, the first environmental management plan for the Seychelles was implemented (RoS, 1990), followed by a plan for 2000–10 which provides guidelines for all activities related to the environment (RoS, 2001). In order to ensure environmental conservation, some 50 per cent of the land area of the Seychelles (230 km^2) was turned into protected areas (RoS, 2001). These areas are of particular importance in creating the image of an eco-island, and they are part of the Seychelles' successful marketing strategy (Gössling and Wall, 2007). Within the archipelago, such an island as Aldabra, a UNESCO World Heritage Site, has no permanent settlement and is accessible only to scientists and special visitors.

St Barthélemy (St Barths)

Another example of successful containment and high per-capita value-added could be of a Caribbean island which is an overseas collectivity of France (and, until 2007, part of the same *department d'outre mer* as Guadeloupe). The island of St Barthélemy has an area of only about 12 km^2 and a residential population of about 3,500 persons. It has long been considered a playground of the rich and famous and is known for its beautiful pristine beaches, gourmet dining in chic bistros, and high-end designer shopping. There are only some twenty-five hotels, most of them with fifteen rooms or fewer, and the largest, the Guanahani, has just seventy rooms (Insiders' Guide, 2006). F. Doumenge (1998: 341) describes the island as follows: "The airport has a very small airstrip, accessible only to smaller planes having not more than 20 seats (including that of the pilot). This drastically limits tourist access, and offers an efficient means of control. In St Barthélemy, you can enjoy a very quiet, traditional way of life, with a very high standard of living, and the islanders control their destiny in a more thorough manner than would otherwise be possible."

A total of 175,055 passengers arrived in St Barths in 2003: "passengers" includes both residents and visitors alike, since there is as yet no system that allows the exact number of tourists to be counted. The number of visitors is thus probably around 50,000 (*St Barths News*, 2004). It is not possible to fly direct into St Barths: the main entry point for commercial flights is via Dutch Sint Maarten, just ten minutes' flying time away. Those ten minutes, apparently, make a world of difference. As Doumenge (1998: 341) candidly continues: "Just in front of St Barthélemy lies Sint Maarten, an island with disaster written all over it, with its mafia barons, gambling racket, and crowds in excess of one million tourists a year channeled through a large international airport."

Galápagos

A third example, this time of how a containment policy can run into serious difficulty, even though it may have started off with the best of intentions, concerns the Galápagos Islands. This island archipelago has been identified as "Evolution's Workshop" following the pioneering work of such bio-geographers and zoologists as Charles Darwin, David Lack, and Peter and Rosemary Grant (Larson, 2002). One-third of the archipelago's vascular land plants are endemic, as are nearly all the reptiles, half the breeding land birds, and almost 30 per cent of the marine species. This has led to an international movement to preserve the islands' unique ecosystem, with the support of the Ecuadorian government, to which the islands belong. The plan was for controlled tourism to help safeguard the rich flora and fauna, while sustaining livelihoods for the locals. The Charles Darwin Research Station, run by the Charles Darwin Foundation, was set up in 1959; UNESCO declared the Galápagos one of its first four World Heritage Sites in 1978; a Biological Marine Resources Reserve was set up in 1986, with a zoning plan in place by 1992; and a 1998 "Special Law" restricted movement of mainland Ecuadorians to the islands. It looked as though the environmentalists had secured the upper hand in the context of a positive-sum game (UNEP/WCMC, 2006).

But the experience has proved exasperating. Hoping to find work, and lured by the prospects of a better life, people from mainland Ecuador have literally invaded the islands. The 1949 resident population was just 800. The 1990 census reported an island population of 9,735. In 2005 the figure had shot up to 28,000, and it is still growing at 6.5 per cent per annum. Tourism has been too successful. Despite high prices – the average cost of a U.S. package to the Galápagos was already around US$3,000 in 2001 (Kerr, 2005), and the National Park charges foreign tourists a US$100 entrance fee – the stream of visitors has never let up. In the 1960s there were around 1,000 tourists annually; some 140,000 visitors turned up in 2006. A third airport has been built, and cruise ships started arriving in 2007. Tourists visiting the park reached some 180,000 in 2008 (Kraul, 2008).

TENSIONS AT WORK

The Galápagos case is illustrative of the many interesting tensions at work in these – and similar[8] – island contexts, reminding us that "development" is always contested since it creates both winners and losers. Although a UNESCO World Heritage Site, this archipelago is witnessing "the mixed blessings of greenery": it is finding it hard to prevent invasions of mainland Ecuadoreans, who threaten its unique environment and species (e.g., Larson, 2002; The Economist, 2008c). Competing visions – an isolated versus an increasingly open archipelago, the first championed by conservation advocates, the second by residents and local authorities – lie at the heart of most conflicts in the Galápagos (Ospina, 2006; González et al., 2008).

Some islands do try to move away from the economic to the ecologic model of development, with industrial and other stakeholders doggedly defending their way of life. Tasmania, for example, continues to struggle to define itself, with a significant business and trade-union lobby intent on commercially exploiting its old growth forests, while other interests are just as determined to protect and preserve them (e.g., Chen and Hay, 2006). In contrast, other island jurisdictions appear to be making an opposite move, from a more ecologic to a more economic logic, promoting some indus-trialization especially to stave off a condition of chronic unemployment, economic stagnation, and regional depopulation: "picturesque poverty," as Harry Rees, a councillor from the Isle of Wight, describes it (Arnold, 2003). The job opportunities, but environmental costs, associated with building an aluminum smelter in Eastern Iceland have divided that island's public (e.g., Hollingham, 2007). Similarly, when the government of the island state of Dominica – said to be the only island that navigator Christopher Columbus would recognize were he to revisit the Caribbean today – decided to accept an offer from its Venezuelan counterpart to build an oil refinery, it sparked keen debates on how this decision would compromise the country's "sustainable development" and its credentials as the "nature island" of the Caribbean (e.g., TheDominican.net, 2007; Shillingford, 2007).[9] The island of Jeju, declared a "special autonomous province" of South Korea in 2006, and home to a World Heritage Site, is now in the sights of the Korean Navy for a potential military base, a development that is being strongly opposed by some of the suspicious, local population (e.g., Koehler, 2007).

Meanwhile, the designation, or "listing," of a place as a UNESCO World Heritage Site creates an interesting twist of responsibility. Each site, of course, stays physically put; it has been nominated for the list by a national govern-ment and is ultimately still in the hands of that same government. And yet there is significant added pressure on national governments to take all mea-sures necessary to preserve any site within their jurisdiction. Should this not happen, and the site is eroded as a result, UNESCO can take measures to place the site on the List of World Heritage Sites in Danger, and perhaps ultimately de-list the site from World Heritage status. Typically, this would be done with the consent of the state party concerned, but UNESCO does have the author-ity to proceed unilaterally and make a new entry on its "World Heritage in Danger" List. The measure could "shame" a government into taking appropri-ate remedial action, as happened in the case of Skellig Michael, in Ireland (e.g., *The Economist*, 2009f). Exceptionally, a site can also be stripped of its status as a World Heritage Site, with or without its government's consent (*The Economist*, 2009g).

World Heritage Sites partake in a project deliberately constructing a common, global history which transcends political, spatial, temporal, and other boundaries: "The listing is an act of dis-embedding and re-embedding that distances heritage sites from former times and spaces in nations, ties them to the evolutionary history of Man [sic] and Nature, and thereby extending their territory to the entire surface of the globe" (Turtinen, 2000: 18). Such responsibilities cannot be taken lightly. The Tasmania Wilderness World Heritage Area was listed in November 1982, at the same time that a major dam on the Franklin River was being proposed for the production of hydroelectric power, threatening the designated heritage site. While the state (that is, provincial) government of Tasmania was in favour of the dam construction, a newly elected Labour government in Australia (under Bob Hawke) was not. When Hawke's government passed the World Heritage Properties Conservation Act, overriding the state legislation, the Tasmanian government appealed the decision. However, the Australian High Court ruled narrowly in the federal government's favour, arguing that the federal government has the power to legislate on any issue, if that is necessary to enforce an international treaty (e.g., Green, 1984).

PROTECTED AREAS, NON-DEMOCRATIC CONTROL, AND PRIVATE ISLANDS

It is much easier for subnational, island territories and jurisdictions to adopt and maintain an ecological approach to their development than an independent state. This is because they can be zoned for such a purpose, while economic development can take place elsewhere, presumably in the metropole. Clearly, it becomes difficult for any jurisdiction to maintain itself on exclusively ecological principles. Although *whole islands and archipelagos* have been ensconced on the UNESCO World Heritage List,[10] no *whole country* has been, and is not likely to be.

Islands, especially smaller ones, can become beacons, or what C. Turner (2007) calls "geographies of hope." Turner is keen to present us with a scattering of islands that are making impressive advances in energy sustainability and serve as beacons of optimism in otherwise dark and gloomy times. Note that Turner uses the word "island" also as metaphor, and so only two of the examples from his "archipelago" of cases are real physical ·

islands. Nevertheless, these two – Samsø (a 100 per cent renewable-energy site) and Aerø, both in Denmark – are clear examples of islands boasting energy sustainability. Other "real island" examples can be added, for good measure: Iceland, with its hydrogen-powered bus fleet and commitment to be (except for its air planes) fossil-free by 2050; and islands like Mackinac (United States), Hiddensee (Germany), Sark (Channel Islands), and Cheung Chau and Lama (Hong Kong, China) remain today without automobiles. The only two vehicles on Heligoland (Germany) are the fire truck and – since 2007 – a police car. Bermuda, which for some time banned the motorcar, now has a strict "one car per household" policy plus no rentable vehicles. On La Digue, the third-largest island in the Seychelles, the local authority restricts the issuing of licences for trucks, cars, taxis, and buses. On Mosquito Island, British Virgin Islands, recently purchased by Sir Richard Branson, everything is designed to reduce, or eliminate, dependence on fossil fuels.

There are three general ways in which islands have been carved out, or enclaved, for the purpose of ecological-development trajectories. The first is via *the crafting of parks or nature/culture reserves*. The world's largest protected marine area, until recently, has been Australia's Great Barrier Reef (which includes many islands and which has been a World Heritage Site since 1981). Since 2006, the Papahānaumokuākea (originally Northwestern) Hawaiian Islands Marine National Monument (United States) is even larger, with an area of some 362,000 km², more than the total area of all current U.S. national parkland (e.g., Eilperin, 2006). The Isle of Wight, England's largest island, has 50 per cent of its land area designated as an "Area of Outstanding Natural Beauty"; more than two-thirds of the island is under some environmental protection (Arnold, 2003). The Andaman and Nicobar Islands, a subnational island jurisdiction of India, and "rediscovered" after the 2004 "Boxing Day" tsunami, have the potential to emerge as the "Organic Islands of the world." They are run by tribal communities using traditional knowledge; forests still cover 85 per cent of their total land area (Nambath, 2005).

There are various international, UNESCO-related listing systems, registries, or networks in the field of heritage. A List of Cultural Property for Protection in the Event of an Armed Conflict was set up in 1954. A listing of Wetlands of International Importance (the Ramsar List) was introduced in 1971. A World Network of Biosphere Reserves, under UNESCO's Man and the Biosphere Program, was launched in 1976. As of May 2009, there were 553 such biosphere reserves in 107 countries, including the whole islands of Fuerteventura (Canaries, Spain) and Flores (Azores, Portugal) as well as the archipelago of Shinan Dadohae (South Korea). More recent listing initiatives – such as the

Memory of the World Register, and the Proclamation of Masterpieces of the Oral and Intangible Heritage of Humanity – were both launched in the late 1990s (UNESCO Listing, 2008).

But perhaps the most prestigious, "enormously popular," and "most successful of all the Conventions" remains UNESCO's 1972 Convention concerning the Protection of the World Cultural and Natural Heritage, which is the basis of the list of World Heritage Sites, numbering 890 places after three decades (Logan, 2008). Some national parks (like Dominica's Morne Trois Pitons) are inscribed onto this list in due course. Inclusion on this high-status list identifies a locale as having cultural and/or natural features that are recognized as part of the common heritage of humankind and therefore merit being preserved for all, beyond the beneficiaries living within the actual political borders where these sites may happen to be situated. Islands, singly or in groups, are the only places that can find themselves *totally ensconced* as World Heritage Sites. Thus, at recent rounds of additions to the list, announced in 2008 and 2009, there were sites *in* Cape Verde, *in* Cuba, *in* Mauritius, *in* New Caledonia, *in* the United Kingdom, and *in* Vanuatu announced; but the *whole island* of Surtsey (Iceland) and the whole Socotra archipelago (Yemen) were also included. The latter join other, wholly endorsed islands or archipelagos: the Aeolian Islands, Aldabra, Baja de California Islands, Fraser Island, Galápagos, Gorée, Henderson, Isla de Cocos, Lord Howe, Mozambique Island, New Zealand Sub-Antarctic Islands, Rapa Nui/Easter Island, Robben Island, Saint-Louis, St Kilda, and Venice. Some of these islands, especially those listed for their natural features, are totally depopulated (as is Surtsey, Iceland); some are accessible only to scientists (Macquarie Island, Australia); some are accessible to tourists but not until special permission is obtained (Aldabra atoll, Seychelles); some are even inaccessible, in name as much as in deed: Gough and Inaccessible Islands (United Kingdom) were inscribed on the list in 1995. (For a complete listing of island-related World Heritage Sites, see Tables 8.3 and 8.4.)

The second route to ecological development, objectionable though it may seem, is via *non-democratic control and non-pluralist governance*. (The designation of land or sea as parks, reserves, or World Heritage Sites is, in itself, a form of wresting such spaces from the at times non-regulatory and laissez-faire tendencies of democracy.) The "political geography" of cold water islands might partly explain why there are lesser pressures to expand tourism on these locations. Extreme island regions of larger states tend to lie on the political periphery, especially when they have smaller populations: they are un/under-represented in the corridors of power, largely forgotten

TABLE 8.3: Whole islands or archipelagos listed as UNESCO World Heritage Sites as of May 2009

1	Lord Howe Island Group (Australia)	15	Isole Eolie (Aeolian Islands) (Italy)
2	Fraser Island (Australia)	16	Portovenere, Cinque Terre, and the Islands (Palmaria, Tino and Tinetto) (Italy)
3	Heard and McDonald Islands (Australia)		
4	Macquarie Island (Australia)	17	Islands and Protected Areas of the Gulf of California (Mexico)
5	Fernando de Noronha and Atol das Rocas Reserves (Brazil)	18	Island of Mozambique (Mozambique)
6	Rapa Nui National Park (Chile)	19	New Zealand Sub-Antarctic Islands (New Zealand)
7	Cocos Island National Park (Costa Rica)	20	Vegaøyan – The Vega Archipelago (Norway)
8	Galapagos Islands (Ecuador)	21	Cultural and Historic Ensemble of the Solovetsky Islands (Russia)
9	Mont-Saint-Michel and its Bay (France)	22	Island of Gorée (Senegal)
10	James Island and Related Sites (Gambia)	23	Island of Saint-Louis (Senegal)
11	Delos (Greece)	24	Aldabra Atoll (Seychelles)
12	Surtsey (Iceland)	25	Robben Island (South Africa)
13	Skellig Michael (Ireland)	26	St Kilda (Scotland, United Kingdom)
14	Venice and its Lagoon (Italy)	27	Socotra Archipelago (Yemen)

by centralized policy makers suffering from "the urban bias," and dismissed as insignificant backwaters other than, perhaps, in strategic (military and resource) terms (Butler, 1993; Wilkinson, 1994). A weak local political influence and a lackadaisical interest from the centre do, in turn, have the potential to create a power vacuum. Local elites can readily fill in this gap and thus assume significant local politico-economic power. These elites also tend to be narrower, less fragmented, and more concentrated in island jurisdictions with smaller populations (e.g., Buker, 2005; May and Tupouniua, 1980; Richards, 1982). Power can rest in the hands of a small, identifiable group: a religious congregation (Solovetsky), a team of scientists (Macquarie), an indigenously controlled corporation (Baffin; Nunivak), an arm's-length enterprise trust (Chatham), or a municipality (Luleå).[11] Such skewed influence creates a situation where there is hardly a plurality of interest groups clamouring to benefit, and benefit fast, from the tourism bandwagon. The oligopolies in power tend to be champions of tradition; they effuse caution and harbour a suspicion of

1 Great Barrier Reef (Australia)

2 Tasmanian Wilderness (Australia)

3 Qal'at al-Bahrain – Ancient Harbour and Capital of Dilmun (Bahrain)

4 Belize Barrier Reef Reserve System (Belize)

5 L'Anse aux Meadows National Historic Site (Canada)

6 SGang Gwaay (Canada)

7 Gros Morne National Park (Canada)

8 Cidade Velha, Historic Centre of Ribeira Grande (Cape Verde)

9 Churches of Chiloé (Chile)

10 Historic Centre of Macao (China)

11 Malpelo Fauna and Flora Sanctuary (Colombia)

12 Stari Grad Plain (Croatia)

13 Old Havana and Its Fortifications (Cuba)

14 Trinidad and the Valley de los Ingenios (Cuba)

15 San Pedro de la Roca Castle, Santiago de Cuba (Cuba)

16 Desembarco del Granma National Park (Cuba)

17 Viñales Valley (Cuba)

18 Archaeological Landscape of the First Coffee Plantations (Cuba)

19 Alejandro de Humboldt National Park (Cuba)

20 Urban Historic Centre of Cienfuegos (Cuba)

21 Historic Centre of Camagüey (Cuba)

22 Paphos (Cyprus)

23 Painted Churches in the Troodos Region (Cyprus)

24 Choirokoitia (Cyprus)

25 Ilulissat Icefjord (Greenland, Denmark)

26 Morne Trois Pitons National Park (Dominica)

27 Colonial City of Santo Domingo (Dominican Republic)

28 Fortress of Suomenlinna (Finland)

29 High Coast / Kvarken Archipelago (Finland and Sweden)

30 Lagoons, Reef Diversity and Associated Ecosystems (New Caledonia, France)

31 Medieval City of Rhodes (Greece)

32 Historic Centre (Chorá) with the Monastery of Saint John "the Theologian" and the Cave of the Apocalypse on the Island of Pátmos (Greece)

33 Monasteries of Daphni, Hosios Loukas and Nea Moni of Chios (Greece)

34 Pythagoreion and Heraion of Samos (Greece)

35 Old Town of Corfu (Greece)

36 National History Park – Citadel, Sans Souci, Ramiers (Haiti)

37 Thingvellir National Park (Iceland)

38 Borobudur Temple Compounds (Indonesia)

39 Komodo National Park (Indonesia)

40 Prambanan Temple Compounds (Indonesia)

41 Ujung Kulon National Park (Indonesia)

42 Sangiran Early Man Site (Indonesia)

43 Lorentz National Park (Indonesia)

44 Tropical Rainforest Heritage of Sumatra (Indonesia)

45 Archaeological Ensemble of the Bend of the Boyne (Ireland)

46 Archaeological Area of Agrigento (Sicily, Italy)

47 Late Baroque Towns of the Val di Noto (southeastern Sicily, Italy)

48 Syracuse and the Rocky Necropolis of Pantalica (Sicily, Italy)

49 Villa Romana del Casale (Sicily, Italy)

TABLE 8.4 (cont.)

50 Su Nuraxi di Barumini (Sardinia, Italy)

51 Buddhist Monuments in the Horyu-ji Area (Japan)

52 Himeji-jo (Japan)

53 Shirakami-Sanchi (Japan)

54 Yakushima (Japan)

55 Historic Monuments of Ancient Kyoto (Kyoto, Uji, and Otsu Cities) (Japan)

56 Historic Villages of Shirakawa-go and Gokayama (Japan)

57 Hiroshima Peace Memorial (Genbaku Dome) (Japan)

58 Itsukushima Shinto Shrine (Japan)

59 Historic Monuments of Ancient Nara (Japan)

60 Shrines and Temples of Nikko (Japan)

61 Gusuku Sites and Related Properties of the Kingdom of Ryukyu (Japan)

62 Sacred Sites and Pilgrimage Routes in the Kii Mountain Range (Japan)

63 Shiretoko (Japan)

64 Iwami Ginzan Silver Mine and its Cultural Landscape (Japan)

65 Jeju Volcanic Island and Lava Tubes (Jeju, South Korea)

66 Tsingy de Bemaraha Strict Nature Reserve (Madagascar)

67 Royal Hill of Ambohimanga (Madagascar)

68 Rainforests of the Atsinanana (Madagascar)

69 Gunung Mulu National Park (Malaysia)

70 Kinabalu Park (Malaysia)

71 City of Valletta (Malta)

72 Hal Saflieni Hypogeum (Malta)

73 Megalithic Temples of Malta (Malta)

74 Banc d'Arguin National Park (Mauritania)

75 Aapravasi Ghat (Mauritius)

76 Le Morne Cultural Landscape (Mauritius)

77 Historic Area of Willemstad, Inner City and Harbour (Curaçao, Netherlands)

78 Te Wahipounamu (New Zealand)

79 Tongariro National Park (New Zealand)

80 Coiba National Park and its Special Zone of Marine Protection (Panama)

81 Kuk Early Agricultural Site (Papua New Guinea)

82 Baroque Churches (Philippines)

83 Tubbataha Reefs Marine Park (Philippines)

84 Rice Terraces of the Philippine Cordilleras (Philippines)

85 Historic Town of Vigan (Philippines)

86 Puerto-Princesa Subterranean River National Park (Philippines)

87 Central Zone of the Town of Angra do Heroismo in the Azores (Azores, Portugal)

88 Laurisilva of Madeira (Madeira, Portugal)

89 Landscape of the Pico Island Vineyard Culture (Azores, Portugal)

90 Natural System of Wrangel Island Reserve (Russia)

91 Brimstone Hill Fortress National Park (St Kitts and Nevis)

92 Pitons Management Area (St Lucia)

93 Vallée de Mai Nature Reserve (Seychelles)

94 East Rennell (Solomon Islands)

95 Ibiza, Biodiversity and Culture (Balearic Islands, Spain)

96 San Cristóbal de La Laguna (Canary Islands, Spain)

97 Garajonay National Park (Canary Islands, Spain)

TABLE 8.4 (cont.)

98 Teide National Park (Canary Islands, Spain)

99 Ancient City of Polonnaruwa (Sri Lanka)

100 Ancient City of Sigiriya (Sri Lanka)

101 Sacred City of Anuradhapura (Sri Lanka)

102 Old Town of Galle and its Fortifications (Sri Lanka)

103 Sacred City of Kandy (Sri Lanka)

104 Sinharaja Forest Reserve (Sri Lanka)

105 Golden Temple of Dambulla (Sri Lanka)

106 Hanseatic Town of Visby (Gotland, Sweden)

107 Agricultural Landscape of Southern Öland (Sweden)

108 Stone Town of Zanzibar (Zanzibar, Tanzania)

109 Castles and Town Walls of King Edward in Gwynedd (Wales, United Kingdom)

110 Durham Castle and Cathedral (United Kingdom)

111 Giant's Causeway and Causeway Coast (Northern Ireland, United Kingdom)

112 Ironbridge Gorge (United Kingdom)

113 Stonehenge, Avebury and Associated Sites (United Kingdom)

114 Studley Royal Park including the Ruins of Fountains Abbey (United Kingdom)

115 Blenheim Palace (United Kingdom)

116 City of Bath (United Kingdom)

117 Frontiers of the Roman Empire (United Kingdom)

118 Westminster Palace, Westminster Abbey and St Margaret's Church (United Kingdom)

119 Canterbury Cathedral, St Augustine's Abbey and St Martin's Church (United Kingdom)

120 Henderson Island (Pitcairn, United Kingdom)

121 Tower of London (United Kingdom)

122 Gough and Inaccessible Islands (St Helena, United Kingdom)

123 Old and New Towns of Edinburgh (Scotland, United Kingdom)

124 Maritime Greenwich (United Kingdom)

125 Heart of Neolithic Orkney (Orkney, Scotland, United Kingdom)

126 Blaenavon Industrial Landscape (United Kingdom)

127 Historic Town of St George and Related Fortifications (Bermuda, United Kingdom)

128 Derwent Valley Mills (United Kingdom)

129 Dorset and East Devon Coast (United Kingdom)

130 New Lanark (United Kingdom)

131 Saltaire (United Kingdom)

132 Royal Botanic Gardens, Kew (United Kingdom)

133 Liverpool – Maritime Mercantile City (United Kingdom)

134 Cornwall and West Devon Mining Landscape (United Kingdom)

135 Pontcysyllte Aqueduct and Canal (United Kingdom)

136 La Fortaleza and San Juan National Historic Site (Puerto Rico, United States)

137 Hawai'i Volcanoes National Park (Hawaii, United States)

138 Chief Roi Mata's Domain (Vanuatu)

139 Ha Long Bay (Vietnam)

change. They are generally aware of the environmental and economic risks of mass tourism and are immune to those populist pressures that may oblige them to consider seriously such investments in that industry. And so there is limited discussion (at best) on whether to take the tourism industry forward. Most of those in power have no stake in tourism – which is not a key industry anyway – and so are more likely to view its intrusion with some grave, even legitimate, concerns. This is well captured in the following statement, uttered by none other than Archimandrite Josef, the head of the monastery on the Solovetsky Islands, Russia. It leaves no room for discussion: "Overgrowth of tourism flows and preservation of divine spirit of the island are incompatible. Nobody even thinks of converting Solovetsky into a trendy resort where the White Sea shore is full of restaurants and … the sky above the Monastery's towers is crossed by para-gliders" (International symposium, *Solovetsky: Future Insights*, 2003; quoted in Nevmerzhitskaya, 2006: 162).

There is here an uncanny similarity to the situation in the Seychelles, which developed the foundations of its tourism strategies in a top-down fashion, and during a period of one-party rule. Meanwhile, both the Seychelles and St Barths have transformed what might at first glance appear to be a brace of awesome physical obstacles (remoteness and "archipelagicity" on one hand; a small airport runway on the other) into strategic tools which help to filter and control access, increasing the distinctiveness of, and maintaining a relatively high price for, the tourism experience.

An extreme rendition of this "governance for exclusivity" is the third approach, which concerns *totally private islands*. Again, this is one island condition that cannot be found, in its totality, on continents. Private islands exist all round the world, and many can be bought, with potential for commercial development or private recreational use.[12] While even private islands operate within the purview of sovereign states, their status as the objects of lease or purchase allows the buyer considerable discretion (which varies from state to state) as to how to manage the island; but this is commonly deployed with the intent to restrict access to a select few, typically some of the owners' relatives and friends, the rich and the famous. They operate as gated communities where geography does much of the gating. Ironically, it is the cash and value-added created in the *economically* successful "hot spots" of the world that are often behind the financing needed to purchase, craft, and preserve *ecological* island enclaves. This becomes another way of tapping the hinterland beyond (Baldacchino, 2006e). And so the two sides of the "eco principle" connect in a rather perverse but symbiotic relationship. The most expensive private island is claimed to be Niihau, in the Hawaiian chain. With around 200 residents, Niihau is owned by the Robinson family. The island is accessible to visitors via expensive helicopter flights and hunting excursions (Yamamoto, 2006: 215)

Perhaps one can modify a proposition made by M. Funk (2008) and schematize a relationship between economic development and ecological development based on the state of "natural capital." In such a model, when countries have significant "natural assets" but then allow their natural-resource endowments, such as banana, bauxite, coffee, copra, cotton, oil and gas, phosphate, sandalwood, sugar, to be mined or harvested and exported, and particularly in a raw state (which means that most of the value-added is reaped in other economies), then they are not likely to "develop" beyond "plantation economy" status. They transform their land into a mono-crop economy, suffer from the "Dutch Disease" (e.g., Paldam, 1997), and are not necessarily much richer for it (rich land but poor economy). If they restructured at all towards, say, tourism and finance, they did so relatively belatedly, after having given up on seeking political solutions to declining terms of trade and intense competition from emerging economies. In contrast, those countries that had no natural capital worth exploiting to start off with – because of poor soils and fishing grounds, as well as limited fresh water, exacerbated by high population densities – would basically have no choice but to promote innovative development policies to survive. These may include high levels of out-migration (resulting in vital remittances being sent back home by the emigrants), attracting foreign investment, or otherwise specializing in such services as tourism and finance. Such locales have typically done better economically, driven by the need to tap hinterlands and markets beyond their shores (e.g., Kakazu, 1994). Such success attracts immigrants and exacerbates population densities. However, barring some "pockets" of nature – such as coastlines, themselves the subject of intense conflict – these countries may have ruined any natural capital which they may have had originally (poor land but rich economy).

Is there, and can there be, a third road that combines the benefits of both these trajectories without their associated costs? Can there be a place that enjoys development but where any "natural capital" remains prized and conserved, and is not adulterated? Can one conceive of an island (rather than the much heralded city) as a fully self-supporting "economy of place" (e.g., Logan and Molotch, 2007)? Low populations, apart from low population densities, help; sustainable management practices by indigenous people might help too. The integration of ecological principles into mainstream development practices is also commendable: for example, applications related to restoration, rehabilitation, conservation, sustainability, reconstruction, and remediation of ecosystems using ecological engineering techniques are now numerous. But how does one make such natural capital pay for itself and its maintenance (rich land but *what* economy?)? The Biosphere Reserve Management Concept, which originated in the early 1970s with UNESCO and its Man and the Biosphere (MAB) program, has evolved to appreciate that the conservation of sites becomes worthwhile in the longer term only if a range of economically viable and sustainable options are afforded to communities contiguous to those sites (e.g., Batisse, 1990). A clearer link between resource management and economic development needs to be established; this link, however, often remains elusive without external financial inputs. Indeed, the preservation of pristine environments often depends on the transfer of rentier income generated elsewhere. Subnational jurisdictions are well placed here: policy options that may be available to them to support such choices involve niche tourism, park use and access fees, domestic transfer payments and international aid, and rent or outright sale of assets to private interests.

Yet many of these touted "solutions" themselves imply negative externalities: for example, both international eco-tourism and wind-turbine construction projects generate high-carbon emissions. Ensuring ecological integrity or ecosystemic health in one place may still imply degradation someplace else.

CONCLUSION

The above is just a beginning to what could become a rich and exciting dialogue on appropriate and eco-friendly development strategies for islands, and especially for those with the jurisdictional capacity to dream and concoct them "in house." There are various, possibly significant, policy lessons and implications lurking in the text. By way of example, one of these concerns the appropriateness of a development policy predicated on population growth. The notion that population growth is good "in principle" needs to be critiqued, with Malthusian concerns about population growth proposed anew for serious discussion. Meanwhile, the export of human resources for long-term sustainability is a policy more easily practised by subnational island jurisdictions, since these are locked into political relationships with larger, continental countries willing to receive – or unable to thwart legally – this human "surplus," and who are themselves beyond entertaining wholesale ecological-development routes.

An Enduring "Rich Seam" of Jurisdictional Capacity

IN THE GRIPS OF AN INFINITE PAUSE

They may all have their quirks and tendencies – for patronage in particular – yet most of today's populated subnational island jurisdictions are functioning democracies and have been so for decades.[1] This suggests that their political economy is working, and that the majority of the population must be benefitting sufficiently from current arrangements so as not to opt for radical change. They are, and remain, as Connell (2003) puts it crisply, in the grips of "an infinite pause."[2] This observation has three main components.

First, it is a widely held axiom that the middle classes in capitalist democracies normally vote their pocketbooks: incumbents are re-elected if the economy does well, not so if it doesn't. The fact that there has been little appetite for major constitutional change in the universe of subnational island jurisdictions for the past three decades, despite countless elections and candidate turnover, suggests that island voters are not unduly frustrated or disappointed by what they have experienced. Admittedly, some may be frustrated by lack of change and leave: as C. Bongie (1998) reminds us, exile is ex-isle. However, while exit hatches remain open, the populations of most subnational island jurisdictions continue to grow (often in spite of already uncomfortably high population densities) and mainly because of immigration, not natural increases (McElroy and Sanborn, 2005).

Second, the average citizen of these jurisdictions tends to be literate and mobile, and so quite aware of the relative socio-economic affluence (or lack thereof) of larger, sovereign neighbours. This is particularly true of the geographically compact Caribbean where there is a long tradition of inter-island transfers and migration. Contrasts in such issues as income, un/employment, life expectancy, crime, and social-service delivery are apparent even to most casual observers. Martinique versus Haiti and French Polynesia versus the Solomon Islands would be extreme comparisons. As a result, and from a crude cost-benefit-analysis perspective, SNIJ residents appear regularly to prefer their obvious socio-economic advantages and tend to ignore or discount the less tangible losses of weaker national identity; full – but mainly symbolic? – political autonomy and international visibility come with their own price tag.

Third, the territorial elite are even more aware of a few specific but major economic benefits associated with their jurisdiction's political affiliation. These include: the "free-riding" afforded them by the protection of the flag (in such areas as international security, currency, law and order); the metropolitan oversight that bestows regulatory legitimacy (particularly to offshore finance, which in turn makes their banking and gaming sectors especially attractive to foreign investors and sales corporations); the seamless connectivity with the labour market of a larger, richer country (which allows the metropole's tourists to visit and support the domestic economy, while ensuring freedom of movement for the islanders for employment, residence, or education in the metropole, even if as a back-up option); and the potential bailout in case of persistent budgetary shortfalls, natural disasters, and other (including military) threats (e.g., Kelman et al, 2006).

INGENIOUS REGULATORY CONSTRUCTS

Michel Foucault recognized that the modern state's main preoccupation was no longer so much its survivability (as with Machiavelli's *Prince*) as its governmentality: its ability to devise, manage, and refine instruments – like taxation or residence regimes – which could very well be geographically differentiated, leading to uneven and heterogenous governmental practices (Foucault, 1991: 99).

Such techniques as statist preoccupations appear to be all the rage. Political separatism has clearly gathered momentum in recent decades. First, the burgeoning number of sovereign states is itself evidence of this dynamic: 84 sovereign states in 1948; over 190 sovereign states just over sixty years later. Statehood has permitted especially smaller, mainly island states also to "go offshore," in the sense that the Bahamas, Bahrain, Liechtenstein, and Vanuatu have used their sovereignty in a very particular manner that enables them to capitalize on the few competitive advantages of their smaller size. This means that overall tax receipts can increase by *reducing* overall rates of tax, rather than raising them, since such policies have tended to expand the tax base of those who introduce them (and contract the tax bases of those who don't). These sovereign states have therefore developed themselves as the "financial equivalent of parking lot proprietors" (Palan, 2003: 60), effectively beyond (hence, offshore to) the regulatory reach of the world's more powerful and affluent states and their organizations (like the G7 and the

OECD). Concurrently, these locales are seen as safe, stable, and so attractive to the rich and powerful, including those located in these same countries: Is this perhaps because these polities thus liberate the rich and powerful from paying much higher taxes? These jurisdictions may have used the (local) instruments and legitimacy of their sovereignty to protect themselves in a regulatory sense, but they have deployed such regulations to facilitate favourable transborder activity. Their laws and regulations belong to the "strictly for export" category, enacted by domestic authorities, to be sure, but often intended and aimed *exclusively* at individuals and institutions located beyond their borders (Conrad, 1973: 633).

Which is why, in spite of "contradictory spatial logics" (Chase-Dunn, 1981; Kratochwil, 1986: 42), there is no inconsistency in stating that these places "are at once on the margins and at the centre of global capitalism's displacement of crisis" (Roberts, 1994: 111). The "unbundling of territoriality" (Ruggie, 1993) allows an increasingly borderless economy to co-exist with a political system based on borders and sovereignty (Palan, 1988). In agreeing with Peter Drucker (1986), one accepts that there is more than just an "intriguing coincidence" of an integrating global economy and a splintering global and national polity. Island enclaves emerge as ingenious regulatory constructions; spaces disposed to political rationality. They are as much geographical as epistemological spaces, outcomes of pragmatic policy making during historically specific conjunctures. They are the consequences of the basic contradiction and incongruity between, on the one hand, the internationalization of capital, and the territorialization, inclusive of mutually exclusive sovereignties, of the modern state, on the other.

Second, the offshore phenomenon is also illustrated by the reworking of contained spaces of regulation by sovereign states, of any size, over a clearly definable part of their own, internal territory. There is, today, much more interest – with a similar intent to facilitate favourable, transborder transactions – in such a "regulatory construction of places" (Hudson, 1998: 919; 2000: 271) *within* an existing sovereign state, rather than in developing enclave status as a fully fledged sovereign state proper. Hence, the existence of special autonomous regions, or subnational jurisdictions: modern versions of the free ports and cities of the past, which oblige a reconsideration not just of the Westphalian concept of sovereignty but of imperialism, colonialism, and development.

A. Alesina and E. Spolaore (2003: 1999) suggest two main reasons for this tendency "on the ground" for the persistence, if not proliferation, of these enclaves, many of which are islands. One is that certain jurisdictions may extract various favours from national governments in order not to break away (even if the threat of secession is not put into action). The presence of independentist political parties on these enclaves helps to strengthen the jurisdictions' hand at negotiation overall. The second is that, even where such regions do *not* press for secession, they demand, and often obtain, more latitude from their national governments. The advantage of many islands today is that geography has given them a significant lead in being considered natural (and almost always unitary) jurisdictions for administrative purposes. If they are relatively smaller units, then what they ask for is also relatively miniscule in the grand scheme of things. Since they are "islanded," and so naturally enclaved, what they ask for, and obtain, is also not necessarily "symmetrical": to be made equitably available to any other players in the federated state. Decentralization without separation maximizes the benefits of self-determination with those of integration. These intended benefits include: larger swathes of autonomy; restrictions on citizenship and residence rights; an expansion of the tax base; opportunities for targetted paradiplomacy; and the creation of sites that are recognized and prized for their distinct environmental (cultural or natural) resources. Paraphrasing Palan (1998), one *can* have the cake and eat it too.

There is no ultimate sanction to be suffered in this political game. Independence cannot be hoisted on any people – though it may very well have been in the past. As T. Carroll (2000: 10) reminds Prince Edward Islanders: "Canada has yet to fire anyone for pushing the envelope on provincial jurisdiction."

There are equally, if not more, compelling reasons to support, by design, a political fragmentation "top down" from the centre of power. Federal principles concerned with the combination of "self-rule" and "shared rule" are typically crafted via a constitutionally sanctioned distribution of power, with the details ironed out in an ongoing process of negotiation and power flexing that becomes the substance of "border skirmishes" (Hudson, 1998) or the bread and butter of federal politics (e.g., Elazar, 1997). These arrangements recognize local differences, and constituent rights to integrity, autonomy, and self-determination, without threatening the unity of the overarching state. This is a shrewd response to the otherwise expected political resistance of nations and other communities to being absorbed, their identity lost and forgotten, into larger state formations. The strategic (re-)engineering of jurisdictional space allows the state to earmark specific territory for equally special, and specialized, services. These include detention camps, quarantine sites, offshore finance centres, low-tax havens, enterprise processing zones, geostrategic military bases, remote weapons test and dump sites, special autonomous regions, duty-free zones, heritage and conservation parks, spaces without right of abode, and various "mix and match" combinations of the above. Judith Butler (2004) is right to note that, in the present imperial moment, we ought to expect more Guantánamo Bays, not fewer (also Reid-Henry, 2007: 632). The decisions to earmark such spaces in this manner would not be possible, feasible, or prudent if extended over a state's total territory and population. These acts of innovative governance share the tenets of David Ricardo's principles of comparative advantage but are extended to the field of jurisdiction. Geography still matters. A lot. There would seem to be a great need for more critical scholarship to examine how such exceptional locales are themselves re-placed (Mountz, 2009).

This geo-political landscape is as much post-sovereign as it is post-colonial. Spaces that are representative and performative of offshoring strategies – and that David Harvey (2003: 14) calls a "sort of outside" – cannot be regarded as "anomalies, annoying or even amusing exceptions" (Stevens, 1977: 178), although it is common for smaller jurisdictions to suffer such a dismissive gaze at the hands of larger actors and larger polities. And yet it may be this ease of succumbing to caricature that facilitates the survival of these excised places. Embassy chapels were "little islands of alien sovereignty" (Ruggie 1983: 279, citing Mattingly, 1964: 244), tolerated by host states for the sake of a greater purpose.

FIVE DILEMMAS

Of course, there are difficulties in this enterprise. Mainland-island relations may be frought with what one hopes is a "constructive tension" (e.g., Osborne, 2005: 27) but which does not always turn out to be so.

First, the "in-betweenity" of such places as Puerto Rico and New Caledonia is awkward, because "it creates a real or imagined responsibility of the metropolis for the internal problems of the territory, which is resented by some, and considered insufficent by others" (Hillebrink, 2008: 347). The same author identifies the issue of international responsibility for wrongful acts (of omission or commission) entertained by subnational jurisdictions as a "general problem" (ibid., 134).[3] Who, for example, is responsible for the non-payment of debts by a subnational government, its default on contractual (domestic or international) obligations, the lack of local law enforcement, its carbon emissions, or the maltreatment of aliens in its territory?

Second, and following from this, are the more mundane, and less easily researched, dynamics between locally elected policy makers and governments, on the one hand, and the "governors," or their equivalents, appointed from the metropole, on the other. With the United Kingdom Overseas Territories in mind, D. Taylor (2005: 20) argues: "Although the Constitution defines the roles of the governor and the government, these often overlap, particularly when the government controls the purse strings for areas for which the governor is responsible, for example, the police. Turf wars are normal." The UKOT governors retain responsibility for managing risks such as crime and disasters but are dependent on funding provided by territory governments. In general, governors "prefer to use their influencing abilities rather than coercive measures" to obtain any necessary funds (Harris, 2008: 353). Governors do have reserve powers to require funding; however, "the use of these powers must be balanced against the need to respect democratically elected local governments" (PAC, 2008: 11).[4] This remains "a grey area in policy making" (Clegg, 2005: 146); the right balance is still – and is likely to remain – elusive, while the policy terrain over which such "dilemmas" pertain (Killingray, 2005: 12) may have widened in recent years. D. Killingray identifies the following as the "hot button" issues, again in relation to the UKOTs: qualities of governance and levels of corruption; judicial policies; and offshore financial dealings. Since 11 September 2001, the list has broadened to include terrorist financing and border security.[5]

Third, offshoring now includes the relocation of not just industrial but also white-collar service jobs to some exotic location (Vlcek, 2008: 158). While the generic notion of "outsourcing" – making arrangements with an external entity for the provision of (duly split) goods or services to supplement or replace domestic efforts – has been around for centuries, the increasing sophistication of information and communication technologies has made the practice virtually pervasive (e.g., Hirschheim, 2006). Thomas Friedman (2005) claims in his best-seller *The World Is Flat* that globalization has levelled the competitive playing field between industrial and emerging economies. Smaller island economies have stood to profit from this broad unbundling, leading to loss of jobs and tax revenue in the developed world. The political response has been significant, in some countries (United States, France) more than in others. In an increasingly protectionist age with no resumption of WTO-level trade talks anywhere in sight, and with voters in no mood to defend "fat cats" – including firms recently bailed out with public funds – who dodge their taxes by tucking their earnings away in "tax havens" (e.g., Leonnig, 2009), "offshore" is being presented as a threat to respectable society. A key competitive advantage of small economies is under threat: the world does not appear any longer so flat after all.

Fourth, and as if to prove that this is the case, there are significant concerns, especially in grappling with the offshore finance sector, that may go beyond the possibilities of careful handling. Tax havens in particular have been portrayed as deliberate state strategies aimed at attracting "hot" (if not criminal) money (Palan, 2002: 157). Various subnational island jurisdictions in the Caribbean have been well placed geographically to become involved, willingly or not, in drug smuggling, gun running, and money laundering. By way of example, in March 1985 three senior members of the Turks and Caicos Islands (TCI) government (including then Chief Minister Norman Saunders) were arrested in Miami, United States. They were found guilty on drug-conspiracy charges and imprisoned (*New York Times*, 1985). A subsequent inquiry led to the resignation of the TCI ministers and a temporary suspension of constitutional government (Killingray, 2005: 12). A 2008 U.K. House of Commons report (PAC, 2008) argued that the UKOTs are still "lacking in regulatory capacity" since they lack the critical mass of regulatory and investigatory expertise necessary to be able to follow up suspicious transaction reports. Places like Montserrat are as much as "31% materially non-compliant with anti-money laundering measures" (Harris, 2008: 354). The former Enron Corporation used nearly 900 offshore entities, mostly in the Cayman Islands, to conceal bogus trades and accounting fraud (Browning, 2008). In a subsection of his book, tellingly titled "Selling Sovereignty and Integrity," R. Crocombe (2007: 163–8) documents various shady "evasion industries" in the Pacific, including: the "Wine Box" scam implicating the Cook Islands government in 1987 and the sale of 1,454 passports by the Marshall Islands up to 1986. Offshore banks in Niue were targetted by various banks located in New York City for the suspension of all transactions in U.S. dollars in 1999–2000 (van Fossen, 2003: 244–51). Smaller island states in these regions, and not just subnational jurisdictions, have been involved in similar episodes. The massive increase in international conventions and standards that apply to financial institutions in the post-9/11 world has been described as a "regulatory tsunami" (Passas, 2006: 321). Arguably, the smaller jurisdictions are very hard pressed to fulfil all their new responsibilities. Indeed, the higher costs of effective supervision and enforcement suggest that the resources of a small jurisdiction could be better spent on other developmental trajectories (Sharman and Mistry, 2008).

Fifth, the near collapse of the banking industry in the 2008 global credit crunch has drastically increased governments' needs to maximize tax revenue and may have thus re-energized the attacks on offshore finance centres generally, since they (ab)use their legislative capacities as "baits" to attract business into their jurisdictions (Aliber, 1976: 182). U.S. President-elect Barack Obama expressed his hostility to the corporate use of offshore stategies for "international tax planning" during his 2008 election campaign (e.g., Houlder, 2008), and a Stop Tax Haven Abuse Bill in the U.S. Congress would, if passed, levy penalties on financial institutions that block tax enforcement (*The Economist*, 2009c).[6]

Such a move would presage a return to the attempted clampdown on tax avoidance in the late 1990s. In the European Union, a Code of Conduct of Business Taxation was adopted in 1997. The Harmful Tax Competition Initiative (HTCI) was launched in April 1998 by the OECD. And in May 1998 the G7 issued a communiqué supporting the OECD initiative and itself setting up a Financial Stability Forum in 1999, in part mandated, along with the Financial Action Task Force (FATF), to look at regulation and money laundering in offshore finance centres (see Biswas, 2002). An internationally agreed-on tax standard, more recently developed by the OECD, requires the exchange of information on request in all tax matters for the administration and enforcement of domestic tax law (OECD, 2009). Meanwhile, a Tax Justice Network brings together organizations, social movements, and individuals as a lobby group committed to a socially just, democratic, and progressive system of taxation, working for international tax cooperation and against tax evasion and tax competition (Hampton and Christensen, 2002; Tax Justice Network, 2008).

Many smaller states and territories have countered these initiatives very strongly. They have claimed that: they undermine one of their few competitive economic advantages; the reputation of their economies remains vulnerable to shaming and denigration (e.g., Roberts, 1994: 110); the "attacks" are illegitimate attempts to intervene in the domestic affairs of other, smaller states, and so threaten the latter's (fiscal) sovereignty; the OECD in particular (composed as it is of developed states) has no right to impose restrictions on the behaviour of non-members; and preaching tax harmonization to others is especially galling and hypocritical when the EU, the FATF, and the OECD have members who have not fully implemented such a principle themselves (Vlcek, 2007: 442; 2008, passim). ("A prime example was when Britain convinced the European Union to exempt the Eurodollar market from the Savings Tax Directive because it did not want to lose this business" [Gallienne, 2007: 100].) These "members" also include the U.S. states of Delaware, Nevada, and Wyoming, whose offer of corporate anonymity rivals that of more familiar offshore financial centres (*The Economist*, 2009d). Within the OECD, Austria, Belgium, Luxembourg, and Switzerland had, by July 2009, not yet adopted the internationally agreed-on tax standard, while various non-OECD members – including Bermuda, Isle of Man, Guernsey, and Jersey – have "substantially implemented it" (OECD, 2009).

Moreover, powerful lobby groups have argued that tax competition is actually healthy; the findings by A.K. Rose and M.M. Spiegel (2007) support the view that "OFC proximity is associated with a more competitive domestic banking system and greater overall financial depth." While most would agree that tax evasion is a crime, tax minimization may not be: in May 2006 Philippe Léger, advocate general at the European Court of Justice, ruled in a non-binding opinion that wanting to minimize tax is not a crime: companies may "happily shop around" for the lowest rate when deciding where to establish subsidiaries (Gallienne, 2007: 117; Houlder and Tait, 2006).

It is difficult to come up with an unequivocal verdict: Is it not the elites and governments in smaller jurisdictions – territories defined away as non-viable, vulnerable, fragile, at the mercy of external donors, with chronic trade deficits (e.g., Prasad, 2004: 59) – that have crafted, copied, discovered, or simply stumbled upon various ingenious competitive niches emergent from their islandness and relative smaller size as their "development strategies" (Baldacchino, 1993)? Are smaller island jurisdictions not using their autonomy to "legislate a space for regulatory arbitrage" (Vlcek, 2008: 159)? Or is the agenda squarely (but more discreetly) in the hands of international global capital and its lackeys in legislatures and in legal and accountancy firms, intent on perfecting and manipulating, even "constructing" (e.g., Hudson, 1998), such jurisdictions in order to exploit legal loopholes? Do not "tax havens" exist because the larger states "allow them to exist"; and is not this in its own turn a consequence of having the rich and powerful as their customers (Kay, 2009)? If the politics of globalization is "all about who has the power to draw boundaries" (Hudson, 2000: 272) and design such exceptional enclaves, it would be pertinent to know who is wielding this power, to say the least. Perhaps we are observing a strategic alliance of a few broadly defined interest groups during this historic conjuncture in the evolution of globalization. Perhaps we are assuming wrongly that these interest groups are indeed distinct (Christensen and Hampton, 1999).

Of course, realistically, any effective clampdown on "tax competition" would spell the demise of the principle of national self-determination and sovereign equality (Palan, 2002: 172–3). It would also have to figure out how to re-territorialize, not just many, extremely mobile, high-net-worth individuals, but also multinational corporations and the international division of labour. It is probably too late for the latter initiatives to have even a remote chance of success. Smaller states and subnational island jurisdictions are merely capitalizing on a worldwide competitive marketplace. This, for better or for worse, "has no moral imperative except to make money" (Gallienne, 2007: 100).[7]

GRADUATED SOVEREIGNTIES

The format that such innovative governance by an SNIJ takes on with the rest of the world, and with any one of a set of larger states in particular, suggests elements of suzerainty, of tributary statehood, of a neo-trusteeship, and of a hierarchy of states generally – and all the more so when what is happening on islands is compared to what has been happening in, and to, such mainland flashpoint milieux as Afghanistan, Bosnia, Gaza, Iraq (and Baghdad's Green Zone), Kosovo, Sierra Leone, and Somalia (e.g., Fearon and Laitin, 2004: 7). In studying export processing zones as responses to the southeast Asian financial crisis of the late 1990s, A. Ong (2004) identifies a wider tendency on the part of governments to condone a progressively more variegated zonal capitalism or "graduated sovereignty": a "complex and uneven experience of selective boundary crossings, subjectivities and exclusions" (Sidaway, 2007b: 352). This device acts to facilitate economic mobility and competitiveness while preserving, or even enhancing, the control of the local state. No contradiction here: it is precisely the "unbundling of territoriality" than enables such an increasingly borderless economy to co-exist with a political system based on borders and sovereignty (Hudson, 2000: 276; Palan, 1998). Key features of the ancient pedigree of this unbundling (inclusive of EPZs) were charted earlier in this book.

Unlike the continental and typically dangerous flashpoints indicated above, however, the agents of larger countries may not wish to exit as fast as possible where smaller, typically more benign, islands are concerned. Granted, the former colonial administrators *may* have an exit strategy; it may be important to show that they do so, in order to silence the inevitable critics, or to appease their citizenry. Yet, in all fairness, the metropolitan players may have every intention of permanently thwarting and postponing the implementation of any such departure plan from their subnational jurisdictions, while the locals of these same jurisdictions may want to make absolutely sure that they do exactly that. Is their alliance an enduring, lingering, post-modern imperialism? "Having 'created' offshore, sovereignty

and self-determination are themselves constrained and (re)enabled in turn"
(Palan, 1998: 625). Such behaviour may continue to fly in the face of rational-
ist theories of international relations (e.g., Amin and Palan, 2001; Cooley,
2005: 167). It looks as though island enclaves, as physical-cum-legal domains,
will be with us for some time yet.

NATURE OF ISLAND SPACES

> Intensified processes and patterns of uneven development are
> increasingly expressed in enclave spaces.
>
> James Sidaway (2007a: 332)

A wave of creative governance is ushering in an unbundling of territoriality that in turn permits both a contracting and expansion in the reach and
clutch of the modern state. This is a deliberate and selective application and
re-crafting of development strategy, so that the state ends up governing over
a differentiated set of regimes as may apply to: excised segments of national
space, excepted segments of populations residing in that national space; and
indeed even to segments of space belonging to, or to populations residing
in, other states (Ong, 2006: 91-2). This is a clear manifestation of "norm
entrepreneurship" (Ingebritsen, 2002) as applied to specific localities. As
"in-between judicial realms" (Palan, 1998: 637), SNIJs are ideally placed to
benefit from, or to serve as the objects of, such clever adventures in "niche
politics" (e.g. Hepburn, 2009).

Where actual, physical islands may not exist to accomplish such a task,
artificial islands now stand temptingly within the realms of technological
possibility. These follow in the wake of Thomas More's *Utopia*, as playgrounds
for human experimentation – reference has been made to Hulhumale as
population platform in the Maldives, and Sealand as platform for extra-
jurisdictional practices off the UK. To these we can add the upscale real estate
"fantasy enclave" of 'The World' archipelago in Dubai; and – soon perhaps
– the *Freedom Ship*, the world's first mobile and extra-territorial community
at sea (Freedom Ship International website; Jackson and Della Dora, 2009).
Excised settlements in the Earth's Ocean, in outer space, and in cyberspace,
all beckon. We have come a long way from the free ports of the 16th century.

This book's discussion of the evolution of international/global political
economy exists parallel to a scholarly tradition about the nature of islands
that resonates with some of the overarching thematics of borders and frontiers, structure and agency. J. Bonnemaison (1994) describes island living by

using the metaphors of the tree and the canoe: the first to represent place, fixity, tradition (read: jurisdiction, law, sovereignty); the second, mobility and exchange (read: market forces, liberalization, globalized capitalism). The ingenuity of these two metaphors lies in the fact that the canoe is carved out of the tree. Trans-territoriality is possible thanks to a very material and territorial resource. In much the same way, one can observe how subnational island jurisdictions deploy domestic laws and regulations for siphoning off, and drawing in, value-added generated elsewhere.

Second, again for islands, as for other smaller jurisdictions, their vulnerability is often a presumed structural feature, and not necessarily borne out by the evidence. Islanders (whether as individuals, household units, or corporate entities) employ considerable "strategic flexibility" in seeking to exploit opportunities and to maximize economic gains in a turbulent, unpredictable, and dynamic external environment (e.g., Midttun et al., 2006). Keeping alive a portfolio of skills and revenue streams enables these actors to migrate both internally and abroad. "Flexible specialization" (e.g., Poon, 1990) and "multifunctionality" (e.g., Farrugia and Attard, 1989) are the key attributes of small, often island economies, as much as of their constituent citizens, households, and firms (Schmitz, 1989; Bertram and Poirine, 2007: 368; Baldacchino and Bray, 2001; Sultana, 2006: 26–7). This assessment contrasts sharply with the "vulnerability thesis" that has dominated scholarship in recent decades (e.g., Briguglio, 1995; Pelling and Uitto, 2001; Vigilance et al., 2008).

The paradigm of vulnerability has followed from pessimistic views about the presumed non-viability of small states (e.g., Harden, 1985; Plischke, 1977). The belief that constraints of small size and geographical separateness render islands particularly "vulnerable" economically is both conceptually and empirically unsatisfactory, in spite of what happened to Iceland in the curent global credit crunch. Conceptually, there are advantages as well as disadvantages in being relatively small and isolated. Empirically, island economies appear on balance quite robust in a globalizing world. Briguglio's "vulnerability index" is positively, not negatively, related to per-capita income: the more "vulnerable" the economy, the higher its per-capita income (Armstrong and Read, 2002). H.W. Armstrong et al. (1998: 644) and W. Easterly and A.C. Kraay (2000: 2015) agree that smaller (mainly island) jurisdictions consistently tend to perform economically *better* than larger (mainly continental) states, while other evidence suggests that smaller landlocked jurisdictions are much more economically challenged than smaller islanded ones (Armstrong and Read, 2005). Proponents of the vulnerability hypothesis have implicitly conceded the point by introducing a countervailing concept of "resilience," placed in a contradictory dialectical relationship to vulnerability to produce indeterminacy of outcomes (Briguglio et al., 2005). Thus, while globalization is generally thought to have diminished the autonomy of smaller jurisdictions, the latter are claimed to have demonstrated remarkable resilience, evolving a suite of "adjustment strategies" (e.g., Held et al., 1999: 9; Woodward, 2006: 685). Peter Katzenstein (1985, 2003) has been more sympathetic to the agency of smaller jurisdictions: he has argued that the creativity and flexibility of their "nimble" governing institutions has "proved extraordinarily adroit at spotting and creating niches" (Woodward, 2006: 686, 694). With an eye on Caribbean island economies, Lloyd Best (1971, 30) explains their economic development as "a problem of management: of timing, sequencing, and manipulating, in an unending effort to perceive or create, and in any case to exploit, a multiplicity of little openings and opportunities."

For such and similar smaller places, sovereignty-derived, place-based, legal powers (read: jurisdiction, instruments and techniques of govern-mentality, or functional sovereignty) are one of their best resource tools for development (Hudson, 2000: 279; Thomson, 1994: 17). These locales are not "fictitious spaces" dealing in/with "fictitious capital" (pace Roberts, 1994), since the outcomes of this engagement are palpable, certainly to their own populations. And, while capitalism is increasingly nomadic, the processes and technologies that fuel, and perhaps even explain, its dynamism remain territorially nested.

Irrespective of metropole and status, subnational island jurisdictions are keen on consolidating their metropolitan connections while securing even greater (or should it be *better*?) autonomy over their local affairs. The latter condition should be consistent with the "self-determination" which, in 1960, in the heyday of decolonization, United Nations Resolution 1514 declared to be a basic right of all peoples. The understanding that such territories can exploit "the resourcefulness of jurisdiction" (Baldacchino and Milne, 2000), while qualifying for many of the tangible benefits from continuing close association with the metropole, is a preferred policy outcome. However, such "sustained autonomy" (Quentin-Baxter, 1994) is, and will remain, a contested domain, subject to constant review and revision, into the forseeable future (Sutton, 2008). Clearly, there is much scope and need for the analysis and dis-section of the various (including unorthodox) options that small territories, and subnational jurisdictions in particular, are increasingly adopting – or being forced to adopt – in order to seek a more satisfactory accommodation within the global political economy (Payne, 2009: 285).

PARTING SHOTS

The privilege of the last word? This book started off with a brief overview of Hong Kong, one of the world's largest (by population) subnational island jurisdictions. It would be fitting to conclude with a commentary from a citizen of one of the world's smallest. I defer to Tony Gallienne, a citizen of the Bailiwick of Guernsey, a British crown dependency, with a population of some 65,000. He has recently articulated the challenges faced by this territory and its people, from the vantage point of it being a subnational island jurisdiction offering financial services in the twenty-first century. Such behaviour may be seen as exemplary of "selling sovereignty" (Crocombe, 2007: 157; Prasad, 2009: 53): part of the set of desperate measures taken by chronically vulnerable jurisdictions that perceive that they realistically have no other development choices to consider (Payne, 2009: 285). Like Gallienne, I am more inclined to consider these acts as expressions of creative governance, a fuller exploitation of political geography for economic or strategic gain.

Gallienne writes:

Guernsey, and every other sovereign, autonomous or semi-autonomous jursidiction, has to operate in the increasingly complex world of the international rule of law ... Guernsey belongs to this world ... It needs to know what is truly going on and be able to fight its corner when needs be... We have to recognize that, even with full sovereignty, we would remain ... beholden to those players who set the rules ... Nothwithstanding all these pressures, we have inherited a jurisdictional space which we have worked hard to maintain, protect and exploit. This is as much a story, at any given time, of [those who] ... mine that "rich seam" of jurisdictional capacity to construct and exploit economic possibilities. (Gallienne, 2007: 70).

Appendix

Listing and Maps of
Subnational Island Jurisdictions

What follows is a selected list of populated, subnational jurisdictions that are islands or on islands. The list, organized by ocean or sea region, briefly identifies their name, political status, geographical location, population, and associated power at the time of compilation (July 2009). The list is accompanied by a three-panel map of the world.

The list is invariably a selective one. It includes overseas territories, provinces, and other units of federal states, and other subnational island units of larger states that enjoy some asymmetric power-sharing arrangements. Most have de jure autonomy (codified at law); but, for others, the level and nature of autonomy may be much less clear, and much more contentious. In such situations – Gozo, Kish, Lofoten – I have preferred to be inclusive. The resulting range of jurisdictional capacities is broad: from quasi-full sovereignty (Bermuda, Cook Islands, Taiwan) to somewhat special, in whole or in part, municipalities (Cape Breton, Macquarie Island, Shetland).

I am also fully aware that the inclusion of some entries on the list may be offensive to some readers. Inclusion in the list is not to be construed as an act of acknowledging the legitimacy or otherwise of any jurisdictional powers, de jure or de facto.

Additional information and data about each entry is available from the Island Jurisdictions Database maintained at the University of Prince Edward Island, Canada, and available at http://utopia.cs.upei.ca/jurisdiction/.

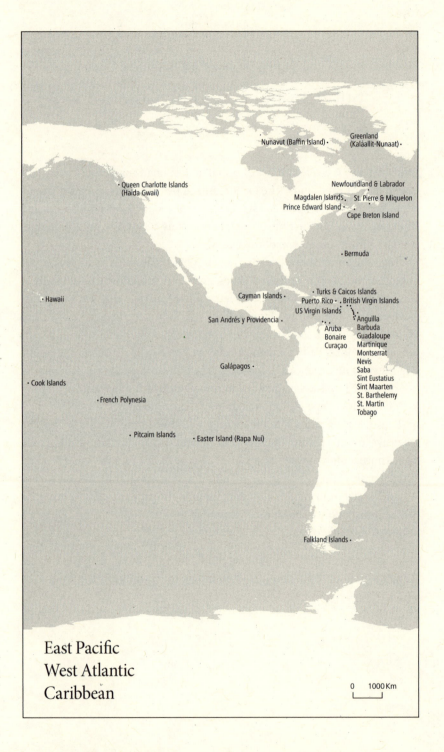

Nunavut (Baffin Island) ·

Greenland
(Kaláallit-Nunaat) ·

· Queen Charlotte Islands
(Haida Gwaii)

Newfoundland & Labrador
Magdalen Islands · St. Pierre & Miquelon
Prince Edward Island ·
Cape Breton Island

· Bermuda

· Hawaii

Cayman Islands ·

· Turks & Caicos Islands
Puerto Rico · · British Virgin Islands
US Virgin Islands ·

San Andrés y Providencia ·

Anguilla
Aruba   Barbuda
Bonaire   Guadaloupe
Curaçao   Martinique
          Montserrat
          Nevis
          Saba
          Sint Eustatius
          Sint Maarten
          St. Barthelemy
          St. Martin
          Tobago

Galápagos ·

· Cook Islands

· French Polynesia

· Pitcairn Islands   · Easter Island (Rapa Nui)

Falkland Islands ·

East Pacific
West Atlantic
Caribbean

0   1000 Km

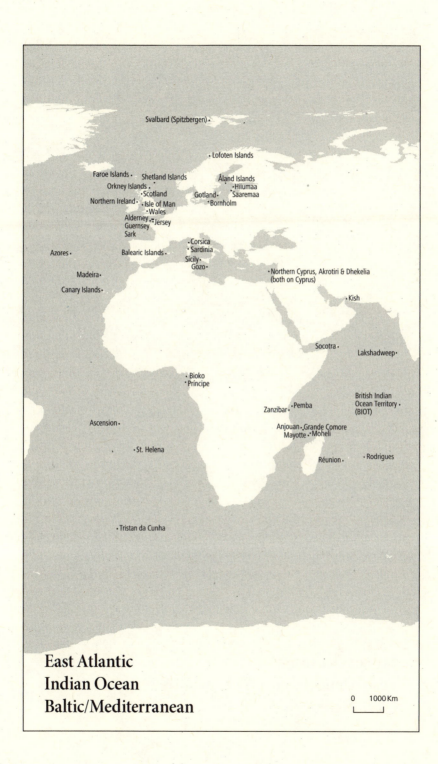

Svalbard (Spitzbergen) ·

· Lofoten Islands

Faroe Islands ·   Shetland Islands ·   Åland Islands ·
Orkney Islands ·   · Hiiumaa
           · Scotland   Gotland ·   · Saaremaa
Northern Ireland · · Isle of Man   · Bornholm
           · Wales
Alderney · · Jersey
Guernsey ·
Sark ·

                              · Corsica
Azores ·   · Sardinia
          Balearic Islands · Sicily ·
                              Gozo ·   · Northern Cyprus, Akrotiri & Dhekelia
Madeira ·   (both on Cyprus)

Canary Islands ·   · Kish

                                                    Socotra ·   Lakshadweep ·

                         · Bioko
                         · Príncipe
                                                         British Indian
                                      Zanzibar · · Pemba Ocean Territory ·
                                                         (BIOT)
Ascension ·
                                      Anjouan · · Grande Comore
                                      Mayotte · · Moheli
          · St. Helena
                                              Réunion ·   · Rodrigues

· Tristan da Cunha

East Atlantic
Indian Ocean
Baltic/Mediterranean

0   1000 Km

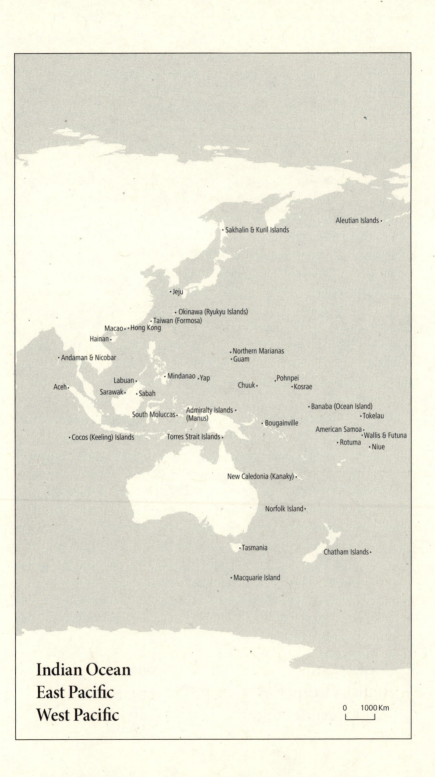

Aleutian Islands .

. Sakhalin & Kuril Islands

. Jeju

. Okinawa (Ryukyu Islands)
. Taiwan (Formosa)
Macao . . Hong Kong
Hainan .

. Northern Marianas
. Guam

. Andaman & Nicobar

Labuan .   . Mindanao . Yap
Aceh .   Chuuk .   . Pohnpei
Sarawak . . Sabah   . Kosrae

. Banaba (Ocean Island)
South Moluccas .   Admiralty Islands .   . Tokelau
                    (Manus)
                                . Bougainville   American Samoa .   . Wallis & Futuna
. Cocos (Keeling) Islands   Torres Strait Islands .   . Rotuma   . Niue

New Caledonia (Kanaky) .

Norfolk Island .

. Tasmania   Chatham Islands .

. Macquarie Island

Indian Ocean
East Pacific
West Pacific

0   1000 Km

TABLE: Sub-National Island Jurisdictions (SNIJs)

SOUTH PACIFIC

SNIJ	DESCRIPTION	POPULATION (APPROX.)	ASSOCIATED POWER
Admiralty Islands (Manus)	Province (2 representatives to PNG parliament)	32,800	Papua New Guinea
American Samoa	Territory administered by US Office of Insular Affairs	57,900	USA
Banaba/Ocean Island	Municipality administered by Rabi Council of Leaders and Elders on Rabi in Fiji	300 + 5,000 on Rabi	Kiribati
Bougainville (North Solomons)	Autonomous Province (4 reps to PNG Parliament); secession referendum pending	185,000	Papua New Guinea
Chatham Islands	Territory and Local Council	760	New Zealand
Chuuk (Truk)	Province of FSM, a sovereign federal state in free association with US	53,000	Federated States of Micronesia, USA
Cocos (Keeling) Islands	Territory (Unicameral Shire Council)	620	Australia, Commonwealth of
Cook Islands	Self-governing, in free association with New Zealand (since 1965)	23,600	New Zealand
Easter Island (Rapa Nui, Isla de Pascua)	1st Governor (1984); Council of Elders (1988); World Heritage Site (1996)	3,500	Chile
French Polynesia (Tahiti, Society Islands)	Overseas Collectivity (5 admin divisions, 130 islands); own President, Legislative Assembly	259,800	France, EU
Galápagos	National Park since 1959; Province since 1973	20,000	Ecuador
Kosrae	Province of FSM, a sovereign federal state in free association with US	7,700	Federated States of Micronesia, USA
Macquarie Island	UNESCO World Heritage Site; part of Huon Municipality, Tasmania	30	Australia, Commonwealth of
New Caledonia (Kanaki, Kanaky)	Sui generis collectivity; 3 provinces (including autonomous Kanak region)	196,000	France, EU
Niue	Self-governing, in free association with New Zealand (since 1974)	2,200	New Zealand
Norfolk Island	Territory with Commonwealth responsibilities administered by Australia	2,100	Australia, Commonwealth of
Pitcairn Islands	Overseas Territory, (local government council 10 seats)	45	United Kingdom, EU

SOUTH PACIFIC

SNIJ	DESCRIPTION	POPULATION (APPROX.)	ASSOCIATED POWER
Pohnpei	Province of FSM, a sovereign federal state in free association with US	34,500	Federated States of Micronesia, USA
Rotuma	Administered by district officer; Rotuma Council	2,600	Fiji Islands
Tasmania	State (province)	456,600	Australia, Commonwealth of
Tokelau	Self-administered territory (3 atolls) moving towards free association	1,400	New Zealand
Torres Strait Islands	Torres Strait Regional Authority, administered by Queensland	8,100	Australia, Commonwealth of
Wallis and Futuna	Territorial Collectivity; two island groups, 3 traditional chiefdoms; Territorial Council & President	15,480	France, EU
Yap	Province of FSM, a sovereign federal state in free association with US	11,200	Federated States of Micronesia, USA

EAST ASIA / NORTH PACIFIC / SOUTH ASIA

SNIJ	DESCRIPTION	POPULATION (APPROX.)	ASSOCIATED POWER
Aceh	Special Autonomous District (in Sumatra) of unitary state	3,799,000	Indonesia
Aleutians	Unorganized borough of Alaska; US military presence	8,200	Alaska, USA
Guam	Organized, unincorporated territory administered by US Office of Insular Affairs; US military base	166,090	USA
Hainan	Province	8,180,000	People's Republic of China
Hawaii	State (8 major islands); homeland compact with US Government	1,210,000	USA
Hong Kong	Special administrative region, semi-autonomous	6,855,000	People's Republic of China
Jeju (Cheju-do)	Special Self-Governing Province since 2006	543,000	Republic of South Korea
Labuan	International Offshore Finance Centre; Territory administered by federal government	78,000	Malaysia
Macao	Special administrative region, semi-autonomous	520,400	People's Republic of China

SNIJ	DESCRIPTION	POPULATION (APPROX.)	ASSOCIATED POWER
Mindanao Autonomous Region	6 Provinces in Mindinao & Sulu Archipelago; autonomous (Muslim) regional government	2,803,000	Republic of the Philippines
Northern Marianas	Self-governing Commonwealth in political union with US (3 main islands)	78,200	USA
Okinawa (Ryukyu Islands)	Prefectures: (Sakashima Islands/ Okinawa Islands); (Amami Islands). Large US military base	1,292,000	Japan
Queen Charlotte Islands (Haida Gwaii)	Council of the Haida Nation to protect, assert Aboriginal Title and land claims	5,000	British Columbia, Canada
Sabah (North Borneo)	State	1,760,000	Malaysia
Sarawak (North Kalimantan)	State	1,846,000	Malaysia
Sakhalin & Kurile Islands	Part of Sakhalin Regional Duma	608,000	Russian Federation
South Moluccas (Maluku)	Province (archipelago of southern Moluccas); militant separatist movement since 1999	1,313,000	Indonesia
Taiwan (Formosa, Republic of China)	Disputed status as sovereign state; rogue province since 1949?	21,336,000	People's Republic of China / USA
Vancouver Island	Island Territory within mainland Province of Federation; site of provincial legislature		British Columbia, Canada

EAST ATLANTIC / MEDITERRANEAN

SNIJ	DESCRIPTION	POPULATION (APPROX.)	ASSOCIATED POWER
Azores	Autonomous Region (9 islands), regional legislative assembly	232,000	Portugal, EU
Akrotiri & Dhekelia	Sovereign Military Bases on Cyprus; administered by UK Base Commander	3,500 military + 5,000 civilians	United Kingdom, EU
Balearic Islands	Autonomous Province; 4 Island Councils: Majorca, Minorca, Ibiza, Formentera	842,000	Spain, EU

EAST ATLANTIC / MEDITERRANEAN

SNIJ	DESCRIPTION	POPULATION (APPROX.)	ASSOCIATED POWER
Canary Islands	Autonomous Region (13 islands)	1,643,000	Spain, EU
Corsica	Regional Government, Collectivité Territoriale de Corse	279,000	France, EU
Gozo	Ministry for Gozo	23,800	Malta, EU
Madeira	Autonomous Region	284,000	Portugal, EU
Northern Cyprus, Turkish Republic of	Democratic secular republic	264,000	Republic of Turkey
Príncipe	Autonomous Province	5,400	São Tomé e Príncipe
Sardinia	Autonomous Region (4 provinces) Sard language legalized in 1991	1,677,000	Italy, EU
Sicily	Autonomous Region – 9 provinces	5,151,000	Italy, EU

INDIAN OCEAN / EAST AFRICA

SNIJ	DESCRIPTION	POPULATION (APPROX.)	ASSOCIATED POWER
Andaman & Nicobar Islands	Union Territory administered by national government	356,000	India
Anjouan (Ndzuwani)	Island sub-jurisdiction within federal state; constitution under development	189,000	Union of the Comoros
British Indian Ocean Territory (BIOT)	Overseas Territory (inhabitants expelled after 1969); Diego Garcia leased as US military base; claimed by Mauritius	1,500 military + 2,000 civilians	UK, US
Grande Comore (Ngazidja)	Island sub-jurisdiction within federal state; constitution under development	234,000	Union of the Comoros
Kish	Kish Free Zone Organization, a company with an autonomous legal status	20,000	Iran
Lakshadweep	Union Territory administered by national government	60,600	India
Mayotte	Territorial Collectivity; to become oveseas department	186,000	France, EU (claimed by Comoros)
Moheli (Mwali)	Island sub-jurisdiction within federal state; constitution under development	24,000	Union of the Comoros
Pemba	Dependency of autonomous province of Zanzibar	641,000	United Republic of Tanzania

SNIJ	DESCRIPTION	POPULATION (APPROX.)	ASSOCIATED POWER
Réunion	Overseas Department	766,150	France, EU
Rodrigues	Autonomous Island Region of Mauritius; agitation for full sovereignty	36,000	Mauritius
Socotra	Province; special conservation area; world heritage site since 2008	44,000	Republic of Yemen
Zanzibar (Unguja)	Autonomous province (mainly Zanzibar and Pemba)	641,000	United Republic of Tanzania

NORTH-WEST ATLANTIC

SNIJ	DESCRIPTION	POPULATION (APPROX.)	ASSOCIATED POWER
Cape Breton Island	Island Territory within Province of Federation	147,000	Nova Scotia, Canada
Îles de la Madeleine (Magdalen Islands)	Island Municipality within Province of Federation	14,000	Quebec, Canada
Newfoundland & Labrador	Province (island and mainland territory) within Federation	511,000	Canada
Nunavut	Self-governing territory (includes Baffin Island); Inuit Homeland	30,000	Canada
Prince Edward Island	Province	140,000	Canada
Saint-Pierre et Miquelon	Territorial Collectivity	6,120	France, EU

NORTH ATLANTIC / BALTIC (RELATED TO SCANDINAVIA)

SNIJ	DESCRIPTION	POPULATION (APPROX.)	ASSOCIATED POWER
Åland Islands	Autonomous Region, via international treaty	26,200	Finland, EU
Bornholm	Regional Municipality, single-tier local government	43,000	Denmark, EU
Faroe Islands	Self-governed autonomy; not in EU	46,000	Denmark
Gotland	Single-tier local government (municipality)	58,000	Sweden, EU
Greenland (Kalaallit Nunaat)	Autonomous dependency; not in EU	56,000	Denmark

NORTH ATLANTIC / BALTIC (RELATED TO SCANDINAVIA)

SNIJ	DESCRIPTION	POPULATION (APPROX.)	ASSOCIATED POWER
Hiiumaa	Hiiumaa County Council	11,000	Estonia, EU
Lofoten Islands	Archipelago of 6 municipalities; declared temporary petroleum-free zone (2003)	24,500	Norway
Saaremaa	Saaremaa County Council	40,000	Estonia, EU
Svalbard (Spitzbergen)	Territory administered by Norwegian Polar Department of Ministry of Justice; Governor in territory	2,700	Norway

ATLANTIC (RELATED TO UNITED KINGDOM / GREAT BRITAIN)

SNIJ	DESCRIPTION	POPULATION (APPROX.)	ASSOCIATED POWER
Alderney	Possession of the British Crown; has own legislature	2,400	Bailiwick of Guernsey, British Crown
Ascension Island	Dependency of St. Helena, an Overseas Territory of UK; Ascension has local Council	1,100	St. Helena, UK
Falkland Islands	Overseas Territory	3,000	United Kingdom, EU (claimed by Argentina)
Guernsey, Bailiwick of	Crown dependency (not in EU): Alderney, Guernsey, Herm, Sark, islets; own parliament	65,000	British Crown
Isle of Man (Mannin)	Crown dependency; not in EU but free access to common market	72,000	British Crown
Jersey, Bailiwick of	Crown dependency (not in EU), largest of Channel Islands; own parliament	90,500	British Crown
Northern Ireland	Home Nation	1,685,000	United Kingdom, EU
Orkney Islands	Island Council; one representative to Scottish Parliament	20,000	Scotland, UK, EU
Sark	Feudal state with hereditary seigneur; appointed legislature	600	Bailiwick of Guernsey, British Crown
Scotland	Home Nation	5,116,900	United Kingdom, EU
Shetland Islands	Island Council; two representatives to Scottish Parliament	43,000	Scotland, UK, EU

ATLANTIC (RELATED TO UNITED KINGDOM / GREAT BRITAIN)

SNIJ	DESCRIPTION	POPULATION (APPROX.)	ASSOCIATED POWER
St. Helena	Overseas Territory (includes Ascension, Tristan da Cunha as dependencies)	7,400	United Kingdom, EU
Tristan da Cunha	Dependency of St. Helena, an overseas territory of UK; Island Council and laws	270	St. Helena, UK, EU
Wales	Home Nation	2,958,600	United Kingdom, EU

CARIBBEAN/ WEST ATLANTIC

SNIJ	DESCRIPTION	POPULATION (APPROX.)	ASSOCIATED POWER
Anguilla	Overseas Territory	13,000	UK, EU
Aruba	Constituent Country of the Kingdom of the Netherlands	71,000	Netherlands, EU
Barbuda	Special Status; Local Council	1,500	Antigua and Barbuda
Bermuda	Overseas Territory	65,000	UK, EU
Bonaire	Constituent member of Netherlands Antilles; to become special municipality	13,000	Netherlands, EU
British Virgin Islands	Overseas Territory	22,000	UK, EU
Cayman Islands	Overseas Territory	44,000	UK, EU
Curaçao	Constituent Country of the Kingdom of the Netherlands	142,000	Netherlands, EU
Guadeloupe	Overseas Department	422,000	France, EU
Martinique	Overseas Department	381,000	France, EU
Montserrat	Overseas Territory	9,000	UK, EU
Nevis	State within Federation; session pressure	38,000	St Kitts and Nevis
Puerto Rico	Self-governing Commonwealth in political union with US	3,676,000	USA
Saba	Constituent member of Netherlands Antilles; to become special municipality	1,500	Netherlands, EU
San Andres y Providencia	Department dominated by executive branch of government	60,000	Colombia

SNIJ	DESCRIPTION	POPULATION (APPROX.)	ASSOCIATED POWER
Sint Eustatius (Statia)	Constituent member of Netherlands Antilles; to become special municipality	2,700	Netherlands, EU
Sint Maarten	Constituent Country of the Kingdom of the Netherlands	42,000	Netherlands, EU
St Barthelemy	Territorial Collectivity	6,800	France, EU
St Martin	Territorial Collectivity	33,000	France, EU
Tobago	Ward of Republic; own House of Assembly	58,400	Trinidad and Tobago
Turks & Caicos Islands	Overseas Territory	19,900	UK, EU
US Virgin Islands	Organized, unincorporated territory administered by US Office of Insular Affairs	108,700	USA

Notes

1 I am deliberately using the term "smaller," rather than "small," resurrecting a usage preferred by Burton Benedict (1966, 1967) and Gerald Berreman (1978) because it alerts readers to a tendency in the literature to equate "large states" with "normal." This is hardly the case in practice. Out of 237 jurisdictions listed in the 2007 edition of the CIA *World Factbook* (CIA, 2007), only 11 have populations exceeding 100 million, 23 have populations of over 50 million, and 158 have populations of less than 10 million (of which 41 have a resident population of under 100,000). Wikipedia has a list of 223 "countries by population," including subnational jurisdictions, which range in descending order from the People's Republic of China to Pitcairn: the median (112th) position is occupied by Finland, with 5,338,000 citizens (Wikipedia, 2009). Clearly, the so-called small state is the typical state size (as it has also been for most of recorded history). In contrast, therefore, it is the *large* state that is the quirk and the anomaly – a fact that often results in the state dealing with some measure of secessionist tendencies (Aceh, Biafra, Chechnya, Okinawa, Scotland, Taiwan, Tibet, West Papua) and other conditions of "giantism" (e.g., Lewis, 1991). There is also "no widely accepted definition of a small state" (Crowards, 2002: 143). Moreover, and as already observed by P.R. Baehr (1975: 466), there is no sharp or self-evident dichotomy between "small" and "large" states.

2 I could also add the notion of an *exclave* to this basic argument. However, the term is not in common use and may serve only to confuse the point. Moreover, an exclave is usually an enclave seen from a different perspective: the enclave of one polity may be an enclave within another: Llívia is an exclave *of* Spain but an enclave *within* France (Muir, 1975: 43–4). As entities completely surrounded by water, all islands are geographical exclaves, though not necessarily political ones.

3 As they also remain in another book with a similar title: Trompf (1993).

4 As D. Gregory (2004: 319; emphasis in original) reminds us, the exception – in Latin, *ex capere* – is literally that which is "taken outside": the result of a process of boundary promulgation *and* boundary perturbation.

5 Offshore finance centres are often mistaken for *tax havens*. The latter are jurisdictions that allow residents or foreigners to minimize their tax payments. While all OFCs are tax havens, not all tax havens are OFCs (Van Fossen, 2003: 268n.1).

6 A Swedish court convicted four men linked to "the notorious internet file-sharing site The Pirate Bay" in April 2009 (*International Herald Tribune*, 2009). And the Pirate Party, which wants to legalize Internet file sharing, won one of

Sweden's eighteen seats in the European Parliament in the June 2009 elections, securing just over 7 per cent of votes cast (*The Guardian*, U.K., 2009).

7 "Myths tell us that islands – be they spent projectiles, coffin lids, fishes turned into stone, or earth thrown down from the sky – are the result of a practice, the outcome of the application of a technique" (Gagliardi, 2009: 47).

CHAPTER 2

1 A third issue, though not as widely commented upon, relates to data protection.

2 I have had interesting debates with my friend David Milne on this issue. He is mainly trained in political science; I, more in sociology. He is thus keener to focus on de jure sovereignty; I am more inclined to broaden the discussion to include de facto sovereignty. We have courteously agreed to disagree.

3 For example, visit British Airways at www.ba.com.

4 The case of Puerto Rico, along with that of New Caledonia, is problematic. There is internal disagreement both in the territories themselves and in their respective metropolitan countries on their political future. Within the current stalemate, their status is one of "in-betweenity": "somewhere between association and integration" (Hillebrink, 2008: 347).

5 As in the cases of the Comoros, even after the "secession" of Mayotte; Tuvalu, which sought and obtained separate statehood, in lieu of remaining attached to Kiribati; and the secession of Anguilla from St Kitts-Nevis and the narrowly thwarted attempt of secession via referendum of Nevis from St Kitts.

6 Various islands and archipelagos have been claimed by different states. One is the Dokdo island chain claimed by (South) Korea – or the Takeshima island chain claimed by Japan, which is one and the same. Perhaps the most dramatic episode associated with such claims in recent years has been the Argentine "invasion" of the Falklands/Malvinas and their subsequent expulsion by a British military force in 1982. But the claim is then typically for the whole island or archipelago, and not for part thereof.

7 Examples of ethnic polarization on islands would include Fiji, Sri Lanka, and the main island of Trinidad within Trinidad and Tobago.

8 Examples include: Canada and Greenland/Denmark (which ironically involves Hans Island); Guatemala and Belize; the Punjab (involving India and Pakistan); and Tibet (assimilated by China).

9 As with Mostar (Bosnia), Kirkuk (Iraq/Kurdistan), Jerusalem (in an eventual Israel/Palestine deal), and Berlin (1945–89). A notable departure from an (equally exceptional) divided island jurisdiction is Nicosia in Cyprus.

10 As in Kosovo, Montenegro, and – should Quebec press for sovereignty – anglophones, allophones, and indigenous peoples in that Canadian province.

11 Russia invaded Georgia via the enclaves of South Ossetia and Abkhazia in August 2008. The self-proclaimed independence of these two enclaves has (so far) been recognized by only four states: the Russian Federation, Nicaragua, Venezuela and, interestingly, Nauru (Barry, 2009).

12 Life Takes Visa. © 2007 Visa U.S.A. Inc.

13 B. Lindström (2009: 16) describes "de facto" competences as those that allow for more informal room for manoeuvre.

CHAPTER 3

1 Confirmed by Paul K. Sutton. E-mail communication of 21 August 2003.

2 Three key exceptions here would be: 1) the Canadian province of Quebec, with its 1980 and 1995 referenda: the first securing 40.4 per cent and the second securing 49.2 per cent of votes cast for independence; 2) the deferred independence referendum on Bougainville, an outcome of the 2002 peace accord with Papua New Guinea (Ghai and Regan, 2006); and 3) the independence referendum expected after 2014 in New Caledonia. Meanwhile, the Scottish National Party-led government in Scotland is committed to a referendum on Scottish independence.

3 This policy stance would also have included returning colonies to appropriate "motherlands" – such as the Falklands to Argentina (Franks, 1983: 5–6, 27) and Hong Kong and Macau to China.

4 One may wish to add to this list the "informal referendum" held in 2002 in Gibraltar (an enclave but not an island), in which 98.97 per cent of voters rejected a motion for shared sovereignty between Britain and Spain (BBC News, 2002a).

5 Before the Second World War, there were 62 independent states; there are now, at the time of writing (January 2010), more than three times as many: 194; and 195 if one includes Taiwan.

6 Including the West Indies Federation and Malaya-Singapore in the late 1950s to early 1960s.

7 Puerto Rico, with a population of over three million, remains a clear, and singular, exception.

8 Other known examples of island autonomies – such as Galápagos (Ecuador); Gozo (Malta); Rapa Nui (Chile); Rotuma (Fiji); Andaman, Nicobar, and Lakshadweep (India); Labuan (Malaysia); Sakhalin (Russia); Svalbard (Norway); and St Helena and its Dependencies (United Kingdom) – need to be investigated further and their "goodness of fit" within the Watts typology considered.

9 Sutton (2008a: 2) identifies fifty-one subnational jurisdictions, including non-island territories.

10 Indeed, in the case of Ireland/Northern Ireland or the Comoros/Mayotte, the contrasting responses to decolonization occurred in the *same* territory. The same had occurred earlier, but on a much larger scale, in late-eighteenth-century British North America, with Canada emerging as the loyalist option to the rebellious Thirteen Colonies (which in turn become the republican United States of America).

11 These "empty islands" included Ascension, Bermuda, Cayman, Falklands, Pitcairn, Réunion, Seychelles, St Helena, and Tristan da Cunha.

12 Thus, the "right of abode" in the United Kingdom was extended in 2002 to the citizens of all the (mainly non-white) residents of its remaining overseas territories. Argentina's invasion in 1982 of the Falkland Islands was reportedly "a godsend" because "it acted as a catalyst for renewed British commitment in the South Atlantic" (Dodds, 2002: 202). The Chagossians – residents of the British Indian Ocean Territory – continue to be thwarted of their right of domicile, in spite of various rulings in their favour by the appropriate courts (e.g., *Telegraph*, 2007); and the Ascension islanders thwarted of the right of abode and property ownership (e.g., Johnston, 2006). More on these in chapter 6 below.

13 More about France and Corsica in chapter 6 below.

14 Such as the Western Isles of Scotland, which form administrative units with parts of the mainland (Skye and Lochalsh; Argyll and Bute); or the Dutch, Danish, Finnish, German, Irish, and Swedish Islands in the Irish, North and Baltic seas, except Gotland. Newfoundland and Labrador, in Canada, may be a similar case.

15 As happened in the case of Cape Breton Island, which was reannexed to the Canadian province of Nova Scotia in 1820. In the late 1960s, Robert Bradshaw, then premier of St Kitts, used the proposed granting of independence to St Kitts-Nevis-Anguilla to tighten central control by St Kitts over the archipelago, leading to the secession of Anguilla and its persisting status as a separate United Kingdom Overseas Territory.

16 Of course, one could argue that such initiatives actually conspire to consolidate rather than erode the dependency of such island regions, and that a high political price could eventually be paid in exchange for any transfer of funds from Brussels resulting from such a recognition.

17 Since the Second World War, only two, newly created, small states have lost their separate identity in a larger state: Zanzibar in Tanzania in 1964; and South Yemen in Yemen in 1990 (Sutton, 2008a: 5).

18 In a sense, all legally identified "reserves" and territories of native peoples constitute enclaves, whether surrounded by water (if on islands) or by other land.

19 Such cases of jurisdictional leverage are not restricted to physical islands. Catalonia, Euskadi/Basque Region, and Andalusia in Spain, as well as Quebec in Canada, are excellent non-island examples.

20 Consider the military interests of the United States in Ascension, Diego Garcia, Guam, Marshall Islands, Hawaii, and Okinawa; and the former interest of metropolitan France in the South Pacific for nuclear-testing purposes.

21 Exclusive Economic Zones can be many times larger than the land area of the island territories that notionally administer them, and they often contain large deposits of untapped resources.

22 The International Whaling Commission has become an obvious platform for such benevolence, as has the cold war relating to the securing of diplomatic relations with either the People's Republic of China or Taiwan.

23 The glaring contemporary exception is Cuba; yet this is a situation imposed by the U.S. trade embargo, and it remains in place because the island is relatively large and its equally large population has been necessarily resourceful.

24 Bongie (1998: 13) goes further: inspired by Lyotard, he prefers the variant "post/colonial" since it better describes an "entangled condition" where neither colonialism nor post-colonialism can be defined as clear-cut entities.

CHAPTER 4

1 I wish to thank Harvey Armstrong for these insights. He has suggested the acronym PROFITT, the second 'T' standing for Tourism (private e-mail communication, 3 March 2004). While I am honoured that the PROFIT acronym is already inviting hybrids (as MIRAB has been doing), this specific suggestion calls for further research.
2 In 2008 the vulnerability of Iceland became evident in the global financial crisis. The Icelandic currency (the króna) fell rapidly in value, while the three main Icelandic banks collapsed, obliging the Icelandic government to take over their operations. See Thorhallsson (2009) for a synthetic review.

CHAPTER 5

1 As Chris Dunn has exclaimed (personal correspondence, June 2006): "What else would one expect with regard to islands, but geography-specific accommodations?"
2 This particular issue is taken up in more detail in chapter 7.
3 This data set, and its analysis, will also be discussed in chapter 7.

CHAPTER 6

1 As we are reminded by Clark (2009): the characteristics of flexibility and adaptability to strategic opportunities in the global arena manifested by subnational island jurisdictions are exactly the same characteristics of capitalist, historical geography emphasized by theorists of uneven development. This issue is revisited in chapter 9.
2 A case in point is Puerto Rico and other "unincorporated territories" of the United States. In a series of decisions that came to be known as the Insular Cases (1902–22), the U.S. Supreme Court created this new category which deemed places like Puerto Rico to be foreign to the United States in a domestic sense, a space belonging to, but not part of, the United States, and whose inhabitants were neither aliens nor citizens (Kaplan, 2005: 841–2; Rivera Ramos, 1996).
3 The U.S. Department of Justice considered other, alternative sites before committing to Guantánamo Bay. These include three "island enclaves" in the Pacific: Tinian (Northern Marianas), Wake Atoll, and Midway Atoll (the latter two being unorganized and unincorporated U.S. territories) (Reid-Henry, 2007: 629).
4 More on this in chapter 9 below.

CHAPTER 7

1 I owe these terms to one of my UPEI graduate students, Jordan Blake Walker.

2 I have personally heard Olafur Ragnar Grimson, president of Iceland, use the same term in 2003, but with some obvious glee rather than any associated contempt.

3 This question becomes even more poignant in the wake of the 2008 financial crisis in Iceland. The British government "used its anti-terrorist law to take over the assets and operations of the two Icelandic banks in Britain ... [and used its influence] to delay the much needed emergency loan from the IMF" (Thorhallsson, 2009: 127). Was this a somewhat belated "payback time" for the embarrassment of the cod wars?

4 Another interesting, and more contemporary, example of "big state versus small state" diplomacy is that of Antigua and Barbuda (population: 68,000) and its willingness to go on the offensive in taking on the United States, defending its interests as an Internet gaming jurisdiction by utilizing the WTO's dispute mechanism (Cooper, 2009).

5 At one point, the United Kingdom's International Development Secretary, Clare Short, accused Montserratian politicians of being "irresponsible" and seeking "golden elephants" as compensation for their plight, a remark for which she later apologized (BBC Politics, 1997).

6 I am grateful to David Fabri for helping me develop the arguments in this section.

7 Readers will tolerate this brief foray into what might have been: the author is Maltese after all, and the whole issue does strike a raw nerve with him.

8 A similar exercise is also available as Table 1 in McElroy and Pearce (2006: 532).

CHAPTER 8

1 Idiosyncratic Antarctica – with a unique, multilateral governance regime that transcends national territorial sovereignty, and is primarily driven by scientific interests – is deliberately excluded from this exercise.

2 "Historically, while garment exporters from other countries faced quotas and duties in shipping to the US market, the CNMI's garment industry benefited from quota-free and duty-free access to US markets for shipments of certain goods in which 50% of the value was added in the CNMI" (Hernandez, 2007).

3 On "modernizers" versus "traditionalists" in Shetland, see Grydehøj (2008).

4 As do the MIRAB and SITE models, both reviewed in Bertram (2006).

5 These five policy areas have been discussed in chapter 4.

6 In sharp contrast to each other, Greenland's population is basically stable, while that of Madagascar is growing at over 3 per cent per annum and is thus likely to double within twenty-two years.

7 Stefan Gössling, private e-mail communication, July 2008.

8 A similar situation is unfolding in Rapa Nui/Easter Island where the population – up now to 5,000 from 3,300 in 2002 – complains that tourism is attracting immigrants from the Chilean mainland. Some 70,000 tourists now visit the island annually, compared to 14,000 in the mid 1990s. The Rapa Nui parliament "is calling for independence" (*The Economist*, 2009e).

9 The refinery project has been put "on hold" since February 2008 (ELAW Advocate, 2008).

10 Or almost whole islands. For example, 97 per cent of the Galapagos land mass is protected.

11 For individual case studies, see Baldacchino (2006f).

12 For a website dealing in private islands, see http://www.privateislandsonline.com/.

CHAPTER 9

1 Until very recently, the island of Sark was the "last feudal outpost in Europe," where its *seigneur* has enjoyed extraordinary powers since 1565, including the right to the *treizième* (one-thirteenth of the sales price whenever one of the island's original forty tenements is sold). Sark is actually a sub-subnational island jurisdiction, since it is a dependency of the Bailiwick of Guernsey (Murphy, 2007).

2 What Quentin-Baxter (2004) calls a political status of "sustained autonomy."

3 For example, in 2006 the competent authority for the island of Bonaire, then part of the Netherlands Antilles (NA), decided to condone the construction of a "Mangrove Village" resort. The governor of the NA, however, annulled both the granting of the emphyteutic lease and the building permit, since the resort was planned to be located within the 500-metre buffer zone of the Lac/Sorobon wetland, a RAMSAR site. The competent authority appealed the governor's decision. The Netherlands crown, in its decision, confirmed the legality of the annulment by the governor (Verschuuren, 2008).

4 Take the events that unfolded in the Turks and Caicos Islands, a UKOT, in August 2009. After an inquiry had found a "high probability of systemic corruption," the U.K. government removed the elected premier, cabinet, and assembly and suspended most of the constitution, passing on the running of the territory to the governor. The removed premier, Michael Misick, has denied any wrongdoing and accused Britain of staging a "coup." His (very brief) successor as premier, Galmo Williams, stated that the territory had been "invaded and recolonized" with a "dictatorship" (*The Economist*, 2009h; Times Online, 2009).

5 The resettlement of four Uighurs, former detainees at Guantánamo Bay, to Bermuda in 2009 created a "political tempest" since Ewart Brown, the premier of Bermuda, allegedly acted without consulting either the British Foreign Office or the governor, who "expressed his displeasure at being kept in the dark" (Eckholm, 2009).

6 For a summary of the proposed act, introduced in March 2009, see: http://levin. senate.gov/newsroom/release.cfm?id=308949.

7 Also, and as discussed earlier in chapter 7, small, low-lying island states have not been successful in using a similar moral argument to wrest concessions from both developed and developing countries with a view to fight sea-level rise. A case of "two weights, and two measures"?

Bibliography

Abara Banaba. 2008. "Our Homeland Banaba." http://www.banaban.com/abarabanaba.html (accessed 8 August 2008).

Abbott, J. 2000. "Treasure Island or Desert Island? Offshore Finance and Development in Labuan." *Development Policy Review* 18, no. 2: 157–75.

ABC American Broadcasting Corporation. 1978. *Fantasy Island.* http://www.tv.com/fantasy-island/show/679/summary.html (accessed 8 August 2008).

Administrative Court of Cologne. 1978. "Re Duchy of Sealand." *International Law Reports*, case no. 9, K 2565/77. http://www.uniset.ca/naty/80ILR683.htm# (accessed 8 August 2008).

Agamben, G. 2005. *State of Exception.* Translated by K. Attell. Chicago, Ill.: University of Chicago Press.

Ahlburg, A., and R.P.C. Brown. 1998. "Migrants' Intentions to Return Home and Capital Transfers: A Study of Tongans and Western Samoans in Australia." *Journal of Development Studies* 35, no. 1: 125–51.

Aldecoa, F., and M. Keating, eds. 1999. *Paradiplomacy in Action: The Foreign Relations of Sub-National Governments.* London: Frank Cass.

Aldrich, R., and J. Connell. 1992. *France's Overseas Frontier: Départements et Territoires D'Outre-Mer.* Cambridge: Cambridge University Press.

— 1998. *The Last Colonies.* Cambridge: Cambridge University Press.

Alesina, A., and E. Spolaore. 2003. *The Size of Nations.* Cambridge. Mass.: MIT Press.

Aliber, R.Z. 1976. *The International Money Game.* London: Macmillan.

Allahar, A. 2005. "Identity and Erasure: Finding the Elusive Caribbean." *Revista Europea de Estudios Latinoamericanos y del Caribe* 79 (October): 125–34.

Amin, A., and R. Palan. 2001. "Towards a Non-Rationalist International Political Economy." *Review of International Political Economy* 8, no. 4: 559–77.

Amoore, L. 2006. "Biometric Borders: Governing Mobilities in the War on Terror." *Political Geography* 25, no. 3: 336–51.

Anckar, D. 2003. "Lilliput Federalism: Profiles and Varieties." *Regional and Federal Studies* 13, no. 3; 107–24.

— 2005. "Decentralization in Microstates: Where, How and Why?" *Canadian Review of Studies in Nationalism* 32, nos. 1–2: 109–20.

Anderson, L.M. 2004. "Exploring the Paradox of Autonomy: Federalism and Secession in North America." *Regional and Federal Studies* 14, no. 1: 89–112.

Angelo, A.H., and A. Townsend. 2003. "Pitcairn: A Contemporary Comment." *New Zealand Journal of Comparative and International* Law 1: 229–51.

Angelo, T., and F. Wright. 2004. "Pitcairn: Sunset on the Empire?" *New Zealand Law Journal*, November. 431–2.

Apostoulopoulos, Y., and D.J. Gayle, eds. 2002. *Island Tourism and Sustainable Development: Caribbean, Pacific and Mediterranean Experiences*. Westport, Conn.: Praeger.

Appadurai, A. 1990. "Disjuncture and Difference in the Global Cultural Economy." In M. Featherstone, ed. *Global Culture: Nationalism, Globalization and Modernity*. London: Sage. 295–310.

— 1996. *Modernity at Large: Cultural Dimensions of Globalization*. Minneapolis: University of Minnesota Press.

Armstrong, H.W., and R. Read. 1998. "The International Political Economy of Micro-States: An Overview." Paper presented at Islands V Conference. Mauritius: University of Mauritius. July.

— 2000. "Comparing the Economic Performance of Dependent Territories and Sovereign Micro-States." *Economic Development and Cultural Change* 48, no. 2: 285–306.

— 2002. "The Phantom of Liberty? Economic Growth and the Vulnerability of Small States." *Journal of International Development* 14, no. 3: 435–58.

— 2003. "The Determinants of Economic Growth in Small States." *The Round Table: Commonwealth Journal of International Affairs* 92, no. 368: 99–124.

— 2005. "Insularity, Remoteness, Mountains and Archipelagos: A Combination of Challenges Facing Small States?" *Asia Pacific Viewpoint* 47, no. 1: 79–92.

Armstrong, H.W., R.J. De Kervenoael, X. Li, and R. Read. 1998. "A Comparison of the Economic Performance of Different Micro-States, and between Micro-States and Larger Countries." *World Development* 26, no. 4: 639–56.

Arnold, J. 2003. "Isle of Wight Hits Stormy Waters." *BBC News*, 14 February. http://news.bbc.co.uk/2/hi/business/2752341.stm (accessed 15 August 2008).

Atauz, A.D. 2004. "Trade, Piracy, and Naval Warfare in the Central Mediterranean: The Maritime History and Archaeology of Malta." PHD thesis. Texas: Texas A&M University. http://handle .tamu .edu /1969 .1 /437 (accessed 6 August 2008). Subsequently published in 2008 by the University Press of Florida.

Atler, R. 1991. "Lessons from the Export Processing Zone of Mauritius." *Finance and Development* 28, no. 4: 7–10.

Augé, M. 1995. *Non-Places: Introduction to an Anthropology of Supermodernity*. Translated by John Howe. New York: Verso.

Australia. Parliament, Senate, 2008. *Norfolk Island*. Senate Select Committee, chapter 7. http://www.aph.gov.au/senate/committee/sgfm_ctte/report/c07.htm (accessed 22 December 2008).

Bacani, B.R. 2005. *The Mindanao Peace Talks: Another Opportunity to Resolve the Moro Conflict in the Philippines*. Special Report. Washington, D.C.: United States Institute of Peace. http://www.usip.org/files/resources/sr131.pdf (accessed 16 July 2009).

Baehr, P.R. 1975. "Small States: A Tool for Analysis." *World Politics* 273: 456–66.

Baglole, H., B. Bartmann, D. Bulger, and H.F. Srebrnik. 1997. *Prince Edward Island and the Canadian Constitution: A Brief to the Standing Committee on the Constitution*. Charlottetown, PEI: Institute of Island Studies, University of Prince Edward Island.

Bahcheli, T., B. Bartmann, and H.F. Srebrnik, eds. 2004. *De Facto States: The Quest for Sovereignty*. London: Taylor and Francis.

Bahn, P. and J. Flenley. 1992. *Easter Island, Earth Island*. London: Thames and Hudson.

Baker, R. 1992. "Scale and Administrative Performance: The Governance of Small States and Micro-States." In R. Baker, ed., *Public Administration in Small and Island States*. West Hertford, Conn.: Kumarian Press. 5–26.

Balasopoulos, A. 2002. "Laputa." In S. Stephanides and S. Bassnett, eds., *Beyond the Floating Islands*. Bologna, Italy: COTEPRA. 58–9.

Baldacchino, G. 1993. "Bursting the Bubble: The Pseudo-Development Strategies of Microstates." *Development and Change* 24, no. 1: 29–51.

— 1997. *Global Tourism and Informal Labour Relations: The Small Scale Syndrome at Work*. London: Mansell.

— 1998. "The Other Way Round: Manufacturing as an Extension of Services in Small States." *Asia Pacific Viewpoint* 39, no. 3: 267–79.

— 1999. "An Exceptional Success: The Case Study of an Export Oriented, Locally Owned, Small Scale Manufacturing Firm in a Small Island Country." *Journal of Pacific Studies* 23, no. 1: 27–47.

— 2000. "The Challenge of Hypothermia: A Six-Proposition Manifesto for Small Island Territories." *The Round Table: Commonwealth Journal of International Affairs* 90, no. 353: 65–79.

— 2002a. "A Taste of Small Island Success: A Case from Prince Edward Island." *Journal of Small Business Management* 40, no. 3: 254–9.

— 2002b. "Jurisdictional Self-Reliance for Small Island Territories: Considering the Partition of Cyprus." *The Round Table: Commonwealth Journal of International Affairs* 91, no. 365: 349–60.

— 2002c. "The Nationless State? Malta, National Identity and the European Union." *West European Politics* 25, no. 4: 191–206.

— 2004a. "Autonomous but Not Sovereign? A Review of Island Sub-Nationalism." *Canadian Review of Studies in Nationalism* 31, nos. 1–2: 77–90.

— 2004b. "The Coming of Age of Island Studies." *Tijdschrift voor Economische en Sociale Geografie* 95, no. 3: 272–84.

— 2004c. "Sustainable Use Practices, including Tourism, in/for Small Islands." INSULA: *International Journal of Island Affairs* 13, no. 1: 5–10.

— 2005. "The Contribution of Social Capital to Economic Growth: Lessons from Island Jurisdictions." *The Round Table: Commonwealth Journal of International Affairs* 94, no. 378: 35–50.

— 2006a. "Innovative Development Strategies from Non-Sovereign Island Jurisdictions: A Global Review of Economic Policy and Governance Practices." *World Development* 34, no. 5: 852–67.

— 2006b. "The Brain Rotation and Brain Diffusion Strategies of Small Islanders: Considering 'Movement' in Lieu of 'Place.'" *Globalization, Societies and Education* 4, no. 1: 143–54.

—2006c. "Islands, Island Studies, Island Studies Journal." *Island Studies Journal* 1, no. 1: 3–18.

— 2006d. "Warm versus Cold Water Island Tourism: A Review of Policy Implications." *Island Studies Journal* 1, no. 2: 183–200.

— 2006e. "Managing the Hinterland Beyond: Two, Ideal-Type Strategies of Economic Development for Small Island Territories." *Asia-Pacific Viewpoint* 47, no. 1: 45–60.

— ed. 2006f. *Extreme Tourism: Lessons from the World's Cold Water Islands.* Oxford: Elsevier.

— 2007a. *Recent Settlers to Prince Edward Island Speak: Positive Selling Points Regarding PEI.* Charlottetown, PEI: Population Secretariat, Government of Prince Edward Island, in association with the University of Prince Edward Island.

— ed. 2007b. *A World of Islands: An Island Studies Reader.* Luqa, Malta, and Charlottetown, PEI: Agenda Academic and Institute of Island Studies, University of Prince Edward Island.

— ed. 2007c. *Bridging Islands: The Impact of Fixed Links.* Charlottetown, PEI: Acorn Press.

— 2008a. "Studying Islands: On Whose Terms? Some Epistemological and Methodological Challenges to the Pursuit of Island Studies." *Island Studies Journal* 3, no. 1: 37–56.

— 2008b. "Islands in Between: Martín García and Other Geopolitical Flashpoints." *Island Studies Journal* 3, no. 2: 211–24.

— 2009. "Governance in Small Places: The Unleashing of Asymmetrical Federalism." In G. Baldacchino, R. Greenwood, and L. Felt, eds., *Remote Control: Governance Lessons for and from Small, Insular and Remote Regions.* St John's Nlfd.: Memorial University of Newfoundland: ISER Press. 114–34.

— 2010. "Upside Down Decolonization." In "Subnational Island Jurisdictions: Questioning the 'Post' in Postcolonialism." *Space and Culture* 13, no. 2, forthcoming.

Baldacchino, G., and A. Spears. 2007. "The Bridge Effect: A Tentative Score Sheet for Prince Edward Island." In G. Baldacchino, ed., *Bridging Islands: The Impact of Fixed Links.* Charlottetown, PEI: Acorn Press. 47–66.

Baldacchino, G., and D. Milne. 2006. "Exploring Sub-National Island Jurisdictions." *The Round Table: Commonwealth Journal of International Affairs* 95, no. 386: 487–502.

— eds. 2000. *Lessons from the Political Economy of Small Islands: The Resourcefulness of Jurisdiction*. Basingstoke and New York: Macmillan and St Martin's Press, in association with Institute of Island Studies, UPEI.

— eds. 2008. *The Case for Non-Sovereignty: Lessons from Sub-National Island Jurisdictions*. London: Routledge.

Baldacchino, G., and G. Bertram. 2009. "The Beak of the Finch: Insights into the Economic Development of Small, Often Island, Economies." *The Round Table: Commonwealth Journal of International Affairs* 98, no. 401: 141–60.

Baldacchino, G., and M. Bray, eds. 2001. Special Issue. "Human Resource Issues in Small States." *International Journal of Educational Development* 21, no. 3: 203–91.

Baldacchino, G., L. Felt, and R. Greenwood, eds. 2009. *Remote Control: Governance Lessons for and from Small, Insular and Remote Regions*. St John's: Memorial University of Newfoundland, ISER Press.

Baldacchino, G., and R. Greenwood. 1998a. "Introduction." In G. Baldacchino and R. Greenwood, eds., *Competing Strategies of Socio-Economic Development for Small Islands*. Charlottetown, PEI: Institute of Island Studies, University of Prince Edward Island. 9–28.

— eds. 1998b. *Competing Strategies of Socio-Economic Development for Small Islands*. Charlottetown, PEI: Institute of Island Studies, University of Prince Edward Island.

Baldacchino, G., and T.I.J. Fairbairn, eds. 2006. Special Issue: Successful Small Business from Small Islands." *Journal of Small Business & Entrepreneurship* 19, no. 4: 331–430.

Baldwin, R. 2006. "Multilateralizing Regionalism: Spaghetti Bowls as Building Blocs on the Path to Global Free Trade." *Discussion Paper No. 5775*. London: Centre for Economic Policy Research.

Barboza, D. 2007. "China's Gamblers Are Prize in Macao's Casino War." *International Herald Tribune*, 25 March. http://www.iht.com/articles/2007/03/25/business/macao26.php (accessed 15 August 2008).

Bard, M. 2007. *Israel's Security Fence*. Jewish Virtual Library. http://www.jewishvirtuallibrary.org/jsource/Peace/fence.html. (accessed 2 August 2008).

Barnes, J.A. 1954. "Class and Committees in a Norwegian Island Parish." *Human Relations* 7, no. 1: 39–58.

Barry, E. 2009. "Abkhazia is Recognized – by Nauru." *New York Times*, 16 December. http://www.nytimes.com/2009/12/16/world/europe/16georgia.html (accessed 14 January 2010).

Barthlott, W., and S. Porembski. 2000. "Why Study Inselbergs?" In S. Porembski and W. Barthlott, eds., *Inselbergs: Biotic Diversity of Isolated Rock Outcrops in Tropical and Temperate Regions*, Ecological Studies no. 146. Berlin: Springer-Verlag. pp. 1–6.

Bartmann, B. 1998. "The Future Political Foundation for Territorial Policy in a Global Context." In B. Lindström, ed. *Den Regionala Utmaningen: Territoriell Politik I ett Europeiskt Norden*. Stockholm, Sweden: NordREFO. 239–50.

— 2002. "Meeting the Needs of Microstate Security." *The Round Table: Commonwealth Journal of International Affairs* 91, no. 365: 361–74.

— 2006. "In or Out: Sub-National Island Jurisdictions and the Antechamber of Paradiplomacy." *The Round Table: Commonwealth Journal of International Affairs* 95, no. 386: 541–60.

— 2007. "Island War and Security." In G. Baldacchino, ed. *A World of Islands: An Island Studies Reader*. Charlottetown, PEI, and Luqa, Malta, Institute of Island Studies, University of Prince Edward Island, and Agenda Academic. 295–322.

— 2008a. "Between *de jure* and *de facto* Statehood: Revisiting the Status of Taiwan." *Island Studies Journal* 3, no. 1: 113–28.

— 2008b. "In or Out: Sub-National Island Jurisdictions and the Antechamber of Para-Diplomacy." In G. Baldacchino and D. Milne, eds., *The Case for Non-Sovereignty: Lessons from Sub-National Island Jurisdictions*. London: Routledge. 57–75.

Batisse, M. 1990. "Development and Implementation of the Biosphere Reserve Concept and Its Applicability to Coastal Regions." *Environmental Conservation* 7, no. 1: 111–16.

Baudrillard, J. 1988. *Selected Writings*. Edited by Mark Poster. Stanford, Calif.: Stanford University Press.

Baum, P. 2006. "Positive Profiling: Common Sense Security." Lead editorial, *Aviation Security International* 12, no. 4. http://publishing.yudu.com/Aqbb/asiaug06vol12issue4/resources/4.htm (accessed 2 August 2008).

Baum, T.G. 1996. "The Fascination of Islands: The Tourist Perspective." In D.G. Lockhart and D. Drakakis-Smith, eds., *Island Tourism: Problems and Perspectives*. London: Pinter. 21–35.

Baum, T.G., with L. Hagen-Grant, L. Jolliffe, S. Lambert, and B. Sigurjonsson. 2000. "Tourism and the Cold Water Islands of the North Atlantic." In G. Baldacchino and D. Milne, eds., *Lessons from the Political Economy of Small Islands: The Resourcefulness of Jurisdiction*. Basingstoke, U.K.: Macmillan in association with Institute of Island Studies, University of Prince Edward Island. 214–29.

Bayliss-Smith, T., R. Bedford, H.C. Brookfield, and M. Latham. 1988. *Islands, Islanders and the World: The Colonial and Post-Colonial Experience in Eastern Fiji*. Cambridge: Cambridge University Press.

BBC Caribbean. 2004. "Saba Voters Go for Breakaway." *BBC News*. London: British Broadcasting Corporation, 6 November. http://www.bbc.co.uk/caribbean/news/story/2004/11/041106_saba-referendum.shtml (accessed 4 August 2008).

BBC News. 2001. "Australia Lands Another Refugee Deal." London: British Broadcasting Corporation. http://news.bbc.co.uk/1/hi/world/asia-pacific/1615903.stm (accessed 9 December 2008).

— 2002a. "QandA: Gibraltar's Referendum." London: British Broadcasting Corporation, 8 November. http://news.bbc.co.uk/1/hi/world/europe/2400673.stm (accessed 2 August 2008)

— 2002b. "Attack Shows Limit to Airport Security." London: British Broadcasting Corporation, 5 July. http://news.bbc.co.uk/1/hi/world/americas/2096081.stm (accessed 2 August 2008).

— 2006a. "Japan Gains Key Whaling Victory." London: British Broadcasting Corporation, 19 June. http://news.bbc.co.uk/1/hi/5093350.stm (accessed 15 January 2010).

— 2006b. "Tokelau Rejects Self-Government." London: British Broadcasting Corporation, 16 February. http://news.bbc.co.uk/2/hi/asia-pacific/4719314.stm (accessed 8 August 2008).

— 2006c. "QandA: Montenegro's Referendum." London: British Broadcasting Corporation, 22 May. http://news.bbc.co.uk/2/hi/europe/4994212.stm (accessed 15 August 2008).

BBC Politics 1997. "Short Defends Handling of Montserrat." http://www.bbc.co.uk/politics97/news/08/0822/short.shtml (accessed 15 August 2008).

Bea, K. 2005. "Political Status of Puerto Rico: Background, Options and Issues in the 109th Congress." U.S. Library of Congress: Congressional Research Service, CRS Report for Congress. http://www.fas.org/sgp/crs/row/RL32933.pdf (accessed 2 August 2008).

Becker, R. 2001. "Noise Regulations Will Break Vieques Accord." *Puerto Rico Herald*, 20 April. http://www.puertorico-herald.org/issues/2001/vol5n16/PRR516-en.html. (accessed 4 August 2008).

Beckford, G.L. 1972/1999. *Persistent Poverty: Underdevelopment in Plantation Economies of the Third World*, 2nd ed. Mona, Jamaica: University Press of the West Indies.

Beckstead, D., and W.M. Brown. 2005. *Provincial Income Disparities through an Urban-Rural Lens: Evidence from the 2001 Census*. Ottawa: Statistics Canada. Cat. no. 11–624–MIE 2005–012. www.statcan.ca/english/research/11-624-MIE/11-624-MIE2005012.pdf. (accessed 4 August 2008).

Bell, A.R. 2002. *The Isle of Man: International Finance Centre*. British American Business. www.gov.im/lib/docs/iomfinance/articles/babi.pdf (accessed 2 August 2008).

Bell, D. 1987. "The World and the United States in 2013." *Daedalus* 116, no. 3: 1–31.

Beller, W., P. D'Ayala, and P.L. Hein, eds. 1990. *Sustainable Development and Environmental Management of Small Islands*. Paris: UNESCO-Parthenon.

Benedict, B. 1966. "Sociological Characteristics of Smaller Territories and Their Implications for Economic Development." In M. Banton, ed. *The Social Anthropology of Complex Societies*. London: Tavistock. 23–34.

— ed. 1967. *Problems of Smaller Territories*. London: Athlone Press for the Institute of Commonwealth Studies.

Bermuda On-Line. 2010. "Bermuda's Single-Family Homes, Condominiums & Apartments." http://www.bermuda-online.org/homes.htm (accessed 15 January 2010).

Berreman, G. 1978. "Scale and Social Relations." *Current Anthropology* 19, no. 2: 225–45.

Bertram, G. 1993. "Sustainability, Aid and Material Welfare in the Small South Pacific Island Economies: 1900–1990." *World Development* 21, no. 2: 247–58.

— 1999. "The MIRAB Model: Twelve Years on." *Contemporary Pacific* 11, no. 1: 105–38.

— 2004. "On the Convergence of Small Island Economies with Their Metropolitan Patrons." *World Development* 32, no. 2: 343–64.

— 2006a. "Introduction: The MIRAB Model in the 21st Century." In G. Bertram, ed., *Asia Pacific Viewpoint* 47, no. 1: 1–13.

— ed. 2006b. Special Issue: Commemorating the 20th Anniversary of the MIRAB Concept. *Asia Pacific Viewpoint* 47, no. 1: 1–160.

— 2007. "Reappraising the Legacy of Colonialism: A Response to Feyrer and Sacerdote." *Island Studies Journal* 2, no. 2: 239–54.

Bertram, G., and B. Poirine. 2007. "Island Political Economy." In G. Baldacchino, ed., *A World of Islands: An Island Studies Reader*. Charlottetown, PEI, and Luqa, Malta: Institute of Island Studies, UPEI, and Agenda Academic. 323–78.

Bertram, G., and O. Karagedikli. 2004. "Are Pacific Economies Converging or Diverging?" In J. Poot, ed., *On the Edge of the Global Economy*. Cheltenham, U.K.: Edward Elgar. 106–22.

Bertram, G., and R.F. Watters. 1985. "The MIRAB Economy in South Pacific Microstates." *Pacific Viewpoint* 26, no. 3: 497–519.

— 1986. "The MIRAB Process: Earlier Analysis in Context." *Pacific Viewpoint* 27, no. 1: 47–59.

Best, L. 1971. "Size and Survival." In N. Girvan and O. Jefferson, eds. *Readings in the Political Economy of the Caribbean*. Kingston, Jamaica: New World Associates. 29–34.

Best, L., and K. Polanyi Levitt. 2009. *Essays on the Theory of Plantation Economy*. Mona, Jamaica: University of the West Indies Press.

Betermier, S. 2004. "Selectivity and the Economics of Independence for Today's Overseas Territories." *Explorations: The UC Davis Undergraduate Research Journal* 7: 63–85. http://faculty.haas.berkeley.edu/beter/betermier_thesis.pdf (accessed 16 July 2009).

Betts, K. 2001. "Boat People and Public Opinion in Australia." *People and Place* 9, no. 4: 34–48.

Bezzina, J. 2005. *Gozo's Government: The Autonomy of an Island*. Rabat, Gozo, Malta: Gozo Local Councils Association.

Bhabha, H.K. 1994. *The Location of Culture*. London: Routledge.

Bigo, D. 2007. "Detention of Foreigners, States of Exception, and the Social Practices of Control of the Banopticon." In P. Kumar Rajaram and C. Grundy-Warr, eds., *Borderscapes: Hidden Geographies and Politics at Territory's Edge*. Minneapolis: University of Minnesota Press. 3–34.

Bikales, G. 2004. "Corsican Capers: Island Separatists Highlight France's Malaise." *Social Contract Journal*. 14, no. 2. http://www.thesocialcontract.com/artman2/publish/tsc1402/article_1195.shtml (accessed 13 December 2008).

Birkett, D. 1997. *Serpent in Paradise*. New York: Anchor Books.

Biswas, R., ed. 2002. *International Tax Competition: Globalization and Fiscal Sovereignty*. London: Commonwealth Secretariat.

Blackadder, A. 1998. "The Case of Oil in the Shetland Islands." In G. Baldacchino and R. Greenwood, eds. *Competing Strategies of Socio-Economic Development for Small Islands*. Charlottetown, PEI: University of Prince Edward Island, Institute of Island Studies. 91–118.

Boissevain, J. 1974. *Friends of Friends: Networks, Manipulations and Coalitions*. Oxford: Blackwell.

Bongie, C. 1998. *Islands and Exiles: The Creole Identities of Post/Colonial Literature*. Stanford, Calif.: Stanford University Press.

Bonnemaison, J. 1994. *The Tree and the Canoe: History and Ethnogeography of Tanna*. Honolulu: University of Hawaii Press.

Borreca, R. 2005. "Proposed Akaka Bill Changes Get Federal OK, Lingle Says." *Honolulu Star Bulletin*, 24 August. http://starbulletin.com/2005/08/24/news/story5.html (accessed 2 August 2008).

Boswell, R. 2005. "France Ready to 'Leapfrog' over Canadian Waters." Canada.com News, 17 November.

Bowcott, O. 2008. "St Helena Smoulders as Airport Plan Is Frozen." *The Guardian* (U.K.), 10 December. http://www.guardian.co.uk/travel/2008/dec/10/st-helena-airport-travel-tourism (accessed 17 December 2008).

Boyes, R. 2008. "Global Warming Could Help Greenland to Independence." *Times on Line*, 7 May. http://www.timesonline.co.uk/tol/news/environment/article3883272.ece (accessed 2 August 2008).

Brathwaite, E.K. 1984. *History of the Voice: The Development of National Language in Anglophone Caribbean Poetry*. London: New Beacon Press.

Braun, B. 2000 "Producing Vertical Territory: Geology and Governmentality in Late Victorian Canada." *Ecumene/Cultural Geographies* 7, no. 1: 7–46.

Briguglio, L. 1995. "Small Island Developing States and Their Vulnerabilities." *World Development* 23, no. 9: 1615–32.

— 2002. "The Economic Vulnerability of Small Island Developing States." In H.H. Hsiao, C.H. Liu, and H.M. Tsai, eds., *Sustainable Development for Island Societies: Taiwan and the World*. Taipei, Taiwan: National Central University. 73–89.

Briguglio, L., B. Archer, J. Jafari, and G. Wall, eds. 1996. *Sustainable Tourism in Islands and Small States – Vol. 1: Issues and Policies*. London: Pinter.

Briguglio, L., and E.J. Kisanga, eds. 2004. *Economic Vulnerability and Resilience of Small States*. Malta: Formatek.

Briguglio, L., and G. Cordina, eds. 2004. *The Competitiveness Strategies of Small States*. Malta: Formatek.

Briguglio, L., G. Cordina, and E.J. Kisanga, eds., 2006. *Building the Economic Resilience of Small States*. Malta and London: Islands and Small States Institute and Commonwealth Secretariat.

Briguglio, L., G. Cordina, N. Farrugia, and S. Vella. 2005. "Conceptualizing and Measuring Economic Resilience." In S. Chand, ed., *Pacific Islands Regional Integration and Governance*. Canberra: Australian National University Press. 26–49.

Brinklow, L., F. Ledwell, and J. Ledwell, eds. 2000. *Message in a Bottle: The Literature of Small Islands*. Charlottetown, PEI: Institute of Island Studies, University of Prince Edward Island.

British Overseas Territories Act 2002. www.opsi.gov.uk/acts/acts2002/20020008. htm (accessed 8 August 2008).

Brittain-Catlin, W. 2005. *Offshore: The Dark Side of the Global Economy*. New York: Farrar, Strauss and Giroux.

Brock, C., and D. Smawfield. 1988. "Education and Development: The Issue of Small States." *Educational Review* 40, no. 2: 227–39.

Brookfield, H.C. 1986. "An Approach to Islands." Unpublished paper, InterOceanic Workshop on Sustainable Development and Environmental Management of Small Islands. San Juan, Puerto Rico.

Brown, D. 2005. "Who's Afraid of Asymmetrical Federalism? A Summary Discussion." Special Series on Asymmetric Federalism. Kingston, Ont.: Canada: Institute of Intergovernmental Relations, Queen's University. http://www.queensu.ca/iigr/working/archive/Asymmetric/papers/16.pdf (accessed 12 August 2008).

Browning, L. 2008. "Madoff Spotlight Turns to Role of Offshore Funds." *New York Times*, 30 December. http://www.nytimes.com/2008/12/31/business/31offshore. html?_r=1&th&emc=th (accessed 31 December 2008).

Brunhes, J. 1920. *Human Geography: An Attempt at a Positive Classification*. Translated by I.C. LeCompte. London: George C. Harrap.

Brzezinski, Z. 1997. *The Grand Chessboard: American Primacy and Its Geostrategic Imperatives*. New York: Basic Books.

Buckley, S. 2005. "Okinawa Base Battle Resolved." *BBC News*, 25 October. http://news.bbc.co.uk/2/hi/asia-pacific/4357098.stm (accessed 2 August 2008).

Buker, P.E. 2005. "The Executive Administrative Style in Prince Edward Island: Managerial and Spoils Politics." In L. Bernier, K. Brownsley, and M. Howlett, eds., *Executive Styles in Canada: Cabinet Structures and Leadership Practices in Canadian Government*. Toronto, Ont.: University of Toronto Press. 111–31.

Bumsted, J.M. 1982. "'The Only Island There Is': The Writing of Prince Edward Island History." In V. Smitheram, D. Milne, and S. Dasgupta, eds., *The Garden Transformed: Prince Edward Island, 1945–1980*. Charlottetown, PEI: Ragweed Press. 11–38.

Butler, J. 2002. "Guantanamo Limbo." *The Nation*, 1 April. http://www.thenation.com/doc/20020401/butler (accessed 4 July 2009)

Butler, R.W. 1980. "The Concept of a Tourist Area Cycle of Evolution." *Canadian Geographer* 24, no. 1: 5–12.

— 1993. "Tourism Development in Small Islands: Past Influences and Future Directions." In D.G. Lockhart, D. Drakakis-Smith, and J.A. Schembri, eds., *The Development Process in Small Island States*. London: Routledge. 71–91.

Cairncross, F. 1997. *The Death of Distance*. Boston, Mass.: Harvard Business School Press.

Caldwell, J.C., G.E. Harrison, and P. Quiggin. 1980. "The Demography of Micro-States." *World Development*. 8, no. 12: 953–68.

Cameron, D.R. 1978. "The Expansion of the Public Economy: A Comparative Analysis." *American Political Science Review* 72, no. 4: 1243–61.

Cameron, S.D. 1998. *The Living Beach*. Toronto: Macmillan Canada.

Camilleri, A. 1995. Address to the State of the European Union Conference. Msida, Malta: University of Malta, European Documentation and Research Centre.

Caribbean Net News. 2003. "French Caribbean Voters Reject Change." 9 December. http://www.caribbeannetnews.com/2003/12/09/voters.htm (accessed 2 August 2008).

— 2005. "Netherlands Antilles Leader Threatens Legal Action over Immigration Limits." 6 June. www.caribbeannetnews.com/2005/06/06/leader.shtml (accessed 4 August 2008)

Carlquist, S. 1965. *Island Life: A Natural History of the Islands of the World*. Garden City, N.Y.: Natural History Press for the American Museum of Natural History.

— 1974. *Island Biology*. New York: Columbia University Press.

Carmel, E., and P. Tjia. 2005. *Offshoring Information Technology: Sourcing and Outsourcing to a Global Workforce*. Cambridge: Cambridge University Press.

Carroll, T. 2000. "Economic Sovereignty for Prince Edward Island." *Policy Options*, December. 7–11. http://www.irpp.org/po/archive/po1200.htm#carroll (accessed 15 August 2008).

Carty, L. 2007. "Camp Closure Hurts Nauru." *Sydney Morning Herald*, 23 December. http://www.smh.com.au/news/national/camp-closure-hurts-nauru/2007/12/22/1198175408703.html (accessed 2 August 2008).

Castells, M. 1996. *The Information Age: Economy, Society and Culture, Vol. 1: The Rise of the Network Society*. New York: Blackwell Publishers.

— 1999. *Information Age: Economy, Society and Culture*. Oxford: Blackwell.

Catt, H., and M. Murphy. 2002. *Sub-State Nationalism: A Comparative Analysis of Institutional Design*. London: Routledge.

CBC News. 2004. "Canada's Caribbean Ambition." 16 April. http://www.cbc.ca/news/background/turksandcaicos/ (accessed 11 December 2008).

— 2008. "UN Condemns Zimbabwe Government as Opposition Leader Seeks Refuge." 23 June. http://www.cbc.ca/world/story/2008/06/23/zimbabwe-election.html (accessed 6 August 2008).

CDNN News. 2004. "Need More Space? Build an Island." *CDNN News*, 11 December. http://www.cdnn.info/industry/i041211/i041211.html (accessed 15 January 2010).

Chamberlain, M.E. 1985. *Decolonization: The Fall of the European Empires.* Oxford: Basil Blackwell.

Chappell, D.A. 1999. "The Noumea Accord: Decolonization without Independence in New Caledonia?" *Pacific Affairs* 72, no. 3: 373–91.

Charney, J.I., and L.M. Alexander. 1998. "Delimitation of Maritime Areas between Canada and France, St. Pierre and Miquelon, Award of June 10 1992." International Maritime Boundaries, American Society of International Law. 2141–58.

Chase-Dunn, C. 1981. "Interstate System and the Capitalist World Economy: One Logic or Two?" *International Studies Quarterly* 25, no. 1: 19–42.

Chasek, P.S. 2005. "Margins of Power: Coalition Building and Coalition Maintenance of the South Pacific Island States and the Alliance of Small and Island States." *Review of European Community and International Environmental Law* 14, no. 2: 125–37.

Chen, H.C.L., and P. Hay. 2006. "Defending Island Ecologies: Environmental Campaigns in Tasmania and Taiwan." *Journal of Developing Societies* 22, no. 3: 303–26.

China Post. 2008. "Diplomatic Ties with Paraguay in Question." 15 July. http://www.chinapost.com.tw/taiwan/foreign%20affairs/2008/07/15/165513/Diplomatic-ties.htm (accessed 11 August 2008).

— 2009. "DOH Minister Yeh Feels 'Terrific' about Making History at WHA." 19 May. http://www.chinapost.com.tw/taiwan/2009/05/19/208639/DOH-Minister.htm (accessed 3 July 2009).

Chomsky, N. 1999. "East Timor, Horror and Amnesia." *Le Monde Diplomatique*, October. http://mondediplo.com/1999/10/02chomsky (accessed 2 August 2008).

Chongyi, F., and D.S.G. Goodman. 1997. "Hainan: Communal Politics and the Struggle for Identity." In D.S.G. Goodman, ed., *China's Provinces in Reform.* London: Routledge. 53–80.

Chowra, M. 2006. "The Living Conditions of Undocumented Aliens 'Waiting' at the Borders of the EU: The Case of the 'Zone d'Attente' in Charles de Gaulle Airport in France." Victoria, B.C., Canada, 6th Biennial Conference of European Community Studies Association, May.

Christensen, J., and M.P. Hampton. 1999. "A Legislature for Hire: The Capture of the State in Jersey's Offshore Finance Centre." In M.P. Hampton and J.P. Abbott, eds., *Offshore Finance Centres and Tax Havens: The Rise of Global Capital.* Basingstoke, U.K.: Macmillan. 166–91.

Christiansen, T. 1996. "Second Thoughts on Europe's 'Third Level': The European Union's Committee of the Regions." *Publius: The Journal of Federalism* 26, no. 1: 93–116.

Christianson, J.R. 1999. *On Tycho's Island: Tycho Brahe and His Assistants: 1570–1601*. Cambridge: Cambridge University Press.

Churchill Semple, E. 1911/2007. *Influences of the Geographic Environment*. Charleston, S.C.: Bibliobazaar.

CIA 2007. *World FactBook 2007*. Washington, D.C.: Central Intelligence Agency.

— 2009a. *World FactBook 2009*. Washington, D.C.: Central Intelligence Agency. https://www.cia.gov/library/publications/the-world-factbook/ (accessed 16 July 2009).

— 2009b. "British Indian Ocean Territory." In CIA *World Factbook 2009*, Washington, D.C.: Central Intelligence Agency. https://www.cia.gov/library/publications/the-world-factbook/geos/IO.html (accessed 16 July 2009).

Clark, E. 2005. "The Order and Simplicity of Gentrification: A Political Challenge." In R. Atkinson and G. Bridge, eds., *Gentrification in a Global Context: The New Urban Colonialism*. New York: Routledge. 256–64.

— 2009. "Island Development." In R. Kitchin and N. Thrift, eds., *International Encyclopaedia of Human Geography*. Amsterdam: Elsevier. 607–10.

Clegg, P. 2005. "The UK Caribbean Overseas Territories: Extended Statehood and the Process of Policy Convergence." In L. de Jong and D. Kruijt, eds., *Extended Statehood in the Caribbean*. Amsterdam: Rozenberg. 125–56.

— 2008. "The Commonwealth Caribbean and Challenges of Institutional Exclusion." *The Round Table: Commonwealth Journal of International Affairs* 97, no. 395: 227–41.

Clifford, J. 1997. *Routes: Travel and Translation in the Late Twentieth Century*. Cambridge. Mass.: Harvard University Press.

CNN News. 2008. "Kosovo Celebrates amid Serb Protests." 18 February. http://www.cnn.com/2008/WORLD/europe/02/17/kosovo.independence/index.html (accessed 2 August 2008).

COFA 1985. Compact of Free Association Act of 1985. Public Law 99–239, 14 January 1986. http://www.fm/jcn/compact/actindex.html (accessed 2 August 2008).

Cohen, R., ed. 1983. *African Islands and Enclaves*. London: Sage.

Cohn, P. 2003. "Economic Independence through Expansion of Private Sector Enterprise: The Prescriptive Unreality of Niue's Development Planning." *Working Paper No. 11*. Melbourne University, Australia: School of Development Studies.

Colombia IndyMedia. 2007. "The Indigenous People of St. Andrew Islands." 17 January. http://colombia.indymedia.org/news/2007/01/55961_comment.php (accessed 13 December 2008).

Commonwealth Consultative Group. 1985. *Vulnerability: Small States in the Global Society*. London: Commonwealth Secretariat.

Commonwealth Secretariat/World Bank. 2000. *Small States: Meeting Challenges in the Global Economy*. London and New York: Commonwealth Secretariat/World Bank, Joint Task Force on Small States. Final report, mimeo. March. http://www.thecommonwealth.org/Shared_ASP_Files/UploadedFiles/03D192EA -CCF2-4FA2-96B3-F7DA64AD245B_taskforcereport.pdf (accessed 16 July 2009).

Congleton, R.D., A. Kyriacou, and J. Bacaria. 1999. *Political and Economic Origins of Asymmetric Federalism: A Model of Endogenous Centralization*. http://selene.uab.es/jbacaria/Economia_Aplicada/asymfed3.pdf (accessed 4 August 2008).

Conlin, M., and T.G. Baum, eds. 1995. *Island Tourism: Management Principles and Practices*. Chichester, U.K.: John Wiley.

Connect-Project.net. 2008. *The British Virgin Islands*. http://www.connect-project. net/british_virgin_islands_2.html (accessed 4 September 2008).

Connell, J. 1987. "New Caledonia or Kanaky? The Political History of a French Colony." *Pacific Research Monograph*, no. 16. Canberra: National Development Studies Centre.

— 1988a. "Sovereignty and Survival: Island Microstates in the Third World." *Research Monograph No. 3*. Sydney: University of Sydney, Department of Geography.

—1988b. "The End Ever Nigh: Contemporary Population Change on Pitcairn Island." *Geo Journal* 6, no. 1: 193–200.

— 1991. "Island Microstates: The Mirage of Development." *Contemporary Pacific* 3, no. 2: 251–87.

— 1994. "Britain's Caribbean Colonies: The End of the Era of Decolonization." *Journal of Commonwealth and Comparative Politics* 32, no. 1: 87–106.

—1995. "In Samoan Worlds: Culture, Migration, Identity and Albert Wendt." In R. King, J. Connell, and P. White, eds. *Writing across Worlds: Literature and Migration*. London: Routledge. 263–79.

— 2003a. "Island Dreaming: The Contemplation of Polynesian Paradise." *Journal of Historical Geography* 39, no. 4: 554–81.

— 2003b. "New Caledonia: An Infinite Pause in Decolonization?" *The Round Table: Commonwealth Journal of International Affairs* 92, no. 368: 125–43.

— 2006. "Nauru: The First Pacific Failed State?" *The Round Table: Commonwealth Journal of International Affairs* 95, no. 383: 47–63.

Connell, J., and R. Aldrich. 1992. *France's Overseas Frontier*. Cambridge: Cambridge University Press.

Connell, J., and R. King. 1999. "Island Migration in a Changing World." In R. King and J. Connell, eds., *Small Worlds, Global Lives: Islands and Migration*. London: Pinter. 1–26.

Conrad, A.F. 1973. "An Overview of the Laws of Corporations." *Michigan Law Review* 4: 623–90.

Constant, F. 1992. "Alternative Forms of Decolonization in the East Caribbean: The Comparative Politics of the Non-Sovereign Islands." In H.M. Hintjens and M.D.D. Newitt, eds., *The Political Economy of Small Tropical Islands: The Importance of Being Small*. Exeter, U.K.: University of Exeter Press. 51–63.

Constitution Act 1982. Part I: Canadian Charter of Rights and Freedoms. Government of Canada: Department of Justice. http://laws.justice.gc.ca/en/const/annex_e.html (accessed 4 August 2008).

Cooley, A. 2005. *Logics of Hierarchy: The Organization of Empires, States and Military Occupations*. Ithaca, N.Y.: Cornell University Press.

Cooper, A.F. 2009. "Confronting Vulnerability through Resilient Diplomacy: Antigua and the WTO Internet Gambling Dispute with the United States." In A.F. Cooper and T.M. Shaw, eds., *The Diplomacies of Small States: Between Vulnerability and Resilience*. Basingstoke, U.K.: Palgrave Macmillan. 207–18.

Cooper, C. 2007. "North Dumpling Island: Segway Inventor Dean Kamen's Island Country." *Associated Content Inc.* 10 October. http://www.associatedcontent.com/article/400202/north_dumpling_island_segway_inventor.html?cat=9 (accessed 4 July 2009).

Corbin, A. 2008. "Kahoʻolawe." http://www.sacredland.org/historical_sites_pages/kahoolawe.html (accessed 16 December 2008).

Corbin, C. 2001. "Direct Participation of Non-Independent Caribbean Countries in the United Nations: A Method for Self-Determination." In A.G. Ramos and A.I. Rivera, eds., *Islands at the Crossroads: Politics in the Non-Independent Caribbean*. Kingston, Jamaica: Ian Randle. 136–59.

Cosgrove, D. 2005. Review of *Islands of the Mind: How the Human Imagination Created the Atlantic World*, by J.R. Gillis. *Geografiska Annaler* 87B, no. 4: 302–3.

Council of Europe. 2007. *Guantánamo: Violation of Human Rights and International Law?* Strasbourg, France: Council of Europe Publishing.

Courchene, T.J. 1995. "Glocalization: The Regional/International Interface." *Canadian Journal of Regional Science* 18, no. 1: 1–20.

— 2005. "City-States and the State of Cities: Political-Economy and Fiscal Federalism Dimensions." *Working Paper Series*, no. 3. Montreal: Institute for Research on Public Policy.

Coutin, S. 2005. "Being En Route." *American Anthropologist* 107, no. 2: 195–206.

CPMR. 2002. *Off the Coast of Europe: European Construction and the Problem of the Islands*. St Malo, France: study undertaken by EurIsles on the initiative of Conference of Peripheral Maritime Regions.

Cracknell, B. 1967. "Accessibility to the Countryside as a Factor in Planning for Leisure." *Regional Studies* 1, no. 1: 147–61.

Crocombe, R. 1979. "Nepotism." In R. Crocombe, ed., *Cook Island Politics*. Suva, Fiji Islands, and Auckland, New Zealand: Institute of Pacific Studies, University of the South Pacific and Polynesian Press. 30–59.

— 2007. *Asia in the Pacific Islands: Replacing the West*. Suva, Fiji Islands: Institute of Pacific Studies, University of the South Pacific.

Cropper, A. 1994. "Small Is Vulnerable." *Our Planet* (UNESCO) 6, no. 1: 9–12.

Crosby, A. 1986. *Ecological Imperialism: The Biological Expansion of Europe: 900–1900*. Cambridge: Cambridge University Press.

Crowards, T. 2002. "Defining the Category of 'Small' States." *Journal of International Development* 14, no. 2: 143–79.

Crystal, *D*. 2000. *Language Death*. Cambridge: Cambridge University Press.

Cullen, R. 1990. *Federalism in Action*. New South Wales, Australia: Federalist Press.

Curr. P. 2009. "We Can Do Better Than Italy's Warehousing on Lampedusa." *Brisbane Times*, 14 October. http://www.brisbanetimes.com.au/opinion/politics/we-can-do-better-than-italys-warehousing-on-lampedusa-20091014-gwh8.html (accessed 15 January 2010).

Dahl, A.L. 1996. *The Eco Principle: Ecology and Economics in Symbiosis*. London: Zed.

Daily Herald. 2006. "Dutch Regulation Is Form of Apartheid." 13 June. http://news.caribseek.com/set-up/exec/view.cgi?archive=111&num=34405 (accessed 14 August 2008).

— 2008. "Zaandam Firmly Opposes Expulsion of Antillean Youth." 19 February. http://thedailyherald.com/news/daily/k233/stzaan233.html (accessed 14 August 2008).

Darwin, C. [1859] 1979. *On the Origins of Species by Means of Natural Selection, or of the Preservation of Favoured Races in the Struggle for Life*. New York: Avenel Books.

Debattista, M. 2007. "The Smart Island in the Making." I-Tech Supplement, *Times of Malta*. Malta, Progress Press, 6 December.

De la Fayette, L. 1993. "The Award in the Canada-France Maritime Boundary Arbitration." *International Journal of Marine and Coastal Law* 8, no. 1: 77–103.

Defoe, D. 1719. *Robinson Crusoe*. London: W. Taylor.

De Kadt, E.B., ed. 1979. *Tourism: Passport to Development?* New York: Oxford University Press.

Deleuze, G. 2004. *Desert Islands and Other Texts: 1953–1974*. Los Angeles, Calif.: Semiotexte.

Deloughrey, E.M. 2001. "'The Litany of Islands, The Rosary of Archipelagoes': Caribbean and Pacific Archipelagraphy." *ARIEL: A Review of International English Literature* 32, no. 1: 21–52.

— 2007. *Routes and Roots: Navigating Caribbean and Pacific Island Literatures*. Honolulu: University of Hawaii Press.

DEME 2008. *Creating Land for the Future*. Zwijndrecht, Belgium: Dredging Environmental and Marine Engineering. http://www.deme.be/projects/maldive_hulhumale.html (accessed 12 August 2008).

Dening, G. 2004. *Beach Crossings: Voyaging across Times, Cultures and Self*. Melbourne, Australia: Miegunyah Press.

Department of Homeland Security. 2008. *Privacy Impact Assessment for the Experimental Testing of Project Hostile Intent Technology*, 25 February. http://www.dhs.gov/xlibrary/assets/privacy/privacy_pia_st_phi.pdf (accessed 4 November 2008).

Depraetere, C. 2008. "The Challenge of Nissology: A Global Outlook on the World Archipelago – Part II: The Global and Scientific Vocation of Nissology." *Island Studies Journal* 3, no. 1: 17–36.

Depraetere, C., and A.L. Dahl. 2007. "Island Locations and Classifications." In G. Baldacchino, ed., *A World of Islands: An Island Studies Reader*. Luqa, Malta, and Charlottetown, PEI: Agenda Academic and Institute of Island Studies, University of Prince Edward Island. 57–105.

Diamond, J. 2005. *Collapse: How Societies Choose to Fail or Survive*. New York: Viking Adult.

Di Castri, F., and V. Balaji, eds. 2002. *Tourism, Biodiversity and Information*. Leiden, The Netherlands: Backhuys.

Diggines, C. 1985. "The Problems of Small States." *The Round Table: Commonwealth Journal of International Affairs* 74, no. 295: 191–205.

Dinstein, Y. 1981. "Autonomy." In Y. Dinstein, ed., *Models of Autonomy*. New Brunswick, N.J.: Transaction Books. 291–303.

— 1993. "The Degree of Self-Rule in Minorities." In C. Brölmann, R. Lefeber, and M. Zieck, eds., *Peoples and Minorities in International Law*. Dordrecht, The Netherlands: Martinus Nijhoff. 221–35.

DMZ. 2008. "Call to Stop the Bombing of Pohakuloa." *DMZ Hawai'i/ Aloha'Aina*, 14 November. http://www.dmzhawaii.org/dev/wordpress/?p=18 (accessed 16 December 2008).

Dodds, K. 2007. "Performing Loyalty: Resisting Decolonization in the Falkland Islands." Paper presented at Islands and Postcolonialism Conference, Northern Ireland, Queen's University Belfast, September.

Dodds, K., and S.A. Royle. 2003. "Introduction: Rethinking Islands." *Journal of Historical Geography* 29, no. 4: 487–98.

Dommen, E.C., ed. 1980. "Islands." *World Development*. Special issue, 8, no. 12: 929–1059.

— 1985. "What Is a *Microstate*?" In E.C. Dommen and P.L. Hein, eds., *States, Microstates and Islands*. London: Croom Helm. 1–15.

Dommen, E.C., and P.L. Hein. 1985. "Foreign Trade in Goods and Services: The Dominant Activity of Small Island Economies." In E.C. Dommen and P.L. Hein, eds., *States, Microstates and Islands*. London: Croom Helm. 152–84.

Doumenge, F. 1989. "Basic Criteria for Estimating the Viability of Small Island States." In J. Kaminarides, L. Briguglio, and H.N. Hoogendonk, eds. *The Economic Development of Small Countries: Problems, Strategies and Policies*. Delft, The Netherlands: Eburon. 39–57.

— 1998. "Considerations for Small Island Development Today." In G. Baldacchino and R. Greenwood, eds., *Competing Strategies of Socio-Economic Development for Small Islands.* Charlottetown, PEI: Institute of Island Studies. 337–46.

Dow Jones Newswires. 2007. "EU Signs Wine Deal with Australia: Protects Champagne, Port." *Food Industry News,* 6 June. http://www.flex-news-food. com/pages/9144/Australia/European-Union/Wine/eu-signs-wine-deal-austra-lia-protects-champagne-port-dj.html (accessed 13 December 2008).

Doxey, G.V. 1976. "When Enough Is Enough: The Natives Are Restless in Old Niagara." *Heritage Canada* 2: 26–7.

Drago, T. 2005. "Spain: From the Berlin Wall to Ceuta and Melilla." *International Press Service News,* 5 October. http://ipsnews.net/news.asp?idnews=30546 (accessed 12 August 2008).

Drower, G. 1992. *Britain's Dependent Territories: A Fistful of Islands.* Aldershot, U.K.: Dartmouth.

— 2002. *Heligoland: The True Story of German Bight and the Island That Britain Betrayed.* Thrupp, U.K.: Sutton Press.

Drucker, P. 1986. "The Changed World Economy." *Foreign Affairs* 65, no. 2: 3–17.

Duchacek, I.D. 1970. "Unions and Associations of States." In *Comparative Federalism: The Territorial Dimension of Politics.* New York: Holt, Reinhart and Winston. 148–87.

— 1984. "The International Dimension of Subnational Self-Government." *Publius: The Journal of Federalism* 14, no. 4: 5–31.

— 1986. *The Territorial Dimension of Politics: Within, Among and Across Nations.* London: Westview Press.

— 1990. "Perforated Sovereignties: Towards a Typology of New Actors in International Relations." In H. Michelmann and P. Soldatos, eds., *Federalism and International Relations: The Role of Sub-National Units.* Oxford: Clarendon. 1–33.

Dunford, G. 2009. "A Mini-History of Micronations." *The Futurist,* 1 May. 34. http://www.allbusiness.com/government/elections-politics-politics/12323562-1. html (accessed 4 July 2009).

Dunn, C. 2004. "Urban Asymmetry: The New Reality in Inter-Governmental Relations." *Policy Options* 25, no. 10: 38–42.

—2005. "Why Williams Walked, Why Martin Balked: The Atlantic Accord Dispute in Perspective." *Policy Options* 26, no. 2: 9–14. Montreal: Institute for Research on Public Policy.

Duval, D.T. 2004. "Conceptualizing Return Visits: A Transnational Perspective." In T. Coles and D. Timothy, eds., *Tourism, Diasporas and Space: Travels to Promised Lands.* London: Routledge. 50–61.

Easterly, W., and A.C. Kraay. 2000. "Small States, Small Problems? Income, Growth and Volatility in Small States." *World Development* 28, no. 11: 2013–27.

Eckholm, E. 2009. "Out of Guantánamo, Uighurs bask in Bermuda." *New York Times.* 15 June. http://www.nytimes.com/2009/06/15/world/americas/15uighur. html (accessed 7 July 2009).

ECLAC 2002. *Globalization and Migration: Canada's Response to the Chinese Boat Refugees.* Santiago, Chile: Economic Commission for Latin America and the Caribbean.

The Economist. 1971. "Damned Dots." 31 July. 16.

— 2002. "The South Atlantic: A Breezy, Squid-Rich Paradise." 30 March. 49–50.

— 2003a. "The End of Elephant Man." 26 July. 75.

— 2003b. "On the World's Rich List." 17 May. 33.

— 2004a. "Norfolk Island: An Island Murder Mystery." 10 July. 38.

— 2004b. "Smallness Pays." 26 February. http://www.economist.com/displayStory. cfm?story_ID=2461814 (accessed 3 August 2008).

— 2005a. "Graduate Emigration." 31 March. 94. http://www.economist.com/ markets/indicators/displaystory.cfm?story_id=E1_PRTDSGR (accessed 2 August 2008).

— 2005b. "A Nearly Final Constitution." 3 September. 41–2. http://www.economist. com/displayStory.cfm?Story_ID=E1_QPVRTGR (accessed 8 July 2009)

— 2005c. "Affirmative Action in Hawaii: Sun, Surf and Secession?" 3 September. 32. http://www.economist.com/displayStory.cfm?Story_ID=E1_QPVDQQG (accessed 8 July 2009).

— 2006a. "Singapore: Self-Replicating." 25 March. 48. http://www.economist.com/ displayStory.cfm?Story_ID=E1_VGGJJNG (accessed 8 July 2009).

— 2006b. "Puerto Rico: Trouble on Welfare Island." 27 May. 25. http://www.economist.com/displayStory.cfm?Story_ID=E1_GJRDDVT (accessed 8 July 2009).

— 2006c. 'Economic Focus: Least Favoured Nation." 5 August. 68. http://www.economist.com/finance/displaystory.cfm?story_ID=E1_SNVNJPT (accessed 8 July 2009).

— 2006d. "Marketing New Zealand: From Fantasy Worlds to Food." 11 November. 73. http://www.economist.com/displayStory.cfm?Story_ID=E1_RTQNRNJ (accessed 8 July 2009).

— 2007a. "Watch That Twitch. Special Report on Air Travel." 16 June. 14. http://www.economist.com/specialreports/displaystory.cfm?story_ID=E1_ JNRPGVT (accessed 8 July 2009).

— 2007b. "One-Horse Race: A Special Report on Hong Kong." 30 June. http://www.economist.com/countries/Hongkong/ (accessed 8 July 2009).

— 2007c. "God's Ambassadors." 21 July. 58–60. http://www.economist.com/world/ international/displaystory.cfm?story_id=9516461 (accessed 8 July 2009).

— 2008a. "Marshall Islands: Home on the Range." 12 January. 37–8. http://www.economist.com/displaystory.cfm?story_id=10498813 (accessed 8 July 2009).

— 2008b. 'Child Abuse in Jersey: Not Seen, Not Heard." 1 March. 58. http://www4.economist.com/displayStory.cfm?Story_ID=E1_TDSGGVTN (accessed 8 July 2009).

— 2008c. "Ecotourism and Economics: Shellshock." 29 March. 97.
http://www.economist.com/finance/displaystory.cfm?story_id=10926493
(accessed 8 July 2009).

— 2008d. "The Cockerel's Cropped Crest." 26 July. 49–50.
http://www.economist.com/displaystory.cfm?story_id=11792951 (accessed
8 July 2009).

— 2008e. "Clouds of Judgment." 25 October. 17. http://www.economist.com/
opinion/displaystory.cfm?story_id=12471098 (accessed 8 July 2009).

— 2009a. "Squaring off for a Seabed Scrap." 9 May. 39. http://www.economist.com/
world/americas/displaystory.cfm?story_id=13611528 (accessed 8 July 2009).

— 2009b. "Obituary: Prabhakaran." 23 May. 92. http://www.economist.com/
obituary/displayStory.cfm?story_id=13687889 (accessed 8 July 2009).

— 2009c. "Tax and the Cayman Islands: Grey Skies in the Caribbean." 23 May.
41–2. http://www.economist.com/world/americas/displaystory.cfm?story_
id=13707671 (accessed 8 July 2009).

— 2009d. "The G20 and Tax: Haven Hypocrisy." 28 March. 87.
http://www.economist.com/businessfinance/displayStory.cfm?story_
id=13382279 (accessed 8 July 2009).

— 2009e. "Easter Island: Rapa Nui Déjà Vu." 10 October. 42

— 2009f. "Skellig Michael: An Irish Riddle Wrapped in a Mystery." 12 September. 94.

— 2009g. "UNESCO and World Heritage Sites: The Limits of Soft Cultural Power."
12 September. 65–6. http://www.economist.com/world/international/display-
story.cfm?story_id=E1_TQQNRVQP (accessed 15 January 2010).

— 2009h. "A Very British Coup." 20 August. 34. http://www.economist.com/world/
americas/displayStory.cfm?story_id=E1_TQNVRJVD (accessed 20 January
2010).

— 2010. "America's Security Treaty with Japan: The New Battle of Okinawa." 14
January. 43-44. http://www.economist.com/world/asia/displaystory.cfm?story_
id=15271146 (accessed 15 January 2010).

Edis, R. 1991. "Punching above Their Weight: How Small Developing States
Operate in the Contemporary Diplomatic World." *Cambridge Review of
International Affairs* 5, no. 2: 45–53.

Edwards, R. 2005. "Secret Nuclear Waste Disposal Sites Revealed." *New Scientist*,
10 June. http://www.newscientist.com/article/dn7504 (accessed 16
December 2008).

Edmond, R., and V. Smith, eds. 2003. *Islands in History and Representation*.
London: Routledge.

Eilperin, J. 2006. "Hawaiian Marine Reserve to be World's Largest." *Washington
Post*, 15 June. http://www.washingtonpost.com/wp-dyn/content/
article/2006/06/14/AR2006061402455.html (accessed 4 August 2008).

Elazar, D.J. 1994. *Federal Systems of the World: A Handbook of Federal, Confederal
and Autonomy Arrangements*, 2nd ed. Harlow, U.K.: Longman Current Affairs.

— 1997. "Contrasting Unitary and Federal Systems." *International Political Science Review* 18, no. 3: 237–51.

ELAW Advocate, 2008. "Dominica: Oil Refinery on Hold." *Environmental Law Alliance Worldwide.* http://www.elaw.org/node/3446 (accessed 5 July 2009).

Emadi-Coffin, B. 1996. "Towards a New Theory of International Organization: The Multinational Corporation, the State, and International Regulation in the Establishment of Enterprise Zones and Export Processing Zones." PHD thesis. Brighton, U.K.: University of Sussex.

Embassy Pages. 2010. *Embassies and Consulates around the World.* http://www.embassypages.com/ (accessed 15 January 2010)

Emmanuel, P. 1976. "Independence and Viability: Elements of Analysis." in V.A. Lewis, ed., *Size, Self-Determination and International Relations: The Caribbean.* Mona, Jamaica: Institute of Social and Economic Research. 1–15.

Encontre, P. 1999. "The Vulnerability and Resilience of Small Island Developing States in the Context of Globalization." *Natural Resources Forum* 23, no. 2: 261–70.

Eriksen, T.H. 1993. *Ethnicity and Nationalism: Anthropological Perspectives.* London: Pluto Press.

European Commission. 2005. "Overseas Countries and Territories." http://europa.eu/scadplus/leg/en/s05034.htm (accessed 4 August 2008).

Everard, J.A., and J.C. Holt. 2004. *Jersey 1204: The Forging of an Island Community.* London: Thames and Hudson.

Fabri, D., and G. Baldacchino, 1999. "The Malta Financial Services Centre: A Study in Microstate Dependency Management?" In M.P. Hampton and J.P. Abbott, eds., *Offshore Finance Centres and Tax Havens: The Rise of Global Capital.* Basingstoke, U.K.: Macmillan. 140–66.

Fabry, M. 2000. "Sovereignty, Territory and Referendum: A Commentary on the Paper Presented by Prof. Jean Laponce." Discussion paper prepared for ISA Convention Workshop "Globalization and Democracy," Los Angeles, 14 March. http://www2.hawaii.edu/~fredr/fabry.htm (accessed 2 August 2008).

Fagerlund, N. 1996. "Autonomous European Island Regions Enjoying a Special Relationship with the European Union." In L. Lyck, ed., *Constitutional and Economic Space of the Small Nordic Jurisdictions.* Copenhagen: NordREFO. 73–89.

Fairbairn, T.I.J. 1988. "Indigenous Entrepreneurship and Business Development in the Cook Islands." In T.I.J. Fairbairn, ed., *Island Entrepreneurs: Problems and Performance in the South Pacific.* Honolulu: East-West Center. 55–76.

Farbotko, C. 2005. "Tuvalu, Climate Change, and the Possibilities for Legal Redress." Paper presented to Clean Air Society of Australia and New Zealand Conference. Hobart, Tasmania.

Farrugia, C.J., and P.A. Attard. 1989. *The Multifunctional Administrator.* London: Commonwealth Secretariat.

Fearon, J.D., and D.D. Laitin. 2004. "Neotrusteeship and the Problem of Weak States." *International Security* 28, no. 4: 5–43.

Federal Court of Australia. 2001. *Federal Court of Australia, Minister for Immigration and Multicultural Affairs and Ors v Eric Vadarlis V1007 of 2001*, and *Minister for Immigration and Multicultural Affairs and Ors v Victorian Council for Civil Liberties Incorporated and Ors V1008 of 2001*.

Feyrer, J., and B. Sacerdote 2006. "Colonialism and Modern Income: Islands as Natural Experiments." NBER *Working Paper No. 12546*. Cambridge, Mass.: National Bureau for Economic Research.

Fife, R. 2004. "PM's New View of Federalism Fractures Party." *Ottawa Citizen*, 22 October, A5.

Financial Action Task Force. 2005a. *Money Laundering and Terrorist Financing Typologies: 2004–2005*. Paris: OECD.

— 2005b. *Annual and Overall Review of Non-Cooperative Countries or Territories*. Paris: OECD.

Firth, R. [1936] 1983. *We, The Tikopia: A Sociological Study of Kinship in Primitive Polynesia*. Stanford, Calif.: Stanford University Press.

Fleming, E. 2002. "Strategic Paths to Competitiveness in Agriculture in South Pacific Island Nations." Geneva: UNCTAD. http://ro.unctad.org/infocomm/ diversification/nadi/study_ver2.PDF (accessed 9 August 2008).

Fletcher, G.P. 2004. "Black Hole in Guantánamo Bay." *Journal of International Criminal Justice* 2, no. 1: 121–32.

Fletcher, L. 2008. "Reading the News: Pitcairn Island at the Beginning of the 21st Century." *Island Studies Journal* 3, no. 1: 57–72.

Fletcher, M. 2008. "Greenland Referendum Offers Break from Links to Denmark." *The Independent* (Ireland), 16 November. http://www.independent.ie/ world-news/europe/greenland-referendum-offers-break-from-links--to- denmark-1552692.html (accessed 6 December 2008).

Fog Olwig, K. 1993. *Global Culture, Island Identity: Continuity and Change in the Afro-Caribbean Community of Nevis*. Reading, Mass.: Harwood Academic Publisher.

Foreign and Commonwealth Office. 2003. *Explanatory Memorandum on the Agreement between the United Kingdom and New Zealand concerning Trials under Pitcairn Law in New Zealand*. London: January. http://www.fco.gov.uk/ en/about-the-fco/publications/treaty-command-papers-ems/explanatory- memoranda/explanatory-memoranda-2003/pitcairn (accessed 16 July 2009).

Foucault, M. 1991. "Governmentality." In G. Burchell, C. Gordon, and P. Miller, eds., *The Foucault Effect: Studies in Governmentality*. Chicago Ill.: University of Chicago Press. 87–104.

Fowler, M.R., and J.M. Bunck. 1995. *Law, Power and the Sovereign State: The Evolution and Application of the Concept of Sovereignty*. University Park: Pennsylvania State University Press.

Fox, A. 1969. *A Sociology of Work in Industry*. London: Collier-Macmillan.

France 24. 2009. "UN Expresses Concern over Italian Refugee Camp." International News. 24 January. http://www.france24.com/en/20090124-un-hcr-italian- refugee-camp-lampedusa (accessed 15 January 2010).

Franks, Lord, and collaborators, 1983. *The Franks Report: Falkland Islands Review*, Cmnd 8787. London: Her Britannic Majesty's Stationery Office.

Fraser, A.B. 1997. "Prince Edward Island." Chapter 17 in *The Flags of Canada*, http://fraser.cc/FlagsCan (accessed 2 August 2008).

Freedom Ship International. http://www.freedomship.com/ (accessed 20 March 2010).

Friberg, E., and L. Holen. 2002. "The Compact of Free Association: The U.S. Experience in Micronesia." Paper presented at "Islands of the World VII" Conference. University of Prince Edward Island, June.

Friedman, T.L. 2005. *The World Is Flat: A Brief History of the Twenty-First Century*. New York: Farrar, Straus and Giroux.

FT Expat. 2002. "Island Life: Buying an Island." *FT Expat*. London: Financial Times, April. 39–42.

Funk, M. 2008. *Mustique Field Notes – I*: 2 April, University of Prince Edward Island. Charlottetown, PEI: Master of Arts in Island Studies Program.

G7 2000. *Review to Identify Non-Cooperative Countries or Territories: Increasing the World's Effectiveness of Anti-Money Laundering Measures*. Paris: G7, Financial Action Task Force on Money-Laundering, June.

Gabilondo, P. 2000. "A Second Creation: In Search of the Island of the Colourblind." In L. Brinklow, F. Ledwell, and J. Ledwell, eds., *Message in a Bottle: The Literature of Small Islands*. Charlottetown, PEI: Institute of Island Studies, University of Prince Edward Island. 85–100.

Gagliardi, P. 2009. "Organizations as Designed Islands." *Island Studies Journal* 4, no. 1: 43–52.

Gallienne, T. 2007. *Guernsey in the 21st Century: A View from the First Decade*. Guernsey, British Isles: Gallant Publishing.

Gardner, R. circa 1939. *Hellcatraz: The Rock of Despair (Alcatraz)*. Self-published.

Garrett, G. 1998. *Partisan Politics in the Global Economy*. Cambridge: Cambridge University Press.

Gaudet, L. 2007. *Safe Haven: The Possibility of Sanctuary in an Unsafe World*. Toronto: Random House.

Gayoon, M.A. 1992. Address by His Excellency Maumoon Abdul Gayoon, President of the Republic of Maldives, at the United Nations Conference on Environment and Development, Rio De Janeiro, Brazil, 12 June. http://www.un.int/maldives/unced.htm (accessed 2 August 2008).

Gensini, G., M. Yacoub, and A. Conti. 2004. "The Concept of Quarantine in History: From Plague to SARS." *Journal of Infection* 49, no. 4: 257–61.

Ghai, Y.P. 2002. "Global Prospects of Autonomies." In H. Jansson and J. Salminen, eds., *The Second Åland Islands Question: Autonomy or Independence?* Mariehamn, Åland Islands: Julius Sundblom Memorial Foundation. 29–54.

Ghai, Y.P., and A.J. Regan. 2000. "Bougainville and the Dialectics of Ethnicity, Autonomy and Separation." In Y.P. Ghai, ed., *Autonomy and Ethnicity: Negotiating Competing Claims in Multi-Ethnic States*. Cambridge: Cambridge University Press. 242–65.

— 2006. "Unitary State, Devolution, Autonomy, Secession: State Building and Nation Building in Bougainville, Papua New Guinea." *The Round Table: Commonwealth Journal of International Affairs*. 95, no. 386: 589–608.

Gillis, J.R. 2004. *Islands of the Mind: How the Human Imagination Created the Atlantic World*. New York: Palgrave Macmillan.

— 2007. "Escape to Alcatraz: Islands in the Landscape of Fear." Paper presented at 3rd International Conference on Small Island Cultures, Charlottetown, Canada, June.

Girvan, N. 2004. "Do Small Islands Have a Future in a Globalized World?" Paper presented at the "Islands of the World VIII" Conference, Kinmen Island, Taiwan, November.

Glick, P., and F. Roubaud. 2005. "Export Processing Zone Expansion in Madagascar: What Are the Labour Market and Gender Impacts?" *Journal of African Economies* 1, no. 1: 192–205.

GLISPA. 2008. Global Island Partnership. http://www.cbd.int/island/glispa.shtml (accessed 4 August 2008).

The Global Game 2006. "Terminal Sadness: Stranded in Time: Ghanaian Plays Football Alone." http://www.theglobalgame.com/blog/?p=200 (accessed 2 August 2008).

Global Shoreline Database 2005. U.S. National Geophysical Data Center. http://www.ngdc.noaa.gov/mgg/shorelines/gshhs.html (accessed 4 August 2008).

Globe and Mail. 2009. "Exports to Statelets." Editorial. 16 June. http://www.theglobeandmail.com/news/opinions/editorials/exports-to-statelets/article1181941/ (accessed 7 July 2009).

Glover, D. 2003. *Elle*. Toronto: Goose Lane Editions.

Golding, W.G. [1954] 1978. *Lord of the Flies: A Novel*. New York: Putnam.

Goldsmith, W.W. 1979. "Operation Bootstrap, Industrial Autonomy, and a Parallel Economy for Puerto Rico." *International Regional Science Review* 4, no. 1: 1–22.

González, J.A., C. Montes, J. Rodriguez, and W. Tapia. 2008. "Rethinking the Galápagos Islands as a Complex Social-Ecological System: Implications for Conservation and Management." *Ecology and Society* 13, no. 2. http://www.ecologyandsociety.org/vol13/iss2/art13/ES-2008-2557.pdf (accessed 5 July 2009).

Gordon, T. 2007. "Salmond Fights for a Scottish Olympic Team." *Sunday Times* (UK), 20 May. http://www.timesonline.co.uk/tol/news/uk/article1813545.ece (accessed 7 August 2008).

Gosden, C., and C. Pavlides. 1994. "Are Islands Insular? Landscape versus Seascape in the Case of the Arawe Islands, Papua New Guinea." *Archaeology in Oceania* 29, no. 1: 162–71.

Gössling, S., ed. 2003. *Tourism and Development in Tropical Islands: Political Ecology Perspectives*. Cheltenham, U.K.: Edward Elgar Publishing.

Gössling, S., and G. Wall. 2007. "Island Tourism." In G. Baldacchino, ed., *A World of Islands: An Island Studies Reader*. Luqa, Malta, and Charlottetown, PEI: Agenda Academic and Institute of Island Studies. 429–54.

Gössling, S., C. Borgström Hansson, O. Hörstmeier, and S. Saggel. 2002. "Ecological Footprint Analysis as a Tool to Assess Tourism Sustainability." *Ecological Economics* 43, no. 2: 199–211.

Gottlieb, G. 1994. "Nations without States." *Foreign Policy* 73, no. 1: 100–12.

Government of Anguilla. N.d. "Introduction to Constitutional Reform." http://gov.ai/images/constitutional%20reform/4.%20Introduction%20final.pdf (accessed 2 August 2008).

Government of Newfoundland and Labrador. 2007. *News Release*: St John's Board of Trade. 12 September. http://www.releases.gov.nl.ca/releases/speeches/2007/premiersept12.htm (accessed 14 January 2010).

Green, R. 1984. *Battle for the Franklin: Conversations with the Combatants in the Struggle for South West Tasmania*, with photographs by Geoffrey Lea. Sydney: Fontana and the Australian Conservation Foundation.

Green, W.A. 1984. "The Perils of Comparative History: Belize and the British Sugar Colonies after Slavery." *Comparative Studies in Society and History* 26, no. 1: 112–19.

Greenhouse, L. 2006. "Justices, 5–3, Broadly Reject Bush Plan to Try Detainees." *New York Times*, 29 June. www.nytimes.com/2006/06/30/washington/30hamdan.html?_r=1andthandemc=thandoref=slogin (accessed 2 August 2008).

Greenpeace. 2007. "Financial Grants and Votes for Whaling: Japan's Fisheries Aid and Links with the St. Kitts Declaration." Briefing, February. http://www.greenpeace.org/raw/content/international/press/reports/japan-fisheries-aid.pdf (accessed 15 January 2010).

Greer, T., and G. Wall. 1982. "Recreational Hinterlands: A Theoretical and Empirical Analysis." In G. Wall, ed., *Recreational Land Use in Southern Ontario*, Publication Series no. 14. Waterloo, Ont.: University of Waterloo, Department of Geography.

Gregory, D. 2004. "Editorial: The Angel of Iraq." *Environment and Planning D: Society and Space* 22, no. 3: 317–24. http://www.envplan.com/epd/editorials/d2203ed1.pdf (accessed 4 July 2009).

Griffith, V., and M. Inniss. 1992. "Environmental Diplomacy: An Effective Tool for Small Island States to Define a More Dynamic Role in International Environmental-Development Negotiations." *Bulletin of Eastern Caribbean Affairs* 17, nos. 1–2: 43–54.

Grove, R.H. 1995. *Green Imperialism: Colonial Expansion, Tropical Island Edens and the Origins of Environmentalism, 1600–1860*. Cambridge: Cambridge University Press.

Grundy-Warr, C. 1989. "Export Processing Zones: The Economics of Enclave Manufacturing." *World Bank Research Observer* 4, no. 1: 65–88.

Grundy-Warr, C., K. Peachey, and P. Martin. 1999. "Fragmented Integration in the Singapore-Indonesian Border Zone: Southeast Asia's Growth Triangle against the Global Economy." *International Journal of Urban and Regional Research* 23, no. 2: 304–28.

Grydehøj, A. 2008. "Branding from Above: Generic Cultural Branding in Shetland and Other Islands." *Island Studies Journal* 3, no. 2: 175–98.

The Guardian (Charlottetown, PEI). 2003. "Immigrants to Canada." 5 September. A5.

The Guardian (U.K.). 2009. "Sweden's Pirate Party Wins EU Seat." Technology Blog. 8 June. http://www.guardian.co.uk/technology/blog/2009/jun/08/elections-pirate-party-sweden (accessed 3 July 2009).

Guillebaud, J.C. 1976. *Les Confettis de l'Empire*. Paris: Seuil.

Guthunz, U., and F. von Krosigk. 1996. "Tourism in Small Island States: From MIRAB to TOURAB?" In L. Briguglio, B. Archer, J. Jafari, and G. Wall, eds., *Sustainable Tourism in Islands and Small States: Issues and Policies*. London: Pinter. 18–35.

Gwyn, R. 2005. "Who Will Speak for Canada Abroad?" *Toronto Star*, 7 October.

Ha, B-J., and N. Prasad. 2008. "Offshore Financial Centres: A Viable Strategy for Small States?" Paper presented at "Islands of the World X" conference, Seogwipo, Jeju Island, South Korea, August.

Hache, J.-D. 2007. "Islands, Fixed Links and the European Union." In G. Baldacchino, ed., *Bridging Islands: The Impact of Fixed Links*. Charlottetown, PEI: Acorn Press. 161–84.

Hagalin, T. 2005. "Real Independence of Microstates in International Organizations and State Relations." Paper presented at 14th Convention of the Nordic Political Science Association, Reykjavik, Iceland, August. http://registration.yourhost.is/nopsa2005/papers/Thorhildur%20Hagalin.doc (accessed 2 August 2008).

Hamilton, J. 2008. "Maldives Build Barriers to Global Warning." National Public Radio, 28 January. http://www.npr.org/templates/story/story.php?storyId=18425626 (accessed 2 August 2008).

Hamilton-Jones, D. 1992. "Problems of Inter-Island Shipping in Archipelagic Small-Island Countries: Fiji and the Cook Islands." In H.M. Hintjens and M.D. Newitt, eds., *The Political Economy of Small Tropical Islands: The Importance of Being Small*. Exeter, U.K.: University of Exeter Press. 200–22.

Hampton, M.P. 1994. "Treasure Islands or Fools Gold: Can and Should Small Island Economies Copy Jersey?" *World Development* 22, no. 2: 237–50.

— 1996. *The Offshore Interface: Tax Havens in the Global Economy*. Basingstoke, U.K.: Macmillan.

— 2004. "Can and Should Small Island Economies Copy Jersey?" Paper presented at "Islands of the World VIII" conference, Kinmen Island, Taiwan, November.

Hampton, M.P., and J. Christensen. 2002. "Offshore Pariahs? Small Island Economies, Tax Havens and the Reconfiguration of Global Finance." *World Development* 30, no. 2: 1657–73.

Hampton, M.P., and J.P. Abbott. 1999b. "The Rise (and Fall?) of Offshore Finance in the Global Economy." In M.P. Hampton and J.P. Abbott, eds., *Offshore Finance Centres and Tax Havens: The Rise of Global Capital*. Basingstoke, U.K.: Macmillan. 1–17.

Handel, M. 1990. *Weak States in the International System*. London: Frank Cass.

Hannum, H., and R.B. Lillich. 1980. "The Concept of Autonomy in International Law." *American Journal of International Law* 74, no. 4: 858–89.

Harden, S., ed. 1985. *Small Is Dangerous: Micro-States in a Macro-World*. London: Frances Pinter.

Hardin, G. 1968. "The Tragedy of the Commons." *Science* 162, no. 3859: 1243–8.

Harrigan, N.E. 1978. "A Theoretical Analysis of the Concept of Microstates: The Raran Model." Paper presented at conference on the development of micro-states, U.S. Virgin Islands, Caribbean Research Institute, April.

Harris, J. 2008. "Risky Territories." *Company Lawyer* (Thomson Reuters) 29, no. 12: 353–4.

Harris, T. 2006. "The Dynamics of International Diplomacy: The Case of China and Taiwan in the Caribbean: 1971–2005." *Journal of Caribbean International Relations* 2 (October): 122–37.

Harvey, D. 1990. *The Condition of Postmodernity: An Enquiry into the Origins of Cultural Change*. Cambridge, Mass.: Blackwell.

— 2003. *The New Imperialism*. Oxford: Oxford University Press.

Harwood, C.J., Jr. 2002. "Diego Garcia: The 'Criminal Question' Doctrine." *War Law*. 1 September. http://homepage.ntlworld.com/jksonc/5_DiegoGarcia.html (accessed 4 August 2008).

Hatziprokopiou, P. 2004. "Balkan Immigrants in the Greek City of Thessaloniki." *European Urban and Regional Studies* 11, no. 4: 321–38.

Hau'ofa, E. 1983. *Tales of the Tikongs*. Auckland, New Zealand: Longman Paul.

— 1993. *A New Oceania: Rediscovering Our Sea of Islands*. Suva, Fiji Islands: University of the South Pacific.

Hay, P. 2000. "Tasmania: The Strange and Verdant Politics of a Strange and Verdant Island." Lecture delivered at the University of Prince Edward Island, 9 July. http://www.upei.ca/iis/art_ph_1 (accessed 2 August 2008).

— 2003. "The Poetics of Island Place: Articulating Particularity." *Local Environment* 8, no. 5: 553–8.

— 2006. "A Phenomenology of Islands." *Island Studies Journal* 1, no. 1: 19–42.

Hein, P.L. 2004. "Small Island Developing States: Origin of the Category and Definitional Issues." In *Is Special Treatment of Small Island Developing States Possible?* Geneva and New York: UNCTAD. 10–22.

Heinze, H.-J. 1998. "On the Legal Understanding of Autonomy." In *Autonomy: Applications and Implications*. London: Kluwer International. 7–32.

Held, D., A. McGrew, D. Goldblatt, and J. Perraton. 1999. *Global Transformations: Politics, Economics and Culture*. Cambridge: Polity Press.

Hepburn, E. 2009. "Introduction: Re-conceptualizing Sub-state Mobilization." *Regional and Federal Studies* 19, nos. 4–5: 477–99.

Hernandez, C.B. 2007. "Politics/Northern Marianas: Saipan's Garment Sector Gasping for Air." *Islands Business*. http://www.islandsbusiness.com/islands_business/index_dynamic/containerNameToReplace=MiddleMiddle/focusModuleID=17445/overideSkinName=issueArticle-full.tpl (accessed 2 August 2008).

Hettne, B., and F. Soderbaum. 2005. "Civilian Power or Soft Imperialism? The European Union as a Global Actor and the Role of Inter-Regionalism." *European Foreign Affairs Review* 10, no. 4: 535–52.

Hickling-Hudson, A., J. Matthews, and A. Woods. 2004. *Disrupting Preconceptions: Postcolonialism and Education*. Brisbane, Australia: Flaxton Press.

Hillebrink, S. 2008. *The Right to Self-Determination and Post-Colonial Governance: The Case of the Netherlands Antilles and Aruba*. The Hague, The Netherlands: TMC Asser Press.

Hintjens, H.M. 1990. "Assimilation, Integration, Citizenship and Decolonization." *Politics* 10, no. 2: 15–19.

—1991. "France in the Caribbean." In P.K. Sutton, ed., *Europe and the Caribbean*. London: Macmillan. 37–70.

—1995. *Alternatives to Independence: Explorations in Post-Colonial Relations*. Aldershot, U.K.: Dartmouth Publishing.

Hintjens, H.M., and M.D.D. Newitt, eds., 1992. *The Political Economy of Small Tropical Islands: The Importance of Being Small*. Exeter, U.K.: University of Exeter Press.

Hinz, E.R., and R. Bendix. *Pacific Island Battlegrounds of World War II: Then and Now*. Honolulu: Bess Press.

Hirsch, A.E. 2009. "Fish Shares and Sharing Fish." *New York Times*, 3 February. http://judson.blogs.nytimes.com/2009/02/03/guest-column-fish-shares-and-sharing-fish/ (accessed 7 July 2009).

Hirschheim, R. 2006. "Information System Outsourcing." In R. Hirschheim, A. Heinzl, and J. Dibbern, eds., *Offshore Outsourcing: Challenge to the Information Systems Discipline*. Berlin: Springer Verlag. 687–99.

Hocking, B. 1993. *Localizing Foreign Policy, Non-Central Governments and Multilayered Diplomacy*. London: Macmillan.

— 1999. "Patrolling the 'Frontier': Globalization, Localization and the 'Actorness' of Non-Central Governments." In F. Aldecoa and M. Keating, eds., *Paradiplomacy in Action: The Foreign Relations of Sub-National Governments*. London: Frank Cass. 17–39.

Hoefte, R. 1996. "Thrust Together: The Netherlands Relationship with Its Caribbean Partners." *Journal of Interamerican Studies and World Affairs* 38, no. 4: 35–54.

Hoefte, R., and G. Oostindie. 1989. "Upside-Down Decolonization." *Hemisphere* 1, no. 2: 28–31.

— 1991. "The Netherlands and the Dutch Caribbean: Dilemmas of Decolonization." In P.K. Sutton, ed., *Europe and the Caribbean*. London: Macmillan. 71–98.

Hogg, P.W. 1977. *Constitutional Law of Canada*. Toronto: Carswell.

Hollingham, R. 2007. "Environmentalists in Uproar as Iceland Pays the Price for Green Energy Push." *The Independent on Sunday* (UK), 21 March. http://www.independent.co.uk/environment/environmentalists-in-uproar -as-iceland-pays-the-price-for-green-energy-push-441141.html (accessed 16 August 2008).

Holm, B. 2000. *Eccentric Islands: Travels Real and Imaginary*. Minneapolis, Minn.: Milkweed Books.

Hooghe, L., and G. Marks. 2003. "Unraveling the Central State, but How? Types of Multi-Level Governance." *American Political Science Review* 97, no. 2: 233–43.

Horowitz, D.L. 1985. *Ethnic Groups in Conflict*. Berkeley: University of California Press.

Horscroft, V. 2005. "Small Economies and Special and Differential Treatment: Strengthening the Evidence, Countering the Fallacies." *Small States: Economic Review and Basic Statistics* 10. London: Commonwealth Secretariat. 41–60.

Hossay, P. 2004. "Recognizing Corsica: The Drama of Recognition in Nationalist Mobilization." *Ethnic and Racial Studies* 27, no. 3: 403–30.

Houbert, J. 1981. "Mauritius: Independence and Dependence." *Journal of Modern African Studies* 19, no. 1: 75–105.

—1986a. "Decolonizing without Disengaging: France in the Indian Ocean." *The Round Table: Commonwealth Journal of International Affairs* 75, no. 298: 145–66.

— 1986b. "Reunion-I: Decolonization in the Mascareignes." *Journal of Commonwealth and Comparative Politics* 18, no. 1: 145–71.

Houlder, V. 2008. "Harbours of Resentment." *Financial Times*, London, 30 November. http://www.ft.com/cms/s/0/464f09e2-bf49-11dd-ae63-0000779fd18c.html (accessed 10 December 2008).

Houlder, V., and N. Tait. 2006. "ECJ Tax Ruling to help Multinationals." *Financial Times*, London, 2 May. http://us.ft.com/ftgateway/superpage.ft?news_ id=ft0050220061412396475 (accessed 11 December 2008)

House of Commons, U.K. 1950. *Debates*. 28 July 910.

Hudson, A.C. 1998. "Placing Trust, Trusting Place: On the Social Construction of Offshore Financial Centres." *Political Geography* 17, no. 8: 915–37.

— 2000. "Offshoreness, Globalization and Sovereignty: A Post-Modern Geo-Political Economy?" *Transactions of the Institute of British Geographers* 25, no. 3: 269–83.

Human Rights Watch. 2009. "Pushed Back, Pushed Around." 21 Sept. http://www.hrw.org/en/node/85582/section/+1 (accessed 20 March 2010).

Hymer, S. 1971/2. "Robinson Crusoe and the Secret of Primitive Accumulation." *Monthly Review* 23, no. 1: 10–26.

The Independent (U.K.) 2006. "Disappearing World: Global Warming Claims Tropical Island." 24 December. http://news.independent.co.uk/environment/article2099971.ece (accessed 2 August 2008).

Ingebritsen, C. 2002. "Norm Entrepreneurs: Scandinavia's Role in World Politics." *Cooperation and Conflict* 37, no. 1: 11–23.

— 2006. "Conclusion: Learning from Lilliput." In C. Ingebritsen, I. Neumann, G. Stöhl, and J. Beyer, eds., *Small States in International Relations*. Seattle, Wash., and Reykjavik, Iceland: University of Washington Press and University of Iceland Press. 286–91.

Ingimundarson, V. 2003. "A Western Cold War: The Crisis in Iceland's Relations with Britain, the United States, and NATO, 1971–74." *Diplomacy and Statecraft* 14, no. 4: 94–136.

Insiders' Guide. 2006. 'The Insiders' Guide to St Barthélemy." http://www.sbhonline.com/ (accessed 4 December 2008).

International Herald Tribune. 2009. "Deal for Piracy Site Jeopardized." 28 Aug. 1–17.

Iran Trade Point Network. 2008. "Free Trade – Industrial Zones." http://www.irtp.com/howto/freetra/mb7.asp (accessed 11 August 2008).

Isfeld, S. [councillor and representative of the Faroe Islands in London]. 2006. Personal correspondence with Barry Bartmann, 22 January.

Island Superlatives 2007. *Island Superlatives*. http://www.worldislandinfo.com/SUPERLATIVESV2.html (accessed 9 August 2008).

ITF. 2008. "What Are Flags of Convenience?" Geneva: International Transport Workers' Federation. http://www.itfglobal.org/flags-convenience/sub-page.cfm (accessed 4 December 2008).

Jackson, J.H. 2003. "Sovereignty-Modern: A New Approach to an Outdated Concept." *American Journal of International Law* 97, no. 4: 782–802.

Jackson, M., and V. Della Dora 2009. "'Dreams So Big Only the Sea Can Hold Them': Man-Made Islands as Anxious Spaces, Cultural Icons and Travelling Visions." *Environment and Planning A* 41, no. 9: 2086–104.

James, K.E. 1991. "Migration and Remittances: A Tongan Village Perspective." *Pacific Viewpoint* 32, no. 1: 1–23.

Janelle, D.G. 1969. "Spatial Re-Organization: A Model and Concept." *Annals of the American Association of Geographers* 59, no. 2: 348–64.

Joenniemi, P., ed. 1997. "Neo-nationalism or Regionality: The Restructuring of Political Space around the Baltic Rim." *Report 1997/5*. Stockholm: NordREFO.

Johns, R.A. 1983. *Tax Havens and Offshore Finance: A Study of Transnational Economic Development*. New York: St Martin's Press.

Johnston, P. 2006. "Ascension Islanders 'Betrayed by Britain.'" *The Telegraph*, 13 February. http://www.telegraph.co.uk/global/main.jhtml?xml=/global/2006/02/13/wascen13.xml (accessed 2 August 2008).

Jolly, M. 2001. "On the Edge? Deserts, Oceans, Islands." *Contemporary Pacific* 13, no. 2: 417–66.

Jonsson, I. 1997. "From Home Rule to Independence? New Opportunities for a New Generation in Greenland." Paper presented at symposium on Dependency, Autonomy and Conditions for Sustainability in the Arctic, Nuuk, Greenland. Institute of Economics and Management, Ilisimatusarfik, March. http://www.bifrost.is/Files/Skra_0008050.pdf (accessed 2 August 2008).

Judicial Committee of the Privy Council, 2006. *Privy Council Appeal No 109/2005.* http://www.privy-council.org.uk/files/other/Pitcairn.rtf (accessed 11 August 2008).

Junemo, M. 2004. "Let's Build a Palm Island! Playfulness in Complex Times." In M. Sheller and J. Urry, eds., *Tourism Mobilities: Places to Play, Places in Play.* London: Routledge. 181–91.

Kaae, B.C. 2006. "Greenland/Kalaallit Nunaat." In G. Baldacchino, ed., *Extreme Tourism: Lessons from the World's Cold Water Islands.* Oxford: Elsevier. 101–14.

Kabutaulaka, T. 2004. "'Failed State' and the War on Terror: Intervention in the Solomon Islands." *Asia Pacific Issues* 72. Honolulu: East-West Center.

Kahnawake Gaming Commission, 2008. http://www.kahnawake.com/gamingcommission/ (accessed 8 August 2008).

Kaiser, R. 2002. "Subnational Governments in International Arenas – Paradiplomacy and Multi-Level Governance in Europe and North America." 5th IPSA Symposium on Globalization, Nations and Multi-level Governance: Strategies and Challenges, Montreal, 24–26 October.

Kakazu, H. 1994. *Sustainable Development of Small Island Economies.* Boulder, Colo.: Westview Press.

— 2000. *The Challenge for Okinawa: Thriving Locally in a Globalized Economy.* Okinawa, Japan: Okinawa Development Finance Corporation, March.

Kanter, J. 2009. "An Air of Frustration for Europe at Climate Talks." *New York Times.* 20 December. http://www.nytimes.com/2009/12/21/world/europe/21scene.html (accessed 15 January 2010).

Kaplan, A. 2005. "Where is Guantànamo?" *American Quarterly* 57, no. 3: 831–58.

Kaplan, R.D. 2009. "The Revenge of Geography." *Foreign Policy*, May/June. http://www.foreignpolicy.com/story/cms.php?story_id=4862 (accessed 3 July 2009).

Kaplinsky, R. 1983. "Prospering at the Periphery: A Special Case – the Seychelles." In R. Cohen, ed., *African Islands and Enclaves.* London: Sage. 195–216.

Karlsson, A. 2006. *Sub-National Insular Jurisdictions as Configurations of Jurisdictional Powers and Economic Capacity: A Study of Åland, The Faroe Islands and Greenland.* Stockholm, Sweden: NordRegio Working Paper.

Kashou, M. 1997. Book Review of E. Davies, *The Legal Status of British Dependent Territories, the West Indies and the North Atlantic Region* (Cambridge: Cambridge University Press 1995). *Stanford Journal of International Law* 33, no. 153: 162–4.

Katzenstein, P.J. 1985. *Small States in World Markets: Industrial Policy in Europe.*
   Ithaca N.Y.: Cornell University Press.
— 2003. "'Small States' and Small States Revisited." *New Political Economy* 8, no. 1:
   9–30.
Kay, J. 2009. "Tax Havens Exist because of the Hypocrisy of Larger States."
   Financial Times, London, 21 March, 13. http://www.johnkay.com/politics/600
   (accessed 8 July 2009).
Keating, M. 1996. *Nations against the State.* London: Macmillan.
— ed., 2004. *Regions and Regionalism in Europe.* London: Edward Elgar.
Kelman, I., M. Davies, T. Mitchell, I. Orr, and B. Conrich. 2006. "Island Disaster
   Paradiplomacy." *The Round Table: Commonwealth Journal of International
   Affairs* 95, no. 386: 561–74.
Kenny, Z. 2007. "Global Warming Refugees: Left to Drown?" *Green Left*, 17 March.
   http://www.greenleft.org.au/2007/703/36535 (accessed 8 August 2008).
Keohane, R. 1971. "The Big Influence of Small Allies." *Foreign Policy* 2, no. 1: 161–82.
Kerr, S.A. 2005. "What Is Small Island Sustainable Development about?" *Ocean and
   Coastal Management* 48, nos. 7–8: 503–24.
Killingray, D. 2005. "British Decolonization and the Smaller Territories: The
   Origins of the United Kingdom Overseas Territories." In D. Killingray and D.
   Taylor, eds., *The United Kingdom Overseas Territories: Past, Present and Future.*
   London: Institute of Commonwealth Studies, University of London. 3–18.
Killingray, D., and D. Taylor, eds. 2005. *The United Kingdom Overseas Territories:
   Past, Present and Future.* London: Institute of Commonwealth Studies,
   University of London.
Kilner, J. 2006. "Visa-Free Norwegian Islands a Haven for Migrants."
   Dawn International, 6 July. http://www.dawn.com/2006/07/05/int11.htm
   (accessed 13 August 2008).
King, R. 1993. "The Geographical Fascination of Islands." In D.G. Lockhart,
   D. Drakakis-Smith, and J.A. Schembri, eds. *The Development Process in Small
   Island States.* London: Routledge. 13–37.
King, R., and J. Connell. 1999. *Small Worlds, Global Lives; Small Islands and
   Migration.* London: Pinter.
Kirch, P.V. 1986. "Introduction: The Archaeology of Island Societies." In P.V. Kirch,
   ed., *Island Societies: Archaeological Approaches to Evolution and Transformation.*
   Cambridge: Cambridge University Press. 1–5.
Kirk, L. 2008. "Finnish Islands Cause Headache for EU Treaty Approval."
   EU Observer, Headline News, 12 August. http://euobserver.com/9/26601
   (accessed 13 December 2008).
Kissinger, H. 1982. *Years of Upheaval.* Boston, Mass.: Little, Brown.
Koehler, R. 2007. "Jeju Residents Protest ROK Navy Base Construction."
   The Marmot's Hole, 6 April. http://www.rjkoehler.com/2007/04/06/
   jeju-residents-protest-rok-navy-base-construction/ (accessed 15 August 2008).

Krasner, S.D. 2001a. "Problematic Sovereignty." In S.D. Krasner, ed. *Problematic Sovereignty: Contested Rules and Political Possibilities*. New York: Columbia University Press. 1–23.

— 2001b. "Explaining Variation: Defaults, Coercion, Commitments." In S.D. Krasner, ed., *Problematic Sovereignty: Contested Rules and Political Possibilities*. New York: Columbia University Press. 323–43.

— 2001c. "Think Again: Sovereignty." *Foreign Policy*, February. http://www.globalpolicy.org/nations/realism.htm (accessed 4 August 2008).

Kratochwil, F. 1986. "Of Systems, Boundaries and Territoriality: An Inquiry into the Formation of the State System." *World Politics* 39, no. 1: 27–52.

Kraul, C. 2008. "Overcrowding, Mismanaged Tourism Threaten Galápagos Islands." *Seattle Times*, 10 October. http://seattletimes.nwsource.com/html/nationworld/2008246694_galapagos10.html. (accessed 15 August 2008).

Kuelhs, T. 1996. *Beyond Sovereign Territory*. Minneapolis: University of Minnesota Press.

Kumar Rajaram, P. 2007. "Locating Political Space through Time: Asylum and Excision in Australia." In P. Kumar Rajaram and C. Grundy-Warr, eds., *Borderscapes: Hidden Geographies and Politics at Territory's Edge*. Minneapolis: University of Minnesota Press. 263–82.

Krugman, P. 1991. "Increasing Returns and Economic Geography." *Journal of Political Economy* 99, no. 3: 483–99.

Kurlansky, M. 1997. *Cod*. New York: Vintage Books.

Kymlicka, W. 1998. "Multinational Federalism in Canada: Rethinking the Relationship." In R. Gibbins and G. Laforest, eds., *Beyond the Impasse: Towards Reconciliation*. Montreal: Institute for Research on Public Policy. 15–50.

Laforest, G. 1998. "Se Placer dans les Souliers de l'Autre dans l'Union Canadienne." In R. Gibbins and G. Laforest, eds., *Beyond the Impasse: Towards Reconciliation*. Montreal: Institute for Research on Public Policy. 55–84.

Lake, D.A. 2003. "The New Sovereignty in International Relations." *International Studies Review* 5, no. 3: 303–23.

Landes, D.S. 1998. *The Wealth and Poverty of Nations: Why Some Are So Rich and Some So Poor*. New York: W.W. Norton.

Lanfant, M.F., J.B. Allcock, and E.M. Bruner. 1995. *International Tourism: Identity and Change*. London: Sage.

Larson, E.J. 2002. *Evolution's Workshop: God and Science on the Galápagos Islands*. New York: Basic Books.

Law, B. 2006. "French Islands Bid for Oil Rich Sea." BBC *Radio 4 News*, 9 March. http://news.bbc.co.uk/1/hi/programmes/crossing_continents/4781886.stm (accessed 13 August 2008).

Lawrence, D.H. 1927. *The Man Who Loved Islands*. Online Literature Library. http://www.literature.org/authors/lawrence-david-herbert/the-woman-who-rode-away-and-other-stories/part-09/index.html (accessed 9 August 2008).

Lawson, D. 2000. "Carrier Hotels Invade Europe." *City Magazine*, summer. http://www.davidlawson.co.uk/Files/webhost-ASP_CIT_MY0.htm (accessed 4 December 2008).

League of Nations. 1920. Report of the Second Sub-Committee to the Fifth Committee, Records of the First Assembly, Plenary Meetings.

Légaré, A. 2002. "The Construction of Nunavut and Its Impact on Collective Identity in the Canadian Eastern Arctic." *Review of Constitutional Studies* 7, nos. 1–2: 55–78.

Leonnig, C.D. 2009. "Bailed-Out Firms Have Tax Havens, GAO Finds." *Washington Post*, 17 January. http://www.washingtonpost.com/wp-dyn/content/story/2009/01/16/ST2009011603928.html (accessed 8 July 2009).

Le Rendu, L. 2004. *Jersey: Independent Dependency?: The Survival of a Microstate.* London: Ex Libris Press.

Le Sueur, J., ed. 2003. *The Decolonization Reader.* London: Routledge.

Levin, M. 2002. *The Prospects for Offshore Financial Centres in Europe.* Brussels: Centre for European Policy Studies, August.

Levine, S., and N.S. Roberts. 2005. "The Constitutional Structures and Electoral Systems of Pacific Island States." *Commonwealth and Comparative Politics* 43, no. 3: 276–95.

Lewis, J.P. 1991. "Some Consequences of Giantism: The Case of India." *World Politics* 43, no. 3: 367–89.

Lindström, B. 1997. "Åland's Challenge to the Baltic Sea Region: Are Territorial Sovereignty and a Common Public Discourse Preconditions for a Functioning Democracy?" In P. Joenniemi, ed., *Neo-Nationalism or Regionality: The Restructuring of Political Space around the Baltic Rim.* Report 1997/5. Stockholm and Copenhagen: NordREFO. 235–52.

— 1999. "Towards a Post-Sovereign Political Landscape?" In B. Poppel and H. Petersen, eds., *Dependency, Autonomy, Sustainability in the Arctic.* Aldershot, U.K.: Ashgate. 79–87.

— 2000. "Culture and Economic Development in the Åland Islands." In G. Baldacchino and D. Milne, eds., *Lessons from the Political Economy of Small Islands: The Resourcefulness of Jurisdiction.* New York: St Martin's Press, in association with Institute of Island Studies, University of Prince Edward Island. 107–21.

— 2009. *Towards the Third Generation of Regional Policy: Lessons from the Nordic Autonomies and Peripheral Regions.* Mariehamn, Åland Islands: Åland Islands Statistical Agency (ÅSUB), Report 2009: 2. http://www.asub.ax/files/Rapport2009.2.pdf (Swedish original, accessed July 2009).

Liou, F.M., and C.G. Ding. 2002. "Subgrouping Small States based on Socioeconomic Characteristics." *World Development* 30, no. 7: 1289–1306.

Lloyd, J. 2002. "Departing Sovereignty." *Borderlands.* 1, no. 2. http://www.borderlandsejournal.adelaide.edu.au/vol1no2_2002/lloyd_departing.html (accessed 2 August 2008).

— 2004. "Departing Sovereignty: Consuming Borders: From the Border Guard to the Contemporary Nation." Paper presented at Crossing Borders conference, Erlangen, Germany, November.

Lockhart, D.G., and D. Drakakis-Smith, eds.. 1996. *Island Tourism: Trends and Prospects*. London: Mansell.

Logan, J.R., and H.L. Molotch. 2007. *Urban Fortunes: The Political Economy of Place*. San Francisco: University of California Press.

Logan, W. 2008. "Cultural Heritage in Asia and the Pacific." Paper presented at "Islands of the World X" conference, Seogwipo, Jeju, South Korea, August.

Lowenthal, D. 1987. "Social Issues." In C.G. Clarke and T. Payne, eds., *Politics, Security and Development in Small States*. London: Allen and Unwin 26–49.

— 2006. Book review of J. Skinner and M. Hills, eds., *Managing Island Life: Social, Economic and Political Dimensions of Formality and Informality in 'Island' Communities* (Dundee, Scotland: University of Abertay Press). *Island Studies Journal* 1, no. 2: 259–61.

Low Tax website. 2008a. "Low Tax Offshore Jurisdictions." http://www.lowtax.net/lowtax/html/jurhom.html. (accessed 3 August 2008).

— 2008b. "Bermuda Residence and Property." http://www.lowtax.net/lowtax/html/bermuda/jbrres.html. (accessed 3 August 2008).

— 2010. "Madeira: Executive Summary." http://www.lowtax.net/lowtax/html/jmdnews.html (accessed 15 January 2010).

Loxley, D. 1990. *Problematic Shores: The Literature of Islands*. New York: St Martin's Press.

Lubin, M. 2003/04. "Perforated Sovereignties in the Americas: The Canada-US Borders and the International Outreach Activities of Québec." *London Journal of Canadian Studies* 19, no. 1: 19–40.

Lyall, S. 2009. "Fondly, Greenland Loosens Danish Rule." *New York Times*, 22 June. http://www.nytimes.com/2009/06/22/world/europe/22greenland.html (accessed 3 July 2009).

MacArthur, R.H., and E.O. Wilson. 1967. *The Theory of Island Biogeography*. Princeton, N.J.: Princeton University Press.

Machiavelli, N. [1515] 1985. *The Prince*. Translated by H.C. Mansfield, 2nd ed. Chicago Ill.: University of Chicago Press.

MacKinnon, M. 2008. "Where Iranians Go to Let Their Hair Down." *Globe and Mail*, 18 October. A3.

Madsen, R. 2001. "The Struggle for Sovereignty between China and Taiwan." In S.D. Krasner, ed., *Problematic Sovereignty: Contested Rules and Political Possibilities*. New York: Columbia University Press. 141–93.

Malaysia. Immigration Department. 2006. Document in Lieu of Passport for Travelling between Sabah/Sarawak. www.imi.gov.my/eng/perkhidmatan/im_DokumenDlmNegeri.asp (accessed 9 August 2008).

Malinowski, B. 1922. *Argonauts of the Western Pacific*. London: G. Routledge and Sons.

Manitoba. Legislative Task Force on Canadian Unity. 1997. Manitoba Legislature: 4th, 36th, vol. 20: Government Resolution. http://www.gov.mb.ca/legislature/hansard/4th-36th/vol_020/h020_4.html (accessed 4 August 2008)

Manning, E.W., and T.D. Dougherty. 1999. "Planning Tourism in Sensitive Ecosystems." In T.V. Singh and S. Singh, eds., *Tourism Development in Critical Environments*. New York: Cognizant Communication Corporation. 1–20.

Marcus, G.E. 1981. "Power on the Extreme Periphery: The Perspective of Tongan Elites in the Modern World System." *Pacific Viewpoint* 22, no. 1: 48–64.

Marguiles, J. 2004. "A Prison beyond the Law." *Virginia Quarterly Review* 80, no. 4: 37–55.

Markham, E.A., ed. 1989. *Hinterland: Caribbean Poetry from the West Indies and Britain*. Newcastle-upon-Tyne, U.K.: Bloodaxe Books.

Markoff, J. 2000. "Rebel Outpost on the Fringes of Cyberspace." *New York Times*, 4 June. http://partners.nytimes.com/library/tech/00/06/biztech/articles/04have.html (accessed 19 August 2008).

Marshall, A.T. 1890. *Principles of Economics*. London: Macmillan.

Martin, P. 1996. "The Death of Geography." *Financial Times*, London, 22 February. http://www.ft.com/cms/s/6fb1b790-6267-11da-8dad-0000779e2340,dwp_uuid=0f82a75a-658a-11da-8f40-0000779e2340.html (accessed 2 August 2008).

Martin, R. 2004. Editorial. "Geography: Making a Difference in a Globalizing World." *Transactions of the Institute of British Geographers* 29, no. 2: 147–50.

Mattingly, G. 1955. *Renaissance Diplomacy*. London: Jonathan Cape.

May, R., and S. Tupouniua. 1980. "The Politics of Small Island States." In R.T. Shand, ed., *The Island States of the Pacific and Indian Oceans: Anatomy of Development*. Canberra: Australian National University. 419–37.

McBride, D. 1999. "Migrants and Asylum Seekers: Policy Responses in the US to Immigrants and Refugees from Central America and the Caribbean." *International Migration* 37, no. 1: 289–317.

McCall Smith, J. 2001. "One Sovereign, Two Legal Systems: China and the Problem of Commitment in Hong Kong." In S.D. Krasner, ed., *Problematic Sovereignty: Contested Rules and Political Possibilities*. New York: Columbia University Press. 105–40.

McElroy, J.L. 1998. "A Propensity for Dependence." *Islander* (U.K.), Habitat Scotland, no. 5: 33.

— 2003. "Tourism Development in Small Islands across the World." *Geografiska Annaler* 85B, no. 4: 231–42.

— 2006. "Small Island Tourist Economies across the Lifecycle." *Asia Pacific Viewpoint* 47, no. 1: 61–77.

McElroy, J.L., and K. de Albuquerque. 1996. "The Social and Economic Propensity for Political Dependence in the Insular Caribbean." *Social and Economic Studies* 44, no. 1: 67–193.

McElroy, J.L., and K.B. Pearce. 2006. "The Advantages of Political Affiliation: Dependent and Independent Small Island Profiles." *The Round Table: Commonwealth Journal of International Affairs* 95, no. 386: 529–40.

McElroy, J.L., and K. Sanborn. 2005. "The Propensity for Dependence in Small Caribbean and Pacific Islands." *Bank of Valletta Review* [Malta], no. 31 (June): 1–16.

McElroy, J.L., and L. Morris. 2002. "African Island Development Experiences: A Cluster of Models." *Bank of Valletta Review*, Malta, no. 26: 38–57.

McElroy, J.L., and M. Mahoney. 2000. "The Propensity for Political Dependence in Island Microstates." *INSULA: International Journal of Island Affairs* 9, no. 1: 32–5.

McElroy, J.L. and W. Bai. "The Political Economy of China's Incursion into the Caribbean and Pacific." *Island Studies Journal* 3, no. 2: 225–46.

McGregor, D.P. 2002. "Recognizing Native Hawaiians: A Quest for Sovereignty." In P. Spickard, J.L. Rondilla, and D. Hippolite Wright, eds., *Pacific Diaspora: Island Peoples in the United States and across the Pacific*. Honolulu: University of Hawaii Press. 331–54.

McKercher, W.R. 2000. "The Isle of Man: Jurisdictional Catapult to Development." In G. Baldacchino and D. Milne, eds., *Lessons from the Political Economy of Small Islands: The Resourcefulness of Jurisdiction*. New York: St Martin's Press, in association with Institute of Island Studies, University of Prince Edward Island. 91–106.

McLuhan, M. 1964. *Understanding Media*. New York: McGraw-Hill.

McPhetres, A. 1983. "Northern Mariana Islands: US Commonwealth." In R. Crocombe and A. Ali, eds., *Politics in Micronesia*. Suva, Fiji Islands: Institute of Pacific Studies, University of the South Pacific. 146–60.

McSmith, A. 2008. "The Big Question: Is Greenland Ready for Independence, and What Would It Mean for Its People?" *The Independent* (U.K.), 27 November. http://www.independent.co.uk/news/world/europe/the-big-question-is-green-land-ready-for-independence-and-what-would-it-mean-for-its-people-1036735.html (accessed 4 July 2009).

Mead, M. [1928] 2001. *Coming of Age in Samoa: A Psychological Study of Primitive Youth for Western Civilization*. New York: Harper Collins.

— [1930] 1973. *Growing up in New Guinea*. Harmondsworth, U.K.: Penguin.

— [1934] 2002. *Kinship in the Admiralty Islands*. London: Transaction Publishers.

Mercer, P. 2008. "Colonial Ties Dominate Polynesia Polls." *BBC News*, 22 February. http://news.bbc.co.uk/2/hi/asia-pacific/7256196.stm (accessed 2 August 2008).

MercoPress. 2009. "Cruise Industry's Trust in Further Growth Suggests Continued Prosperity in Falklands." *South Atlantic News Agency*. 11 April. http://en.mercopress.com/2009/04/11/cruise-industrys-trust-in-further-growth-suggests-continued-prosperity-in-f (accessed 15 January 2010).

Messineo, F. 2009. "Italy: Lampedusa, the Island of Europe's Forgotten Promises." *Amnesty International*, 6 July. http://asiapacific.amnesty.org/library/Index/ENGEUR300082005?open&of=ENG-ITA (accessed 15 January 2010).

Micallef, J.V. 1979. "Mediterranean Maverick: Malta's Uncertain Future." *The Round Table: Commonwealth Journal of International Affairs* 68, no. 275: 238–51.

Middleton, J. 2005. "Picking up the Pieces on Pitcairn Island." *New Zealand Herald*, 22 March. http://www.nzherald.co.nz/section/story.cfm?c_id=2andobjectid=10116489 (accessed 4 August 2008).

Midttun, A., K. Gautesen, and M. Gjølberg. 2006. "The Political Economy of Corporate Social Responsibility in Western Europe." *Corporate Governance* 6, no. 3: 369–85.

Miles, W.F.S. 1985. *Elections and Ethnicity in French Martinique: Paradox in Paradise*. New York: Praeger.

Mills, G.E. 1972. *The Environment of Commonwealth Caribbean Bureaucracies*. Mona, Jamaica: University of the West Indies, Department of Government.

Milne, D. 1992. "Challenging Constitutional Dependency: A Revisionist View of Atlantic Canada." In J.N. McCrorie and M.L. MacDonald, eds., *The Constitutional Future of the Prairie and Atlantic Regions of Canada*. Regina, Sask.: University of Regina, Canadian Plains Research Centre. 208–17.

— 2000. *Ten Lessons for Economic Development in Small Jurisdictions: The European Perspective*. Charlottetown, PEI: University of Prince Edward Island, Institute of Island Studies.

— 2005. "Asymmetry in Canada: Past and Present." Asymmetry Series, Kingston, Ont.: School of Policy Studies, Queen's University. http://www.queensu.ca/iigr/working/archive/Asymmetric/papers/1.pdf (accessed 4 August 2008).

Milne, S. 1992. "Tourism Development in Niue." *Annals of Tourism Research* 19, no. 3: 565–9.

More, T. [1516] 2002. *Utopia*. http://etext.lib.virginia.edu/toc/modeng/public/MorUtop.html (accessed 2 August 2008).

Morgan, G. 1996. *Images of Organization*. London: Sage.

Morgan, K. 2004. "The Exaggerated Death of Geography: Learning, Proximity and Territorial Innovation Systems." *Journal of Economic Geography* 4, no. 1: 3–21.

Mørkøre, J. 1996. "The Faroese Home Rule Model: Theory and Reality." In L. Lyck, ed., *Constitutional and Economic Space of the Small Nordic Jurisdictions*. Stockholm: NordREFO 1996. 162–91.

Morris, T.A., Jr. 2008. "A Brief History of the Ilois Experience: 1962–2008." http://www.zianet.com/tedmorris/dg/chagossians.pdf (accessed 16 December 2008).

Moseley, R. 1999. "Refugee Refuses to Leave His Paris Airport Home." *Chicago Tribune*, 21 September. http://archives.californiaaviation.org/airport/msg02138.html (accessed 2 August 2008).

Motzfeldt, J. 1997. "Home Rule in Greenland." In L. Lyck, ed., *Constitutional and Economic Space of the Small Nordic Jurisdictions*. Stockholm: NordREFO. 192–5.

Mountz, A. 2009. "Islands as Enforcement Archipelago: Off-Shore Migration Processing, Graduated Sovereignty and Borders." Paper presented at the annual meeting of the International Sociological Association, New York, 15 February. http://www.allacademic.com/meta/p314136_index.html (accessed 5 July 2009).

Mrgudovic, N. 2005. "The French Overseas Territories in Change." In D. Killingray and D. Taylor, eds., *The United Kingdom Overseas Territories: Past, Present and Future*. London: University of London, Institute of Commonwealth Studies. 65–86.

MSNBC. 2009. "Cabinet Makes Splash with Underwater Meeting: Maldives Calls Attention to the Threat Climate Change Poses to Island Nation." 17 October. http://www.msnbc.msn.com/id/33354627/ns/world_news-weird_news/ (accessed 15 January 2010).

Muir, R. 1975. *Modern Political Geography*. London: Macmillan.

Mukherjee, A. 1993. "First World Readers, Third World Texts: Some Thoughts about Theory and Pedagogy." *Gulliver* 33, no. 1: 24–36.

Munro, D. 1990. "Transnational Corporations of Kin and the MIRAB System." *Pacific Viewpoint* 31, no. 1: 63–6.

Murphy, K. 2007. "Tiny Island Is a Feudal Time Warp." *Los Angeles Times*, 8 March. http://www.globalpolicy.org/nations/micro/2007/0308feudalism.htm (accessed 6 August 2008).

Mushkat, R. 1997. *One Country, Two Personalities: The Case of Hong Kong*. Hong Kong: Hong Kong University Press.

Mynott, A. 2005. "UK Waves in Kenya Airport Dweller." *BBC News*, 29 June. http://news.bbc.co.uk/2/hi/africa/4635011.stm (accessed 2 August 2008).

Nadkami, D. 2007. "Views from Auckland: Chequebook Diplomacy Gets Some Serious Notice." *Islands Business*. http://www.islandsbusiness.com/ islands_business/index_dynamic/containerNameToReplace=MiddleMiddle/ focusModuleID=17653/overideSkinName=issueArticle-full.tpl (accessed 15 January 2010).

Naipaul, V.S. 1972. *The Overcrowded Barracoon and Other Articles*. London: André Deutsch.

Nambath, S. 2005. "Andamans Can Be Developed as Organic Islands of the World." *The Hindu*, 25 May. http://www.hindu.com/2005/05/25/ stories/2005052508041200.htm (accessed 15 August 2008).

National Aeronautics and Space Administration (NASA). 2003. "Eruption. Space Station Science Picture of the Day," 23 May. http://science.nasa.gov/ppod/y2003/23may_eruption.htm?list955889 (accessed 9 August 2008).

National Geographic. 2006. *Destinations Rated: Islands*. http://www.national geographic.com/traveler/features/islandsrated0711/islands.html# (accessed 14 August 2008).

NationMaster. 2008. "Population Statistics." http://www.nationmaster.com/graph/ peo_pop-people-population (accessed 2 August 2008).

Nature Conservancy. 2008. *Micronesia. Palau: A Champion of Coral Reefs.* http://www.nature.org/wherewework/asiapacific/micronesia/features/mcpalau. html (accessed 14 August 2008).

Neuman, G.L. 2007. "The Military Commissions Act and the Detainee Debacle: A Response." *Harvard International Law Journal* 48, 12 February. http://www.harvardilj.org/attach.php?id=100 (accessed 9 December 2008).

Neumann, I.B., and S. Gstöhl. 2004. *Lilliputians in Gulliver's World? Small States in International Relations*, Working Paper 1–2004, Reykjavik, Centre for Small State Studies, University of Iceland. http://www.hi.is/solofile/1008303 (accessed 9 December 2008).

Nevmerzhitskaya, J. 2006. "The Solovetsky Archipelago, Russia." In G. Baldacchino, ed., *Extreme Tourism: Lessons from the World's Cold Water Islands.* Oxford: Elsevier. 159–68.

Newitt, M.D.D. 1992. "Introduction." In H.M. Hintjens and M.D.D. Newitt, eds., *The Political Economy of Small Tropical Islands.* Exeter, U.K.: University of Exeter Press. 1–17.

Newmark, W. 1987. "A Land-Bridge Island Perspective on Mammalian Extinctions in Western North American Parks." *Nature* 325, no. 6103: 430–2.

New York Times. 1985. "Arrested Island Leaders Appear in Court in Miami." 7 March. http://query.nytimes.com/gst/fullpage.html?res=9C06EFDB1139F934 A35750C0A963948260 (accessed 11 December 2008).

Ng, E., and J. Whalley. 2008. "Visas and Work Permits: Possible Global Negotiating Initiatives." *Vox*, 4 October. http://www.voxeu.org/index.php?q=node/1891 (accessed 13 December 2008).

Nobbs, A. 2008. *From the Desk of the Chief Minister*, Norfolk Island, 5 December. http://www.info.gov.nf/news/Media%20Releases/20081205%20%20From%20 the%20desk%20of%20the%20Chief%20Minister%20No%2017.pdf (accessed 13 December 2008).

Norwegian Ministry of Agriculture and Food. 2010. *Svalbard Global Seed Vault: Description of the Facility.* http://www.regjeringen.no/en/dep/lmd/campain/ svalbard-global-seed-vault/description.html?id=464076 (accessed 15 January 2010).

Nunn, P.D. 1994. *Oceanic Islands.* Oxford: Blackwell.

OAS (Organization of American States). 2002. *Special Security Concerns of Small Island States of the Caribbean.* AG/RES. 1886 XXXII–0–02. Adopted at 4th plenary session held on 4 June 2002. http://www.oas.org/juridico/English/ga02/ agres_1886.htm (accessed 9 December 2008).

Oberst, A., and J.L. McElroy. 2007. "Contrasting Socio-economic and Demographic Profiles of Two, Small Island, Economic Species: MIRAB versus PROFIT/SITE." *Island Studies Journal* 2, no. 2: 164–76.

Oberthür, S., and H.E. Ott. 1999. *The Kyoto Protocol: International Climate Change Policy for the 21st Century.* Berlin: Springer.

O'Brien, R. 1992. *Global Financial Integration: The End of Geography*. London: Pinter.

OECD (Organization for Economic Cooperation and Development). 2004. *The OECD's Project on Harmful Tax Practices: The 2004 Progress Report*. Paris: Centre for Tax Policy and Administration, OECD, February.

— 2009. *A Progress Report on the Jurisdictions Surveyed by the OECD Global Forum in Implementing the Internationally Agreed Tax Standard*, 8 July. http://www.eecd.org/dataoecd/50/0/42704399.pdf (accessed 8 July 2009).

OECS (Organization of Eastern Caribbean States). 2008. Member States of the OECS. http://www.oecs.org/membs.html (accessed 4 August 2008).

Ogden, R.M. 1993. "Locating Technology in the Development Debate: From MIRAB to MIRTAB." Chapter 6 in "Islands on the Net: Technology and Development Futures in Pacific Island Microstates," PHD thesis. Honolulu: Department of Political Science, University of Hawaii.

Ohmae, K. 1990. *The Borderless World: Power and Strategy in the Inter-Linked Economy*. New York: Harper Collins.

— 2000. "How Regions Can Prosper from Globalization." In A. Scott, ed., *Global City Regions: Trends, Theories, Policy*. New York: Oxford University Press. 33–43.

Olafsson, Á. 2000. "Constitutionalism and Economics in the Faroes." In G. Baldacchino and D. Milne, eds., *Lessons from the Political Economy of Small Islands: The Resourcefulness of Jurisdiction*. New York: St Martin's Press, in association with Institute of Island Studies, University of Prince Edward Island. 121–40.

O'Neil, P. 2009. "France Seeks Settlement to St-Pierre Offshore Claim." Canwest News Service, 12 May. http://www2.canada.com/france+seeks+settlement +pierre+offshore+claim/1588566/story.html?id=1588566 (accessed 4 July 2009).

Ong, A. 1999. *Flexible Citizenship: The Cultural Logics of Transnationality*. Durham, N.C.: Duke University Press.

— 2004. "The Chinese Axis: Zoning Technologies and Variegated Sovereignty." *Journal of East Asia Studies* 4, no. 1: 69–96.

— 2006. *Neoliberalism as Exception: Mutations in Citizenship and Sovereignty*. Durham N.C.: Duke University Press.

Online Casino City. 2008. Malta. http://online.casinocity.com/jurisdictions/juris-diction.cfm?start=1andid=6 (accessed 10 August 2008).

Online Casino Locator. 2008. "Where Are Internet Casinos Located?" http://www.online-casinos.com/beginnersguide/faq6.asp (accessed 5 July 2009).

Online Encyclopedia. 2006. Entry for Diplomacy. http://www.encyclopedia.jrank. org/DIO_DRO/DIPLOMACY_Fr_diplomatic_.html (accessed 20 March 2010).

Oostindie, G. 2006. "Dependence and Autonomy in Sub-National Island Jurisdictions: The Kingdom of the Netherlands." *The Round Table: Commonwealth Journal of International Affairs* 95, no. 386: 609–26.

Oostindie, G., and I. Klinkers. 2003. *Decolonizing the Caribbean: Dutch Policies in a Comparative Perspective*. Amsterdam: Amsterdam University Press.

Ordeshook, P. 1986. *Game Theory and Political Theory*. New York: Cambridge University Press.

Ordeshook, P.C., and O. Shvetsova. 1997. "Federalism and Constitutional Design." *Journal of Democracy* 8, no. 1: 27–42.

Osborne, J. 2008. "In the Land of the Longer Living." *Globe and Mail*, 22 March, T5.

Osborne, R.P. 2005. "The United Kingdom Overseas Territories Relationship: An Overview." In D. Killingray and D. Taylor, eds., *The United Kingdom Overseas Territories: Past, Present and Future*. London: Institute of Commonwealth Studies, University of London. 25–44.

Ospina, P. 2006. *Galápagos: Naturaleza y Sociedad: Actores Sociales y Conflictos Ambientales*. Quito, Ecuador: Universidad Andina Simón Bolívar and Corporación Editora Nacional.

Owen, J. 2007. "'Smallest Country' for Sale: Sea Views Included, Land Extra." *National Geographic News*, 18 January. http://news.nationalgeographic.com/news/2007/01/070118-sealand.html (accessed 6 December 2008).

PAC 2008. *Foreign and Commonwealth Office: Managing Risk in the Overseas Territories*. London: House of Commons, Public Accounts Committee, Session 2007–08, 17th Report, HC 176. http://www.parliament.the-stationery-office.com/pa/cm200708/cmselect/cmpubacc/176/176.pdf (accessed 20 December 2008).

Page, S., and P. Kleen. 2004. *Special and Differential Treatment of Developing Countries in the World Trade Organization*. London: Overseas Development Institute.

Palan, R. 1998. "Trying to Have Your Cake and Eating It: How and Why the State System Has Created Offshore." *International Studies Quarterly* 42, no. 4: 625–43.

— 2002. "Tax Havens and the Commercialization of State Sovereignty." *International Organization* 56, no. 1: 151–76.

— 2003. *The Offshore World: Sovereign Markets, Virtual Places and Nomad Millionaires*. Ithaca N.Y.: Cornell University Press.

Palan, R., and J. Abbott, with J. Deane. 1996. *State Strategies in the Global Political Economy*. London: Pinter.

Paldam, M. 1997. "Dutch Disease and Rent Seeking: The Greenland Model." *European Journal of Political Economy* 13, no. 3: 591–614.

Parry, C.E., and J.L. McElroy. 2009. "The Supply Determinants of Small Island Tourist Economies." *ARA: Journal of Tourism Research* 3, no. 1: 13–22.

Passas, N. 2006. "Fighting Terror with Terror: The Counter-Productive Regulation of Informal Value Transfers." *Crime, Law and Social Change* 45, nos. 4–5: 315–36.

Payne, A. 2004. "Small States in the Global Politics of Development." *The Round Table: Commonwealth Journal of International Affairs* 93, no. 376: 623–35.

— 2009. "Afterword: Vulnerability as a Condition, Resilience as a Strategy." In A.F. Cooper and T.M. Shaw, eds., *The Diplomacies of Small States: Between Vulnerability and Resilience*. Basingstoke, U.K.: Palgrave Macmillan. 279–85.

Pearce, D. 1989. *Tourism Development*. New York: Wiley.

Pearn, J., and P. Carter. 1995. *Islands of Incarceration: Convict and Quarantine Islands of the Australian Coast*. Brisbane, Australia: Amphian Press.

Peckham, R.S. 2003. "The Uncertain State of Islands: National Identity and the Discourse of Islands in Nineteenth-Century Britain and Greece." *Journal of Historical Geography* 29, no. 4: 419–515.

Pelling, M., and J.I. Uitto. 2001. "Small Island Developing States: Natural Disaster Vulnerability and Global Change." *Global Environmental Change Part B: Environmental Hazards* 3, no. 2: 49–62.

Perera, S. 2002. "What Is a Camp?" *Borderlands* 1, no. 1: 1–10. http://www.borderlandsejournal.adelaide.edu.au/issues/vol1no1.html (accessed 4 July 2009).

— 2007. "A Pacific Zone? Security, Sovereignty and Stories of the Pacific Borderscape." In P. Kumar Rajaram and C. Grundy-Warr, eds., *Borderscapes: Hidden Geographies and Politics at Territory's Edge*. Minneapolis: University of Minnesota Press. 201–27.

Péron, F. 1993. *Des Îles et des Hommes: L'Insularité Aujourd'hui*. Rennes, France: Editions de la Cité/Editions Ouest-France.

Picciotto, S. 1997. "International Law: The Legitimation of Power in World Affairs." In P. Ireland and P. Laleng, eds., *The Critical Lawyers' Handbook 2*. London: Pluto Press, 13–29.

— 1999. "Offshore: The State as Legal Fiction." In M.P. Hampton and J.P. Abbott, eds., *Offshore Finance Centres and Tax Havens: The Rise of Global Capital*. Basingstoke, U.K.: Macmillan. 43–79.

Pilger, J. 2004. "Paradise Cleansed." *The Guardian* (U.K.), 2 October. http://www.guardian.co.uk/comment/story/0,,1317945,00.html (accessed 4 August 2008).

— 2006. *Freedom Next Time*. London: Bantam Books.

Pirotta, G.A., R. Wettenhall, and L. Briguglio. 2001. "Governance of Small Jurisdictions." Guest Editors' Introduction. *Public Organization Review* 1, no. 2: 149–65.

Pirotta, J.M. 1985. "Unruffled Persistence: Borg Olivier's 1952 Negotiations with the British Government." *Melita Historica* 9, no. 2: 171–84.

Pitcairn Islands. Supreme Court. 2004. "R V Seven Named Accused," 19 April, *Pacific Islands Legal Information Institute*. http://www.paclii.org/pn/cases/PNSC/2004/1.html (accessed 2 August 2008).

Pitt, D. 1970. *Tradition and Economic Progress in Samoa*. London: Oxford University Press.

— 1980. "Sociology, Islands and Boundaries." *World Development* 8, no. 12: 1051–9.

Planistat Europe and Bradley Dunbar Associates. 2003. *Analysis of the Island Regions and Outermost Regions of the European Union, Part I: The Island Regions and Territories*. Final report. March.

Plantegenest, M., M. Iosipescu, and R. Macnab. 2003. *The French Islands of St-Pierre et Miquelon: A Case for the Construction of a Discontinuous Juridical Continental Shelf?* http://st-pierre-et-miquelon.org/docs/marc_plantegenest.pdf (accessed 13 August 2008).

Plischke, E. 1977. *Microstates in World Affairs: Policy Problems and Options.* Washington, D.C.: American Enterprise Institute for Public Policy Research.

Plunkett, T.J. 2004. "A Nation of Cities Awaits Paul Martin's 'New Deal': Federal Funds for 'Creatures of the Provinces.'" *Policy Options*, February. 19–25.

PMO (Prime Minister's Office, Canada). 2006. "Prime Minister Harper and Premier Charest Sign Historic Agreement Establishing Formal Role for Quebec in UNESCO." Media release, 5 May. http://pm.gc.ca/eng/media.asp?id=1151 (accessed 4 August 2008).

Poirine, B. 1998. "Should We Hate or Love MIRAB?" *Contemporary Pacific* 10, no. 1: 65–107.

— 1999. "A Theory of Aid as Trade with Special Reference to Small Islands." *Economic Development and Cultural Change* 47, no. 4: 831–52.

Polèse, M., and R. Shearmur. 2002. *The Periphery in the Knowledge Economy.* Montreal: Institute Nationale pour la Recherche Scientifique.

Pollock, E. 2005. "Rough Cut: Tuvalu – That Sinking Feeling. Global Warming, Rising Seas." *Frontline World*, 6 December. http://www.pbs.org/frontlineworld/rough/2005/12/tuvalu_that_sin_1.html# (accessed 4 August 2008).

Poon, A. 1990. "Flexible Specialization and Small Size: The Case of Caribbean Tourism." *World Development* 18, no. 1: 109–23.

Poot, J., ed. 2004. *On the Edge of the Global Economy.* Cheltenham, U.K.: Edward Elgar.

Porter, M. 1990. *The Competitive Advantage of Nations.* New York: The Free Press.

Power, H. 2007. "Pitcairn Island: Sexual Offending, Cultural Difference and Ignorance of the Law." *Criminal Law Review*, August. 609–29.

Prasad, N. 2004. "Escaping Regulation, Escaping Convention: Development Strategies in Small Economies." *World Economics* 5, no. 1: 41–65.

— 2009. "Small but Smart: Small States in the Global System." In A.F. Cooper and T.M. Shaw, eds., *The Diplomacies of Small States: Between Vulnerability and Resilience.* Basingstoke, U.K.: Palgrave Macmillan. 41–64.

Premdas, R.R. 2001. "Identity and Secession in a Small Island State: Nevis." *Canadian Review of Studies in Nationalism* 28, nos. 1–2: 27–44.

Private Islands Online. 2008. "Celebrity, Movie Stars, The World's Most Exclusive Property." http://www.privateislandsonline.com/celebrities-islands.htm (accessed 6 August 2008).

Quammen, D. 1996. *The Song of the Dodo: Island Biogeography in an Age of Extinctions.* London: Pimlico.

Quentin-Baxter, A. 1994. "Sustained Autonomy: An Alternative Political Status for Small Islands?" *Victoria University of Wellington Law Review* 24, no. 1: 1–18.

Quinn, T. 2008. "One Man on a Rock." *New Statesman*, 2 July. http://www.newstatesman.com/society/2008/07/hill-islands-carmichael (accessed 12 August 2008).

Ramassamy, A. 1987. *La Réunion: Décolonisation et Intégration*. Saint-Denis, La Réunion, France: AGM.

Ramesh, R. 2008. "Paradise Almost Lost: Maldives Seek to Buy a New Homeland." *The Guardian* (U.K.), 10 November. http://www.guardian.co.uk/environment/2008/nov/10/maldives-climate-change (accessed 4 December 2008).

Ramos, A.G., and A.J. Rivera, eds. 2001. *Islands at the Crossroads: Politics in the Non-Independent Caribbean*. Kingston, Jamaica: Ian Randle.

Redondan Foundation. 2008. "Redonda: A Brief History of the Island Kingdom." http://www.redonda.org/history.html (accessed 12 August 2008).

Reid-Henry, S. 2007. "Exceptional Sovereignty? Guantánamo Bay and the Re-Colonial Present." *Antipode* 39, no. 4: 627–48.

Reuters Foundation. 2005. "FactBox: Problems Dog Tsunami Effort." *AlertNet*, 26 August. www.alertnet.org/thefacts/reliefresources/112506559193.htm#andamans. (accessed 9 August 2008).

Reuters UK. 2009. "UPDATE 1 – Canada Raps France Bid for Atlantic Shelf Rights." 25 March. http://uk.reuters.com/article/IDUKN2544485120090325 (accessed 4 July 2009).

Rezvani, D. 2007. "False Self-Determination by Design: The 'Sham-Federacy' Phenomenon." Paper presented at annual meeting of the International Studies Association, 48th Annual Convention, Chicago, Ill. http://www.allacademic.com/meta/p179307_index.html (accessed 12 August 2008).

RFI 2009. "Politicians Welcome Referendum Result in Mayotte." *Radio France Internationale*. 30 March. http://www.rfi.fr/actuen/articles/111/article_3322.asp (accessed 4 July 2009).

Richards, J. 1982. "Politics in Small, Independent Communities: Conflict or Consensus?" *Journal of Commonwealth and Comparative Politics* 20, no. 2: 155–71.

Ritchie, J.E. 1977. "Cognition of Place: The Island Mind." *Ethos* 5, no. 2: 187–94.

Rivera Ramos, E. 1996. "The Legal Construction of American Colonialism: The Insular Cases 1902–1922." *Revista Jurídica de la Universidad de Puerto Rico* 65: 227–328.

Roberts, S. 1994. "Fictitious Capital, Fictitious Spaces: The Geography of Offshore Financial Flows." In S. Corbridge, R. Martin, and N. Thrift, eds., *Money, Power and Space*. Oxford: Blackwell. 91–115.

Robertson, R. 1995. "Glocalization: Time-Space and Homogeneity-Heterogeneity." In M. Featherstone, S. Lash, and R. Robertson, eds., *Global Modernities*. London: Sage. 25–44.

Robinson, M., and R. Kalakota. 2004. *Offshore Outsourcing: Business Models, ROI and Best Practices*. Alpharetta, Ga.: Mivar Press.

Rosalie, M. 2002. "Tourism and Social Development in the Seychelles." *Development Bulletin*, no. 60, November. 95–8.

Rose, A.K., and M.M. Spiegel. 2007. "Offshore Financial Centres: Parasites or Symbionts?" *Economic Journal* 117, no. 523. 1310–35.

Rose, I.N. 2005. "Internet Gaming: United States Beats Antigua at World Trade Organization." *Gaming Law Review.* 9, no. 5: 437–48.

Rosecrance, R. 1986. *The Rise of the Trading State: Commerce and Conquest in the Modern World.* New York: Basic Books.

— 1999. *The Rise of the Virtual State: Wealth and Power in the Coming Century.* New York: Basic Books.

Rosenau, J.N. 2003. *Distant Proximities: Dynamics Beyond Globalization.* Princeton, N.J.: Princeton University Press.

Rosenblatt, P.R. 1998. "What Is Sovereignty? The Cases of Taiwan and Micronesia." *New England Law Review* 32, no. 3: 797–800.

Roston, A. 2005. "Iran's Bizarre Military Bazaar." *The Walrus* (Canada) 2, no. 4: 21–3.

Royal Society of Canada (RSC). 2005. "Who's Afraid of Asymmetrical Federalism?" 12 May. http://www.rsc.ca/index.php?lang_id=1andpage_id=196 (accessed 9 August 2008).

Royle, S.A. 1989. "A Human Geography of Islands." *Geography* 74, no. 1: 106–16.

— 1997. "Industrialisation in Indonesia: The Case of Batam Island." *Singapore Journal of Tropical Geography* 18, no. 1: 89–98.

— 2001. *A Geography of Islands: Small Island Insularity.* London: Routledge.

— 2006. "The Falkland Islands." In G. Baldacchino, ed., *Extreme Tourism: Lessons from the World's Cold Water Islands.* Oxford: Elsevier. 181–92.

— 2007a. "Islands off the Irish Coast and the Bridging Effect." In G. Baldacchino, ed., *Bridging Islands: The Impact of Fixed Links.* Charlottetown, PEI: Acorn Press. 203–18.

— 2007b. "Postcolonial but not Post-Colonial: The UK's Overseas Territories." Paper presented at Islands and Postcolonialism Conference, Belfast, Northern Ireland, Queen's University Belfast, September.

Royle, S.A., and D. Scott. 1996. "Accessibility and the Irish Islands." *Geography* 81, no. 2: 111–19.

Ruggie, J.G. 1983. "Continuity and Transformation in the World Polity: Toward a Neorealist Synthesis." *World Politics* 35, no. 2: 261–85.

— 1993. "Territoriality and Beyond: Problematizing Modernity in International Relations." *International Organization* 47, no. 1: 139–74.

Russell, B. [1938] 2004. "Economic Power." In B. Russell, *Power.* Oxford: Routledge.

Ryan, C. 2006. "Towards Self-Determination: A Self-Government Document for Pitcairn." *Revue Juridique Polynesienne* 12, 83–112; Université de la Polynésie Française, http://www.upf.pf/recherche/IRIDIP/RJP/12/7-RJP12-ryan.pdf (accessed 11 August 2008).

Saba Tourist Bureau. 2008. "Time for Dutch Government to Show Political
  Commitment." Community News, 29 January. http://www.sabatourism.com/
  communitynews527.html (accessed 14 August 2008).

Sacks, O. 1997. *The Island of the Colourblind*. New York: Knopf.

Sahlins, M. 1987. *Islands of History*. Chicago, Ill.: University of Chicago Press.

Said, E. 1979. *Orientalism*. New York: Vintage.

— (with B. Robbins, M.L. Pratt, J. Arac, and R. Radhakrishnan). 1994. "Edward
  Said's Culture and Imperialism: A Symposium." *Social Text* 40 (autumn): 20–4.
  http://www.asienundeuropa.uzh.ch/aboutus/persons/assistenzprofessuren/
  trakulhun/teaching2/Robbins1994.pdf. (accessed 4 July 2009)

Salter, M.B. 2006. "The Global Visa Regime and the Political Technologies of the
  International Self: Borders, Bodies, Biopolitics." *Alternatives: Global, Local,
  Political* 31, no. 2: 167–89.http://www.sfgate.com/cgi-bin/article.cgi?file=/
  chronicle/archive/2006/05/17/EDGDOIJKNT1.DTL (accessed 8 August 2008).

Sanders, R. 2005. "Bermuda: Independence or Not?" *Caribbean Net News*, 8 March.
  http://www.caribbeannetnews.com/2005/03/08/sanders.shtml (accessed 14
  August 2008).

San Francisco Chronicle. 2006. Editorial, "A Big Casino Bet," 17 May.

SARTMA (South Atlantic Remote Territories Media Association). 2005. "An
  Airport for St Helena." Media release, 14 March. http://www.sartma.com/
  artc_1479_SH_9_1.html (accessed 4 August 2008).

— 2007. "Ascension: Ascension's Former Councillor's Joint Statement." Media
  release, 28 March. http://www.sartma.com/artd_4012_03_2007_2.html
  (accessed 15 August 2008).

Saunders, M. 2001. "Take Boat People Back, Court Orders." *The Australian*, 12
  September. 4.

Schengen Visa. 2008. *Your Visa to Europe*. http://www.schengenvisa.cc/ (accessed
  2 August 2008).

Schmidt, M. 2008. *List of Countries and Territories*. http://www.geocities.com/
  marcoschmidt.geo/countries.html (accessed 2 August 2008).

Schmitt, C. [1922] 1985. *Political Theology: Four Chapters on the Concept of
  Sovereignty*. Cambridge, Mass.: MIT Press.

Schmitz, H. 1989. "Flexible Specialization: A New Paradigm of Small-Scale
  Industrialization." *Discussion Paper No. 261*, Brighton, U.K.: Institute of
  Development Studies.

Scoop News 2006. "Tokelau Referendum Does Not Produce Two-Thirds Majority."
  Media release, New Zealand Government, 16 February. http://www.scoop.co.nz/
  stories/PA0602/S00232.htm (accessed 2 August 2008).

— 2007. "Voting under Way in Tokelau Self-Goverment Ballot." Media release, New
  Zealand Government, 23 October. http://www.scoop.co.nz/stories/WO0710/
  S00518.htm (accessed 10 December 2008).

Scott, S. 2003. "Loneliest Island May Hold Key to Asthma." *National Post* (Toronto),
  18 January. http://www.sk.lung.ca/content.cfm/xtra46 (accessed 9 August 2008).

Sealand, Principality of. Website. 2008. "History of Sealand." http://www.sealandgov.org/history.html (accessed 10 August 2008).

Second Life 2009. Private Regions (Islands). http://secondlife.com/land/ privatepricing.php (accessed 5 July 2009).

Sehdev, P.S. 2002. "The Origin of Quarantine." *Clinical Infectious Diseases* 35, no. 9: 1071–2.

Seychelles, Republic of (ROS). 1990. *Environmental Management Plan of Seychelles* EMPS, *1990–2000, Achieving Sustainable Development*. Victoria, Mahé, Seychelles.

— 2001. *Environment Management Plan of Seychelles,* EMPS, *2000–2010: Managing for Sustainability*. Victoria, Mahé, Seychelles.

Shah, N.J. 2002. "Bikinis and Biodiversity: Tourism and Conservation on Cousin Island, Seychelles." In F. di Castri and V. Balaji, eds., *Tourism, Biodiversity and Information*. Leiden, The Netherlands: Backhuys. 185–96.

Shakespeare, W. 1611/1987. *The Tempest*, edited by Stephen Orgel. Oxford: Oxford University Press.

Sharafutdinova, G. 2003. "Paradiplomacy in the Russian Regions: Tatarstan's Search for Statehood." *Europe-Asia Studies* 55, no. 4: 613–29.

Sharman, J.C., and P. Mistry. 2008. Considering the Consequences: The Development Implications of Initiatives on Taxation, Anti-Money Laundering and Combating the Financing of Terrorism. London: Commonwealth Secretariat.

Sherwood, B. 2008. "Island Thrives by Looking Outwards. Doing Business in Guernsey 2008." London: *Financial Times*. http://www.ft.com/cms/s/0/ dfb641b6-845e-11dd-adc7-0000779fd18c,s01=1.html?nclick_check=1 (accessed 20 September 2008).

Shetland Island Council. 2007. "Shetland and Oil: Energy from the Edge." http://www.energyfromtheedge.com/shetland-and-oil (accessed 15 August 2008).

Shillingford, M. 2007. "An Oil Refinery and Dominica's Sustainable Development." *TheDominican.net*, vol. 1, no. 95, 27 March. http://www.thedominican.net/ articles/refinerytwo.htm (accessed 14 August 2008).

Sidaway, J.D. 2007a. "Enclave Space: A New Metageography of Development?" *Area* 39, no. 3: 331–9.

— 2007b. "Spaces of Postdevelopment." *Progress in Human Geography* 31, no. 3: 345–61.

Simberloff, D.S., and E.O. Wilson. 1969. "Experimental Zoogeography of Islands: The Colonization of Empty Islands." *Ecology* 50, no. 2: 278–96.

Simeon, R. 2002. "Federalism in Canada: A Visitor's Guide." Government of Canada, http://www.pco-bcp.gc.ca/aia/index.asp?doc=why_e.htmandlang=enga ndpage=federalandsub=why#2 (accessed 4 August 2008).

Simon, J. 1998. "Refugees in a Carceral Age: The Rebirth of Immigration Prisons in the United States." *Public Culture* 10, no. 3: 577–607.

Singa Boyenge, J.-P. 2003. *ILO Database on Export Processing Zones*. Geneva: International Labour Organization, Sectoral Activities Department.

Singham, A.W. 1968. *The Hero and the Crowd in a Colonial Polity*. New Haven, Conn.: Yale University Press.

Skelton, T. 2000. "Political Uncertainties and Natural Disasters: Montserratian Identity and Colonial Status." *Interventions: International Journal of Postcolonial Studies* 2, no. 1: 103–17.

Skinner, J. 2006. "Formal and Informal Relations on Colonial Montserrat and Gibraltar." In J. Skinner and M. Hills, eds., *Managing Island Life: Social, Economic and Political Dimensions of Formality and Informality in 'Island' Communities*. Dundee, Scotland: University of Abertay Press. 181–205.

Skinner, J., and M. Hills, eds. 2006. *Managing Island Life: Social, Economic and Political Dimensions of Formality and Informality in 'Island' Communities*. Dundee, Scotland: University of Abertay Press.

Slack, E., and R.M. Bird. 2007. "Cities in Canadian Federalism." http://ideas.repec.org/p/ttp/itpwps/0603.html (accessed 4 August 2008).

SLRF (Sea Level Rise Foundation). 2008. http://www.sealevel-rise.org/ (accessed 12 August 2008).

Sloterdijk, P. 2005. *Écumes: Sphérologie Plurielle*. Paris: Maren Sell Éditeurs.

Smith, A. 2002. "The Discourses re. Constructing the Sacred Geography of Kahoʻolawe Island, Hawaii." PHD thesis, University of Hawaii, Department of Geography.

Smith, S.C. 2007. "Conflict and Co-operation: Dom Mintoff, Giorgio Borg Olivier and the End of Empire in Malta." *Journal of Mediterranean Studies* 17, no. 1: 115–34.

Smyth, M. 1995. "Borders within Borders: Material and Ideological Segregation as Forms of Resistance and Strategies of Control." Three Conference Papers on Aspects of Sectarian Division, "Borders within Borders," Northern Ireland, *Conflict Archive on the Internet* (CAIN). http://cain.ulst.ac.uk/issues/segregat/temple/confer2.htm (accessed 2 August 2008).

Sopoanga, S. 2003. Statement by The Hon. Saufatu Sopoanga OBE, Prime Minister and Minister of Foreign Affairs of Tuvalu, 58th UN General Assembly, 24 September. http://www.un.org/webcast/ga/58/statements/tuvaeng030924.htm (accessed 2 August 2008).

Sorensen, T. 2006. Book review of J. Poot, ed., *On the Edge of the Global Economy*. *Urban Studies* 43, no. 12: 2351–2.

Srebrnik, H.F. 2004. "Small Island Nations and Democratic Values." *World Development* 32, no. 2: 329–42.

Srinivasan, T.N. 1986. "The Costs and Benefits of Being a Small, Remote, Island, Landlocked or Ministate Economy." *World Bank Research Observer* 1, no. 1: 205–18.

States of Alderney. E-Commerce, 2008. "Alderney: A Safe Bet for Offshore E-Commerce Operations." http://www.alderney.gov.gg/index.php/pid/68 (accessed 10 August 2008).

Statistics Canada, 2006. *2006 Census Canada Release on Immigration and Language Data, Part 1: Immigration and Non-Official Languages*. Ottawa: Research Unit, Strategic Policy and Management Branch, Citizenship and Heritage Sector, 22 slides.

St Barths News. 2004. "More Visitors in 2003 Than in 2002." http://www.st-barths.com/editorials/cecil-lucot/04_03_06.html (accessed 15 January 2010).

Stefanidis, I.D. 1999. *Isle of Discord: Nationalism, Imperialism and the Making of the Cyprus Problem*. London: Hurst.

Stefanou, S. 2005. "Foreign Military Bases in Cyprus." *Military Bases in Europe*. http://militarybases.twoday.net/stories/763647/ (accessed 10 August 2008)

Steinberg, P., and S. McDowell. 2003. "Mutiny on the Bandwidth: The Semiotics of Statehood in the Internet Domain Name Registries of Pitcairn Island and Niue." *New Media and Society* 5, no. 1: 47–67.

Stepan, A, 1999. "Federalism and Democracy: Beyond the US Model." *Journal of Democracy* 10, no. 4: 19–34.

Stevens, R.M. 1977. "Asymmetrical Federalism: The Federal Principle and the Survival of the Small Republic." *Publius: The Journal of Federalism* 7, no. 4: 177–203.

Storper, M. 1997. *The Regional World*. New York: Guilford Press.

St Pierre and Miquelon, 2008. "Défendre les Droits de St Pierre et Miquelon." http://st-pierre-et-miquelon.org/petition/index.php (accessed 10 August 2008).

Stratford, E. 2003. "Editorial: Flows and Boundaries: Small Island Discourses and the Challenge of Sustainability, Community and Local Environments." *Local Environment* 8, no. 5: 495–9.

— 2006. "Isolation as Disability and Resource: Considering Sub-National Island Status in the Constitution of the New Tasmania." *The Round Table: Commonwealth Journal of International Affairs* 95, no. 386: 575–87.

Streeten, P.P. 1993. "The Special Problems of Small Countries." *World Development* 21, no. 2: 197–202.

Stuart, K. 2006. "Energizing the Island Community: A Review of Policy Standpoints for Energy in Small Island States and Territories." *Sustainable Development* 14, no. 2: 139–47.

— 2008. "A Global Listing of Sub-National Island Jurisdictions." In G. Baldacchino and K. Stuart, eds., *Pulling Strings: Policy Insights for Prince Edward Island from Other Sub-National Island Jurisdictions*. Charlottetown, PEI: Island Studies Press. 173–86.

Suhrke, A. 1973. "Gratuity or Tyranny? The Korean Alliances." *World Politics* 25, no. 4: 508–32.

Sui, C. 2009. "Taiwan Approves Gambling Enclaves." *BBC News*, 12 January. http://news.bbc.co.uk/2/hi/asia-pacific/7823825.stm (accessed 6 July 2009).

Sultana, R.G. 2006. *Challenges for Career Guidance in Small States*. Msida, Malta: Euro-Mediterranean Centre for Educational Research.

Summers, M. 2007. "Falklands Forum 2007: Self-Determination and Constitutional Development." Falkland Islands Government, 18 April. http://www.falklands.gov.fk/forum2007/self-determination.pdf (accessed 15 August 2008).

Sutton, P.K. 1987. "Political Aspects." In C.G. Clarke and T. Payne, eds., *Politics, Security and Development in Small States*. London: Allen and Unwin. 3–25.

— 2008a. "Non Independent Territories and Small States: Retrospect and Prospect." Keynote address at conference on Governance in the Non-Independent Caribbean: Challenges and Opportunities, San Juan, Puerto Rico, April 2008.

— 2008b. "'The Best of Both Worlds?': Autonomy and Decolonization in the Caribbean." *Caribbean Studies Working Paper*, no. 2. London: London Metropolitan University, August. http://www.londonmet.ac.uk/londonmet/library/h16097_3.pdf (accessed 5 July 2009).

Swift, J. 1726. *Gulliver's Travels: Or, Travels into Several Remote Nations of the World*. http://www.jaffebros.com/lee/gulliver/contents.html (accessed 2 August 2008).

Sydney Morning Herald. 2004. "Pro-Independence Leader Becomes French Polynesia's President." 15 June. http://www.smh.com.au/articles/2004/06/15/1087244909424.html?from=storylhs (accessed 2 August 2008).

Tamil Eelam News. http://www.tamileelamnews.com (accessed 20 March 2010).

Tarlton, C.D. 1965. "Symmetry and Asymmetry as Elements of Federalism." *Journal of Politics* 27, no. 4: 861–74.

Taussig, M. 2004. *My Cocaine Museum*. Chicago Ill.: University of Chicago Press.

Tax Justice Network. 2008. "Tax Havens Cause Poverty." http://www.taxjustice.net (accessed 11 December 2008).

Taylor, D. 2005. "The British Overseas Territories in the Caribbean: Recent History and Current Policy." In D. Killingray and D. Taylor, eds., *The United Kingdom Overseas Territories: Past, Present and Future*. London: Institute of Commonwealth Studies, University of London. 19–24.

Telegraph. 2007. "Chagos Island Exiles Win Right to Return Home." 24 May. http://www.telegraph.co.uk/news/uknews/1552445/Chagos-Island-exiles-win-right-to-return-home.html (accessed 2 August 2008).

TheDominican.net 2007. "Venezuela to Build Oil Refinery in Dominica: Editorial." Vol. 1, no. 91 (26 February). http://www.thedominican.net/articles/refineryone.htm (accessed 16 July 2009).

Thibodeau, W. 2005. "P.E.I., Feds Working toward Energy Deal." *The Guardian* (Charlottetown, PEI), 8 October, A5.

Thom, B. 1999a. "Aboriginal Rights and Title in Canada after Delgamuukw: Part One: Oral Traditions and Anthropological Evidence in the Courtroom." *Native Studies Review* 14, no. 1: 1–26.

— 1999b. "Aboriginal Rights and Title in Canada after Delgamuukw: Part Two: Anthropological Perspectives on Rights, Tests, Infringement and Justification." *Native Studies Review* 14, no. 2: 1–42.

Thomas, R., B. Pigozzi, and R. Sambrook. 2005. "Tourist Carrying Capacity Measures: Crowding Syndrome in the Caribbean." *Professional Geographer* 57, no. 1: 13–20.

Thompson, E. 2006. "Quebeckers a Nation: Harper." *Gazette* (Montreal), 23 November. http://www2.canada.com/montrealgazette/news/story. html?id=aac10143-cba1-48ec-92ed-950685dd45f0&k=26107 (accessed 8 July 2009).

Thompson, M., J.B. Rose, and A.E. Smith. 2003. *Beyond the National Divide: Regional Differences in Industrial Relations.* Kingston Ont., School of Policy Studies, Queen's University.

Thomson, J. 1994. *Mercenaries, Pirates and Sovereigns: State-Building and Extraterritorial Violence in Early Modern Europe.* Princeton, N.J.: Princeton University Press.

Thondavadi, N., and G. Albert. 2005. *Offshore Outsourcing: Path to New Efficiencies in IT and Business Processes.* Chennai, India: Thomson.

Thorhallsson, B. 2000. *The Role of Small States in the European Union.* Aldershot, U.K.: Ashgate.

— 2009. "Can Small States Choose Their Own Size? The Case of a Nordic State – Iceland." In A.F. Cooper and T.M. Shaw, eds., *The Diplomacies of Small States: Between Vulnerability and Resilience.* Basingstoke, U.K.: Palgrave Macmillan. 119–42.

Thorndike, T. 1987. "Antigua and Barbuda." In C.G. Clarke and T. Payne, eds., *Politics, Security and Development in Small States.* London: Allen and Unwin. 96–112.

— 1989. "The Future of the British Caribbean Dependencies." *Journal of Interamerican Studies and World Affairs.* 31, no. 3: 117–40.

Thucydides. [431BC] 1972. *History of the Peloponnesian War.* Translated by Rex Warner. London: Penguin Classics.

Tiffin, H. 1988. "Post-Colonialism, Post-Modernism and the Rehabilitation of Post-Colonial History." *Journal of Commonwealth Literature* 23, no. 1: 169–81.

Time Magazine. 1968. "The Concept of Sanctuary." 28 June. http://www.time.com/ time/magazine/article/0,9171,841355,00.html (accessed 6 August 2008).

Times Online. 2008. "Jersey Child Abuse Inquiry Focuses on Bricked up Cellar." 25 February. http://www.timesonline.co.uk/tol/news/uk/article3432338.ece (accessed 12 August 2008).

— 2009. "Michael Misick Says Britain Guilty of Turks & Caicos Coup." 3 September. http://www.timesonline.co.uk/tol/news/world/us_and_americas/ article6819103.ec (accessed 20 January 2010).

Toafa, M. 2004. "Statement by the Hon. Maatia Toafa, Acting Prime Minister
and Minister of Foreign Affairs of Tuvalu, 59th UN General Assembly," 24
September. http://www.un.org/webcast/ga/59/statements/tuveng040923.pdf
(accessed 15 January 2010).

Treadgold, M L. 1999. "Breaking out of the MIRAB Mould: Historical Evidence
from Norfolk Island." *Asia Pacific Viewpoint* 40, no. 3: 235–49.

Treaty of Amsterdam. 1999. Brussels, European Commission.
http://www.eurotreaties.com/amsterdamtreaty.pdf (accessed 12 August 2008).

Trenwith, A. 2003. "The Empire Strikes Back: Human Rights and the
Pitcairn Proceedings." *Journal of South Pacific Law* 17, no. 2, Pacific
Islands Legal Information Institute. http://www.paclii.org/journals/
jspl/042003Volume7Number2/EmpireStrikes.html (accessed 11 August 2008).

Trimble, W.R. 1946. "The Embassy Chapel Question: 1625–1660." *Journal of Modern
History* 18, no. 2: 97–107.

Trompf, G., ed. 1993. *Islands and Enclaves: Nationalisms and Separatist Pressures in
Island and Littoral Contexts*. New Delhi: Sterling Publishers.

Tuan, Yi-Fu 1990. *Topophilia: A Study of Environmental Perception, Attitudes and
Values*, 2nd ed. New York: Columbia University Press.

Turner, A.K. 1993. *The History of Hell*. New York: Harcourt Brace Jovanovich.

Turner, C. 2007. *The Geography of Hope: A Tour of the World We Need*. Toronto:
Random House.

Turtinen, J. 2000. "Globalizing Heritage: On UNESCO and the Transnational
Construction of a World Heritage." *SCORE Rapportserie No. 12*. Stockholm:
Stockholm Centre for Organizational Research. http://www.score.su.se/
pdfs/2000-12.pdf (accessed 15 December 2008).

Tweedie, N. 2009. "Carteret Islands: 'The Sea Is Killing Our Island Paradise.'"
The Telegraph (U.K.). 9 December. http://www.telegraph.co.uk/earth/carteret-
islands/6771651/The-sea-is-killing-our-island-paradise.html (accessed 14
January 2010).

UK Chagos Support Association. 2006. "Support the Chagos Islanders."
http://homepage.ntlworld.com/carlene.lyttle/home.htm (accessed 2 August
2008).

UN. 1945. *Documents of the UN Conference on International Organization*, Vol. 6.
New York: United Nations Information Division.

— 1999a. Special Session of the General Assembly for the Review and Appraisal
of the Implementation of the Programme of Action (POA) for the Sustainable
Development of Small Island Developing States (SIDS), 27–28 September. http://
www.iisd.ca/sids/ (accessed 9 August 2008).

— 1999b. *Standard Country or Area Codes for Statistical Use, ST/ESA/STA/
SER.M/49/Rev.4, M.98.XVII.9, 4th Revision. New York: United Nations Statistical
Division.*

— 2006. *Indigenous People*. Geneva: Office of the United Nations High Commissioner for Human Rights. http://www.unhchr.ch/indigenous/main.html (accessed 9 August 2008).

— 2008. Special Committee on Decolonization: 2008 Session. http://www.un.org/depts/dpi/decolonization/main.htm (accessed 15 August 2008).

— Earthwatch Island Directory website. http://islands.unep.ch/Tidensit (accessed 9 August 2008).

UNCTAD. 2004. "Is Special Treatment of Small Island Developing States Possible?" UNCTAD/LDC/2004/1. New York and Geneva: UNCTAD.

Underwood, R.A. 2003. "The Amended U.S. Compacts of Free Association with the Federated States of Micronesia and the Republic of the Marshall Islands: Less Free, More Compact." *Working Paper No. 16*. Hawaii: East-West Center, Pacific Islands Development Series. http://pidp.eastwestcenter.org/compacts/PIDP_WP16.pdf (accessed 2 August 2008).

UNEP/WCMC 2006. "Galápagos National Park and Marine Reserve: Ecuador." *United Nations Environment Programme and World Conservation Monitoring Centre*. http://www.unepwcmc.org/sites/wh/galapago.html (accessed 2 August 2008).

UNESCO. Listing 2008. *International UNESCO-Related Listing Systems, Registries or Networks in the Field of Heritage*. Paris: UNESCO. http://portal.unesco.org/ci/en/files/24695/11810299601uneso_listing_en.doc/uneso_listing_en.doc (accessed 15 December 2008).

— 2009. *World Heritage List*. Paris: UNESCO World Heritage Centre. http://whc.unesco.org/en/list (accessed 3 July 2009).

Unger, R.W. 1980. *The Ship in the Medieval Economy: 600–1600*. Montreal and Kingston: McGill-Queen's University Press.

U.S. State Department. 2007. *Background Note: Tuvalu*, Bureau of East Asian and Pacific Affairs, October. http://www.state.gov/r/pa/ei/bgn/16479.htm (accessed 15 August 2008).

— 2008. Background Notes, Under Secretary for Public Diplomacy and Public Affairs. http://www.state.gov/r/pa/ei/bgn/ (accessed 2 August 2008).

U.S. Supreme Court. 2004. *Rasul et al. v. Bush, President of the United States et al.* Decided: 28 June. http://www.humanrightsfirst.org/us_law/inthecourts/gitmo_briefs/Rasul_sct_Decision.pdf (accessed 2 August 2008).

van Fossen, A.B. 1992. *The International Political Economy of Pacific Islands Flags of Convenience*. Mimeograph. Centre for the Study of Australia-Asia Relations. Brisbane, Australia: Griffith University.

— 2002. "Norfolk Island and Its Tax Haven." *Australian Journal of Politics and History* 48, no. 2: 210–25.

— 2003. "Money Laundering, Global Financial Instability and Tax Havens in the Pacific Islands." *Contemporary Pacific* 15, no. 2: 237–75.

Vashistha, A., and A. Vashistha. 2006. *The Offshore Nation: Strategies for Success in Global Outsourcing and Offshoring*. New York: McGraw Hill.

Verne, J. [1874] 1965. *The Mysterious Island*. New York: Airmont.

Verschuuren, J. 2008. "Ramsar Soft Law Is Not Soft at All: Discussion of the 2007 Decision by the Netherlands Crown on the Lac Ramsar Site on the Island of Bonaire." Originally published in Dutch in *Milieu en Recht* 35, no. 1: 28–34. Social Science Research Network. http://papers.ssrn.com/sol3/papers.cfm?abstract_id=1306982 (accessed 4 July 2009).

Vertovec, S. 2001. "Transnationalism and Identity." *Journal of Ethnic and Migration Studies* 27, no. 4: 573–82.

Vesilind, P. 2000. "In Search of the Vikings." *National Geographic*, May. 5–27.

Vigilance, C., G. Cordina, L. Briguglio, and N. Farrugia. 2008. *Small States and the Pillars of Economic Resilience*. London: Commonwealth Secretariat.

Villamil, J.J. 1977. "Size and Survival: Planning in Small Island Systems." *Microstate Studies* 1, no. 1: 1–7.

Vital, D, 1967. *The Inequality of States: A Study of the Small Power in International Relations*. Oxford: Oxford University Press.

Vladi Private Islands. 2008. http://www.vladi-private-islands.de/sales_islands/sites/worldmap_e.html (accessed 9 August 2008).

Vladivostok News. 2005. "Sakhalin Natives Protest Industrial Invasion." 21 January. http://vn.vladnews.ru/Arch/2005/ISS450/News/upd21_2.HTM (accessed 2 August 2008).

Vlcek, W. 2007. "Why Worry? The Impact of the OECD Harmful Tax Competition Initiative on Caribbean Offshore Financial Centres." *The Round Table: The Commonwealth Journal of International Affairs* 96, no. 390: 331–46.

— 2008. "Competitive or Coercive? The Experience of Caribbean Offshore Financial Centres with Global Governance." *The Round Table: Commonwealth Journal of International Affairs* 97, no. 396: 439–52.

Voice of America. 2009. "Japan to Tell Obama It Wants Okinawa Marine Base Closed." 11 December. http://www1.voanews.com/english/news/a-13-2009-11-11-voa13-69822947.html (accessed 15 January 2010).

Von Neumann, J., and O. Morgenstern. 1953. *Theory of Games and Economic Behaviour*. Princeton, N.J.: Princeton University Press.

Wainhouse, D.W. 1964. *Remnants of Empire*. New York: Harper and Row for the Council on Foreign Relations.

— 1966. *International Peace Observation: A History and Forecast*. Baltimore, Md.: Johns Hopkins University Press.

Wallace, A. [1880] 1975. *Island Life, or the Phenomena and Causes of Insular Faunas and Floras, including a Revision and Attempted Solution to the Problem of Geological Climates*. New York: AMS Press.

Warleigh, A. 2002. *Flexible Integration: Which Model for the European Union?* Sheffield, U.K.: Sheffield Academic Press.

Warrington, E. 1998. "Introduction: Gulliver and Lilliput in a New World Order: The Impact of External Relations on the Domestic Policies and Institutions of Micro-States." *Public Administration and Development* 18, no. 2: 101–5.

Warrington, E., and D. Milne. 2007. "Island History and Governance." In
    G. Baldacchino, ed., *A World of Islands: An Island Studies Reader*. Luqa, Malta,
    and Charlottetown, PEI: Agenda Academic and Institute of Island Studies.
    379–427.

Watson, I. 2004. "Iran Island Resort Is an Experiment in Free Trade." Audio. NPR
    News, 7 December. www.npr.org/templates/story/story.php?storyId=4206243;
    www.kishisland.com/ (accessed 15 August 2008)

Watters, R.F. 1987. "MIRAB Societies and Bureaucratic Elites." In A. Hooper, ed.,
    Class and Culture in the South Pacific. Suva, Fiji Islands: Institute of Pacific
    Studies. 32–55.

Watts, R.L. 1999. *Comparing Federal Systems*, 2nd ed. Kingston, Ont.: Institute of
    Intergovernmental Relations, Queen's University.

— 2000. "Islands in Comparative Constitutional Perspective." In G. Baldacchino
    and D. Milne, eds., *Lessons from the Political Economy of Small Islands: The
    Resourcefulness of Jurisdiction*. Basingstoke, U.K.: Macmillan. 17–37.

— 2005. "A Comparative Perspective on Asymmetry in Federations." *Asymmetry
    Series*. Kingston, Ont.: School of Policy Studies, Queen's University.
    http://www.queensu.ca/iigr/working/archive/Asymmetric/papers/4.pdf
    (accessed 15 August 2008).

— 2008. "Island Jurisdictions in Comparative Constitutional Perspective." In
    G. Baldacchino and D. Milne, eds., *The Case for Non-Sovereignty: Lessons from
    Sub-National Island Jurisdictions*. London: Routledge. 25–44.

Weale, D. 1992. *Them Times*. Charlottetown, PEI: Institute of Island Studies,
    University of Prince Edward Island.

Weaver, D. 1998. *Ecotourism in the Less Developed World*. New York: CABI.

Weber, M. 1949. *The Methodology of the Social Sciences*. Translated by E. Schils and
    H. Finch. New York: The Free Press.

Weiler, J.H.H. 1991. "The Transformation of Europe." *Yale Law Journal* 100: 2403–83.

Weisman, A. 2007. *The World without Us*. New York: Harper Collins.

Wells, H.G. [1896] 1999. *The Island of Dr. Moreau*. http://etext.lib.virginia.edu/toc/
    modeng/public/WelIsla.html (accessed 2 August 2008).

Wente, M. 2005. "Oh Danny Boy, Pipe Down." *Globe and Mail* (Toronto),
    6 January, A19. http://www.rantandroar.ca/wente-boy-o-boy.htm (accessed
    16 July 2009).

Westlake, D.E. 1972. *Under an English Heaven*. New York: Simon and Schuster.

Whittaker, R. 1999. *Island Biogeography: Ecology, Evolution, and Conservation*.
    Oxford: Oxford University Press.

Whyte, J. 1990. *Interpreting Northern Ireland*. Oxford: Clarendon.

Wikipedia. 2007. *List of Sovereign States*. http://en.wikipedia.org/wiki/List_of_
    countries (accessed 16 July 2009).

—2009. *List of Countries by Population*. http://en.wikipedia.org/wiki/
    List_of_countries_by_population (accessed 16 July 2009).

Wilkinson, P.F. 1994. "Tourism and Small Island States: Problems of Resource
Analysis, Management and Development." In A.V. Seaton, ed., *Tourism: The
State of the Art*. Chichester, U.K.: John Wiley. 41–51.

Willoughby, W.W., and C.G. Fenwick. 1974. *Types of Restricted Sovereignty and of
Colonial Autonomy*. Washington, D.C.: General Printing Office.

Winchester, S. [1985] 2003. *Outposts: Journeys to the Surviving Relics of the British
Empire*. Sevenoaks, U.K.: Sceptre Books.

Wisner, B., P. Blaikie, T. Cannon, and I. Davis. 2004. *At Risk: Natural Hazards,
People's Vulnerability and Disasters*, 2nd ed. London: Routledge.

Wolfson, P. 2006. "Bush Authorizes Fence for US-Mexico Border." Voice of
America News. 4 October.www.voanews.com/english/2006-10-04-voa60.cfm
(accessed 2 August 2008).

Wood, D. 2008. "Writing Tasmania's 'Different Soul.'" *Island Studies Journal* 3,
no. 2: 153–62.

Wood, D.P.J. 1967. "The Smaller Territories: Some Political Considerations." In
B. Benedict, ed., *Problems of Smaller Territories*. London: Athlone Press for the
Institute of Commonwealth Studies. 23–34.

Woodward, R. 2006. "Offshore Strategies in Global Political Economy: Small
Islands and the Case of the EU and OECD Harmful Tax Competition Initiatives."
Cambridge Review of International Affairs 19, no. 4: 685–99.

Woolf, S. 1989. "French Civilization and Ethnicity in the Napoleonic Empire."
Past and Present 124, no. 1: 96–120.

World Bank. 1992. *Mauritius: Expanding Horizons*. Washington, D.C.: World Bank.

— 2001. *Export Processing Zones in Sub-Saharan Africa*, Findings Report no. 193.
Washington, D.C.: World Bank, Economic and Social Policy Department.
http://www.worldbank.org/afr/findings/english/find193.pdf (accessed
8 August 2008).

World Tourism Organization. 2004. *Indicators of Sustainable Development for
Tourism Destinations*. Madrid: World Tourism Organization.

— 2005. *Making Tourism Work for Small Island Developing States*. Madrid: World
Tourism Organization.

World Trade Organization (WTO). 1999. "Proposals for Addressing Concerns
on Marginalization of Certain Small Economies." WT/GC/W/361, 12 October.
Geneva: WTO.

Worsley, P. 1957. *The Trumpet Shall Sound: A Study of 'Cargo' Cults in Melanesia*.
London: MacGibbon and Kee.

Wriggins, H.W. 1975. "To the Highest Bidder: Malta, Britain and NATO: *The Round
Table: Commonwealth Journal of International Affairs* 64, no. 1: 167–85.

—1976. "Up for Auction: Malta Bargains with Great Britain." In W. Zartman, ed.,
The Fifty Per Cent Solution. New York: Doubleday. 208–34.

Wright, F. 2005. "Pitcairn: The Saga Continues." *New Zealand Law Journal* 295,
no. 2: 295–6.

Yamamoto, L. 2006. *Kauai'i*. New York: Lonely Planet Travel Guide.

Yeats, W.B. 1899. *The Lake Isle of Innisfree*. http://www.poetryarchive.org/ poetryarchive/singlePoem.do?poemId=1689 (accessed 8 August 2008).

Young, L.B. 1999. *Islands: Portraits of Miniature Worlds*. New York: W.H. Freeman.

Young, R.J.C. 2003. *Postcolonialism: A Very Short Introduction*. Oxford: Oxford University Press.

Zeng, H. 2003. "Hong Kong's Autonomy: Concept, Developments and Characteristics." *China: An International Journal* 4, no. 2: 313–25.

Zimmermann, E. 2000. "Algerian Refugee Commits Suicide in Frankfurt Airport's Asylum Zone." World Socialist Web-Site, 24 May. http://www.wsws.org/ articles/2000/may2000/asyl-m24.shtml (accessed 2 August 2008).

FILMOGRAPHY

Lioret, P., director. 1993. *Tombés du Ciel* [Lost in Transit], 91 minutes, Bymages/ Canal Plus/CNC/ Epithete Films/ Filmania/ Procirep/Sogepaq. http://www.allmovie.com/cg/avg.dll (accessed 2 December 2008).

Sellers, P., director. 1959. *The Mouse That Roared*, 83 minutes, Columbia Pictures/ Open Road Productions. http://www.allmovie.com/cg/avg.dll?p=avgandsql= 1:33517 (accessed 2 December 2008).

Spielberg, S., director. 2004. *The Terminal*, 128 minutes, DreamWorks Pictures/ Amblin Entertainment. http://www.allmovie.com/cg/avg.dll?p=avg&sql= 1:289945 (accessed 2 December 2008).

Zemeckis, W., director. 2000. *Castaway*, 143 minutes, DreamWorks/Image Movers/ Playtone. http://www.allmovie.com/cg/avg.dll?p=avg&sql=1:229030 (accessed 2 December 2008).

Index

Iceland: and cod wars with U.K., 151–2
identity, 115–17; marketing of, 84
Ilois: plight of, 107
imaginative geographies, 5
imperial temptation, 95
"in-betweenity," 6, 170, 192
"inbordering," 28
independence referenda: failure of,
    44–5
The Independent (U.K.), 17
independentist political parties, 191
India: and independence, 53
Indian Gaming Regulatory Act, U.S.
    (1988), 105
indigenous people: absence of, 57;
    and rights of, 60–1, 104–5; and
    sovereignty, 120–1
Indonesia: and development contrasts,
    169
infra-nationalism, 104
Ingebritsen, C., 140, 198
Ingimundarson, V., 151–2
innovative governance, 117–34; by
    islands, 117–23; on islands, 123–34
Insiders' Guide, 175
insular particularism, 56
International Business Activities Act,
    Malta (1989), 158–9
International Business Centre, Madeira,
    159
International Court of Justice, 151
International Olympic Committee
    (IOC), xxi, xxii, 103, 104
International Organization for
    Standardization (ISO), 31
international political economy, 76
International Whaling Commission,
    156
Internet Assigned Numbers Authority
    (IANA), 31
Iran: and its unofficial oasis of fun, 131
Iran Trade Point Network, 131
Irridex, 17

Isfeld, S., 145
island allure, 19
islanders: as mobile citizenry,
    62–3; as transnationals, 116; and
    Westernization, 58, 67
island geographies, 12–14
island identity, 115–16
islanding, 15
island jurisdictional enclaves, 19–21
island-mainland relations, 91, 141, 192;
    constructive tension, in 192–7
islandness: and subnational
    jurisdiction, 100–1
island parks and reserves, 179–80
island political economy, 88
islands: and autarchy, 62; carving
    out of 4–5; and clairvoyancy, 16;
    and economic performance, 75;
    and enclaves, 34–6; and energy
    sustainability, 178–9; as entrepôts,
    170; as flywheels of evolution,
    16; as fortresses, 170; as frontline
    zones, 15–19; as geographies of
    hope, 178; and high population
    density, 18, 167–8; and literary and
    fictive insights, 18–19; as material
    or spiritual hinterlands, 18; and
    metaphors, 36; and natural-science
    insights, 16–17; and nodal location,
    170; as non-spaces, 37–8; not
    insular, 115; as novelty sites, 14–15;
    and peripheral location, 170;
    and post-colonial theory, 63–4;
    and offshoring of waste, 168; as
    reimagined spaces, 113; and sea-level
    rise, 16–17; and social engineering,
    18; and social-science insights, 17–18;
    and subnational jurisdictions, 32–4;
    and tapping hinterlands, 65–88; as
    uninhabited spaces, 168
island studies, xxviii–xxx, 91
island superlatives, 18
island tourism, 18

leapfrogging from primary to tertiary
sector, 168
legal limbos, 128–30
Légaré, A., 61
Leonnig, C.D., 193
Le Rendu, L., 37, 77, 81
Le Sueur, J., 64
Levin, M., 159
Levine, S., and N.S. Roberts, 46
Lewis, J.P., 215
Liechtenstein, 46
Lilliput (Swift), 87
Lindström, B., 27, 80, 108, 217
Lionel Jospin (France, prime minister),
141
Lioret, P., director, 27
Liou, F.M., and C.G. Ding, 100
local hinterland: absence of, 66–9
localization economics, 139
Lockhart, D.G., and D. Drakakis-Smith,
18
locus amoenus (beautiful place), 33
Logan, J.R., and H.L. Molotch, 186
Logan, W., 180
loopholes: closing of, 141
Lowenthal, D., 35, 63, 116
low tax, 76, 81, 160
low-tax jurisdictions, 76–8
Loxley, D., 87
Lubin, M., 143
Lyall, S., 120

Macapagal International Airport,
Philippines, 27
MacArthur, R.H., and E.O. Wilson, 13,
34
Machiavelli, N., 149, 189
MacKinnon, M., 131
MacLauchlan, W.H, xxv
Madeira: and Free Trade Zone, 159;
versus Malta 158–60; as offshore
finance centre (OFC), 159
Madsen, R., 147, 148

mainland-island relations, 91, 141
Malaysia Immigration Department, 118
Maldives: and development contrasts,
169; and environmental diplomacy,
154–5
Malinowski, B., 15
Malta, xxx–xxxi; and EU membership,
159; and integration with Britain,
69; and permanent derogation over
property purchase, 81
managed dependency, 112; management
of external relations, 173
Manitoba Legislative Task Force on
Canadian Unity, 92
Manning, E.W., and T.D. Dougherty, 83
manufactured societies, 58
Marcus, G.E., 63, 70
Marguiles, J., 129
Maritime union, xxvi
marketing of identity, 84
Markham, E.A., 62, 116
Markoff, J., 137
Marshall, A.T., 139
Marshall Islands, 46; as geo-strategic
site, 127
Martin, P., 23
Martin, Paul (Canada, prime minister),
93, 97
Martin, R., 139
Martin-Williams deal and showdown,
93–4, 96
Mattingly, G., 192
Mauritius: and integration with Britain,
69
Mauritius International Review
Meeting (2005), 156; Declaration,
149
maximization of tax revenue post-
2008, 194–5
May, R., and S. Tupouniua, 181
McBride, D., 128
McCall Smith, J., xxii
McElroy, J.L., 82, 86, 174

McElroy, J.L., and K. de Albuquerque, 44
McElroy, J.L., and K.B. Pearce, 220
McElroy, J.L., and K. Sanborn, 102, 108, 162–4, 188
McElroy, J.L., and L. Morris, 71
McElroy, J.L., and M. Mahoney, 46, 55, 72
McElroy, J.L., and W. Bai, 148
McGregor, D.P., 122
McKercher, W.R., 73, 77
McLuhan, M., 23
McPhetres, A., 29
McSmith, A., 120
Mead, M., 15, 34
Mercer, P., 43
Merchant Marine Act, U.S. (1920), 80
MercoPress, 160
Merodia (imaginary country), 87
Messineo, F., 130
metropolitan links as insurance, 72
Micallef, J.V., 151
Michel, James (Seychelles, president), 153–4
Middleton, J., 91
Midttun, A., et al., 199
Miles, W.F.S., 58, 66, 70, 116
Mills, G.E., 164
Milne, D., xxvi, 76, 77, 96, 172, 216
Milne, S., 80
minority rights: promotion of, 97, 104–5
Mintoff, Dom (Malta, prime minister), 151
MIRAB model and economy, 17, 65, 70–6, 83–7, 90, 155
MIRAGE, 70
MIRTAB, 70
Mohawk Council of Kahnawake, 105
Montevideo Convention (1933), 30
Montgomery, Lucy Maud, xxv
Montserrat, 44, 68; evacuation of, 157; and money laundering, 194; and paradiplomacy, 143–4

More, Thomas, 6, 198
Morgan, G., 10
Morgan, K., 23, 139
Mørkøre, J., 59
Morris, T.A., Jr, 126, 128
Moseley, R., 27
Motzfeldt, J., 145
Mountz, A., 128, 129, 192
Mrgudovic, N., 56, 67, 112
MSNBC, 154
Muir, R., 20, 215
Mukherjee, A., 63
Munro, D., 70
MURAB, 70
Murphy, K., 6, 221
Mururoa and Fangataufa: cession of, 126–7
Mushkat, R., xxii
Mynott, A., 27

Nadkami, D., 148
Naipaul, V.S., 58
Nairobi International Airport, 27
Nambath, S., 179
Nasheed Mohammed (Maldives, president) 154, 157–8
National Aeronautics and Space Administration (NASA), 16
National Geographic, 169
NationMaster, 48
nation-state and autonomy, 99
nations without states, 100
natural capital, 186
nature conservancy, 169
nature-culture relationship, 167
Netherlands: and sea-level rise, 155
Netherlands Antilles, 43; and relations with Netherlands, 161
Neuman, G.L., 129
Neumann, I.B., and S. Gstöhl, 150
Nevis Tourist Board, 82
Nevmerzhitskaya, J., 185
New Caledonia/Kanaky, 43

tacit knowledge, 23

Taiwan: and paradiplomacy, 147–8; status of, 147–8

Talake, Koloa (Tuvalu, prime minister), 153

Tamil Eelam, 30, 134

Tampa incident, Australia, 37–8

Tarlton, C.D., 92

Tasmanian Wilderness: as UNESCO World Heritage Site, 178

Taussig, M., 12

tax competition: as healthy, 196

tax havens, 113, 139, 193; "allowed to exist" by larger states, 196; and attracting "hot money" 194

Tax Justice Network, 195

tax policies of SNIJs, 189

Taylor, D., 193

Telegraph (U.K.), 218

The Tempest (Shakespeare), 87

terra nullius (empty land), 33

territorial innovation systems, 23–4

territoriality: unbundling of, 190, 197

Territorial Sea Act, U.K. (1987), 137

territory: reinvention of, 142

terrorism: and illegal migration: 25

TheDominican.net, 177

Thibodeau, W., 97

Thom, B., 122

Thomas, R., et al., 169

Thompson, E., 96

Thompson, M., et al., xxvi

Thomson, J., 200

Thondavadi, N., and G. Albert, 41

Thorhallsson, B., 150, 219, 220

Thorndike, T., 91, 164

Thucydides, 149

Tiffin, H., 64

Time Magazine, 8

Times online (U.K.), 133, 221

Toafa, M., 153

Toafa, Maatia (Tuvalu, acting prime minister), 153

Tokelau: and sea-level rise, 158

Torres Strait Islands: and sovereign rights of indigenous people, 121

TOURAB, 70

tourism: and cold water islands, 17; and "trickle down" effects, 174

Tourism Area Life Cycle, 173

"tragedy of the commons," 155, 173

transferability of sovereignty, 158

transnational corporations of kin, 63, 70

Treadgold, M L., 70, 86, 135

Treaty of Amsterdam (1997), 158

Treaty of Rome (1957), 106

Trenwith, A., 133

trickle-down effects of tourism industry, 174

Trimble, W.R., 8

Tristan da Cunha: evacuation of, 157

Trompf, G., 47, 60, 72, 215

Tsunami (Boxing Day, 2004), 157

Tuan, Yi-Fu, 36

Turkish Republic of Northern Cyprus (TRNC): and paradiplomacy, 122–3

Turner, A.K., 8

Turner, C., 13, 178

Turtinen, J., 178

Tuvalu: and environmental diplomacy, 153; and sea-level rise, 153, 156

Tweedie, N., 17

Tycho Brahe, 13

"tyranny of the weak," 150

U.K.: and cod wars with Iceland, 151–2

U.K. Chagos Support Association, 126

ultra-peripheral regions of the EU, 158

UN, 15, 31, 52, 91, 121, 165; observer mission at, 144; and sea-level rise 153, 154; unbundling of territoriality, 190

unconstrained migration, 81

UNCTAD, 166

Underwood, R.A., 29